SPRING
MOON

SPRING
MOON

A Novel of China

BETTE BAO LORD

BOOK CLUB ASSOCIATES LONDON

TO
My Chinese and American parents,
My husband, Winston Lord,
AND
My editor, Corona Machemer
Debts I can never repay

Printed in Great Britain by
Richard Clay (The Chaucer Press) Ltd,
Bungay, Suffolk

Contents

PRINCIPAL CHARACTERS

THE HOUSE OF CHANG, IN SOOCHOW:

Bold Talent, son of Old Venerable and his first wife, the Matriarch

Sterling Talent, son of Old Venerable and his second wife

Noble Talent, son of Old Venerable and his third wife, Silken Dawn

Fragrant Snow, wife of Sterling Talent

Spring Moon, daughter of Sterling Talent

Golden Virtue, wife of Bold Talent

August Winds, distant relative

Resolute Spirit, son of tenant Farmer Lee

Fatso, faithful servant

THE HOUSE OF WOO, IN PEKING:

Fierce Rectitude, Hanlin Scholar

Lotus Delight, his wife

Glad Promise, their son

Lustrous Jade, daughter of Glad Promise

Enduring Promise, adopted heir of Fierce Rectitude

Dummy, mute handmaiden

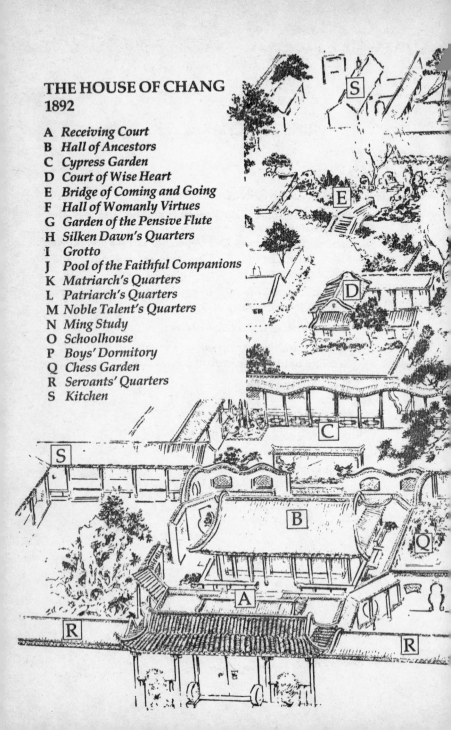

THE HOUSE OF CHANG
1892

A *Receiving Court*
B *Hall of Ancestors*
C *Cypress Garden*
D *Court of Wise Heart*
E *Bridge of Coming and Going*
F *Hall of Womanly Virtues*
G *Garden of the Pensive Flute*
H *Silken Dawn's Quarters*
I *Grotto*
J *Pool of the Faithful Companions*
K *Matriarch's Quarters*
L *Patriarch's Quarters*
M *Noble Talent's Quarters*
N *Ming Study*
O *Schoolhouse*
P *Boys' Dormitory*
Q *Chess Garden*
R *Servants' Quarters*
S *Kitchen*

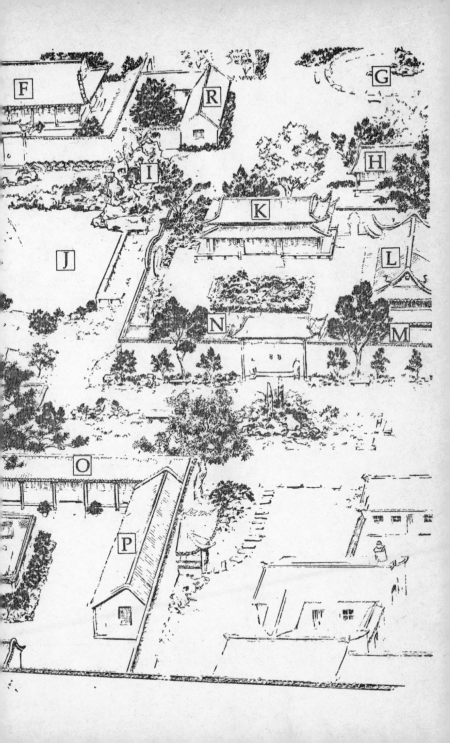

PROLOGUE

Before the beginning there was chaos. All sounds but none heard; all shapes but none seen. Darkness pursuing darkness for an endless age.

When the moment was true, out of chaos emerged the sleeping giant Pan Koo. Upon awakening, he was angered by the void and shattered it with a blow. That which yields floated upward while the unyielding sank, forming the Heavens and the Earth.

The breath of Pan Koo became the winds and clouds, his voice the rolling thunder, his left eye the sun, his right the moon, the hairs of his head and beard the stars, and the sweat of his brow the rain and dew. The fleas on his body became men and women. Thus the world began.

Three Divine Rulers appeared to help mankind. They taught the black-haired people to build a fire; to fish, hunt, and tame the animals; to cultivate the land. Each reigned for thousands of years. Then chaos returned, for their successors were princes of inferiority. And without order, men knew no peace and were no better than beasts.

At last, the Yellow Emperor ascended the throne, restoring civility. From him the people of the Huang Ho learned to mine and to mint, to heal the sick and to record the wisdom of men and the passage of time. His Empress shared the secret of silk making.

Thereafter, for more than four thousand years, empires waxed and waned, dynasties rose and fell, clans flowered and faded, season after season, year after year. And always more feared than tigers or floods or spirits were the times of chaos, luan, when kings were not kings, nor subjects subjects; fathers were not fathers, nor sons sons; husbands were not husbands, nor wives

wives; brothers were not brothers; friends were not friends.

In the days of the great sage Confucius, the Prince of Wu, seeking glory, spoke thus to his Prime Minister: "Build me a new capital for my kingdom, one that will mirror the Heavens and the Earth, where virtuous men of letters and beautiful women will dwell, and in time of danger subjects and goods will be safe from the enemy."

And so, on a site between lush hills and fertile plains, where flowers bloomed ten months in every year, the walled city of Soochow was built and encircled by a moat. Like heaven, it had eight water gates; like earth, eight foot gates. On the hillocks a crown of pagodas, and in the vale fretted with canals, gardens of infinite perspective.

Two thousand years passed like the seasons. Then, during the reign of Wan Li, a poor scholar and his aged mother stopped in Soochow on the way to Peking, where he hoped to succeed in the Imperial Examinations. But the woman fell ill. Before she died, she commanded her son to bury her in the first convenient spot and thence journey on to meet his destiny. He did as she asked. The site was near a pool, the home of a pair of ever-faithful mandarin ducks; the grave was marked with a sprig of cypress.

In the capital, the scholar won all honors, but not once in twenty-seven months did a smile touch his face. Grieved by his servant's sorrow, the Emperor inquired. The Senior Wrangler explained. All who heard were moved.

The Emperor sent him to serve in Soochow, where he could be near his beloved mother. On his arrival, he saw that her resting place had not been disturbed and the sprig had become a sapling.

South of the tree he ordered the gates of his home to be built, and around it the garden walls.

—Clan story

AS THE SUN BLAZED in the western skies, Spring Moon slept. Her room was cool, shaded by the green-tiled roof that arched gracefully away from the ancient walls, and she curled contentedly in the far recesses of her bed, enveloped by its pink silk curtains and the scent of camphor. Her breathing was imperceptible.

Suddenly a ray of sunlight, slipping under the eaves and through an open shutter, found a crack in the curtains and splashed across the bed. At its touch, Spring Moon stirred, pulling the coverlet over her head. She could still just see the red box and willed herself to dream again. But it was no use.

"Plum Blossom," she called, throwing off the covers and sitting up. "Why did you leave the curtains open? I was having the most wonderful dream, and now it is spoiled."

It had been the best kind of dream, magical and shivery. Bearers had come from far away, bringing a red lacquer chest. On its lid were strange gold characters not even Eldest Uncle could read. "It is a present for Spring Moon," the bearers said. They warned that she must wait three days and nights, until at the exact hour of her birth, the box would pop open like a roasted chestnut.

And she had waited. But when at last the hour of the monkey approached, the sun had wakened her. Now she would never know what was inside.

Spring Moon sighed. It must have been something most marvelous. An enchanted peachstone to sing to her, perhaps, or a potion for turning peppers into sweets. Plum Blossom should not have left the curtains open, even a little.

"Plum Blossom?"

Still there was no reply. Spring Moon raised her voice.

"Plum Blossom, I am through napping. You must not sleep when I am awake. Answer me."

She parted the curtains. There was no one in the room.

"Plum Blossom? Are we playing hide and seek?" Spring Moon scrambled out of the bed and peeked underneath. Only a thimble was there, and the gourd placed beneath the spot where her head lay, to ward off ghosts.

Spring Moon straightened and paused for a moment, her brow furrowed. Then, quickly pushing her cloth-bound feet into a pair of pink embroidered shoes and pulling on her *ta chin p'ao*, she stepped out onto the gallery that bordered the garden of the Court of Wise Heart. The garden was a small one and contained no hiding place, so she walked from door to door, looking into each room of the three wings of her family's quarters. Plum Blossom was not in any of them. No one was.

Where could the girl be? A sudden fear quickened Spring Moon's heart. Only a two-headed snake could have sent Plum Blossom away. Unless . . . what if Fragrant Snow had needed her? Had not Fatso complained that morning of a headache? Perhaps Plum Blossom had been called to wait on Mother in Fatso's place.

Quickly the child slipped through the Fan Gate, past the Court of Silent Bamboos, which belonged to the family of Great-Uncle Number Three, past the several courts of the Venerable's nephews, to the Bridge of Coming and Going and the Court of Womanly Virtues. As she neared the tall red columns that marked the entrance of the Hall, she could hear the hum of gossip and the clatter of gaming tiles within. For a moment she hesitated. What if Mother was losing again to Great-Aunt Number Three? But she could also be winning, and in good spirits. Resolutely Spring Moon walked the few steps across the gallery to the open door.

At the threshold, she paused once more, trying to locate Plum Blossom or Fragrant Snow among the grandmothers, mothers, widows, wives, concubines, daughters, slave girls, and servants who lived together in the thirty courts beneath the ancestral roofs. Her gaze passed quickly over the three betrothed and over Auntie from Tientsin, who was painting flowers on a silk fan. Auntie did not see her sister-in-law mimic her pursed look of concentration behind her back for the benefit of the Matriarch. Nor did that wizened woman give any sign that she noticed, although everyone knew she missed nothing. She sat, flanked by two slave girls whose delicate features and fine clothes were proof of the wealth and standing of the household, in the precise center of the room.

To Spring Moon's relief, Fragrant Snow was not among the mah jong players with Great-Aunt Number Three, who, from the sound of triumph in her voice, was surely winning. But there was no sign of the slave girl either, and as Spring Moon's eyes darted from one group to the next, the fear stirred once more. Finally she spotted the plum silk that, years ago, Fragrant Snow had decided was her best color and now wore exclusively. She was embroidering by the west window where she could catch the last of the afternoon light. Spring Moon slipped through the crowd.

"Mother!" She tugged at Fragrant Snow's sleeve. "Mother!"

Fragrant Snow slapped the offending hand. "What are you doing, naughty girl? Rushing in like a gust of wind, interrupting your elders without so much as a greeting! Everyone will think that I have neglected my duties. You will heap shame upon our ancestors!"

Spring Moon bowed her head. "A thousand pardons, my mother." She turned away and walked slowly toward the Matriarch.

The old woman's full attention was now given to Grandniece Number Five, who stared at the hem of her tunic while being instructed on the conduct proper during expectant happiness.

". . . and remember, no hashed foods lest the baby have a careless disposition . . ."

Spring Moon waited to be acknowledged.

". . . and no sad thoughts lest the baby be infected." The Matriarch nodded. "You may go now and take tea." She turned to Spring Moon.

Spring Moon blushed, remembering all at once that she had neglected to wash after her nap. Grandmother would know, of course. She always knew. But you could never tell what she was thinking, for the rice powder hid her expressions as completely as the opera mask hid the face of the doll Eldest Uncle had given her before he went away. With the Matriarch looking at her, Spring Moon always felt as small as a sesame seed.

"Well?"

The child swallowed hard, then bowed deeply. "Good afternoon, my grandmother. Forgive me for not paying you proper respect when I came in just now."

The Matriarch smiled, careful not to part her lips and reveal her toothless gums. "You seem excited, indeed."

Spring Moon breathed easier.

"What is it, my child?"

Thus invited, the words rushed out. "Oh, Grandmother, Plum Blossom is lost. I cannot find her anywhere."

As though a ghost had spoken, the women stopped their sewing and chatting, eating and playing, to look her way and listen.

"Do not be foolish, child." The Matriarch no longer smiled. "She must be somewhere within our homestead. Perhaps she is in your room looking for you."

Unable to move, Spring Moon watched her grandmother sip her tea, feeling as if she herself had been swallowed.

"Well? Is there anything else?" The Matriarch waited. When no answer came, she spoke more harshly. "Speak up, child. Speak up!"

In a quivering voice, Spring Moon obeyed. "But Grandmother, she was not there when I woke up. I thought she might be here, but I do not see her. Something must have happened. I am afraid something . . ."

She faltered. The Matriarch's eyes had narrowed until they were only slits, searching the room for the responsible parent. At once, Fragrant Snow rose to take charge, pulling her impudent daughter by the ear toward the door. All eyes followed the retreat. There was no sound except for the jangle of Fragrant Snow's gold bracelets.

Safely beyond the red columns, the mother scolded. "You are forever meddling in family affairs, Spring Moon. A good girl never asks such impertinent questions." She waved the child away.

Spring Moon opened her mouth to protest, but her mother arched an eyebrow, daring her to utter the smallest sound. It was no use. She bowed and walked away. Slowly, she retraced her steps to her family's quarters. Perhaps Grandmother was right, and the slave girl would be in her accustomed place.

But as before, the painted stool was empty. She checked inside the rosewood wardrobe and opened the sandalwood chests, although they were much too small to hide anyone bigger than the monkey that belonged to Cousin Number Six. At last she paused, sitting on the slave girl's bamboo k'ang to rest. Could Plum Blossom have run away like the neighbor's girl? She shook her head emphatically. No, Plum Blossom would never do that.

Her golden lilies ached, and she tried to massage her calves as Plum Blossom always did, but there was no strength in her fingers. Wearily, she lay back, brushing away a tear before it could fall. She was much too old to cry. Had it not been more than two years since her seventh summer, when the bandages were first used to bind her feet? She had screamed and screamed then, as the four smaller toes were curled underneath the sole, and the sole forced toward the heel until the feet were bent almost in half. "It is for your own good, child," her mother had said. "No matter how beautiful, how rich, how filial, no man will marry feet that flop like yellow pike."

It was Plum Blossom who had comforted her and bathed her feet in medicinal waters, making certain that no toes were lost to infection. Every day the slave girl had carried her on her back to the Pool of the Faithful Companions, where she could lie on the cool rocks and play with the golden carp . . .

Suddenly Spring Moon smiled and sat up. The grotto! Why had she not thought to look there before? Once, long ago, Plum Blossom had said it was her favorite place to release *chi*. Perhaps she had gone there and forgotten the time.

Sliding quickly from the bed, Spring Moon hurried out.

When she reached the terrace she heard something, and paused to listen. There! Once more she heard it, a sound as faint as the footfall of a ghost. "Plum Blossom?" she called sharply. "Plum Blossom, is that you?" There was no answer.

Gingerly she made her way to the other side of the miniature mountain. There, huddled on her knees, her face raised to her young mistress, was Plum Blossom. She wiped away tears with the back of her hand.

"Plum Blossom?" Spring Moon whispered. She had never seen the slave girl cry, except at funerals, when everybody wailed. Only that morning, Plum Blossom had been unable to stop smiling, for the betrothed cousins had rated her a third-grade beauty, citing only the roundness of her face and the closeness of her eyes as demerits. She reached out to touch the older girl's cheek, but Plum Blossom pulled away.

"Please let me be, Small Mistress. I will come to you in a while."

"But what is the matter, Plum Blossom? Are you sick? Mother will call for the doctor."

"No, I am not sick."

"Then why are you crying?"

"I am not crying. I just have some thinking to do."

"About what?"

"It is of no importance."

"Then come and play."

Plum Blossom shook her head.

"You must! You are my slave girl. You must do everything I say."

Plum Blossom bowed her head. "Yes, it is true. I am only your worthless slave girl."

She had never spoken in that way before, whatever her mistress said. Quickly Spring Moon took her hand and held it to her heart. "No, Plum Blossom, you are my sister. I am sorry I was angry. It is just that I have been looking for you everywhere. What is wrong? Tell me, please?"

Plum Blossom only shook her head.

Spring Moon leaned closer and whispered into her ear, "Did Grandmother say something to make you cry?"

"Shhh!" Plum Blossom put her hand to the child's lips.

"So it *is* Grandmother. . . ."

"We must not speak of her—"

"I do not care. Tell me at once!" Spring Moon's voice rose.

The slave girl hesitated, then shrugged. "The Matriarch said that I am to go to another house."

So Plum Blossom's tears had not been real tears, after all, but ritual ones, like those shed at departures. Spring Moon clapped her hands, applauding the performance, too relieved to be angry at the trick. How beautifully the slave girl wept! She had been even more convincing than the female impersonators at the New Year's opera.

"But that is wonderful news, Plum Blossom," she cried. "Grandmother has chosen a husband for you! You will soon be married and free, and I—"

She broke off. Her friend shook with silent sobs, burying her face in her hands again. Spring Moon was more puzzled than ever. All slave girls were married before they were twenty, and Plum Blossom was already seventeen.

"Why do you cry, Plum Blossom?" she asked finally. "We have been expecting this to happen. You can come back for visits. I shall invite you. We shall have tea in the garden, and I . . ."

She stopped, for as she spoke, Plum Blossom had grown strangely calm, and when she looked up her eyes no longer glistened with tears but were dull, like those of the blind storyteller.

"You do not understand, Small Mistress. I am not going to be married."

"But you just told me—"

"I said another house, not a marriage. Your family has promised me as a concubine to Old Yeh."

But Spring Moon still did not understand. True, Old Yeh's wife was as shriveled as a cooked shrimp, but it could be worse. Plum Blossom could have been given to Lame Loo or the cross-eyed barber. Old Yeh was a scholar and very rich.

"Do not cry, Plum Blossom, please. Think of the dowry Grandmother will give you. . . . And you will never be poor again. You will never have to sell even one of your daughters. Old Yeh is as rich as . . . as we are. You will give him a son. And your son will be a scholar, I know he will. He will pass all the Imperial Examinations, be Senior Wrangler, even enter the Hanlin Forest of Pencils. All his honors will also be yours, and someday you will be the Patriarch's mother. Fate will see to it. You may even be more honored than I. Then you will invite me to tea."

But the look on Plum Blossom's face never changed, and when Spring Moon paused for breath, she said only, "Please go." Her voice was smooth as *koo* melons, and as bitter.

"May I not stay here with you?"

"Please go. I will be along to help you dress for dinner."

Reluctantly, Spring Moon walked away, stopping every few steps to look back to see if Plum Blossom had changed her mind. The slave girl crouched motionless beside the small mountain, her dark eyes like windows shuttered against the light.

Spring Moon was determined to understand but dared not disturb the women a second time. That left the men of the clan, and the boy cousins. The boys would be in school and would scorn to tell her even if they knew. One by one, she dismissed the men too. Grandfather was ill. Her father, at this hour, was studying with scholar Tang. The granduncles were prepared to indulge her, but none, she knew, would tolerate an interruption. Except . . . except, perhaps, Young Uncle. He was not like the others, and he favored her. Who else had received a fan painted with a map of the Empire upon his return from the Military Academy? No matter that Fatso had told everyone it was only because the colored blobs and squiggly lines reminded him of the sorry state of Spring Moon's embroidery.

Quickly, the girl made her way toward the Cypress Garden, which linked the outer and inner courts of the sprawling family compound. At the marble screen she stopped and, retreating a few steps, sat down on the stone bench in the shade of the clan treasure to wait.

She came here almost every day, Plum Blossom by her side, to eavesdrop on the clan school on the other side of the wall, trying to make sense of the sounds the boys made reciting aloud at the same time, but never from the same page. She knew that beginners read the Three-Character Mottoes; and the advanced studied the tenets of Confucius from the Four Great Books and the Five Classics. And she knew that the students did not understand what they chanted any better than she; their teacher did not explain a text until every word was committed to memory. Of course the teacher would never explain anything to her, a girl, yet for Spring Moon the sounds of learning were spellbinding, and she made up stories to go along.

Today, however, she did not listen but waited impatiently for a servant to appear, one who could go into the forbidden outer courts and ask Young Uncle to come and see her. Finally, when there was a silence in the classroom, she heard the sound of shuffling footsteps. The ancient gardener had come to air Second Grandaunt's lark.

Spring Moon stood up and waved. "Old Gardener, please, come here." There was no response, and she called again, more loudly this time. "Come here, Old Uncle. Please?"

The gardener, however, continued at his original pace. When at long last he reached her, he mumbled, "I am not deaf. I heard you the first time, Small Mistress. But why should I waste breath answering when we will be toe-to-toe soon enough?"

"You are right." Spring Moon knew she could not offend him if she wanted a favor. Old servants, her mother said, were to be respected, not commanded. She patted his arm, sinewy and browned by the sun. "You must save your strength for pruning the garden."

"I have been doing just that since I came here four generations ago." The old man nodded his head, as if an argument had been won.

She bowed deeply. "Old Uncle, you have served here longer than anybody else. The clan is honored." His eyes softened. She bowed again and then, glancing up at him, said, "Old Uncle, will you do something small for me? It will take no time "

When he said nothing, she went on.

"Please, go and find Young Uncle and tell him that I must see him. It is urgent." She smiled hopefully.

He grumbled. "How can anything be urgent to an infant like you?"

"Please? Before it is too late!"

"You are always hurrying. If not yourself, someone else. Listen to an old man. Nature holds the answers. Nothing fruitful ever comes when plants are forced to flower in the wrong season. So how can my wintry legs run as they did in my spring, hm? Even for you! Have you thought of what would happen to this hibernating heart?"

Spring Moon swallowed her impatience. "You are right, Old Gardener. There is no hurry. Walk as slowly as you wish. I will keep the songbird for you."

He stroked his long wispy beard, considering her offer. At last he said, "Now, why did you not mention that before? We would not have wasted all this time. I could have gone and been back by now. But you talk too much."

He shuffled off, shaking his head so that his beard swayed.

Certain he was on his way, Spring Moon sat again upon the bench. Carefully she placed the bamboo cage beside her and watched the small brown bird jump from perch to perch. After a few moments it paused on the tiny swing to trill its evening song. When the last note hung in the air, it cocked its head and bowed to Spring Moon, inviting her song in reply. She sang the first one she had ever learned, about a man from Plum Blossom's village.

> Snow drops at New Year's,
> Red lamps lit at every door,
> All families are united,
> But he has gone to build the Great Wall.

The bird bowed again and had opened its beak to repeat its own song when the gardener returned with Noble Talent. How stern Young Uncle looked when he was not smiling! For a moment Spring Moon wondered whether she should ask him after all. But there was no other choice. She bit her lip, then jumped to her feet and bowed respectfully. "Thank you for coming, my uncle. Thank you for all your trouble, Old Gardener."

"It was nothing, Young Mistress. Besides, I had promised to show the Master the progress I have made with the lark in his absence." Uncle and niece watched as Old Gardener bent down to unlatch the door of the cage. The bird hopped to the stoop. Suddenly it flew up and out of sight beyond the garden wall. The gardener chuckled at their amazement, then picked up the cage. "Patience. Just a matter of patience, my youthful friends. The lark awaits me by the rockery." The two watched him disappear through the Clover Gate.

"You wished to see me, Spring Moon?" Noble Talent asked.

She stared up at him, so straight and tall in his long gown of burgundy silk, like the banners that hung from the rafters in the Hall of Ancestors at New Year's. She wondered how to begin.

"Well, what is it, Small Niece?"

Spring Moon took a deep breath. "Young Uncle, why have you changed out of your uniform? It was wonderful to look at."

He laughed. There, that was better. He should laugh more often. She took him by the hand and pulled him down to sit beside her on the bench while he answered her question.

"Well, it seems that you and my father are the only ones who think so. The rest of the clan thinks the uniform is only fit for a barbarian or a man of the lowest class."

"Why do they think that, Young Uncle?"

"Surely you have heard that 'Good iron is not made into nails; good men are not made into soldiers.' "

"Is that true, my uncle?"

"No. I do not think it is always so, but then I do not think as most people do." He smiled, as if they were sharing a secret.

"But you sent for me, my niece. What is the matter?"

The encouraging squeeze he gave her hand sent the question forth at last. "Please, oh, please tell me why Old Yeh is taking my slave girl."

At once he no longer smiled. In Young Uncle's stead, it seemed, there was the sternest general. "Our family has promised," he said, "and we must all honor our bond."

"But Plum Blossom is so unhappy. She cries and cries. She has never cried before, not like the others. Can we not give Honey Buds or Blessed Flower? They twitter and screech every time a stranger comes to the back gate."

"That may be so, but they will not redeem our word—"

"It is not fair. Good girls are not sent to be old men's concubines!"

Noble Talent stood up abruptly. She dared not move. What had she said to anger him? He took several steps in the direction of the marble screen, then stopped and stood very still, poised like an acrobat about to perform his most difficult trick. Please, she prayed, do not go. She held her breath until, at last, he returned to his seat and took her hand again. It was a moment before he spoke.

"My niece, you will not understand this, and I should not discuss such things with one so young, but . . . I was the youngest once, and it is not easy, never being told. . . ." He cleared his throat. "Last night Second Granduncle went to a party with Old Yeh. He lost every round of Go. When it was almost dawn, Old Yeh suggested a final game. If Second Granduncle won he would win back everything, but if he lost, Plum Blossom would become Old Yeh's concubine. It was agreed. Second Granduncle lost again."

The explanation made no sense to Spring Moon. It still was not fair. "Why should Old Yeh get what is mine?" she asked.

"Because, my niece, Plum Blossom is not yours," he said softly, almost sadly. "She belongs to the House of Chang. You are old enough to know that nothing we have is ours alone."

"But . . ." Her eyes filled with tears and, though she blinked quickly, one escaped and began to roll down her cheek.

He stiffened and stood. "Spring Moon, now I must go."

It was useless to say any more. She rose too and bowed formally, then watched his back until he disappeared behind the screen again. He was right. She did not understand.

She sat awhile in thought. Perhaps Old Yeh did not know how unhappy Plum Blossom was. Perhaps if someone told him, he would change his mind. But who? Finally she decided to risk another scolding from her mother and made her way slowly back to the family court.

When she peeked into her parents' bedroom and saw that the servant Fatso, now apparently in excellent health, was dressing her mother's hair, her courage ebbed. Fragrant Snow prided herself on the new hairstyle she created every week and disliked having her toilette interrupted. But the hair still formed the wide petals of a lotus, as it had at tea. Fatso was merely tucking in a few stray wisps.

Spring Moon approached the dressing table, which was bare except for the open cosmetic box. "Mother, may I speak with you?"

"It is almost dinnertime," said Fragrant Snow, with a knowing glance at her servant. "What is so urgent that you disturb me now?"

Fatso, who ruled the family court as well as her husband, Old Hawk, never failed to express her opinions. "Your daughter, Mistress, should be called 'Galling Goat.' Nervy and stubborn. Here she gets away with it because of those big black eyes, but at her mother-in-law's they will win no more favor than the beady eyes of a mouse. Please"—Fatso posed in angelic prayer like a portly Buddha—"let me be around to see it!" Both women laughed.

Spring Moon yanked at the servant's black tunic. "Go away, Fatso, I want to talk with my mother."

"Daughter." Fragrant Snow's voice rose in pitch as it always did when she was annoyed. "Watch your manners!"

"Oh, she is only playing, Mistress." Fatso was as quick to forgive as she was sharp-tongued.

"Children should not be so encouraged. Tell me, my daughter. What is it?" Dipping a finger into the rouge, Fragrant Snow consulted the mirror on the cosmetic box.

"Mother, please make Old Yeh give Plum Blossom back to me!"

Fragrant Snow glared at the image of Spring Moon in the mirror. "You are being impertinent, child. This is adult business, no concern of yours. A promise was made. The affair is settled."

"The promise must be broken!"

At that both women swiveled about, and the daughter quickly moved behind the bulk of Fatso, out of her mother's reach.

"How can you even think such a thing?" As if she heard herself, Fragrant Snow paused, and when she went on her voice was no longer high-pitched but as cold as water from the well. "What would everyone say if we were to dishonor our name over a trifling slave girl? We would lose face for generations. Stop your meddling, my daughter, before it is bandied around town that you are indiscriminate and indiscreet. Do you want to ruin your chances for a good marriage? Not even the biggest dowry can persuade a family to take in a troublemaker." Fragrant Snow turned back to her mirror. "Another pin here, please, Fatso."

There was nothing more to say. Spring Moon turned and left the room, walking slowly along the gallery toward her father's library and, beyond it, her own chamber. When she reached Sterling Talent's door she stopped. He was seated, as usual just before the dinner hour, at his desk, reading one of the thousands of string-bound books that were neatly stacked on shelves along three walls. She almost never talked with him, for he was always studying. Still, he would soon be joining the elders for dinner; perhaps he would not mind being interrupted. Perhaps this once he would help.

With a quick glance to make sure her mother and Fatso were not looking, she stepped inside the room.

"Please, my father, may I speak with you?"

Sterling Talent did not respond. She was not surprised. His mind was always somewhere else, at the Court of Duke Ting perhaps, listening to the Sage.

She spoke up again. When again she got no answer, she walked boldly to the desk and placed her hand on the page he was reading.

At this he looked up, mildly startled. His gentle eyes slowly focused on the upturned face of his only child. "Oh, it is you. Has your mother sent for me? Have I forgotten an honored guest or a clan conference?"

"No, Father, I came to speak of my troubles."

"Go to your mother. She will know what to do."

"But she cannot do anything about it."

"What do you expect from me, then?"

"It is Plum Blossom, Father. She has been given to Old Yeh. I do not want her to go!"

Perplexed, he fingered the worry beads of jade he kept on his desk. "But what do you mean? Who is Plum Blossom?"

"My slave girl!"

"Oh, then it is nothing, Spring Moon. Your mother will replace her."

"I do not want anyone else."

"My daughter"—Sterling Talent put his hand on her shoulder—"the Great Sage has said that the higher type of man seeks all that he desires in himself; the inferior man seeks all that he desires from others."

"Yes, my father," said Spring Moon, and waited for him to explain. When he did not, she asked, "If that is so, my father, why does Old Yeh want my Plum Blossom?"

But Sterling Talent had already looked away. His long, pale face was bent once more over his book, a thin finger tracing the characters as he read.

Spring Moon bowed. "Thank you, my father." She turned and walked slowly from the study, along the gallery to her own room.

"Where have you been?" asked Plum Blossom. She was seated on the painted stool, rolling a fresh set of foot bindings.

"I have been everywhere trying to undo the promise. But no one will help." Spring Moon sat down on the slave girl's k'ang, watching her hands.

"Your elders are right," Plum Blossom said. "Who can retrieve words already spoken? I shall weep no more."

"I do not understand you, Plum Blossom. What does it mean?"

"How could you understand?" asked the girl. She rolled the bindings faster and faster. "You have a home. You have never been beyond these garden walls."

"But I would give . . . I would give my good luck charms to see what is out there."

"No, you would not!"

She is farther away than the Emperor, Spring Moon thought, as the disgraceful tears welled up once more. "Please, Plum Blossom. You are making me cry."

At that the slave girl put aside the bandages and turned toward Spring Moon, gently lifting the child's face until she could look into her eyes. "You are too young, my mistress, to understand. But perhaps someday, you will remember. . . ." Plum Blossom's voice trailed off.

"Plum Blossom?" asked Spring Moon.

The girl started. "Yes?" she said, and then, "Always before today, even after my father sold me and sent me away, I dreamed every night that if I were good-natured and worked hard the Matriarch would wed me to a young artisan from town or to the son of a clan retainer. I dreamed that we would be well matched and have sons. I would have a home and my rightful place as daughter-in-law, wife, and mother. My dream made being a slave girl seem unimportant.

"Then today, while you napped, my dream was ended. I will never be a wife—only a concubine. When you said that I would have a son and through him be honored, your words pierced my heart like a skewer. You see, I shall never have sons, never. Old Yeh is too old. He has a wife and many concubines already, but no child. I shall be an empty vessel. I shall never have a rightful place. When Old Yeh dies, or if I displease him, I may be cast out, as easily as bath water. There will be no more dreams for me."

The slave girl rose. Spring Moon did not know the stranger who collected the bandages and carried them to the wardrobe.

At dinner Spring Moon ate little and said nothing. She was conscious that the others at her table did not take their usual delight in teasing her, the youngest of the girls, but watched her quietly as if she had returned to their midst after a long sickness. Plum Blossom walked to and fro, serving her mistress as usual.

Then, halfway through the third course, she noticed that the Matriarch was missing from the seat of honor. She turned to Sixth Cousin and spoke for the first time. "Where is Grandmother, Sister?"

"Grandfather grows restless. She attends him."

I should have gone to him at once, she thought. Even though he was ill, Grandfather was the head of the clan. Anything he decided would be done without question, without delay. If only she could get in to see him.

With a gesture, she summoned Plum Blossom and sent her to request an audience with Old Venerable.

The Patriarch of the House of Chang lay in his rosewood bed. Around him hovered physicians and servants. He wished they would go away, for he was dying and they served no purpose. He would tell them to leave if he thought they would do so, but they would not. They would only humor him, whose every word had once been law throughout entire provinces. As an official wearing the insignia of the White Crane, he had been treated with deference and respect, according to strict codes of etiquette. Now . . .

Wearily, he closed his eyes, remembering the sanctuary this room had once been, not only for him but for all the Patriarchs before him. He could see it without looking, every detail. All within it was symmetrical, balanced, in harmony: the folding wooden lattice screens that served as doors; the gentle curves of the high-backed chairs that stood in pairs beside the desk with its shiny brass pulls; the scrolls on the walls, painted and penned with poetry exchanged between friends through generations; the porcelains his grandfather had collected, the jade his father had treasured, and the bronzes which he so prized displayed in identical open cabinets; the books the clan valued above all their other possessions.

An old man needed order, not this chaos that had invaded the sanctum of his bedroom. Servants, priests, spirits, his senior wife—

all conspired against him. He was never alone; someone was always there, even as he slept.

Now Fatso had joined the crowd, delivering a special broth brewed by her husband from the udder of a cow. He could smell it.

"Take it away!" he said, opening his eyes wide. There was a commotion by the door. He signaled to the Headman. "What is it? I am not so sick that I cannot be told what is going on!"

"It is nothing, sir, nothing for you to worry about. It is only Plum Blossom, a slave girl. She says she has a message for you. I have told her to go away."

Presumptuous fool. Perversely, he decided to see the girl.

As Plum Blossom approached the bed, he beckoned to her until she stood nearer than anyone else in the room, in the place of honor beside the cushions that propped his head up.

"Well, girl? Why have you come?" His voice, to his annoyance, cracked.

"Please, sir, I am Spring Moon's girl. Your granddaughter has sent me to request an audience. She would like to wish you better health."

Spring Moon. Even her name was beautiful. The Venerable smiled. Strict with their children, Chinese men could indulge the whims of their grandchildren. He would see her. But before he could speak, the Matriarch had decided. "Impossible! The father of my children needs rest, not company!"

The old man glared at her. "Tell my precious she may come," he said. "Everyone else out! Including the mother of my eldest son. Out! Out!" He waved his hand. They scurried away like partridges frightened by a shadow. He was still grinning to himself when Spring Moon reached his door, though he was fighting sleep. His head bobbed on his thin neck, and his eyes blinked rapidly.

"Grandfather, may I have permission to enter?"

"What? Oh, it is you, Granddaughter." He was suddenly acutely conscious of dying. She was so young.

"Come, child. Come. Sit next to me and warm my hands, my heart." The little girl hastened to obey, climbing up beside him on the bed, cupping his once graceful fingers, now knotted and speckled, in her own, and placing her cheek tenderly on his breast. The old man sighed.

Careful not to move, Spring Moon said, "I am so sorry that you are not feeling well, Grandfather. What sickness do you have?"

"The ills of mortality."

"But you will be well soon. I know it."

"Perhaps. Tell me, why have you come to see me?"

"Grandfather." Spring Moon forgot herself and raised her head. "Something terrible is about to happen. My Plum Blossom has been promised to Old Yeh. I do not want her to go. Please let her stay, or I shall die from unhappiness."

The Venerable sighed again. The girl was so innocent. "No, my child, you will not."

"But I shall. I know I shall."

For a moment he closed his eyes, trying to recall his first disappointment. It was no use. He could not remember.

"Grandfather?"

He roused himself. "No, child, you will not die. Remember that we are not gods who can fashion events to our desires. We are mere mortals who must learn not to contend with life but to yield to it."

"But why must I yield to Old Yeh's desires?"

"Because of honor and duty. This matter is more, much more, than it seems, Spring Moon."

"But it is only a gambling debt, Grandfather. Young Uncle told me."

"Young Uncle should have held his tongue. Besides, he knows only the skin that covers the bones. Believe me, I cannot undo what has been done. I must not even try."

The old man saw that there were now tears in his granddaughter's eyes. A last gift from the gods, he thought, this sublime portrait of all that was young. A last sorrow that he must spoil it.

"Come, Spring Moon. You are too old to cry. Let Grandfather dry those eyes and tell his favorite a story."

His fingers trembled as he dabbed away the tears.

"Once upon a time," he began, "very long ago, there lived a

man and his wife who wanted a son more than anything else in the world. But none was born. After the first barren years, the good wife pleaded with her husband to take a concubine. At first he refused. Finally, he agreed. Still, there was no son.

"Though they.lived in a large house, owned land, had riches, and he was a respected official, even the beggars felt sorry for the childless couple. For the most terrible fate in life is to be without living descendants. Since the man was the last of his family line, even adoption was impossible. He and his wife had to have a son or be doomed to roam as vagabonds in the everlasting. With no heir to sweep their graves, make offerings, and perform services, they had no way to ensure their spiritual welfare in the other life. The couple prayed day and night for a son.

"Sadly, their prayers were not answered. Desperate, they prayed for a mere girl, thinking a large dowry would buy the daughter a husband from a poor family who would take their clan name. But not even a girl was born.

"While the official served in Loyang, far from his *lao chia*, he and his wife lived next door to another family, who had a son. One year, at a time when both husbands were away on the Emperor's business, an epidemic struck. People in every household died. Fear gripped all hearts. Death came so often, so relentlessly, that few remained to bury the dead, and bodies rotted on the streets. Both the mother next door and her son were infected. All their loyal servants had already succumbed, the others had run away. It was the childless neighbor who took care of them—cooking, cleaning, and nursing. She never left their side. She never closed her eyes.

"On the evening of the third day, without warning, the boy turned pale, closed his eyes, stopped breathing, and grew cold. But the good neighbor would not accept death. She seized the boy's coat and ran into the streets, where scavengers, ghosts, and bandits roamed at will, waving the garment and calling, 'Boy spirit, come back. Boy spirit, come back.' Hour after hour she circled the dark alleys littered with putrid flesh, calling, calling. Only when her voice was hoarse and her feet raw did she turn toward the house again. There she found the boy, flushed but breathing.

"The good neighbor had captured the boy's spirit from the dead. And he was not even hers.

"Now the good neighbor is old. She and her husband remain childless. But recently she dreamed that if a certain slave girl, whom she knew to be bright and strong, were to become his concubine, the girl would have a son to be the heir. The good woman believed that her dream was an omen from the Goddess Kwan Yin.

"At first, the husband ignored her wishes. But his wife grew frail, and finally he agreed to devise a way of approaching the clan to which the girl belonged. It had to be indirect, for to ask for anything of consequence from friends who cannot refuse is uncivilized."

Old Venerable paused, closing his eyes for a moment. There was too much pain: in her eyes, in his heart. When he looked again, he could barely see. But the story must be finished. He whispered hoarsely, unable to clear his throat.

"My granddaughter, the boy in the story was my eldest son, your uncle, Bold Talent. The slave girl is Plum Blossom, and the good neighbor is the senior wife of Old Yeh." The old man waited for the child to respond. When she did not, he continued. "Spring Moon, this story has no ending yet. What ending would you give it?"

For many minutes there was no sound save the old man's labored breathing. Then the child said in a small voice, "Grandfather, I wish I had never heard your story. I knew what was right before. Now you have mixed me all up. I do not know who is right, who is wrong. I do not want to choose."

"There is no choice, my child. There is but one proper ending. We must honor our debts. Only the gods can alter fate. You, my precious, must yield. Simply yield."

"You make it sound so easy, Grandfather, but my heart is breaking." Spring Moon was sobbing openly now.

"If your heart did not break now and then, Spring Moon, how would you know it is there? Hearts break, then mend and break and mend again in a cycle without beginning, without end. As surely as dawn sows the evening, twilight sows the morn."

He brushed away her tears. Her sobs quieted until finally she was still.

"You make it sound beautiful, Grandfather."

"It is," he said to her and to himself. "Now it is late. I must sleep."

She slid from the bed and bowed. "Good night, Grandfather."

His eyes were already closed.

Spring Moon walked slowly from the room, postponing the moment when she would have to explain to Plum Blossom what had happened.

How changed her life would be, she thought, when Plum Blossom left. Her earliest memories were not of her mother or her father but of riding on the slave girl's back. Even after she could walk, she had often preferred being carried, soothed by the rhythm of Plum Blossom's gait. She had guided the slave girl by pulling on her pigtails as if they were reins. For the first time, Spring Moon wondered if that had hurt.

She crossed the threshold. Plum Blossom waited just outside the door, standing with her arms at her sides, straight and tall, like a tree that would not bend before the wind.

Spring Moon wanted to run to her, but did not, and was relieved when Plum Blossom remained silent, following a few steps behind her as they made their way back to the home court. It was an unseasonably warm evening, with the scent of jasmine lingering in the air. The heavens were clear, salted with stars. Beyond the garden walls someone was playing a flute.

When they reached their quarters, the slave girl undressed the child and prepared her bed. Suddenly Spring Moon was exhausted, slipping beneath the coverlets as if already in a dream. The older girl smoothed the quilt, brushed the hair from her mistress's face, and turned to go.

"Good night, Plum Blossom."

"Beautiful dreams, Young Mistress."

The next voice was her mother's. "Make sure she stays in her room. She must not see. Quickly now!"

Spring Moon sprang up and parted the curtains. Fatso was at the door, panting, wiping her round face with her apron.

"What is the matter? Why are you here?" cried the child.

Fatso began to wail.

"Stop that, and tell me what has happened! Where is Plum Blossom?"

Fatso blew her nose and muttered a prayer. "Your mother is coming. She will tell you herself."

"Tell me now. What has happened?"

When Fatso only shook her head, Spring Moon leaped out of bed and rushed toward the door. Fatso grabbed for her, but the girl squirmed free and escaped. Outside the court, people were running. She followed.

In the Cypress Garden the crowd was silent, gaping at the old tree. Spring Moon could not see, and no one moved to let her pass. Frantic, she climbed onto the back of the stone turtle. From there, she saw.

Plum Blossom dangled from a limb. She had dressed for her journey in the finest silks, a holiday scarf around her neck.

The slave girl achieved her revenge; the House of Chang was shamed. In honoring one debt, the clan had incurred another.

The cypress was cut down.

Within the week Old Venerable was dead.

This happened in Soochow, under the reign of Kuang Hsu of the Ch'ing Dynasty, during the fifth moon in the Year of the Dragon, 1892.

WEST
WIND

⊷§ 1 §⊷

The New Patriarch

It is told that Yung Wing was the first to be called a returned student.

In his village, he spoke Cantonese. At the mission school, he learned English. After he swallowed the foreign religion, he was sent to study at Yale, where he graduated in the class of 1854.

Upon his return, he took upon himself the "responsibilities which the sealed eye of ignorance can never see" and dreamed of sending more and more Chinese boys to study in America. Eighteen years later, his dreams came true. The government sent 120 boys to homes in Hartford, Connecticut. It was Yung Wing's plan that each receive fifteen years of western education before returning to serve China.

Before long they, like Yung Wing, were transformed. More Congregational than Confucian, they wore western clothes instead of the gowns of the Flowery Kingdom. Before long, sensing danger, the Emperor recalled them.

But already it was too late.

Already, the Empire was infested with treaty ports where barbarians ruled, sowing foreign ways.

Already, farsighted gentlemen of Han sent their sons to be schooled in the alien methods, hoping thereby to save China.

Already, countless thousands of poor peasants from Yung Wing's home district in the South had sailed to Golden Mountains throughout the world, sending home remittances, foreign goods, and new ideas from lands that did not kowtow to the Emperor.

One among them would be known as the Father of the Chinese Revolution. Sun Yat-sen sailed at thirteen to Honolulu, where

27

he too swallowed the foreign religion. Upon his return, he smashed temple idols, and though he studied to be a doctor, he practiced ger ming, *the severing of life.*

—Chinese history

BOLD TALENT REACHED for the envelope the landlady held out to him and put it in his pocket.

"Aren't you going to open it?" There was concern as well as curiosity in her voice.

"I already know what it will say."

"Not bad news, I hope."

"Nothing unexpected. Thank you for waiting up." He bowed slightly and started up the stairs.

"Are you all right, Mr. Chang?"

"Yes, quite all right, thank you." He climbed slowly to his room on the third floor. As always, the smell of bacon grease grew more insistent with each step, but now, for the first time since he had come to live in this house, it made him queasy. He fumbled with the key.

Except for the desk near the west window, still lit by a faint glow from the setting sun, the room was in shadow. He did not turn up the lamps, but removed his coat and tie before sitting down at the desk, propping the telegram against the base of the brass inkwell. For a long time he stared at the envelope. It had been seven years since he had bid his father farewell. Now he would never see him again.

The loss had been anticipated. He himself had lovingly presented to his father on the Venerable's sixtieth birthday the massive coffin made of wood from the forests of Liu Chow. The funeral robes, sewn exclusively by women doubly blessed, by the artistry of their embroidery and by the happiness that their fathers, husbands, and sons all still dwelled in this life, had long been ready. And the Venerable, after much deliberation, had selected a favorite volume of odes to take with him beyond the Yellow Springs. Graced at birth by name and clan, in his time he had enhanced the honor of the ancestors through distinguished service and filial piety. He had lived in harmony. He must have died content. No son could ask for more. Bold Talent looked forward to mourning him.

Opening the envelope, he read, OLD VENERABLE RIDES THE STORK. He checked the date of the telegram and his calendar. There was no time to lose. If he was to reach Soochow before the forty-ninth day, he must leave New Haven as soon as possible.

With an effort, he rose and lit the lamps. He pulled a trunk from the closet and began packing, mechanically filling the empty spaces with the belongings collected in the past seven years, his mind astir with memories that fizzed, then faded, like sparklers on a black night. The pride in his father's eyes when his eldest son stood before him dressed for the first time in official robes with the insignia of the rank of Noble Egret embroidered front and back. . . . The softness of his father's fur-lined coat, and the day he had hidden in its voluminous folds for an afternoon after overturning Old Gardener's prize chrysanthemums. He smiled to himself. The cloak had not saved him from the old servant's righteous wrath. "Each bloom is like a child to him," his father had said. "Do not forget."

So many memories. The touch of his father's hand on his brow when he returned to Loyang to discover that his son had almost died. . . . The Patriarch's exact words on the night, soon after the sinking of the southern fleet by the French, when his father had asked to see him:

"My son, I am sending you to America," he had announced.

Stunned, Bold Talent had stared speechless at the smoke that swirled from the Venerable's water pipe. Had he been such a failure as a district magistrate that he must now be sent away? There was no denying that his rulings had pleased no one, not the Manchu authorities, not the Han merchants, not the foreigners whose languages and ways he had studied.

The Patriarch drew on his pipe. "I see I have surprised you. Then let me simply ask how long it will take for me to finish smoking this pipe."

Bold Talent hesitated.

"Well? How long a smoke?"

29

"Ten minutes?"

"Think. In less time than that, our southern fleet was sunk. If she is to recover, China must modernize. But the Conservatives in Peking have shut down the Tung Wen Kwan for foreign studies and recalled all government students from abroad. We who oppose them must now send our people to study independently. You, my son, are a logical candidate. Your betrothed is dead, and no other can be chosen for several years out of respect for her clan. You have an inquiring mind."

"My brothers? Will they be going too?"

"No. I have other plans for Noble Talent. China needs modern soldiers. He will enroll in the new military academy established by the governor of Shantung province. We are fortunate that not all officials follow the Conservative line of Peking."

"And Sterling Talent?"

"He is a book swallower and will stay home."

The Venerable had smoked silently until the pipe was finished, then put it aside and stood and faced Bold Talent, who had not moved. With the solemnity heard only at clan rituals, the father prescribed the future of his son.

"You will travel to the West. You will study the sciences of the foreigner. You will return to teach our clan and share with our countrymen the secrets of their strength."

Weeks later, on the day of his departure, the Venerable had honored him by accompanying him to his sedan. He had walked with him to the gate and waited by the screen which concealed the entrance of the house from evil spirits as his eldest took his seat in the chair. He had stood beside the bronze lions, watching as the porters bore his son away, until Bold Talent could no longer make out his features in the distance. He was still standing there, a slender, erect figure, his gold-embroidered gown glistening in the evening light, when the chair turned the corner by the Ink Pagoda.

The gesture had been more eloquent than any words his father could have spoken.

It was dawn when, with the shelves and drawers almost emptied, the trunks packed, and the crates filled with books, Bold Talent retrieved the small leather suitcase from beneath the four-poster bed, where it had lain undisturbed, except by the landlady's broom, since the day he arrived at Yale nearly six years ago. Into it he put the clothing he would need on his journey and then, very carefully, his most precious possessions. They had accompanied him from hotel to hotel, from Athens to Paris to London, everywhere he had gone during the twelve months of the obligatory grand tour of Europe, and finally to New Haven.

First, wrapping them in silk, he placed on the left side of the case the Four Treasures of Literature: the thick brushes of fox hair, their stand of jade, the inkstone carved into the shape of a lotus leaf, and the inksticks which his father had prized.

Then, between two gowns, the family photograph. The picture had been taken just before he left Soochow: three generations, 54 clansmen. In the center his father and mother posed stiffly in their rosewood chairs. At their feet, far from her rightful place among the children, the Venerable's favorite, Spring Moon.

Finally, he took from its place upon his nightstand the cloisonné box. The firs of the cypress, drawn on the lid in copper threads and colored Mohammedan blue, were as bright as they must have been the day the Emperor Wan Li presented the chess set to the original Patriarch of the House of Chang. Until he had received it from the Venerable on the thirtieth anniversary of his birth he had now and then wondered if his father would indeed choose his eldest to succeed him. There had been times during the 300 years recorded in the Clan Book when a nephew had been deemed more worthy than a son.

He opened the box and passed his fingers over the Stone-Drum Inscription characters engraved on the thick ivory disks. Foot soldier, horse, cannon, minister, general, and king. He still knew them by touch. Once more he smiled, remembering a certain Mid-Autumn Festival, when his father had returned after several years' absence in the capital. He had been twenty; second brother, three years younger. The Patriarch had announced a chess tournament to be held after the Banquet of the Moon Hare, and both sons, wanting to impress their father, had slipped away from the festivities to practice in the Chess Garden. Third brother, anxious to prove himself too, had tagged along, although the three piglet tails on his shaven crown just reached the top of the table, and he did not yet understand the moves.

Suddenly, through the Bamboo Gate had come the Venerable, resplendent in a crimson gown embroidered with flying cranes. The players sprang to their feet. The boy started to run.

"Stay!" their father had said sternly, but with laughter in his eyes.

Noble Talent had stopped short and peeked around and, at the Patriarch's nod, scrambled back, bowing three times, his pigtails bobbing.

"Resume play!" Father had commanded, but the players did not dare sit down until he waved them to their stools. Silently he watched a few moves, then pronounced, "Bold Talent, do not become too enamored with the process; remember the goal."

"Sterling Talent, stop memorizing all possible moves from books; play more games."

"Noble Talent, remember the most effective attack is not always the direct one; cultivate subtleties."

Then he had turned and walked on, passing from the court through the Maple Leaf Gate so quickly that his three sons had had no chance to respond. The Venerable had never before seen them play. . . .

So many memories. Bold Talent gently closed the box and, wrapping it in soft linen, placed it in the suitcase. Would his father still have been able to identify each chessman with his eyes closed, or had age deadened his fingertips before he died? The question would never be answered. The game he had dreamed of would never be played.

One week later, in San Francisco, the new Patriarch of the House of Chang boarded Her Majesty's Steamship *City of Peking*, bound for Shanghai.

The purser, a rotund Englishman with a ruddy complexion,

greeted him politely, although he could not entirely conceal his dismay at finding an Oriental among the first-class passengers, nor his relief when Bold Talent indicated that he would not be dining with the others at either sitting. With exaggerated courtesy, he summoned one of the Cantonese stewards who stood at the ready, their queues tucked neatly into the vest pockets of their starched white uniforms. "Show Mr. Chang to Number Eight. Be certain to see to his every need."

In his cabin, Bold Talent stood gazing out through the porthole while the steward fussed, passing his gloved hand over the woodwork, pocketing a bruised rosebud, straightening a pillow, placing the small leather suitcase on a stand, opening the drapes which hid the dressing alcove and washroom. The early morning fog that had enveloped the city had lifted, revealing the sun poised atop the hills across the bay like a giant gold coin on its edge.

He wished, suddenly, that he had had more time. This was his first visit to San Francisco. Now he would never know it.

When would he be able to roam again as he pleased, free of the demands of Confucian conformity and clan responsibilities? In forty years? Stooped, with a wispy white beard, could he live out his days as a hermit wandering through misty mountains according to the Taoist ideal?

The Venerable had never been free. His son had had seven years. Perhaps too much freedom for any man. He would need the forty-nine days, now only thirty-six, to become Chinese once more.

"Master, there has been a mistake. Only one suitcase is here. If you will give me your baggage checks, I will see to the others immediately."

Bold Talent roused himself and turned. "There is no mistake. Everything I need for the voyage is in that one suitcase. The rest can stay in the hold."

"I hope you are pleased with your accommodations, sir."

"Yes, they are fine." He nodded, noticing the cabin's appurtenances for the first time. "But I will need a large rectangular table, waist high, in place of that desk. Can you find one for me?"

"Certainly."

33

"Will there be anyone on deck at dawn?"

"No, sir, only the groom who exercises the horses of the English lord, and the watch."

"I shall walk every morning, returning to this cabin by six. Please bring my breakfast to me here at that time. My noon meal is also to be served here, at twelve; tea at four; and dinner at seven. Otherwise, I do not wish to be disturbed."

"The menus?"

"It does not matter. Rice, fresh and pickled vegetables, and fruit will do. No wine."

"If that is all, I will see to the table." The steward bowed and closed the cabin door noiselessly behind him.

Bold Talent opened the suitcase and drew from it a long gown of beige silk. Quickly he shed the coat, vest, and pants, the stiff shirt of the foreigner.

As he buttoned the gown's high collar, there was a knock.

"Enter."

The steward opened the door. "Your table, sir."

During the exchange of furniture, Bold Talent washed up. When he came again into the bedroom, he was alone.

He took a roll of white rice paper from the suitcase and draped it across the table so that the excess lay at his feet. Then he removed the Four Treasures and placed them beside the paper, on the left.

Rolling up his flowing sleeves, he poured water from the decanter on the bedside stand into the glass. Carefully he carried the glass to the table and poured some of the water onto the inkstone, droplet by droplet, for he must not exceed the correct amount. Adjusting his stance, he took the brush in his right hand, the inkstick in his left. To screen out extraneous thoughts, he closed his eyes and drew a deep breath.

Now to begin.

He ground the inkstick round and round on the inkstone until the glistening black liquid was the proper consistency. Then he moistened the brush in the ink, drawing a few strokes on the inkstone until the feel of the hairs satisfied him. With the brush firmly gripped, he paused, his arm outstretched above the paper.

Speckles of black blotted the clean sheet. His hand was shaking. It was no wonder. When had he last practiced the old arts? He could not recall. There had been time only for the new studies. They had seemed so important . . .

He had dutifully reported in letters home his progress in mathematics and in the physical sciences, as well as his studies in the philosophies of the West, which in truth he preferred to physics and engineering. But not a word of his growing misgivings. The more he had learned, the less he had dared tell his father. How could he possibly make the Venerable understand that the machines he had been sent to study were only the manifestations of foreign strength, not its source? The roots were deep in western thought, in a way of life infinitely more alien than railroads and reapers, infinitely more difficult for China to absorb.

Now, at least, he would be spared that conversation.

Suddenly he attacked the paper, sculpting the words with his brush—words he had first drawn as a boy under the watchful eye of his father. Over and over and over, repeating the strokes of *na* and *p'ieh* and *k'ou*, the sheep's leg, the vertical like dropping dew, the eagle's beak, the hook like a dragon's tail.

He did not notice when the ship set sail.

After a voyage of thirty-two days, at noon on the second day of the Fortnight of the End of Hot Weather, the *City of Peking* dropped anchor in the deep water beyond the estuary of the Whampoo. Within an hour her passengers had boarded the lighter *Chiang Yung,* which was to carry them the twelve miles to Shanghai.

That morning Bold Talent had dressed carefully in a gown of dove-gray silk, remaining before the mirror for many minutes until satisfied that nothing of the excitement within was revealed, that a Chinese was returning. And if anticipation had impelled him toward the lighter's bow, as if being there would bring him home more quickly, his demeanor was serene, and his long tapered fingers rested lightly on the rail, as befitted a man from Soochow.

The Whampoo River was as it had been the day he had sailed

away, standing then, too, at the bow. The same lorchas, steamers, tugs, sampans, and junks, many with huge round eyes painted on them to watch out for the demons of the river, bustled about in a cacophony of sirens, whistles, and horns. On board the sampans, barefoot women squatted beside charcoal stoves while children in bright smocks, blocks of wood or hollowed gourds tied to their small figures in case they tumbled over, fetched or bailed water. Sea gulls and ragged men with nets vied for the garbage dumped by the foreign steamers.

Ahead, very near now, was Shanghai, its skyline more London than Cathay. The Tricolor of France and Victoria's Union Jack, not the Imperial Dragon, flew from the standards that lined the quay, and on the wide boulevards in the British sector he could see the tall mahogany Sikhs in red turbans directing traffic.

The boat gently nudged the dock as ropes were secured. Moving to a place near the gangplank, Bold Talent waited patiently for whoever had come for him, while his fellow passengers scrambled about, collecting luggage and children, exchanging good-byes, jostling one another as they surged ashore. To his left a group of boisterous American sailors shouted and whistled at people on the quay. When one of them leaned dangerously far over the railing, his friends hoisted him off his feet and pretended to dump him overboard, to the delight of onlookers. Bold Talent shook his head. How like children the Americans were, with their pranks and easy warmth! Men who offered their hands for strangers to shake, ladies who sat and chatted at dinner with gentlemen they had never seen before, children who threw snowballs at adults no matter what their station. He would miss them.

And yet, he had never quite felt at ease with them. Not as he was, for example, with his young friend Glad Promise, when they sat across the chessboard from each other, speaking not a word.

It had been barely a year since the Venerable had written him that Glad Promise was on his way to New Haven to commence studies at Yale, asking that he "be an elder brother to the son of my old colleague." He had not found the task difficult. The youth had a carefree charm that seemed to complement his own reserve.

He was full of enthusiasm for all things western, even that dreadful activity called sports, and as the months went by had contracted an almost romantic optimism about the future. Most unusual, but in a man of his age, delightful.

Bold Talent smiled wryly to himself. The one true friend he had made in all his years abroad. A Chinese.

"Master, Master." The voice behind him spoke in the accents of Soochow, and he turned to find Old Gardener.

"My friend," said Bold Talent, moved by the smile on the servant's face, the eyes glistening with devotion to the son returning and the father departed.

The two men bowed formally.

"Oh, Master, you have been away too long, too long."

"To see you is to be home."

Together, they made the rest of the journey by yuloh up the Soochow Creek. Sixty miles. Three days and three nights. Each day Bold Talent sat on the deck, lulled by the sounds of the boatman's fishtail oar in the stern, only half listening to Old Gardener's discussion of the ritual soon to be performed.

To the man who had been away, life along the meandering stream seemed to unfurl like an endless scroll, as it always had. Blindfolded buffaloes turned the waterwheels and men poled bamboo rafts on which leashed black cormorants perched, searching the brown waters for fish to fill their masters' baskets. Across the bows of the houseboats that hugged the shores, shirts and pants of faded blue flared in a summer breeze that wafted to the traveler now faintly, now more insistently, the cries of children and the familiar smell of frying fish. In the fields, farmers swung their hoes with a rhythm more ancient than the gentle sway of the yuloh in the water, and wherever the creek eddied about a rock or two, the women crouched, chatting, slapping laundry on the stones, plucking feathers from limp chickens. To the horizon stretched the paddies of the province of Kiangsu, emerald and jade, with a sprinkling of snow-white geese.

At the end of each day, when golden threads of light wove through the trees, flocks of starlings rushed to perch on the telegraph poles and wires. Only these were new. And the fact that he, the student, was now the Patriarch. His father had said that even in reunion there is parting.

It was early afternoon on market day when the yuloh, after much maneuvering, finally squeezed into a berth at the northeast water gate of Soochow. In the square a hundred brown-skinned farmers stood beside oversized baskets, hawking produce; a hundred peddlers, displaying their wares on straw mats, shouted no less loudly.

Shoppers, the shirtless ones and those in gowns sewn with gold alike, haggled for a better price. By the monument of the chaste Widow Kung, a blind musician stood in the shade of the stone arch, strumming, blowing, tapping on his Busy-Ten.

Buffeted by the sounds and smells of the unruly crowd, Bold Talent shifted his weight impatiently, waiting for Old Gardener to settle accounts with the boatman. How many times had he passed this way and never noticed the vermin and the offal, the unholy din? Markets did not change, he reasoned. It was his eyes and ears that were new.

"Peaches, as sweet as the nectar of immortality, peaches . . ."

"Cloud ears, dragon eyes, lily buds . . ."

"Lotus roots guaranteed to please even the bureaucracies of heaven . . ."

"Silks from the loom of the Spinning Maid!"

". . . and to please your mother-in-law too!"

"Ducklings . . ."

"Bones culled from the tables of the finest families in town!"

He tightened his grip on the suitcase he had insisted on carrying and edged toward an opening between two clusters of bored men, one watching the barber shave and the other the letter writer write. In the small space, he brushed the dust from his gown and was breathing somewhat easier when, from behind, a stench enveloped him so repulsive he was nauseated. Covering his nose, he swung around. A vile beggar sidled furtively toward him. Barber, letter writer, and onlookers scattered as the man drew near.

Quickly Bold Talent reached into his pocket for a coin to pitch, but it was empty. What in the world could be keeping Old Gardener? This was no time to be without a single *cash* to ward off the heap of dung and rags headed his way. But suddenly, the beggar stopped advancing and inexplicably withdrew the foul hand he had held out. For a long moment, the man stared, his rheumy eyes as empty and hard as the stone sockets of the guardians of tombs. Then he spat on the ground and scuttled away, dropping down beside a porter who was slurping soup from a bowl by the canal steps.

"Honorable sir, give me a mouthful, just a mouthful."

"Get away, get away!"

The beggar hitched himself closer. "Please, I have not swallowed for days."

"Get going! You spoil my appetite!" The porter lowered the bowl to fend off the scurvy presence. It was the beggar's opportunity. Quick as lightning, he spat into the soup, then cocked his head and grinned into his victim's face. The porter sprang up. Slowly, deliberately, he poured his lunch onto the dirt and walked away with his head high.

Bold Talent watched him fade into the crowd. How Chinese, how admirable, he thought. Only soup was spilled. In the West, nothing short of blood could have settled such a score.

Laughing, the beggar snatched the bits of greens and meat off the ground and stuffed his mouth. When he was done, he stared again at Bold Talent, his face once more expressionless as stone.

Minutes passed. Still, the beggar made no move, either to go or to approach. Bold Talent grew increasingly uneasy. Why should he warrant such a long and tiresome scrutiny? He glanced toward the yuloh to see what was keeping the gardener. The old man, already headed his way, quickened his pace.

"Master, everything is settled. Your trunks will follow us by cart after the cargo has been unloaded. We can proceed directly to the sedans."

Leading the way, the servant nodded politely over and over as they zigzagged through the shoppers. "Honorable citizens, please lend light." The crowd, one by one, fell silent as they passed, the beggar's stare on every face.

Bold Talent glanced down at his gown. It was as before. He was not wearing foreign shoes. What then could be wrong? He called out to Old Gardener.

"Yes, Master?"

"What are they looking at?"

"Begging your pardon, sir. They are looking at you."

"Do they know me?"

"No, Master."

"Then what is there to see?"

"Pay no heed, sir. They are merely idlers with itchy eyes." The old man tried to wave them away, but the townsmen stood fast.

Bold Talent tried nodding at those who now lined the route to the sedans. None responded. Determined not to show his misgivings, he walked on toward the banner that displayed the cypress, ignoring the eyes that followed him and the crowd closing in from behind. He could not remember another time when he had felt so affronted. Even in America, no one had stared at him so. Had he suddenly sprouted feathers and scales? More and more distressed, almost frightened, he wondered what these people would do to such a beast.

At last, he reached the sedans. The porters bowed respectfully, then straightened. In their eyes, the same void.

What could it be? He turned again to the gardener. "Do not hesitate, Old Friend. Please tell me why they stare so."

Head bowed, the old man replied, "Seldom have they seen someone of your distinction. Your fine features reflect the nobility and character of your illustrious clan."

"Get to the point."

"But my words are as pure as the water from the Imperial Well. Your gown is as elegant as those the eunuchs buy for the Court, and yet . . ."

"And yet?"

Old Gardener was now openly grinning. "It is your hair. They are all wondering how it is that an honorable Hanlin scholar has

no queue. Your hair, Master, is as short as a barbarian monkey's."
Suddenly recollecting his manners, the old man hid his mouth
behind his hand, but he could not help tittering.

Bold Talent smiled ruefully. So that was it. He had not had
his hair cut since leaving New Haven, but even so there was not
enough to make a queue.

"Foreigner!" The stares accused him. "Swallower of the foreign
religion." He had tried so hard to become Chinese again, yet as
his hair had grown longer day by day on the voyage, he had not
thought of a queue at all, but of the need for a haircut as soon
as he reached home.

"Master, you must not take such things to heart."

Had he become so American that his emotions now showed
on his face? He forced a laugh. It sounded a bit hollow to himself
but seemed to convince the old man. "My friend, they are right.
My hair is much too short." Blushing, the gardener helped his
master into the chair and then clambered into his own. The two
sedans started off, leaving the crowds behind.

Aye ya! He had forgotten what riding in a sedan chair was like.
It was as bad as that sailboat outing an acquaintance had insisted
he join last summer. Even now, he could feel the beer and hardboiled eggs sloshing about inside. Another hundred years in America, and he still would fail to appreciate those strenuous activities
foreigners seemed to love. To him, there was something distinctly
incoherent about risking one's well-being to no purpose and calling
it fun. He chuckled. Perhaps he was Chinese after all.

But it was not until the sedans turned off the main streets of
town to sway down the quiet lanes between garden walls that
he began to feel in harmony, reciting to himself the names of
friends who lived in the compounds beyond the carved entrances
and the spirit screens. The Yangs had been calling on his clan
for centuries; the Soongs were the family of his deceased betrothed;
the patriarch of the Tangs had been in the stall next to his for
the three days and three nights they had labored over the poem
and essay of the Imperial Examinations. Both had qualified for
the title of Budding Scholar.

Suddenly, his chair lurched to a halt. Before him was the Ink Pagoda, as familiar as the ancestral roofs on which its lengthening shadow rested.

Taking the suitcase in hand, he alighted, for he must approach his *lao chia* respectfully, on foot. Slowly he walked along the stone walls toward the gate and the bronze lions that had guarded it since the last years of the Ming Dynasty. Everything was as it had been on the day he left, except for the blue and white streamers that hung from the roof of the entry, announcing to the world that a clansman had died.

He was halfway there when a sudden breeze stirred the streamers and swirled dust into his eyes. Blinking, he hesitated. There was a figure standing at the gate, a man dressed not for summer but cloaked in a crimson cape embroidered in gold. Did the ghost of Old Venerable wait for his son, watching as he had done from that very spot so long ago? He could not make out the features in the distance and started to run. Oh, Father, do not tire yourself. Your son is home.

But before he could reach him, the dust rose again, and this time, when he opened his eyes, the streamers hung limp. The vision was gone.

In another moment he was at the gate. He placed his free hand on the bronze lion to steady himself. It felt alive, warmed by the sun.

Old Gardener, out of breath, slipped past him silently and went ahead to prepare the way. At once the sound of gongs and drums assaulted Bold Talent's ears, announcing the return of the son, recalling the death of the father. He took a deep breath. He was home.

Proceeding slowly around the spirit screen into the receiving court, he stopped just inside and searched the square expanse, hoping for another glimpse of his father. Only the hired musicians were there, and Old Gardener, waiting by an empty guardhouse. The entire household attended the departed one.

"Please, Master," the gardener begged. "This way."

"Yes, of course." Bold Talent nodded absently. In the shadows cast by the willow, was it he? No, there was no one.

"It is late, Master. We must hurry."

He obeyed, trailing a few steps behind the old man, who led him through the second set of open doors into the Great Court of the House of Chang. Again, he paused, seeing as if in a dream the sloping green-tiled roof and the eight vermilion columns of the Hall of Ancestors directly ahead. Again he felt the ghost of his father, beckoning now from the other side of the closed shutters. He started forward to meet him.

Old Gardener's voice stopped him. "Master, please. This way."

"Forgive me, Old Friend. I am not myself. I seem lost here."

"It is most understandable, sir. Please then, shall we proceed to your quarters?"

"Yes, lead the way."

Through the Bottle Gate, past the Chess Garden and the school-house, around the marble screen . . . Suddenly, Bold Talent stopped again. He could not be mistaken. This must be the Cypress Garden. But the tree was gone. Instead, a pool of lotus blocked their path. "Old Friend, please wait. What happened here?"

The old man opened his mouth as if to explain, then closed it again and hurried on. "This way, Master, this way."

Bold Talent did not persist. He should have known better than to ask the servant. Only his brothers could be expected to report ill fortune.

At last they reached his quarters. In the doorway he stopped. Here, nothing was changed. The spare elegance of the Ming period, unadorned except for the blue and white vases in the open cabinets, still had the power to lighten his heart. Silently, Old Gardener showed him the mourning gown, cap, and slippers of white hemp that had been laid out in the sleeping alcove. Then, ceremoniously, he straightened and stood for a moment with his hands at his sides before bowing and taking his leave.

As he unpacked the small case and changed into the mourning clothes, Bold Talent rehearsed the rituals once more in his mind. Old Gardener had been persistent despite his master's inattention. As if he could ever really forget such traditions. As if any Chinese ever did.

When the chanting began, he was ready.

Through the Moon Gate and the Clover Gate, around the marble screen, he retraced his steps to the Hall of Ancestors. The sound of chanting grew, filling the courts. The shutter doors were now open. He paused on the threshold to straighten his gown and smooth back his hair.

More than a hundred clansmen dressed in white sackcloth with coiffures and queues undone, cheeks unshaven, knelt in rows beneath the carved and vaulted ceiling, men on the left, women on the right. Along the sides stood scores of holy men—Buddhist monks in robes of saffron, Taoists in black. The coffin, draped in red satin, lay upon a trestle at the end of the room behind the altar. Since the third day his father, wrapped in the gold-threaded cloak embroidered long ago, had lain in the wooden box.

Reverently, with eyes lowered, Bold Talent walked toward the altar until he reached the table set before the bier. On it stood a portrait of his father and a wood tablet painted with his father's name. He kowtowed three times. The chanting ceased.

A servant appeared with a tray of food. Using the taper already burning, Bold Talent ceremoniously lit the candles and the sticks of incense, then placed the bowls of meat, vegetables, and fruit and a pair of chopsticks on the table. He stepped back. Three times he cried out, "Oh, my father." Three times he kowtowed. His head pressed to the wood floor, he heard the others in the room stir. All the men of the House of Chang, and all the women, kowtowed three times as the priests intoned the prayers for the dead, punctuating their words with cymbals and bells. The women wailed and sobbed, lest the Venerable, gone far beyond the Yellow Springs, not hear their sorrow.

As darkness fell, the mourners left the hall one by one, until Bold Talent was alone. Still on his knees before the coffin, he vowed to bring honor to the house of his father and fulfill his duties in the care and worship of their ancestors, as his father had vowed to his father, and he to his.

When there was peace within the hall and within the son, Bold Talent rose and proceeded to his mother's quarters.

He commanded the servant at the entrance to request an audience for him. Almost at once he was motioned inside the private reception room, where the old woman, attended by her slave girls, sat upon her ornate rosewood chair, her golden lilies resting on a matching stool. Mistress and servants alike were swathed in white hemp.

He had barely risen from his kowtow when his mother began scolding. "So it took this to bring you home. You are nothing but a vagabond, my son." Her adoring eyes belied the sharpness in her voice. "Come! Quick! Let me get a good look at your ugly face."

He drew nearer. "Well, my mother?" He almost smiled. She at least would never change.

She reached out to touch his cheek, then thought better of it and shook a finger at him instead. "Son, grow a queue! People will think you have been caught wandering in the inner courts." The slave girls giggled. Swift as an adder, the Matriarch turned from one to the other, her eyes ablaze, searing both to the core.

Bold Talent thought it wise to change the subject. "You, my mother, are looking well."

She turned back to him. "Liar! I have not closed my eyes these seven weeks, what with hundreds of mourning guests to attend to and feed, and the distant relations I never heard of—all poor, of course—who had to be housed and given an allowance as well. Not to mention the priests. We have had to hire twenty-five more hands. If you had been here all along, doing your share, I would look better."

He bowed his head. "Forgive this unworthy son. I promise never to neglect clan affairs again."

She threw up her hands. "Ha! You have not even given me a grandchild. I warned your father not to let you go away to the edge of the earth without first marrying you off. Now, with mourning, nothing can be done for another three years. By that time you will be a man of forty, an age when any normal filial son would be presenting me with great-grandsons."

My beloved mother continues exactly where she left off seven years ago, he thought. He must change the subject again. "Honored

Mother, has everything been done for the funeral tomorrow?"

The old woman pretended not to hear. She motioned for the girls to fan her.

He repeated his question, louder this time.

She winced at the volume, then spoke. "Oh, we may not have the funeral so soon. The geomancers favor a later date, perhaps another year."

"But forty-nine days is customary, and also Father's wish. You remember that, do you not, my mother?"

"Since when do you concern yourself with customs? By custom, I should be weighing offers from marriage brokers for my grandson. Besides, geomancers know what is best. Why, soon after you left us. some foreign devils came and peered at our lands through witch glasses and put up tall poles with wires. Every geomancer in town warned the officials against such practices, but they would not listen." She sighed dramatically. "What happened?" She paused again, awaiting his answer. When he said nothing, she answered for him. "Only what one would expect. The waters rose and crops were lost. Beware, I say, of offending the dragon spirits. Is that not right, my girls?"

The girls nodded emphatically.

No use challenging his mother's faith in the geomancers' magic. It would never work. He said humbly, "My mother, how can I object when you have obviously given this much thought?"

A smile barely touched her eyes, but anyone who knew her could tell she was most pleased.

Checked at one point, the player makes another move. After a moment, Bold Talent asked, "How is everybody?"

"Fine now. Until today, they were busy running in and out of here asking about you."

Was she as off guard as she seemed?

"Are many of my cousins with happiness?"

"Oh, several. At least two will have boys. I can tell by the way they walk."

Here was his opening. "Then, Mother, I must quickly locate a house outside the city gates, for you have always said it is bad luck to give birth under a roof where the dead still sleep."

He saw from the expression in her eyes that he had succeeded, but otherwise she revealed neither her pride in his agility nor her exasperation at her predicament. She merely turned to the nearest slave girl and ordered her to tell the priests to prepare for the funeral.

At dawn on the appointed day, the cortege left the courtyards, winding its way through the city, out the western foot gates, along the country roads—the Banners of Condolence, the Venerable's sedan chair, his umbrella and coat, his portrait and spirit tablet; eighteen Buddhist monks, eighteen Taoist priests, seven Lamas, two full bands of musicians, a hundred porters of heavenly gifts, ten sweepers of evil spirits, eighteen flashing swordsmen to ward off unfriendly devils, and thirty-two bearers in green brocade coats and red-plumed hats carrying the giant silk house that shrouded the catafalque. All these were followed by Bold Talent, the only living son of the senior wife; Sterling Talent, the only living son of the deceased second wife; and Noble Talent, the only living child of the third wife, leading all the males of the family on foot and all the females in closed carts; and then the entire household staff, friends, officials, and farmer tenants of the House of Chang.

Crowds lined the streets. Coolies smacked their foreheads in disbelief as more and more passed in review, and merchants bowed respectfully before the wealth ot the Changs. The eyes of young women and girls sparkled behind slits in windows and doors; thus they maintained the proper distance without missing the display. Old women gossiped and giggled, pointing now at this mourner, now at that one, all the while keeping a halfhearted eye on the urchins who ran to and from the popping firecrackers like moths attracted to the light and then singed. Scores of shopkeepers and artisans had erected paper houses on altar tables along the route; in tront of each was a white mat on which the Chang sons knelt to reciprocate the honor thus given their father. Only the beggars were missing; the clan had given a generous donation to the head of the Beggars' Guild to prevent their odious and macabre presence from spoiling the great occasion.

Half the day had passed before the entire procession arrived at the ancestral graveyard, where generation upon generation of Changs had been interred. According to the geomancers, these grounds enjoyed a perfect correspondence between the course of the stream, the trend of the mountains, the curve of the road, the spirits of the trees, and the paths of the sun and the winds.

When the last servant stood within, a hush fell, broken almost at once by the shrill lament of the musicians. As the dirge rose to the heavens, the male mourners on the inside, the females in their carts on the outside, formed a circle to watch the transfer of the coffin from the catafalque into the shallow hole prepared for it. Then each male mourner in turn threw a handful of earth into the grave, and when the coffin was fully covered, the priests burned the gifts, sending papier-mâché horses, servants, carts, pigs, hens, food, money, lutes, books, chess sets, houses, and other comforts of life to the Western Skies for the use of the departed.

Finally, as the assembled fell to their knees, Bold Talent drew the red dot upon the spirit tablet that would grace the altar at home, signifying that one of the three spirits of the Venerable would now reside within the House of Chang forever, while the second slept within the ground, and the third flew to the Land of the Shadows.

Holding the tablet before him, the new Patriarch eulogized his father. "My sins are many and heinous, and for them I should die. My life, however, is spared. The gods have punished me by causing the death of my father. He died on the fifth day of the fifth moon of this year under the ancestral roofs. I and my brothers shed tears of blood and bow our hearts to the earth with grief.

"My father was born . . ."

Bold Talent's voice was hoarse by the time he had finished extolling all the particulars of Old Venerable's virtuous life and exhorting the mourners to follow his example.

"We dedicate our lives to you, O Father, as you have dedicated yours to the House of Chang."

Thus ended one man's sojourn in this world; thus began his homecoming in the land of the ancestors.

Death and duty were undeniable.

The Year of the Dragon would pass, and the Year of the Snake, and of the Horse, and throughout that time the members of the House of Chang would mourn the death of Old Venerable, dressing and eating simply, renouncing all celebrations of births and marriages, retiring from public life and official posts. Not until the Day of Pure Brightness in the Year of the Sheep, 1895, when the descendants would gather to sweep the ancestral graves with branches of willow in bloom, would the clansmen return to the world.

❧ 2 ❧

The Reforms

The sadness of the Chinese!
Ah, what I am speaking about is the sadness of being Chinese.
Not because foreigners have insulted me,
Nor because my compatriot has oppressed me:
He does not point out my name and beat me
Nor does he call out my name and abuse me,
He only comes upon me face to face,
Humming a nameless tune, and passes on.
But when I sleep at home,
He in his house beyond the garden wall
Begins to fire off double-popping crackers.
                                    —Chon Tso-jen, about 1910

BOLD TALENT SHIVERED and thrust his hands deeper into his sleeves as he made his way along deserted pathways toward the gate. It was still not too late to turn back. His brazier was warm, and a new shipment of books had just arrived from Shanghai. Nothing would delight him more than to spend the morning reading. But the Patriarch could not indulge himself so.

The receiving court was deserted, except for the porters huddled against the wall, smoking. In the icy air, their breath was as white as the cigarette smoke. Seeing him, they jumped to their feet and bowed. He nodded in return.

No one could remember such cold. Even the Widow Wang was not at her usual post by the spirit screen, waiting to pour out her grievances against this or that tenant of the House of Chang. The poor woman had no children and made it her business to be the landlord's eyes and ears, hoping to win favor. No one took her seriously, least of all himself. Nevertheless, he must remember to send Fatso to her tomorrow with a rasher of bacon in return for the duck egg the widow had brought him with yesterday's report. He sighed. Landlords could ill afford the generosity of their tenants. At least, with no petitioners today, he was able to see Farmer Lee for the first time in a fortnight and thereby fulfill his responsibilities in the most agreeable way. Lee was the only tenant who never assumed the privileges of the tributary; his words and deeds were always what they seemed, not entwined with hidden intents.

Picking up the skirt of his gown, Bold Talent stepped into his sedan chair. The head porter bowed, closed the door, then snapped an order to the country boy who had recently been hired. The youth did not move from his position by the wall but flung himself into a groveling kowtow. "Please, Master, do not make me. I will do anything else you ask. But Old Uncle, please . . ."

The porter repeated the command in a low growl. The boy continued to press his head to the paving stone. Obligingly, Bold Talent pulled the curtains of the chair, smiling to himself. Now the porter, unobserved, could speak his mind.

"You cowardly, mangy abortion of blithering baboons!" The words were followed by the sound of scuffling, then a howl of pain.

"Ow! Ow! Let go of my queue! Ow! Ow! Ow!" The boy's shrieks were punctuated by the porter's somewhat breathless curses as he yanked the wiry body into place at the rear of the chair. For a moment there was an ominous silence. Then a hacking cough. Bold Talent was beginning to wonder whether it was time to intervene when suddenly the boy loosed another healthy bellow.

"Ow! Please, Master, don't make me walk under washing again. Something terrible will happen this time for sure!"

"You superstitious spawn of camel's dung! This is a great and learned house. If you wish to work here, you walk straight and pay no mind to what is hanging overhead."

"Please . . ."

"Aye ho! Aye ho!" cried the head porter as he took his place in the front.

"Aye ho!" wailed the boy.

The sedan lurched into the air and swayed around the spirit screen. Bold Talent broke into a wide grin. Here was progress! How many months had it taken him to convince the head porter that pants overhead did not portend disaster? Five? Ten? A pity that such persuasive language was beneath his dignity.

If only he could speak so to the tutor, who had threatened to quit rather than teach mathematics. "Traffic in numbers," he called it, "the work of petty clerks and mendacious merchants." Bold Talent imagined the teacher's learned mouth agape, emptied at last of pedantic couplets and oblique metaphors, after a word or two from the head porter's repertoire.

A few such epithets during the Patriarch's next lecture on hygiene to the kitchen staff might at least make them stop to think before spitting into their palms and wiping them dry on the back of their grimy trousers. He imagined them in spotless aprons, scrubbing their hands at the basins he had had installed more than two years ago, for once using the soap he had taught them to make instead of selling it under the table to merchants.

Still smiling, he settled back in the seat, enjoying the rare solitude. It reminded him of the tranquility of his life across the seas. There, no one had plagued him with squabbles to mediate or debts to pay, and he had grown used to living alone among strangers and to the dulcet rhythms of English.

He shook his head. Three years home, and he still could not accustom himself to the shrill sounds of his native tongue. Chinese, with its constantly changing pitch and staccato monosyllables, seemed to him like drums, cymbals, gongs, and bells—exclamatory by nature. Even in the dialect of Soochow, the sweetest of all, ordinary conversation lapsed into fortissimo, and though he was able to escape the presence of callers now and then by leaving the Patriarch's quarters for his beloved Ming study, he could not escape the sounds of daily life among the Changs.

Perhaps he would not mind so much if anyone had anything of interest to say. But his relatives, at least during these years of mourning, had had little to do but savor certain subjects, enjoying the same conversations over and over again. Constantly they argued about the ability of various cooks, the insolence of a servant, the boorish ways of a neighbor's friend. Gossip. Endless gossip.

Whenever he was present at the evening meal in the men's dining room, the subject sooner or later was foreigners. Eldest Cousin would begin, shaking his head in sorrow. "The Barbarians do not know the first thing about *jen*. How can they ever hope to become civilized? Just last week, the brother of our kitchen maid was fired by his Englishman. That is the employer's privilege. But if he were also a man, instead of a Barbarian, he would give the boy face, allow him to resign instead. Even the dirtiest gutter-snipe in China does not step on his drowning enemy!"

Third Uncle or Second Cousin would then shrug and declare, "But how could they behave otherwise, when their own rulers set such bad examples? Victoria's ministers sell opium to Chinese while banning its use in England. If the Queen is not virtuous, how can her people be so?"

Then all would bemoan China's losses in the Opium Wars, the burning of the Summer Palace, the granting of the Concessions—all fifty-six of them, one by one.

If Bold Talent reminded them of the murders of defenseless missionaries or of the Imperial Edict that commanded foreign emissaries to kowtow before the Yellow Emperor although they did not kowtow to their own kings, they were quick to retort:

"Who asked them to come? Did Emperor Chien Lung not warn them at the start that neither their goods nor their presence would be welcome? If they would simply go home, all under the Heavens would be harmonious once more."

On and on the harangue went, an endless sport. No one disagreed that China was like an overripe fruit, neglected and humiliated, poised to fall into the mouths of foreign jackals. No one, except Bold Talent and Noble Talent, thought there was anything that could be done to prevent it. The litany was, "Poor China! Poor sons of Han! A big-footed Manchu concubine behind the throne. And big-nosed Barbarians throughout the Celestial Empire."

Sterling Talent was no help at all. "Yes," he would say, "who asks them to stay? They ridicule our ancient culture and our sages, while preaching about the virtues of a dead carpenter. They laugh at our ancestors' tablets but worship a god of three spirits. They deride the food we sacrifice to commemorate our departed parents, yet declare that bread is the flesh of God, and wine his blood. Cannibals! Chinese converts? Aye ya! Ten years of strife and twenty million dead before the rebellion of the Christian-led Taipings was put down."

If Fatso was serving, it was she who always had the last word. "Any no-neck, no-eyed turtle can see that they are spies. Why else would anyone stay where he was not wanted? Spies, nothing but spies! If one of those *yang kwei* ever tells me that *I* am going to hell, I'll spit in his pasty face and say, 'Show me the way!' " And all would guffaw as if they heard her words for the first time.

In the beginning, Noble Talent had been his ally at these discussions. He understood the need to modernize and had great respect for the English and German instructors at the military academy. But in the last few months, as the evidence mounted that Japan was intent on taking Korea, his young brother had become obsessed, pressuring him constantly for permission to return to his ship, though the period of mourning had not yet ended. "I am a soldier. I belong at sea fighting the enemy. What good are reforms if the country is occupied?"

As Patriarch, Bold Talent had had to reject these appeals. How could he permit one of his family to break the most sacred of traditions? Especially when the clan never failed to point out that "Even the honored ancestor, the minister to the Emperor, retired to Soochow for the duration of mourning."

Now Noble Talent sat in stony silence during family gatherings or withdrew to his quarters, counting the days, no longer pretending the smallest interest in the Patriarch's efforts to introduce reforms here at home. "What does a soldier know of farming?" he would say. Meaning, perhaps more to the point, What does a returned student from the West know of it either?

Sighing, Bold Talent pulled open the curtains of his sedan.

They had passed through the city gates and were now on one of the many toe paths that crisscrossed the farmlands belonging to the House of Chang. The paddies on either side oozed brown mud at this time of year, during the planting.

The noon sun had broken through the clouds, warming the air and sending the tenants home from chores in the fields for a bowl of soup. As his chair passed, they stepped aside and bowed low. He inclined his head and smiled.

The peasants were always respectful and, for the most part, silent in his presence. Even Farmer Lee, who always volunteered to try an innovation, did not talk much. He would laugh and scratch his head and bow, only rarely making a suggestion of his own. But when the others saw that no unhappy ghosts haunted Lee after the mechanical pump was installed in the field near his ancestors' grave, they too wanted use of the contraption.

A few weeks ago, he and the farmer had started a cooperative effort to repair the crumbling dikes, which corrupt officials had neglected. As it had from the first, reluctantly, the clan humored him and paid for the tools and the materials; Lee supplied the men. With the dikes mended and the new pump working, the fields would be thick with rice shoots by spring, each well-watered row a luxuriant green.

As the sedan swayed around the bend toward the mud-and-straw-thatched cottage of Farmer Lee, the sound of a young voice roused Bold Talent from this satisfying reverie.

"Mother, Mother, Honored Master is here! Honored Master is here!" It seemed to come from beneath his chair. Leaning out, he spotted the boy waving and running alongside, his short queue flapping. It was Resolute Spirit, Lee's four-year-old son.

By the time he alighted, the child had disappeared around the corner of the house and the Lees were standing in a welcoming group, like a patch quilt of faded blues, with a touch of red on the toddlers. They bowed from the waist; the wadding of straw stuffed between their many layers crunched. "Welcome, Master! We do not deserve such honor."

"Good day, my friends. Have you eaten today?"

"We are well, Master." They answered in unison, bowing again. "Have you eaten today?"

"I am well also." He nodded.

The toothless grandmother then came forward and presented him with a bowl of hot water, while two skinny uncles shouldered each other aside for the honor of bringing up the stool and placing it in the shade by the wall. As the Patriarch drank, the Lees grinned and nodded their approval.

Suddenly, from the back of the house, Resolute Spirit appeared in a whirl of dust, pulling a black piglet by a rope. The boy was already taller than his two older brothers, though he still wore his mother's thin gold loop earrings to fool the jealous gods into thinking he was a mere girl and unworthy of their interest. Around his neck were strung amulets to ward off the sickness that had nearly killed him several weeks before.

"Look, Honored Master, look how big Ham has grown!"

"Indeed, the pig is truly worthy of an Emperor." Bold Talent inclined his head with suitable gravity.

Resolute Spirit would have said more, but his sturdy mother quickly hoisted the sleeping baby higher on her back and stepped forward to take hold of his hand. Her son must not overstep his place.

"Please do not take the child away," Bold Talent protested. "I enjoy his company."

Resolute Spirit stood taller and his clan laughed, but then there was an awkward silence. The mother broke it, bowing. "My stupid third son refuses to allow anyone near that pig. He feeds it by hand and washes its feet as if they were the Buddha's."

"Honored Master." Resolute Spirit bowed solemnly, very low. Bold Talent tried hard not to laugh at the boy's small naked bottom, which peeked through the slit in his pants when so raised. "I want to make Ham taste good, Master."

"And you can be assured that I will pay an extra special price for his extra special taste!"

"Oh, no, sir!" The boy shook his head so hard that his queue whipped about his face. "Ham is a present."

"A present for me?"

Everyone nodded.

"If it were not for you, Honored Master," said the grandmother, "Resolute Spirit would have gone to his ancestors."

"It was nothing. The least I could do."

The mother wiped away the tears which inevitably flowed at the thought of how sick her favorite son had been. "You could have walked away, Master, when I quarreled with you. I thought the foreign hospital was an evil place. I did not believe you when you said they would not take my child to make gold. Can you forgive this ignorant woman?" She fell to her knees.

"Please, get up. There is nothing to forgive."

Thus was the ritual conversation ended. Bold Talent stood up and asked for Farmer Lee.

"My husband is not here. He felt sick and went straight to the same hospital."

"When?"

They looked at one another. An old uncle said it had been on the day of the full moon; the wife thought it was a few days before.

All were certain he would be back soon, completely cured. They nodded their heads emphatically.

Their recently acquired but clearly absolute faith in the magic powers of the mission hospital dismayed Bold Talent. Quickly he said his good-byes and, when he was out of hearing, gave the order for the porters to take him there at once.

Built in part with funds he had insisted the Chang treasury provide, the hospital was a small two-storied red brick building which looked as if it had been picked up by some zealous wind in New Haven, Connecticut, and deposited haphazardly in Soochow. Its only concession to its surroundings was the high wall that enclosed it. Instead of a spirit screen there was, over the entry, a wooden plaque with the name SOOCHOW MEN'S MISSION HOSPITAL inscribed in English and Chinese.

Waving aside the porter at the door, Bold Talent swept down

the hallway, dodging worried relatives who had come with special foods, which the patients were forbidden to eat, and who now squatted along the walls wailing and quarreling with the staff. His nose twitched at the smell of sickness and disinfectant mingled with herbal brews and chicken soup. The gray-haired Bible woman who served as receptionist, translator, and traffic director sent him to a back room upstairs, room 16.

The door was open. Farmer Lee lay, propped on pillows, in the narrow bed.

The peasant's large frame, which only two weeks before had been full of vitality, seemed hollow and frail, and his face was the color of a dried husk. His eyelids twitched. From somewhere deep inside him came low, intermittent groans.

Slowly Bold Talent drew near the sick man. The tiny room was full of hovering spirits, so that unconsciously he whispered. "Old Friend, it is I, the Patriarch. Are you in pain? Can you talk?"

With great effort, the eyes opened and focused, and a glimmer of a smile came to the dry lips. "Master . . ."

Bold Talent bent closer. "Do not worry. I shall speak to the doctor. You will have the best care. I promise."

"Yes . . . thank you . . ." Suddenly Lee's breathing quickened and with each breath the labored groans grew louder.

Bold Talent turned to leave; he must get help.

"Stay . . . please . . ."

"Yes, of course." The farmer who did not fear the ghosts in his fields feared being alone. "Yes, of course I will stay."

Bold Talent took his handkerchief from his sleeve and leaned over to wipe the sick man's brow, then hesitated. Perspiration was dripping from the end of Lee's queue onto the floor. Surely there should be an attendant present, someone who could ease the pain.

Putting the handkerchief instead to his own lips, Bold Talent hurried out to call for help.

He saw the physician coming up the stairs. "Doctor, you must come. It is Lee."

"Yes, I know." The man paused, out of breath. He met Bold Talent's eyes.

"Is there nothing you can do?"

"We . . ." The doctor shook his head. "The man came too late."

At the hour of the cock, Farmer Lee died. The following evening, his youngest son came to the courtyards to sell his black piglet, too small to be of any value. The Patriarch paid a handsome price. The money went for the funeral.

On the way home from the burial, the new porter, walking down the street with his eyes fixed on a pair of trousers hanging overhead, tripped over a loose stone and broke his leg.

❦ 3 ❧

Winged Shoes

My niece, who is six years old, is called "Miss Tortoise";
My daughter of three, little "Summer Dress."
One is beginning to learn to joke and talk;
The other can already recite poems and songs.
At morning they play clinging about my feet;
At night they sleep pillowed against my dress.
Why, children, did you reach the world so late,
Coming to me just when my years are spent?
Young things draw our feelings to them;
Old people easily give their hearts.
The sweetest vintage at last turns sour;
The full moon in the end begins to wane.
And so with men the bonds of love and affection
Soon may change to a load of sorrow and care.
But all the world is bound by love's ties;
Why did I think that I alone should escape?
                        —Po Chu-I, Tang Dynasty

A FEW WEEKS AFTER the death of Farmer Lee, as the sun passed its
zenith, Bold Talent sat on a taboret beside the pond in the Garden
of the Pensive Flute. It was the fortieth anniversary of his mother's
suffering, and all day he had felt trapped in Heaven's web. Now
his eyes followed restlessly one of the golden carp that darted
from lily to lily, flashing chiffon skirts.

At least, he thought, he was spared the good wishes people believed appropriate to this occasion in America; in China, everyone's birthday was celebrated on the seventh day of the First Moon. A most civilized custom. Or was it? He shook his head. He did not know anymore. Nothing seemed in harmony, not since the death of Farmer Lee. Letters from his "progressive" friends were piled high on his desk awaiting answers, but he had nothing to say any longer in response to their pleas for support and encouragement. The morning of Lee's funeral, the pump had frozen. Later, when the ceremonies were over, he had not even been able to persuade a neighbor of Farmer Lee's to take his daughter to the hospital, although everyone could see that her leg was already black, foul with gangrene. The man had been quite logical. "Tell me who would take a bride with one leg? Better she walk to the other side of the Yellow Springs than live the life of a beggar." He did not say that neither the foreign doctor nor the Patriarch's reforms had helped Farmer Lee, but that was what he meant, as well.

Now the girl, too, was underground. Since her death, Bold Talent had read and reread Shen Chu-lien's letter to his dead daughter until he knew it by heart. The words haunted him.

"When you see the Judge of the Lower World, hold your hands together and plead to him, 'I am young, and I am innocent. I was born in a poor family and I was content with scanty meals. I never wasted a single grain of rice, and I was never willfully careless of my clothing and my shoes . . .' Now I am composing this, but you do not yet know how to read. I can but cry for you and call your name."

Words penned three hundred years ago, but the ink had not dried! So many little ghosts.

Suddenly, there was a faint sound. He looked up, startled. It came again, stronger this time, but still soft. "Ooooo! Ooooo!"

Where had it come from? He glanced about. No one was there.

"Ooooo! Ooooo!"

"Who is calling?"

"Me."

"Who is me?" The voice sounded suspiciously mortal.

"Spring Moon!" she said, peering at him from behind a rock.

"You almost undid me. What if you had sent me splashing into the pool?"

"Then I would have run away."

"Would you have left me to drown?"

"Are you not wearing the magic steam pants from America to pump, pump you back to shore?" she countered, laughing at him. He shook his head, unable to resist her impertinence. Several times he had come upon her in the Cypress Garden, perched on the stone bench beside the schoolhouse wall. She must have been listening yesterday to the story he had concocted to explain a point in mathematics, the subject no one else would teach.

She offered him a handful of crumbs, and they fed the fish together.

What a merriment she is, he thought. So different now from the sad-eyed creature he had found when he first returned from America. So different from others her age, those short replicas of their mothers and aunts. Spring Moon was joy and just as elusive.

"Look, Uncle!" She tugged at his sleeve, then pointed into the pool. "That one with the bulging eyes. I named him Eldest Uncle, after you."

"Because . . ."

"Because—" She brushed the last crumbs from her hands and turned to look up into his face. "You will not like it," she warned.

"Of course not! Otherwise, you would not have done it."

"Well"—she leaned closer—"every time another fish comes along, that one runs away and hides. When no one is around, he sneaks out and swims all alone, shaking his head. Just like you."

The Patriarch laughed. "Your mother is right. You are trouble."

"But you still like me, do you not?"

He nodded, smiling. It was true. He enjoyed the girl's company more than that of any other relative, although their paths did not often cross. Until the farmer's death he had been preoccupied with his reforms, she with whatever young girls did. Sewing for her trousseau, he supposed, though he doubted that Spring Moon bent willingly to the task.

"Can I come later to borrow the picture book?"

"The one with the steam engines?"

She nodded eagerly.

"Why does that one interest you above the others?"

She must not have heard the question, for she asked, "If steam can paddle the boats in that book, Eldest Uncle, and the cars that run on rails, why could it not make winged shoes that would go without hurting my feet?"

He glanced down at her golden lilies. "Do they still pain you?"

"Not that much, not really. Almost never. I am not a baby anymore, you know."

She drew herself up and with a lofty look challenged him to deny it. He could only shake his head in appreciation.

Suddenly, she remembered something else. "Eldest Uncle?"

"Yes?"

"Grandmother thinks the telegraph poles scratch the back of the dragon and make him angry enough to ruin the crops. But I agree with you. I think we should build a telegraph of our own."

"How could we do that?" He was genuinely curious.

"Well, I could tie a string to your bedpost and pull it until it reaches mine. Then you would buy two bells, small ones, to tie at each end. At night, when the ghosts come, I can pull on the string and you can pull back. The bells ringing will frighten them away."

"Might it not be simpler just to wake up your slave girl?"

At once the look on her face changed, as thoroughly as if she had donned a wooden mask. Slowly, she shook her head.

"But why?"

She shrugged. "Because . . . because I have no slave girl."

"No one wants trouble, is that it?"

"No." Her voice was almost a whisper. "I could have had anyone. Mother said so. But those that came, I sent away. I told everyone that I did not want a slave girl, not then, not ever."

He asked gently, "Did something happen, Spring Moon?"

For a long time, she did not respond, her eyes cast down. Nor did he intrude. She was not too young for private thoughts.

Finally, she looked up and said, "Something did happen before you returned. My Plum Blossom died, in the Cypress Garden. No one can ever take her place. No one. I would rather be afraid at night than let another come into her bed."

Sterling Talent had not told him that the dead slave girl had been Spring Moon's. "I am truly sorry. It must have been very sad for you."

She managed a slight nod. He took her small hand in his and held it tight.

"Do not think of that anymore. It happened so long ago."

"But I can never forget her!"

"No, you are right. You should not." She must have been a tiger to have defeated her mother and the Matriarch.

He should say something. She was too young to be haunted by ghosts. *I am young, and I am innocent. I was born—*

All at once, he knew the answer. "Spring Moon?" She looked up. "How would you like to learn to read and write?"

"Could I?"

"Of course you could."

"But the boys would laugh at me. The tutor would resign again."

"No," he said, "I shall teach you myself."

"What will Grandmother say?"

"You need not be concerned about that."

"But—"

"I am the Patriarch, am I not?" He struck the most formal pose, like that of an ancestor portrait. She jumped to her feet and bowed solemnly. Then, with head tilted to one side, eyes dancing, she said, "Oh, Eldest Uncle, I think you are trouble too!"

So it began. Every morning, after her calls on the elders and breakfast, Spring Moon came to Bold Talent's study, where a table and a stool had been placed between the two cabinets of Ming porcelain. There she worked on new characters and read while he dealt with his correspondence. Every afternoon, they took tea together. Then he would answer any questions she had and explain the lesson for the next day. He was delighted with her intelligence.

within a month she was able to read and write simple texts. And unlike the boys, she understood what she had learned.

The family was scandalized, of course.

"Too much learning for a girl is dangerous and spoils her chances for a good marriage. Educated ones are malcontents who disturb the virtuous harmony of the household."

"Girls belong in the inner courtyards with their mothers, learning the arts of homemaking."

The Matriarch relentlessly pursued the subject. "Have you no consideration for my grandchild's future? Before, she pestered everyone with *why* this, *why* that. If you keep this foolishness up, as certainly as the Goddess Kwan Yin is merciful, she will *dare* this, *dare* that."

Bold Talent understood their fears, but he would not bend. Even after the period of mourning ended, Spring Moon continued to study. She was his only success, his one hope.

❧ 4 ❧

The Soldier

*In the world today, what position do we occupy? Compared to
the other peoples of the world we have the greatest population
and our civilization is four thousand years old; we should therefore be advancing in the front rank with the nations of Europe
and America. But the Chinese people have only family and clan
solidarity; they do not have national spirit. Therefore, even
though we have four hundred million people gathered together
in one China, in reality they are just a heap of loose sand. Today
we are the poorest and weakest nation in the world, and occupy
the lowest position in international affairs. Other men are the
carving knife and serving dish; we are the fish and the meat.*

—Sun Yat-sen

THE LAST RAYS of the sun clung to the far edges of the Po Hai as
Noble Talent walked toward the sea. The northeast wind howled,
and along the shore the giant fishing nets flared and flapped like
the tangled gray tresses of a faceless witch. Here and there men
worked, scraping the barnacles from the bottoms of boats, hauling
baskets of fish or driftwood on their backs toward the shelters
of woven straw where ragged children warmed their hands at sputtering fires.

He walked as if there were no wind, and he did not stop at
the water's edge but waded straight into the waves, plunging in
against the tide until the water of the bay licked his boot tops.

The rabble gathered behind him. He could hear their shouts amid the mewling of the gulls that flew overhead.

"*Lai! Lai!* A crazy in the water. Quickly, before he dies," an urchin cried.

"Who is he?"

"What is he up to?"

"Hey, you!"

Suddenly the voice of a man. "I know him. From the military academy. See? The same leather boots as the foreign devils who teach there."

"See what monkeys these students of the Barbarian are!" A wild chorus of agreement arose.

"Hey! Is that what the foreign devils told you to do to become *ping,* a soldier?"

The crowd jeered.

"You idiot running dog, standing in freezing water is what you do to become *ping,* ice." The onlookers guffawed at the pun. "Did your mother never tell you the difference between a soldier and an icicle?"

"*Ping ping!* Ice soldier, ice soldier!"

Noble Talent could no longer pretend not to hear and swung around. A Manchu bannerman strutted as if on parade before the children, who, eyes crossed, slapped themselves on the cheeks in the manner of madmen. The others, huddling together against the wind, blew into their fists to warm them, watching.

For the first time in his memory he lost control. It was as if the excesses within that he battled always had grown like a viper in his bowels, too deadly to digest, and he had no choice except to spit them out, with only the wind and the rabble to hear.

"Go away!" he shouted. "Let me be! I stand here to honor the patriots who fought and died at sea, to bid my friends farewell. A few more minutes and I will be gone." He could see that his words commanded, but he felt no victory. Without control the commander is without virtue, like the madman they thought him to be.

Still, the bannerman, who had lost comrades himself perhaps, stopped mocking and with a gesture dispersed the others. "Go along now. There is nothing to see."

The children lingered a moment, as if they could not believe the game had ended. Then they too marched off, one after the other, swinging their arms, stamping a single set of footprints in the sand.

As darkness swallowed them, Noble Talent turned again and stared out to sea. The remnants of breakers sloshing and swirling at his feet were like ice, but he welcomed the cold. It numbed the senses, masking the shame, the fury. For he had come too late. Just like the father of his mother! Or so the whispers went.

During all those months of waiting, he had imagined that he, one of the few who had been trained to fight a modern war, might make a difference. Others would shoot arrows at ironclad hulls and think to stop cannonballs with bamboo sticks. He was a master of ballistics and naval strategy.

He spat scornfully into the water. What difference did his training make now? This morning, when he had reported for duty, the base had been almost deserted. His comrades had died in battle or were recuperating from wounds. There was not a ship left, not even one on which he could help train others for another war.

The swordfish had speared the whale. The Middle Kingdom was dead.

"Three years! Three wasted years!" His voice was hoarse.

Go home and wait, his superiors had said. Go home and wait with the others.

Wait a year, perhaps two. Wait for more ships to be built in the dry docks of Great Britain and Germany. Wait for the Dowager Empress to complete her Summer Palace and Marble Boat so that there would be funds again for the military. Wait for a change of heart among the ruling Manchus and the eunuchs, who lied and misled the Court while lining their sleeves with bribes and the people's taxes. Perhaps then there would be adequate supplies and no more papier-mâché bullets in the ammunition store.

Wait another year or two? He threw back his head and gave an angry laugh. No, he had been fool enough. He would not wait forever.

He shut his eyes, seeing the two ironclads that had gleamed in the harbor broken on the ocean floor, the scattered limbs of his captain and classmates rotting beneath the mute waters, eviscerated Chinese buried in a common grave while the living kowtowed to a Brown Dwarf.

No, he would not wait.

Making a fist with his right hand, he held it high, clenched tight as if to hold shut the jaws of the viper within, and shouted aloud the vow in his heart. His voice cracked.

"Hear this, departed comrades—you who died in the Korean Bay when your transport was sunk by the Japanese before war was even declared. Hear this, departed comrades—you who died at Yashin, Pyongyang, Chenhwan, and Seoul at the hands of the Japanese army. Hear this, departed comrades—you who died in the naval battle of Yalu. Hear this, departed comrades—you who died at Port Arthur and Weihaiwei, Haich'eng and Kaip'ing. Here this, my ardent vow. Your deaths will be avenged. China will be free and strong. I dedicate my life to the cause you have fought and died for. Hear this, departed friends, and know peace!"

He stood for a moment more, then dislodged his feet from the sand and slowly pushed his way through the water to shore. He limped until he could walk, and then he ran.

During the eight days of the journey back to Soochow, he practiced endlessly the speech he would make when he reached home.

The sedan stopped. "Are we there?" Noble Talent called to the head porter.

"No, Master. Another thirty paces, but people are gathered in the way."

"I informed no one of my return."

"Master, they are not members of your illustrious family."

"Let me down. I will walk."

He pushed his way through the crowd. Before the entrance, a short, sturdy woman screeched and danced like a trapped monkey, battering the air with a ferocity that was all the more terrible because her hands were no larger than a small child's. Her face was so contorted with anger that it was impossible to distinguish her features, and a purple vein swelled from her hairline to her throat. She wheezed like a mouse-eaten bellows. "Dogs, sheep, goats, it does not matter to these sons of turtles who they lay!" She spat at the spirit screen.

Noble Talent gritted his teeth and tried to slip by, but the woman was too quick and grabbed his sleeve. "Do not go in." Then she recognized him, let go her hold, and raised her arm as if to ward off a blow. Did she think that he would soil himself by striking a demented old woman? Giving no sign that he had noticed her, he walked past, around the spirit screen into the receiving court.

As soon as he was out of sight, she resumed her tirade. "There goes one of those rotten abortions! Chickens, snakes, rabbits, and toads. . . ."

The court was empty except for Fatso, who had her ear pinned to the screen. She did not see him and suddenly, before he could speak, she scooted through the entrance to the Great Court, shaking her head and waving her hands in horror. He ran after her, to the women's quarters.

As she approached the open doors of the Hall of Womanly Virtues, she began shouting. "Oh, oh, if only you had heard, if only . . ." and by the time he had reached the red columns, the entire female household was in an uproar. Slave girls scurried to and fro with ginger water to revive the elderly, who were swooning because of the report they had eagerly waited to hear. Several mothers looked toward heaven. "To think I let that woman near my husband's child," he heard one say, and the others nodded agreement. Second Grandaunt's voice rose above the hubbub. "I always knew that Amah Liu was up to no good. If you, my sisters, had listened, it might not have come to this. Amitabha!" Her fan snapped. "Attacking the cook with a knife!"

Noble Talent carefully stayed out of view, waiting to catch Bold Talent's eye.

It would not be easy. His brother stood in the center of the room with his back to the columns, facing the Matriarch. Their voices were not raised but somehow could be heard above the din.

"My son, do something! You are the Patriarch. You must do something!"

Bold Talent clasped his hands and bowed. "Mother, dear, I have explained a hundred times. It is the tradition—one that our clan has always abided by. The dismissed must be allowed the right to revile the employer. It is a good rule. It protects those who need protecting."

"But she can be heard in Shanghai!"

"That may be so, but imagine the shame if I gagged her and had her spirited away. The entire Yangtze delta would talk."

"I do not care for your excuses. Do something!" She waved a slave girl over to dab her brow, while Bold Talent looked toward the ceiling tiles, as if seeking inspiration from the Immortals. Then, slowly, he nodded. "Fatso, come here."

"Yes, Master."

"Go tell the head porter to take Amah Liu home in style, in our best sedan chair. Quickly, before she faints from her exertions!"

The Matriarch frowned, then brightened. "Clever, quite clever!"

"I am overcome by your praise." Bold Talent bowed again, visibly swallowing a laugh.

"It is all those chili peppers," she explained. "They give out the wrong *chi* and cause great imbalances, reducing . . ."

But Noble Talent was no longer listening. A war had been lost and they vented their spleen over a gnat! He decided to wait for his brother in the Ming study.

On the Bridge of Coming and Going he collided with Spring Moon, who was hurrying toward the commotion with several of her mother's plum silk handkerchiefs in hand.

"Young Uncle, what are you doing back so soon? Where is your uniform?" Without waiting for his answer, she went on. "Never mind, come with me now to the women's hall. You must not miss the excitement. It is like a feast day, so much is happening."

He stared at the girl. Her cheeks were flushed and the yellow ribbons in her long braid unraveling.

"Oh, Uncle, do not just stand there. Come with me."

"Spring Moon, you should be ashamed of yourself—taking delight in distress."

She recoiled as if he had splashed her with tub water.

What was the matter with him? Could a girl of thirteen behave otherwise? He cleared his throat, wanting to say something to reassure her. "Spring Moon . . ."

"I meant no harm, Young Uncle, truly I did not." She smiled tentatively. He nodded, trying to smile too.

At once she was cheerful again. "Oh, please come. Grandmother will be so happy to see you. She and my greataunt went to the convent to say prayers for you last week."

"No, Spring Moon. I shall see everyone later. First I must speak to the Patriarch. You run along."

"Shall I send him to you?"

"That would be most thoughtful, my niece." He nodded, grateful that he would be spared the squeals of feminine delight. "Tell him privately. I do not want anyone to know yet of my presence. I shall be waiting for him in his study." He reached out, then resisted the impulse to pat her cheek.

"Oh, I shall keep your secret." She smiled. "Young Uncle, I am glad you are home and safe."

He nodded and watched her prance away, down the steps of the bridge, along the zigzag walk.

At twilight, after Amah Liu was royally on her way, the two brothers sat together in the study, Bold Talent at his desk, Noble Talent in one of the rosewood chairs against the wall. Resolutely calm, the younger man began the speech he had so carefully rehearsed, talking first of the pride and hope he had felt when the Venerable sent them both to learn from the West. But as he recounted the events that had led to the sudden end of the war, his anger swept over him again and he jumped to his feet and paced the floor, hands clasped behind his back, each stride flipping the hem of his gown, open and shut, open and shut.

Only at the end of his tirade did the soldier realize that through it all Bold Talent had sat impassive, now and then puffing on his water pipe, seemingly more engrossed in watching the smoke drift than in anything being said.

Impatiently Noble Talent swatted the smoke, then sat down again when his brother's mild gaze met his. With nothing more to say, he waited.

There was a long silence.

Outside the garden walls, the night watchman was making his rounds. They could hear his wooden clapper and the cries of "Coming! Coming!" So too would the evildoer hear him and a confrontation in the dark be avoided.

At last the elder brother spoke. His words were true enough but to the soldier seemed as insubstantial, as little to the point, as the wreaths of smoke. "I think, perhaps, the fault lies with us, with our love of literature, of the past and the family. We choose men to administer our welfare, conduct wars, and dispense justice solely on the basis of eight-legged essays and poems they write by rules laid down in the philosophy of the ancients. We . . ."

But Noble Talent was no longer listening. As if by its own will, his right hand clenched into a fist. As vividly as when he had stood upon the beach he saw the bodies of his comrades, and then a new vision, the Patriarch of the House of Chang kowtowing to the Brown Dwarfs. No!

But his cry must have been entirely within, for Bold Talent merely struck a match and relit his pipe. He spoke thoughtfully, between puffs. "The modern world will not let us be, but we do not know it. We sleep, like the coolie in the gutter—dirty, despised, and dying, dreaming all the while that he is king and sage."

" 'We,' my brother?" Noble Talent heard himself shouting. Again he fought for control. "You and I are not part of that 'we'! Our father did not sleep. Nor can you and I. We must act!"

Bold Talent shrugged. "What would you have us do? You have seen how I have tried. Yet not even the smallest change has come to our own courtyards. You saw how little it took today to throw the household into utter chaos!"

"And you just stood there, listening to the nonsense. I do not understand you at all!"

The Patriarch smiled ruefully. "The fact is that I no longer see it as nonsense, if I ever did. The women had a right to be upset.

The amah had a right to speak her mind. There is merit in the middle way." He spoke as if to himself. "What right do I have to wake that coolie? What harm is there in dreaming, if it eases pain? What good is reality, if it blots out hope? Can a man's mind be washed without bleaching his soul?"

Slowly Noble Talent stood. He forced himself to speak deliberately, to tame the animal within, the animal that howled. "What matter the whiteness of the soul, my brother, if the coolie is attacked in his sleep by carnivorous dogs? In the morning his bones will be scattered and buried, to be gnawed again and again at leisure."

He waited, searching Bold Talent's face, reading nothing there, pleading silently with him.

The older man studied the younger for a moment, then he too stood. "There is a chill. Do you not feel it?" He walked to the charcoal burner, lifted off the top, and stirred the ashes, probing for the glowing red nuggets.

The soldier marched over and dumped in new coals. "Let me do that."

Together they stood beside the brazier while warmth filtered into the room, inappreciably at first, then layer by layer, in the silence.

"Young Brother?"

"Yes?"

"The hour is late. I still have Spring Moon's lessons to correct. We will speak of this again." Bold Talent turned back to his desk and picked up some papers. When he lowered his eyes, it seemed a door had shut.

He was being dismissed! Looking quickly away, afraid that he would speak, say what must never be said, Noble Talent turned on his heels and left the room.

After a sleepless night he was up at dawn, dressing and slipping out of the courts like a fugitive. No more than last night could he bear the prospect of the women's greetings, their chatter, the smiles upon their faces.

He walked, not caring where, as long as the route took him away from home.

When the sky had turned a pale blue, he found himself at the government compound. It was still early and the gates were locked. Only a few petitioners were about. One or two read the posted sheets. The others stood near the entrance, each hoping to be first inside. The notices were the usual ones—of tax levies, the rulings of district magistrates, lists of personal grievances, announcements of births and deaths, advertisements, even old news. He walked along, reading one after another, searching for—he was not sure just what it was he sought. As he neared the Yamen's main gate, a servant of the compound appeared to paste up a new poster, and he went to take a closer look. He scanned the headlines, then bought a copy from the man to read.

It was not possible! Even after all her defeats, China could not have agreed to such peace terms as these! Clutching the paper, he ran toward home.

He found Bold Talent moving through his *tai-chi* exercises in the rose garden beside the Patriarch's quarters, apparently so lost within himself that he was oblivious to the intrusion.

"Eldest Brother—"

He was still breathless from his run, and could not say more.

"Can it not wait a few more minutes?" Bold Talent lifted his right heel slowly to his left knee while making a graceful circle with his arms.

"No! This cannot wait." He thrust the paper into his brother's hand.

Reluctantly, Bold Talent took it and walked over to sit on the stone bench beside the screen of climbing yellow roses. Noble Talent, sitting beside him, waited restlessly for him to finish reading. His hand would not be still; it tapped upon his thigh, beating the muffled drums for China's losses: Hong Kong, Ili, Liu-ch'iu, Annam, Burma, Korea, Quemoy, Matsu, Taiwan. How could his brother read with that infuriating calm, revealing nothing? He felt like a derelict pupil, his palms burning from the tutor's punishing cane. Each territory signed away, another stroke.

At last Bold Talent put down the paper. "Where will the two

hundred million taels of silver come from?" He shook his head, as if in sorrow. "It is more than three times Peking's total annual revenue. My brother, where could it possibly come from?"

Noble Talent stared at him in disbelief. The reparations were the least of it. This was not a treaty to end a war. It was the end of a nation. Eldest Brother had turned into a book swallower too, counting the hairs and not knowing the nature of the beast. "I do not know, my brother," he said. He turned on his heel and walked away.

Even as he passed through the Moon Gate, he had decided what he must do, and within the hour his plans were made. He would go south to Canton, where lived those farthest from the Emperor's sway, and search out the rumored secret societies, dedicated to revolution. He would tell the clan only that he had recently had an offer from the import-export firm of the Sui Brothers of Kwangtung, relatives of a classmate. The last part, at least, was true. He could arrange the first. And the clan would not be displeased. Even a merchant was preferred to a soldier.

Once the path of honor was clear, Noble Talent became calm; now that he knew he would soon be leaving, there was no need to hurry.

For the first time since he was a child, he sought the company of his mother, Silken Dawn. Every day they sat together side by side near the west window of her chamber, he with a book, she at work on the exquisite embroidery that was her chief preoccupation. Whenever she had hidden a final stitch, she would ask him to find the telltale sign of a beginning or an end. He never could, and each time she smiled and said, "It is as it should be."

She could not recall her age when she had come to live in the House of Chang, only that her feet were not yet bound. Her father had been killed while in the service of the Venerable and her mother was already dead. She had had nowhere else to go. The clan took her in.

The Venerable's first wife grew to love the orphan, and when the second wife died of cholera, she suggested that he take Silken

Dawn as his third wife. It was an ideal solution, for the Venerable was soon to leave Soochow to take up a post in Shantung. He needed a wife, and the older woman should not go herself, for tradition expected that, having borne a son, the first wife of the heir of the Patriarch would remain in the *lao chia* to serve her mother-in-law.

Perhaps this history explained why Silken Dawn was so compliant, often acting more like a servant than the mother of the third son of the Venerable. Or had she too heard the whispers about the man who was her father, how he had served as the Venerable's personal guard, how he died? Neither mentioned him to the other, neither ever knew or asked his name. For his grandson it was as if he had never existed except in stories, half heard, half imagined. Was it the same for his daughter?

One story said that when the guard was in the service of the family, he had run away from his post and caused the wounding or the death of men in his charge. Sometimes the whispers said that the bandits cut off a finger for a ring; sometimes, that they slit the throat of an old man or stabbed five youths in the back. All the rumors told how the derelict had returned to receive his punishment. The Venerable had made him his personal bodyguard instead. Years passed. Finally, the guard died while saving the Venerable's life. Sometimes, the whispers said, he shielded his patron from a bullet; sometimes he diverted a tiger and was mauled to pieces, or hid the Venerable in a stream and did battle with a pack of wolves.

Still other whispers said that these heroic accounts were all figments of the Venerable's imagination, for he had had to say something to soothe his young wife, to comfort their son; that the guard had gone mad and shot himself or been shot when he ran from duty again.

A few days in every year the soldier was certain that none of the stories were true. How many times had he wanted to say just that to his mother? But he never had.

Now that he was about to leave her, he wondered what her life had been like, married at sixteen to a man three times her age and widowed before forty. What dreams did she dream now?

That her son would rise to serve the Emperor someday, he thought. That her many descendants would sweep her grave, honoring the chaste widow who had lived all the years of her long life eternally loyal to her departed husband.

But he would never serve the Emperor. And he would not marry or have sons, for the soldier and revolutionary must be prepared to die.

Perhaps she had known all the time. When he had been still too young to read, he had more than once seen tears slide from her eyes—one, then another, each politely waiting its turn.

Lately, she had embroidered only chrysanthemums. He must ask her to stitch a daffodil or some other spring flower. He meant to say, "No more of those that bloom in fall." But he never did.

No peace can be bought, and the Treaty of Shimonoseki was an open invitation; when a cat overturns a jar, the dogs are assured of a meal.

The next year, the Heavenly City of Soochow became a treaty port, the twenty-second city in the Empire to be subject to the unequal treaties that exempted foreigners from Chinese law, granted foreigners the right to determine Chinese tariffs, ceded Chinese lands to foreign control without reciprocity.

At last Bold Talent acted, joining with other concerned scholar-gentry in a Self-Strengthening Society, to explore avenues of reform. As in similar societies in many cities, discussion was lively. The gentlemen met once a fortnight to read the words of Thomas Jefferson and the life of Napoleon, seeking a way of reinterpreting Confucianism to foster Westernization.

By the Year of the Dog, 1898, thirteen of China's eighteen provinces had become foreign spheres of influence.

Those within garden walls lived as before, growing older.

❧ 5 ❧

Red Letters

*When a son is born, what is desired of him is that he may have
a wife; when a daughter is born, that she may have a husband.
All men as parents have this feeling. If, without awaiting the
instructions of their parents and the arrangements of the interme-
diary, they bore holes in the garden wall to steal a sight of each
other, or climb over the wall to be with each other, their parents
and all others will despise them.*

—The Book of Rites

EYES FIXED on the open book, Spring Moon braided her hair absently,
savoring the scene from the *Dream of the Red Chamber* in which Black
Jade renounces her unhappy love.

The copybook in which the beauteous Black Jade had recorded
the poems of her heart was already afire when the servant Snow-
goose returned bearing the footstool made of *hua-li*. Heedless of
the flames, she pulled the burning book from the brazier, trampling
it with her golden lilies until the last sparks were out. But alas,
only a sorry charred remnant survived. Black Jade closed her eyes,
content, and sank back upon her pillows. . . .

Suddenly, from the other side of the closed door, a voice intruded.
"I have no hands. Open up."

"Come back later, Fatso. I am busy."

"I am busier than you, Galling Mule. Open up or else!"

The wily old servant was a worthy opponent, knowing exactly when to cajole, command, trick, reason, plead, or simply pull by the ear. Spring Moon put aside her book and opened the door.

Fatso dashed in, mixing a bowl of cold water and thin shavings of *wu-mu*, lifting the spatula to check the consistency of the jelly. Her pockets bulged with hairbrushes, pins, and combs.

"You know that I do my own hair," Spring Moon protested.

"Not today, Whining Mule. Sit down!" Fatso set the *wu-mu* on the dressing table and proceeded to lay out the implements she needed. "Your mother has ordered your hair put up. She says it is time to reflect your womanhood."

At last! Spring Moon had thought it would never happen. Now everyone would see what she had already known for months— that she was no longer a mere girl but a woman of infinite possibilities, a woman who would be off any day now to Heavenly Lane, or the Yamen, or even to faraway Shanghai in her red bridal chair!

She sat down with a show of great dignity and watched in the mirror as Fatso combed the jelly through every inch of her waist-length hair. When the servant was almost finished she spoke up again.

"Fatso?"

"Mmm?" Fatso had an extra comb in her mouth.

"Fatso, then perhaps it is also time you stopped calling me this and that mule. It is time you called me 'Young Mistress.'"

"Is that so?" The servant gave an extra-hard yank on the comb.

Spring Moon smiled her sweetest smile at the old woman's reflection. "Please?"

"So be it," said Fatso. "Now turn around, so that I can see what I do." She worked swiftly, drawing the comb down the exact center of Spring Moon's head to make the part and twirling a long shining rope of hair into a perfect circle above her left ear. With one hand she held the coil awkwardly, fetching hairpins from her mouth to fasten it in place, then repeated the procedure over the other ear. At last she stepped back to judge her work. "Not ugly! Not ugly!" The barest hint of a smile touched her round cheeks. "Young Mistress, you are not too grotesque when you behave and keep still."

Spring Moon turned and stole a quick glance in the mirror, then looked again. Was it really she? The twin coils of maidenhood accented her high cheekbones, the oval contours of her face. The reflection could be that of the legendary beauty Black Jade, escaped from the pages of her book.

Fatso interrupted the reverie. "No time to stare at yourself. Your mother and the Matriarch are waiting." The servant opened the sandalwood chest and laid out the new clothes. "Come, come!"

"I shall dress myself as usual. Please wait outside."

Fatso threw her hands up but stomped out without protest. When she had gone, Spring Moon removed her dressing gown. Swiftly she pulled on the tunic of lavender silk that fell gracefully below the knees and stepped into the long purple skirt, pleated at the hips. On the wide, flowing sleeves and high collar of the tunic, sixteen butterflies in shades of pink and green had been embroidered by her mother.

Smiling to herself, she walked slowly around the room, swaying on her tiny golden lilies, carefully balancing the maiden's coils as if they were a jeweled headdress. Before the mirror, she dipped gracefully in obeisance—her neck bent forward, her back straight, the right knee barely grazing the floor, both hands gently touching the left hip. With eyes downcast, she spoke: "This daughter of the House of Chang feels most unworthy of your kind words. I am not the fairest of the fair . . ."

The door flew open. "But the slowest of the slow! Come along now! Come along."

For once, Spring Moon did as she was told, meekly trailing the servant, who hurried toward the Matriarch's private quarters. But her golden lilies could not keep up with Fatso's big feet, and deliberately she slackened her pace. Why should she exert herself? She was no porter padding the streets for an extra *cash* or two. She was Young Mistress. On the terrace she stopped altogether. "Slow down, Fatso! It is not yet time for dinner, you rice bin!"

Fatso, who had already disappeared through the Moon Gate, dashed back, dipped elaborately. "This daughter of the House of Yu is most unworthy of your kind words."

So Fatso had seen and heard! Impudent servant! Spring Moon

walked past her, head high. Thank Buddha that the woman, no matter how insolent, could be trusted not to tattle of her foolishness.

At the Matriarch's quarters, she waved Fatso away. Then she turned to face the open door. She straightened her skirt and smoothed her sleeves. Pretend, she told herself, pretend this is a day like any other and not the beginning of your life. Taking a deep breath, she crossed the gallery and passed between the ancient dwarf cypresses that marked the entrance of the Matriarch's reception room.

Inside, she stopped. Where were the marriage brokers? Where was the go-between? There was only Grandmother and Mother, embroidering. Aye ya! She had been presumptuous. It was to be just another day after all.

"Good morning, my grandmother. Good morning, my mother." She bowed.

"Where have you been?" Fragrant Snow asked, her eyes on the length of silk in her hand.

"My hair . . ."

"It is most charming, is it not?" the old woman remarked to the younger.

The mother finished knotting the thread and put aside her needle. Then she looked at her daughter. It was a moment before she spoke. "Aye ya, she looks different . . . civilized."

She continued to stare until a gentle nudge from the Matriarch reminded her of her duty.

"Spring Moon, you may sit down. Your grandmother and I have important matters to discuss with you."

"With me?" The girl quickly sat down on a stool beside the large embroidery frame. She tried to smile but could not.

"My daughter, you are invited to tea in the Hall of Womanly Virtues."

"Why?" There was always tea.

"Is that the only word you know? Never mind why! We expect you to be at tea this morning."

"This morning?"

"Yes. In a few minutes."

"But Eldest Uncle expects me for my lessons." She could not hide her disappointment.

"For once, you will be at tea with the rest of us, do you understand?"

"Yes, my mother."

"You will behave properly. You will not speak unless spoken to. You will not drift off, dreaming about whatever it is you are always dreaming of."

"And my afternoon lessons, must I forgo them as well?"

Fragrant Snow clapped her hands sharply. "Lessons! Always lessons! If I had wanted a second bookworm, I would . . ."

Spring Moon lowered her eyes and shut her ears. She had heard her mother's lecture many times. The words never varied.

She had so hoped that this day would be special, as memorable as the day Black Jade and Pao-yu met. . . . How did it go?

The precious stone that Pao-yu wore was the size of a sparrow's egg and shone with the rose light of morning clouds. On it was inscribed:

Never lose me, never lose me!
Glorious life—lasting prosperity.

Then Black Jade showed him her gold amulet, on which these words were written:

Never leave me, never reject me!
Precious youth—everlasting bloom.

And Pao-yu exclaimed, "Our verses complement one another and form a perfect . . ."

"Spring Moon, are you listening?"

She looked up. "Yes, Mother." Fragrant Snow shook a finger at her. "Now remember. Do not speak of your lessons."

"No, my mother."

"Remember the dictum of the Sage: 'A silent woman is a virtuous one.'"

"Yes, my mother."

The Matriarch, who had not spoken during the mother's tirade, now beckoned to Spring Moon, summoning her to stand near the rosewood chair. When the girl was beside her, the old woman leaned over and whispered in her ear. "You must make a most proper impression upon our guest, my granddaughter, for Pan Tai Tai has come especially to see you. This will not be an ordinary tea but an occasion of consequence."

Spring Moon flushed with joy and embarrassment. She had been right after all! Today would be the first day of her true life.

The Matriarch smiled broadly, for once, in her pleasure, forgetting to conceal her gums. "Now that you understand, my granddaughter, let us join the ladies."

Throughout the hour of the snake, as her mother and the aunts chatted with Pan Tai Tai about everything but the purpose of the visit, Spring Moon sipped her tea demurely, eyes downcast, though her heart was clicking faster than Fourth Grandaunt's knitting needles. The guest seemed pleasant enough, perhaps just a bit toothy. She wondered if the son favored the mother. Third Cousin claimed that was the rule.

The ladies rose. The tea was over. She had not spoken a word throughout.

They stood together, grandmother, mother, daughter, and all the female relatives and their servants, and waved good-bye. "Let us meet again!" cried Pan Tai Tai triumphantly. Like a peddler who has sold all her wares, Spring Moon thought. "Let us meet again!" The women returned to their chairs, chatting brightly, already planning the festivities to come, paying no attention to the prospective bride. Weddings were clan affairs, the province of elders.

Unnoticed, Spring Moon slipped away and walked quickly in the direction of the servants' quarters.

In her daydreams, her betrothed was a man of a thousand names, as changeable as the weather. She discarded one, chose another, according to her fancy.

But, of course, there would be no choice.

One stranger. What if the Pan boy's face were pockmarked, like a sesame bun? What if his legs were skinny like chopsticks? What if?

She found Fatso squatting in the doorway of her room, her upper arms jiggling as she scrubbed a pair of Old Hawk's pants against the washboard in the wooden tub. "Fatso . . ." The servant started and looked up. Spring Moon knelt down beside her on the dirt floor.

"Your new dress!"

"It is no matter. Please, may I speak with you?"

"Now?"

"Please." Deliberately Fatso finished rinsing and wringing out the pants and dropped them into the basin. She wiped her hands dry on her apron. She felt the girl's forehead.

"Are you sick?"

Spring Moon shook her head.

"You want to talk in your room or in mine?"

"In yours."

Fatso's room had not changed since Spring Moon and Plum Blossom had first hidden there to escape Fragrant Snow's summons to the embroidery frame. There were the two stools, the battered trunk, Old Hawk's pipe, and, on the wall, the baskets filled with the strings, feathers, papers, and dried bones Fatso collected for sale to the Odds and Ends Dealer. After the slave girl's death, Spring Moon had come here often, helping Fatso sort her treasures. Thus had she thanked Fatso for assuming Plum Blossom's duties without complaint, making it possible for her to refuse another slave girl. Neither spoke of appreciation; it was understood.

Today, she pulled her stool close to Fatso's, until their knees touched. "Old Friend." She took the thick sausage fingers in her own. "Old Friend, you must help me before it is too late. Tell me what this son of Pan Tai Tai looks like. Is he a scholar? Does he frequent teahouses?"

Fatso shook her head, pulling out her handkerchief to blow her nose.

It is even worse than I imagined, Spring Moon thought. Fatso only blew her nose like that when she was upset. "Well, Old Friend, well?"

Fatso hesitated, checked outside the door—as if an eavesdropper would dare to cup an ear to Fatso's business—then spoke quickly.

"If you want my opinion, Young Mistress, you ought to shave your head, trade your trousseau for some prayer beads, and be done with it."

"Be serious, Fatso!"

"I am serious. Pan Tai Tai is a terror. Once when she was here for tea, I poured before she thought it was properly brewed. She accused your mother, in front of everyone, of being too lenient with her servants." Fatso curled her lower lip under and assumed a toothy look, smiling falsely. " 'If you let servants get away with one thing, dear Elder Sister, before long they will have you running around for them!' "

Spring Moon laughed. "Nothing like that happened today, Old Friend. Perhaps you have let one incident mislead you."

Again Fatso shook her head. "Today she wanted to impress your clan, Young Mistress. But I have heard terrible stories from one of her kitchen girls who is from my village."

"Perhaps her son is not like her."

Fatso spat. "What does he have to do with it? It is the mother-in-law who counts. The Pan woman wears two faces—one for influential families like ours, another for the rest of the world."

Could Fatso be right? Suddenly Spring Moon wished she had not been so virtuous at tea. If only she had talked incessantly, told of her lessons, of how, in the rain, when everyone else was running in, she went running out. . . . But perhaps it was not too late.

"Old Friend." She clasped Fatso's hand again, and voiced her thought aloud. "Perhaps it is not too late. Go and tell the Pans' kitchen girl the worst, the most terrible things you can about me, about how often I am scolded, about how badly I embroider, about how much I have to say. Make some up, too!"

But Fatso only shook her head, and blew her nose again. "That will not change Pan Tai Tai's mind, little one. She wants an alliance with a family of breeding and scholarship to make her money shine." As she spoke, she caressed Spring Moon's cheek, wiping away tears that had yet to fall. It was as if the gentle hand of the old servant told a truth her words could not convey.

There was no hope. This match was Spring Moon's destiny.

Now she would never see Wu Shi Lake or Hangchow, only the

neighboring gardens of Pan Tai Tai and the toothy grins of her mother-in-law and her husband . . . or the convent walls.

She did not know until Fatso reached over and pulled her hands down that she had begun to undo her maiden coils. Saying nothing, the old servant repaired the damage. Spring Moon did not resist.

When the coils were in place again, Fatso leaned over to whisper in her ear.

It was many minutes before she understood the true meaning of the servant's words. "In an upright house, inferiors must obey superiors, children their parents, parents their elders, elders the Patriarch."

Spring Moon shook her head. "More than anyone else in the world, Fatso, I want Eldest Uncle to think well of me. If I speak of the arrangement of my marriage, he will think me shameless— with the ways of the lowest class, of an actress or . . . worse. He will think me wanton!"

Slowly, she stood and started for the door. But Fatso ran over and blocked the way and, placing her hands on the girl's shoulders, spoke again, urgently.

"No, he would not think any such thing! For he has lived with foreigners, and it is said that foreign women court many suitors for themselves, and with their parents' blessing. What you say cannot shock him. You must tell him quickly, now, before things go too far."

At the hour of the cock, Bold Talent was at his desk in the study, awaiting Spring Moon, rereading the poem she had written the day before.

> Entering the bold world
> I awakened to see
> Only upon
> leaving my universe
> the courtyard
> can I know
> the sounds of homecoming
> and the relentless hooves of my own steed.

He smiled. It was not an unworthy effort. He would never have believed that she would come so far in three short years, though she did work every day and often into the night. What pleasure he had had, watching her powers grow!

Her voice interrupted him, and he looked up.

"Eldest Uncle?" she repeated, standing in the doorway.

For a moment, he could not answer. She was beautiful. Why had he not realized it until now? Was it the new maiden's coils? Or that particular shade of lavender? He was sure she had never worn it before.

She spoke again. "My uncle, why are you looking at me so?"

"Am I?" He shuffled the papers on the desk to one side. "Come in, my niece."

She sat in the chair by his desk with her hands folded and her head bowed.

"Well? Speak up."

"I do not know how to tell you."

He waited, strangely disturbed, as if he had walked through a mirror and found everything the same, and yet nothing similar.

"Have you heard Mother talking of me lately?" Her voice was very soft.

"She complains three times a day about your studies, but that is nothing new."

Spring Moon hesitated a moment more; then the words burst forth. "She wants to have me married!"

So it has come, he thought. He had known it would. Yet he had hoped life would continue for a while as it had been. He could not imagine what it would be like to look up from his correspondence and not see her. . . .

He said only, "Why are you unhappy? Everyone must be married."

"You are not, my uncle."

"No, but I would be if the girl the Venerable chose had lived." Three times married, if the Matriarch had had her way, he thought to himself. Again he felt the old ambivalence. If he were already married, he would think it fine, he was certain. But he was not, and so that was fine too. It was as if he had passed a crossroad where he should have turned so long ago that now returning there would take more effort than he wanted to expend. Yet the longer he walked alone, the greater the distance, the more formidable the effort. And, he knew, he could not put off the trip back forever. Why, then, had he tarried these three years since the end of mourning?

Because they had been most agreeable years, he answered himself. Almost idyllic.

". . . Eldest Uncle, please, you must listen. I was introduced to Pan Tai Tai today. I do not like her. I do not want to be her daughter-in-law."

Amitabha! What was his sister-in-law thinking of? Pan Tai Tai had no breeding. And her boy was hardly more satisfactory. He was, in fact, nothing but a prince of leisure. Probably even smoked the foreign mud. Yes, he was sure he had heard that Pan Tai Tai's son was an addict. The marriage would not do, not at all.

He rose from his chair and handed Spring Moon some papers. "My niece, you stay and look over these corrections. I will speak to the women."

He found the Matriarch in her private quarters.

Seeing that her son had something delicate on his mind, she sent the slave girls to fetch tea. When they were gone, he said, "I hear that Spring Moon is to be married."

"I wondered when you would hear of it. If you paid more attention to clan affairs, you would be better informed."

He bowed. "My shortcomings are indeed grave, my mother. It is to remedy them that I come to you."

"Well?" She waved him to the chair next to hers.

He obeyed, wondering if he had been wise to address the issue so directly. Now, he had no choice but to proceed. "Is it true, then, about the Pan boy?"

"I cannot deny that your sister-in-law speaks enthusiastically of him."

"That boy is not worthy of your granddaughter. Tell my sister-in-law that the match is unsuitable."

She did not answer immediately but seemed to be weighing

his words, nodding. Finally, she said, "You agree, my son, that Spring Moon is of age."

"She is only sixteen."

"I was married at fifteen." Her shrewd eyes seemed to read his every thought. "But then, you would feel the same if she were twenty!"

"Certainly! The boy is unworthy!" His tone was more vehement than he had intended, echoing in his ears like a coin clattering across a brass tray What was the matter with him?

His mother furrowed her brow in silent disapproval. He had not felt so rebuked since he was twelve and had deliberately allowed Sterling Talent to get lost at the fair. But before he could make an apology, the Matriarch spoke again. "My son, you are incapable of judging this matter."

"What do you mean, my mother? I, myself, have seen the Pan boy near the House of the Reclining Willows."

Now she sat up very straight, her eyes the angry slits her son, unlike the women, seldom saw. "Listen to me, my son. It is time for Spring Moon to leave this house. It is time for her to serve her mother-in-law. It is time for those who should be married to marry."

"Do not try to spear two fish with one lance, my mother. Whether it is time or not is another matter. She must not go to someone who will not appreciate her."

"To someone who will not appreciate her as you do, you mean."

"That is exactly what I mean." Hearing himself, he went on quickly. "After all, I have taught her much. She is not just another pretty girl."

"No, you have seen to that." The Matriarch's spirits now were visibly improved. "And since she is so special, my son, it is you who must choose a husband for Spring Moon."

"I?" He was genuinely surprised. "Why, I could not—"

"You must. And quickly, or your sister-in-law will have her way." The old woman's small eyes now sparkled with triumph, though her lips were without a trace of a smile. He almost laughed, realizing how carefully she had planned it all.

He stood up and bowed. "As you wish, my mother."

In the light from the window, her skin seemed like antique silk, without sheen but still fine. He bowed again and withdrew.

During the following weeks, Bold Talent and Sterling Talent systematically invited the fathers and sons of the most respected families of Soochow to dinner on one pretext or another, but neither he nor his brother found any of the candidates worthy. Before long Sterling Talent withdrew to his library. Making any decision was difficult for him, much less one which would inevitably displease his wife and perhaps his daughter.

After that, Bold Talent acted alone, discreetly consulting members of the Self-Strengthening Society, careful not to arouse the interest of those who had eligible bachelors in their own families. But each nominee was found wanting. This one had no character; that one was sickly; this one had no learning; that one had a penchant for opera stars.

The search soon attracted the ambitious matchmakers of Soochow, intrepid women with tongues of honey. They had to be dealt with diplomatically but firmly, and Bold Talent, knowing they would be too much for him, enlisted Fatso to hold the interviews while he eavesdropped from behind a screen.

"Big Sister, are Spring Moon's feet little red peppers?"

"You might say that," Fatso would bellow.

"And her face? I have heard that she is beautiful!"

"Well, if you like that sort of face."

"What sort?"

"I have been with this family, on and off, for twenty years. Can you expect me to say more? The girl is unique, and that is all I can say."

"But . . . naturally, she has a lovely disposition and does the most intricate embroidery."

Fatso would stifle a laugh and agree, too eagerly.

"And how would you compare her to her cousin who married one of my clients some years ago?"

"No comparison. No comparison."

Each morning when Bold Talent paid his respects, the Matriarch would ask for an accounting. Day after day, no name was forthcoming.

Then, one afternoon in April, his old school friend Magistrate Tang came to call. Since Tang now followed Peking's conservative line, Bold Talent was not displeased, thinking the visit might portend some small changes, even the beginning of support for the Self-Strengthening Society's goals. But after several rounds of wine, the Magistrate stood and assumed the most formal posture. He bowed deeply. "Old Friend, it is my pleasure to come today to represent the honorable family of Pan and to give to you, the Patriarch of the illustrious clan of Chang, this Red Letter inscribed with the name of their eldest son along with the year, month, day, and hour of his birth. And in my humble role of go-between, I will be honored to carry the Red Letter of your virtuous niece, Spring Moon, to the Pan family, who have entreated me to request formally their beauteous union."

By not a flicker of an eyelid did Bold Talent reveal his dismay. Clearly Fragrant Snow had been busy while he delayed. She had, no doubt, encouraged the Pans' hopes. To deny their request now would be unseemly. There was no choice but to comply, according to tradition.

And so the Red Letters were exchanged, and the credentials of Pan Tai Tai's son were laid on the table before the rosewood altar in the Hall of Ancestors. If, after three days' time, there had been no contrary sign, it would be assumed that the union had the blessing of the ancestors of the House of Chang. Then the horoscopes would be cast and Spring Moon's fate sealed.

Fragrant Snow had planned well, dropping hints of the gifts and favors that the Pans would soon be presenting to the Changs, so that the household buzzed with enthusiasm for the match. None too soon, the elders said. Alas, it was true. Bold Talent had had limited success in building up the clan treasury.

Only Spring Moon had little to say. After the day of Pan Tai Tai's visit she had never again spoken or even hinted of the arrangements for her marriage, though she often asked to be excused from her lessons. Now, when they met, she barely managed a smile, and even the Matriarch was cold. Each knew that he had failed her.

The crucial hours slipped by, and he had no more idea of what he could do to stop the match than when the go-between had first come. On the last night, sleepless, he walked from one garden to another, hoping for inspiration. In the Court of Wise Heart, he stepped up onto the veranda and stopped by Spring Moon's opened window. Her room, like the others, was dark, but he could see her bed curtains rippling in the moonlight and smell the lilacs in the vase on the tea table. Absently, he passed his hand over the smooth lacquer surface of the sill.

Only a trick would do now, something that would put an end to the alliance without hurting a friendship, without revealing his handiwork, without compromising honor. It would be useless to bribe a fortune-teller; his sister-in-law had already gathered many glowing reports. What then?

He thought at first that he had imagined the sharp intake of breath. Then he heard it again. Spring Moon was not asleep but crying softly, unaware that anyone was near. He almost called her name but knew he should not. What could he say to comfort her?

At dawn, he stood on the threshold of the Hall of Ancestors. In the dimness he could just see the offerings on the altar table. Beside the bowls of food lay the Red Letters, waiting for the blessing of those beyond the Yellow Springs. If only they could truly speak! Surely such a marriage would not be their wish, not the wish of the Venerable, who had so dearly loved Spring Moon. For a long time he stood there, while the sky lightened. The pear in the bowl of fruit seemed to catch the glow. Pears were rare at this time of year, and thus a special gift. . . .

Suddenly, he gave a shout of laughter. Perhaps the gods existed after all, for he had the answer. He was still chuckling to himself as he slipped into the empty room.

As the hour of the snake approached, Bold Talent stood by the marble screen and watched the women of the House of Chang gathering near the pool of lotus. They looked like a flock of cardinals, cocking their heads and mingling, greeting one another, and for an instant he felt like a cruel cat about to pounce and spoil the day's pleasure. No one noticed him as he followed the procession into the Hall of Ancestors and took up a position behind a coromandel screen to watch the Matriarch and Fragrant Snow lead the women to the altar to collect the credentials. Only Spring Moon was absent. According to tradition, the lucky girl awaited the news in her quarters.

Suddenly the Matriarch gasped, then cried out, "Amitabha! Aye ya! Amitabha!"

"What is the matter?" Fragrant Snow asked.

"Look!" The Matriarch pointed. The pear had tumbled from the basket of fruit on the altar and rested on top of the Red Letters.

Everyone pushed forward to see. Palms flew to mouths to muffle cries of shock.

The Matriarch clapped her hands for silence. A hush fell. For a moment it seemed that no one breathed, as all waited to hear what she would say.

When she finally spoke, her tone forbade anyone to doubt her words. "The noble ancestors have imparted their wisdom to us. There will be no alliance between the Pans and the Changs."

The other women nodded left and right, exclaiming to no one in particular until a chorus of assent filled the room. Only Fragrant Snow was apparently uncertain about what to think. She reached out to touch her mother-in-law's sleeve. "Perhaps it does not mean anything at all, Por Por. Surely there can be no reason to disapprove the son of Pan Tai Tai."

The Matriarch picked up the pear and shook it in front of her daughter-in-law's nose. "What is this, then?"

"A *li*," replied Fragrant Snow.

"And what does *li* mean?"

"A pear, Por Por."

"Yes, yes, but what else can *li* signify?"

"*Li* . . . *li* also means to depart."

"And so . . ."

"But, Por Por, the pear could merely have rolled out of the basket of offerings."

The Matriarch gave the pear to Fragrant Snow to hold and then, drawing herself up, pronounced in a manner most grand, "That is precisely what happened. But it is, nevertheless, a sign. A sign of the undeniable wish of our wise ancestors. There must be no marriage. No other interpretation is possible." She stared into her daughter-in-law's eyes, daring her to protest further.

Fragrant Snow could do nothing but hold her tongue. Reluctantly, she nodded assent, studying the pear in her hand.

"Fatso," the Matriarch called. "Send for the go-between, so that we may advise him of what has happened here." The servant hurried out the door, grinning from cheek to cheek.

Fragrant Snow looked up again at her mother-in-law. "Por Por?"

"Yes?"

"What will I say to Pan Tai Tai?"

The Matriarch snatched the pear and put it back on top of the oranges in the bowl, where it had been the night before. "Say that there has been a sign. What is the purpose of the three days, if not to consult the ancestors? If the situation were reversed, the Pan family would be compelled to do exactly as we are doing. No one has lost face. The wishes of the august ancestors must be obeyed."

As he slipped out, Bold Talent smiled to himself, relishing his victory. But the trick would never work again. There could be no further delay.

Doubting his resolve, he imposed upon himself an arbitrary deadline and sifted through the old list of candidates behind closed doors. When the day was done, the reluctant decision was made. His choice was a member of the Self-Strengthening Society, grandnephew of the renowned judge called Butterfly, who fined every offender fifty butterflies because "time spent with nature rehabilitates best." He and Sterling Talent had rejected the young man originally, for he had an unexceptional mind. But he was a likable soul whose clansmen had gentle dignity, were usually monogamous, and enjoyed singular longevity. While his niece might be bored, she would never be mistreated. Besides, he told himself, Butterfly owned a fine library and had taught his own wife to read. And Spring Moon had the zest and wit to season the most prosaic of lives.

He glanced at his watch. An hour or so must pass before the clansmen would gather for the evening meal and he could present his choice for their approval. To fill the time, he turned to the stack of letters that had accumulated while his mind was on family affairs. There were several from acquaintances in the West, many from the Yamen—soliciting funds, no doubt—a few from boyhood classmates now serving in far-off provinces, and one from Glad Promise. Surprised to see that it came from Peking, he opened it first. The closely written pages told of his friend's return from America sooner than expected. "Father has not been well, and I am my mother's only son. . . ." He had found work as a translator with the Reform Society, and the letter was full of hope. "Our friend K'ang Yu-wei has been summoned for consultations at the Court with increasing frequency, to the chagrin of the Dowager and the Imperial Councilors. It would not surprise me if the Young Emperor adopts a more progressive outlook. Write our mutual friends in the South of this latest development." For once, Bold Talent thought, some good tidings!

He smiled, remembering his first meeting with Glad Promise at the train station in New Haven. He had been so full of talk, of wonder at the iron horse, the self-coming water, the kiss he had received from a churchwoman in Springfield. His enthusiasm was like Spring Moon's when she had mastered a concept.

Slowly, almost reluctantly, the idea formed itself: Glad Promise and Spring Moon. Why not?

Weeks ago, when he had first explored the possibilities for his niece, he had dismissed Glad Promise because he knew his friend was planning to stay abroad and work at the embassy. Now . . .

The Woos were not known for their wealth, but Chinese still valued scholarship above silver, and Glad Promise's father was a Hanlin Scholar. Furthermore, he was an old friend of the Venerable, from the days when the two had worked together to help found the Tung Wen College for interpreters, the first of its kind. The Matriarch, especially, would appreciate that. And Glad Promise had studied abroad and would welcome a wife with a lively mind.

All at once the stale air of the study became intolerable, and Bold Talent got up from his desk and went out onto the terrace.

But the night breeze that ruffled the surface of the waters failed to refresh him, and in a few minutes he returned to his study to compose a letter to the Hanlin.

Again and again he dipped his brush into the ink, only to let it dry. The words did not come. He had progressed no farther than the greeting when there was a light rapping on the door.

Spring Moon stood at the threshold, her hands behind her back. "Eldest Uncle, may I come in?" Her eyes were dancing, and a smile hovered on her lips.

He nodded, and she entered the room, stopping beside the desk.

"You have saved my life, Uncle."

"Have I now?" His own words seemed to come from far away, as if spoken by another. "How have I accomplished such a feat?"

"Oh . . ." She tilted her head to one side. "By telegraph!"

He raised an eyebrow in puzzlement.

"By telegraph, my uncle!" she insisted. "I think you have built a new telegraph line . . . all the way to our ancestors."

He thought, I have begun to miss her already.

"Since the hour of the snake I have been waiting," she went on, "to give you this special token of my gratitude." She leaned forward and, bringing her hands out from behind her back, presented him with a fragrant pear.

He took it carefully, then held it up to the lamp, studying it as if it were one of the blue and white porcelain vases in his cabinets, not seeing it at all. It was minutes before he was certain he could control his voice, and when he did speak it was almost a whisper. "Your gift is like no other," he said, and, to himself, I shall treasure it always.

She dipped gracefully in obeisance—her neck bent forward, her back straight, the right knee barely grazing the floor, both hands gently touching the left hip.

In a moment, she was gone.

Within a month, the Red Letters and contract had been accepted by both clans, and the Matriarch and Fragrant Snow sent for Spring

Moon. Although, as go-between, Bold Talent sat in the room, he preferred to remain in the background. It was his mother who made the announcement, as if Spring Moon had not been informed by Fatso at every stage of the negotiations. "My granddaughter, a marriage has been arranged for you by your Eldest Uncle. You will be a member of a Hanlin family, the Woos of Peking. It is most suitable."

As custom demanded, Spring Moon began to weep. "Oh, please, please do not send me away. I do not want to leave my dear family. I want to stay in Soochow. I do not wish to go to the capital."

Until this moment, he had not realized how well Spring Moon could play the parts tradition assigned to her, so unlike other women had she seemed to him. He would have preferred to think that her professed sentiments were real, but though she played well, she gave herself away when she peered through her handkerchief, judging the effect she had on her audience.

The older women and their slave girls seemed satisfied, however, especially after she motioned for a second handkerchief. "I will never have another home like my *lao chia,"* she sobbed. "Nothing on earth or in heaven can equal the goodness, the honor, and the care I have known within these courtyards."

The Matriarch, her words muffled by the painted fan she held to her face, whispered to Fragrant Snow, "Not quite the bucketful I shed, but adequate, adequate."

Fragrant Snow nodded, dabbing away her own tears.

Thus encouraged, Spring Moon wailed, "Oh-oh-oh, the capital is so far away. I will never be back again, not even on the traditional days—not on the third day after my wedding, not at New Year's, not on any of the feast days. Peking is almost twenty-five hundred *li* from here!"

All the women gasped at the figure, and Fragrant Snow cried out despairingly, "It is so far! I did not know it was so far!"

At that Spring Moon sniffed and ran to embrace her mother. "Not a day of my life will pass that I will not think of you, my mother, and weep."

She was no longer acting. Probably afraid her mother would

change her mind, Bold Talent thought wryly. Afraid she would never go beyond the garden walls after all.

He left the room, unnoticed.

The astrologer determined two lucky dates for the couple—the twentieth of June, in six weeks, or the twentieth of December, in eight months. Since ice might block a winter passage, the summer day was chosen, and phoenix and dragon cakes on which the auspicious date was painted in red sugar were delivered to the homes of family and friends announcing the marriage.

The early wedding precluded most of the traditional pomp and ceremony. Nevertheless, from the day the news went out, the Chang residence was packed from dawn to dusk with agitated relatives, noisy workmen, nearsighted tailors, and bubbling well-wishers. Fatso and Old Hawk volunteered to accompany the bride to Peking and continue in her service there. The Patriarch rewarded their loyalty with a generous sum; the Matriarch with a pipe inlaid with silver and a gold brooch set with blue kingfisher feathers.

Until the last possible moment, Fragrant Snow was busy overseeing the preparation of her daughter's trousseau and the gifts for the Woos, coming frequently to ask Bold Talent for additional funds. "The parade must dazzle everyone in Peking, do you not agree?" For the first time since he could remember, she was up and about during his early morning *tai-chi*. And throughout the day it seemed he spied a plum-colored dress in every court as she rushed about checking on the tailors, bargaining with the peddlers who lined up outside the gate, instructing the artisans camped by the spirit screen on the design to be painted in red and gold on the twenty-four leather trunks. To all of them she said, "Now, four of everything, one for each of the Gods of Marriage," until it became a litany.

Spring Moon, too, was everywhere. And everywhere it seemed he felt her joy and was touched. Yet he was bewildered, as well, for she never came for a lesson and mentioned several times how much she regretted having neglected her needlework.

Only once did he see either Fragrant Snow or the betrothed sitting still. They were huddled together on a taboret in the Garden of the Pensive Flute, whispering. A slow flush blossomed on Spring Moon's cheek, and he knew that Fragrant Snow was relating to her daughter some plum-colored version of the apple tree and the peach tree.

Ten days before the appointed date, lanterns, gold foil symbols of double happiness, red scrolls, and family treasures of porcelain, jade, and bronze were brought out from their purple sandalwood cabinets to bedeck halls and gardens lit with scarlet candles for the Maiden's Feast.

When all the family, except Spring Moon, and the invited guests were seated in the Cypress Garden, the men and boys at their tables and the women and children at theirs, five pyrotechnists set off a display of fireworks so magnificent that it filled the night with wonder in anticipation of the bride. She appeared in the Clover Gate as the red sparks of the last skyrocket faded, a woman in a rose-colored gown trimmed with pearls, peonies in her ebony hair.

Acrobats hurtled through the air, musicians played, and storytellers sang their ballads, but Bold Talent's eyes returned to her again and again as she led her attendants from one guest to another, from one table to the next, performing the ritual of serving wine and offering a toast to all who had come to celebrate.

"Welcome! Your distinguished presence illuminates our obscure residence."

"I drink to your happiness, Daughter of the House of Chang."

"I drink to yours, Honored Guest."

They raised the wine cups in the air and put them to their lips, but Spring Moon only pretended to drink, handing the cup to a designated attendant who actually emptied it. It would not do for her to drink too much, to reel about in public like the Idlers of the Bamboo Brook.

Watching her, Bold Talent imagined a bridal chamber and Spring Moon smiling, flushed with wine, her long hair loose. Carelessly open on the bed a volume of verses by Li Po, the lusty Idler who was her favorite poet. Quickly, he banished the image. But the words of one of Li Po's poems would not leave him:

> Night after night I ever keep for her the half of my quilt
> In expectation of her spirit coming back to me. . . .

As she approached the women's tables, the ladies ceased gossiping and serving tasty morsels to their neighbors to coo praises of her loveliness and whisper tender reassurance. He could not hear, but it was always so. When she came to toast her bachelor cousins, seated at the table next to his, each in turn serenaded her with snippets of arias from the "Palace of Eternal Youth" and the "Peach Blossom Fan," according to the custom.

He could see that she was beginning to droop. Her golden lilies must ache, he thought, remembering the afternoon so long ago when she had dreamed of winged shoes. Today she dreamed of Glad Promise. And tomorrow she would go for the first time beyond the garden walls.

At last she approached him. He stood and raised his wine cup to meet hers.

"Eldest Uncle, you look so solemn."

"Do I?"

"Are you worried that your unworthy pupil will be trouble to the Woos?"

He did not answer her but raised his cup again. "I drink to your happiness, daughter of my brother."

"I drink to yours, my uncle."

When the last guest had gone and the scraps had been put aside for the beggars, Bold Talent went alone to his study. The shutter doors had been folded back, and he could see the half-moon in the sky. A breeze rustled some papers held fast with a jade weight, and he ran his fingers over the symbol of yin and yang carved in the stone, thinking how empty the room looked now, without the other desk.

He turned up the lamp and poured droplets of water from the

quartz vessel onto the inkstone. Deliberately he ground the ink-stick, took up the brush and wrote.

My brother—
We missed you at the Maiden's Feast. Everyone in Soochow came. Many asked for you.
It is my wish that you act as my go-between. Kindly call on the Merchant Sui and ask for his daughter, Golden Virtue, to be my wife.

The short letter sealed, he stayed for several more minutes at his desk, staring vacantly across the study. Then, his heart full of melancholy weariness, he went to his bedroom and mechanically undressed. The curtains of the bed puffed and swayed like long flowing sleeves of lightest gauze.

He slept fitfully.

The scent of pear blossoms startled him, and he opened his eyes. A beauty he had never seen before hovered in the doorway like a fox spirit, reciting a poem. Her gown was the color of willows in spring, and her voice filled the air with delight. She smiled as if they had known each other intimately.

"Who are you?" he asked.

"You know who I am."

"Why are you here?"

"Because it is time."

"For what?"

"To play."

"Play?"

The beauty tilted her head to one side, tied a ribbon in her hair, and ran away. He was alone. He waited. On the table beside him was her fan. When he waved it, she reappeared, carrying two amber goblets on a silver tray. With each step, the glasses kissed.

They drank the wine, but it did not quench his thirst. She strummed a lute, singing songs.

"Now it is time to play," she said again.

"What are the rules?"

"The rules are here." The beauty lifted the pillows. There was a garden. Men and women lay intertwined, as in the Book of the Cloud and Rain.

Suddenly he was shrinking. Smaller and smaller he became until he was imprisoned inside her goblet. She was still smiling, but now her voice boomed. "It is time! It is time! . . ."

"It is time to wake, my master," said the servant.

SPRING
FIRE

❧ 6 ❧

The Bride

Anxiously chirps the cicada,
Restlessly skips the grasshopper.
Before I saw my lord
My heart was ill at ease.
But now that I have seen him,
Now that I have met him,
My heart is at rest.
           —The Book of Songs

THE COURTYARDS of the House of Chang resounded to the music of horns, cymbals, flutes, and drums as Spring Moon began her ten-day journey to Peking. Her face, beneath the jeweled headdress, was veiled, and the windows and doors of the red bridal chair were sealed. The bride must not be seen until her husband lifts the veil, the women said.

And so the curtains were drawn in the cabin of the yuloh to Shanghai, in the suite on the northbound steamer, and in the compartment of the train from Tientsin to the capital. When Spring Moon changed from one conveyance to the next, the bridal veil was donned again and the bridal sedan sealed. Throughout, no sights, only the sounds of cities, of water rushing past, of wheels that clattered and engines that thundered like the heart of a giant.

At first she pleaded with Fatso and with Old Hawk, who stood guard outside her chamber, just to let her peek. But when they would not, she became resigned and her spirits lifted.

She thought not so much of what was to come but of her *lao chia*. The feast had gone well. Grandmother had not laughed so much since she lost her teeth, and Mother had talked incessantly of all the grandsons she would have. Even Father had written two poems, one for Glad Promise, one for her. The two scrolls would hang in her new home. "Spring is gone, before I knew her at all . . ." the one for her began. It was the first sign of his care for her she could remember receiving. Young Uncle had sent his apologies and a ceramic Tang horse. He had bought it, she thought, not for its beauty but as a symbol of military preparedness. No matter. She would treasure it because it came from him.

Only Eldest Uncle's laughter had been missing, and she wondered what had troubled him in her hour of happiness.

While the train stood in the station in Peking she was enveloped for the last time in the layers of brocade and satin, blinded by the red silk veil and jeweled headdress, sealed in the sedan. Then the chair lurched into motion, swaying endlessly along unknown paths until at last it was still, and music filtered through the suffocating blackness. She had arrived in the courtyards of her betrothed.

She longed to open the door, to breathe freely, to see something, if only the light of day tinted pink by its passage through her veil. But custom required the playing of three songs to test her virtuous patience before the door of the chair could be opened. She would rather die than be thought too anxious.

The music ended. There was a moment's silence. And then—the three taps she had waited for! She heard the sound of paper tearing. A breeze lifted the corners of her veil. The air was fragrant with incense.

The crowd she had known would be there clapped and shouted, "The bride! The bride!" She tried to catch a glimpse of them, but all she could see, looking down, were the embroidered phoenix and peonies on her red bridal gown and the tips of her tiny red shoes. Gentle female hands guided her descent and helped her stand. For a moment she wondered if her cramped legs would support her. How humiliating if she were to stumble, if anyone thought, even for a minute, that the Changs had sent a weakling! But the hands held her until she steadied. Then, slowly, she moved, guided by the strange women who would soon be her sisters and cousins.

Red carpets covered the walks. The floor of the ceremonial hall was of wood, deeply scarred. As she crossed the threshold, she saw in front of her, only a few feet away, the white-soled shoes of a man and the hem of his blue silk gown.

A deep voice announced the commencement of the wedding rites, and the music began. All cymbals and drums—or was it only her heart? Unable to see and forbidden to talk, she was led here and there, to kneel and kowtow again and again before the members of the family that would be hers and their guests.

She wondered, almost absently, how they knew she was the right bride and not some other girl bundled in red who had gotten into the wrong sedan. Or perhaps it was she who was mistaken. Perhaps she had wandered into another's place. Strangely, the thought did not trouble her. She felt as if she were in a kind of dream, as if she had lived this day before, in another incarnation. What was it the Venerable had said? . . . Yield, my child, yield.

Suddenly the music stopped and the crowd broke into thunderous applause and cheers. She was now the wife of the man who had walked and kowtowed with her. The sound of firecrackers and music filled the air.

As the ovation continued, she was led out of the hall by attendants, along garden walks, across the thresholds of strange courts. Always, just ahead, she could see the hem of the royal blue gown and the white-soled shoes of her husband. At last, they entered a room, and she was told to sit down at a table. There were choruses of soft laughter, low whispers, the clatter of dishes, and the continual coming and going of golden lilies. Then a door closed and all was silence.

She waited, not knowing why everyone had gone or when they would return. She willed herself to be calm, listening. Suddenly the weight of the headdress was unbearable. She reached up to massage her neck.

Someone cleared his throat, startling her. Glad Promise had been there all along. She bowed her head and closed her eyes, wondering when he would speak. She must not, until he did. He walked over and sat down on the settee next to her. Still he said nothing. For a moment she felt giddy. Not now, merciful Kwan Yin, she prayed. She must not swoon and touch his clothing. Abruptly he stood up and began pacing back and forth, muttering to himself.

The words were meaningless, but she recognized the sounds. Bold Talent, too, had argued with himself in English. All at once she was at ease.

As suddenly as he had begun, he stopped pacing and returned to sit beside her. Again they waited. At long last he said, too loudly, "Little Sister, how is my friend Bold Talent?"

Now she could speak. "So, you are not a deaf-mute."

"What made you think I was?" His voice pleased her.

"Well, you have not said a word."

"Neither have you." His response was quick.

"But I am not supposed to speak first."

"How do you know?"

"I was told so."

"Then did they not inform you that I have all my faculties?"

"No," she lied. "I did not ask."

"You did not ask?"

"No, I did not ask any questions, not a single one. I do not know if you are a hunchback or a giant, a dandy or a bull."

"So you were willing to marry anyone?"

"Of course!" Did he think that she was not well brought up? "I would marry anyone chosen by my elders," she said virtuously.

There was a pause. She heard him sigh. "And I the same," he said at last. "I know nothing about you either."

"Nothing?" Was he lying too?

"Nothing. Like you, I left the matter completely to my parents."

"Then you, too, would have married just anyone?"

"Just anyone."

"Oh." Disappointed, she sat even taller.

Silence returned.

Finally Glad Promise got up and pulled the table closer. She smelled the aroma of Peking duck.

"We might as well eat. The guests will be coming soon and may stay all night. If we do not eat now, we may not have another chance."

"But I cannot eat with this on."

"Then take it off."

"No."

"Why not?"

"You must."

"I suppose you were told that too."

She nodded.

"Well, then, perhaps you should stand up first."

"Please, Older Brother, help me out from behind the table. I cannot see."

Glad Promise walked to the other side of the table and pulled it away from her. "It is all right now to stand."

Spring Moon stood absolutely still, her eyes lowered, while he carefully lifted the jeweled headdress, then the veil, from her head and set them on the end table. For a moment she shut her eyes, blinded by the brightness of the light. Then, slowly, she opened them. She raised her head. At eye level a gold button. She lifted her gaze, counting two more buttons before she saw the face of her husband. He was very tall. His skin was smooth. He smiled when he saw her face.

Blushing, Spring Moon quickly sat down. "Our dinner is getting cold."

Suddenly she was starving. He started to say something, then stopped. She picked up her chopsticks to reach for a prawn, remembered her manners, and quickly laid them back on their stand. She glanced his way. Their eyes met. He looked confused, absently twisting the ring he wore on the third finger of his right hand. She eyed the food longingly. Finally, he marched to the other side of the table and sat down. The food looked delicious!

Neither moved. Was he never going to? If he did not, she would! Simultaneously, both picked up their chopsticks and tried to spear the same quail's egg.

"Please, you take it," she said.

"No, please. You are the guest."

"Am I?" She paused. "Well, if you insist, I will."

She ate with relish. He picked at the food silently, piling morsels on his plate that he did not touch. He watched her eat four duck-filled pancakes, five prawns, two dumplings, two thousand-year eggs, three helpings of spicy beef, six stuffed mushrooms, and the entire serving of sweet and sour pork.

"Do you always eat this much?" he asked.

"Do you always eat this little?"

Glad Promise blushed.

A knock, and the attendants returned to remove the table. One ran out at once, crying, "A beauty! A beauty!" Bride and groom sat stiffly, saying nothing, until the oldest servant motioned for him to step outside.

While the women retouched the rouge on Spring Moon's lips and tucked a loose strand of hair into a comb, she looked around the room, seeing it for the first time. Was it really so much smaller than the receiving room in the Court of Wise Heart or was it just that there was so much furniture? Perhaps after the birth of her first son, her mother-in-law would permit her to change it a little.

As the servants left, the prettiest paused at the door to summon Glad Promise. "Lucky groom," she called in a singsong voice, "you may take your place beside the bride now. Your family and friends will be coming soon to warm up the wedding chamber."

Glad Promise came as he was bid, muttering, "Another barbaric custom."

Spring Moon whispered, "Will it be terrible?"

"I pray not. All I can suggest is that we go along with the pranks. Do whatever they ask, or else they will become stubborn and stay for the entire three days and three nights."

The parents of the groom entered first. Although Lotus Delight and Fierce Rectitude were both dressed expensively, her clothes looked stylish, Spring Moon thought, his borrowed. She was unusually tall, elegant, and considerably younger than her husband. He was round, though not fat, with a yellowing beard and a pockmarked but friendly face.

Lotus Delight spoke first. "Well, well, well, I had no idea that she would be this pretty. Did you, my honorable husband?"

"No. Oh, no, of course not. My son, you are fortunate that your ugly father has comely friends." Spring Moon wondered at this reply. Fatso had told her that Eldest Uncle had sent the Hanlin the photograph he had taken of her under the willow tree by the Pool of the Faithful Companions. Clearly her father-in-law had not shown it to his wife.

With a smile on her lips, but not in her voice, the mother-in-law said, "We shall see if your comely friends have obedient granddaughters."

Perhaps it would be wiser to wait until the birth of her second son before asking about the furniture, Spring Moon thought.

As her parents-in-law left the room the women of the Woo clan surrounded her. In a moment she felt like nothing so much as a plucked duckling they planned to cook for dinner.

"My, my, is that all your hair?"

"Let us have a good look at your golden lilies."

"A bit skinny, do you not think?"

"Oh, actually a bit pudgy, in my opinion."

"Do you think she will be a *hwa tou*, like so many Southerners?"

"An embroidered pillow, perhaps. Decorative with nothing inside. I would not be surprised if she will have to think twice before deciding which side of the cup to drink from."

Let them talk. She was a Chang!

While the ladies poked and prodded, the men stood apart and fixed their eyes upon her, congratulating Glad Promise with hearty laughs.

These older guests did not stay long, however. When they had left it was the turn of the bachelors, who galloped in with whoops and shouts. A number carried tables and chairs and immediately settled down to play mah jong, while others heckled, mocked, aped, and taunted the couple, according to tradition. They tried repeatedly to trick Spring Moon into losing her composure, to make her laugh, cry, or lash out in anger. In truth, though, she continued to be as serene inside as she appeared. Their teasing was no match for Fatso's.

When one of them told a bawdy tale, Glad Promise ground

his teeth, but Spring Moon merely whispered, "Remember what you told me. We do not want them here for three nights and three days."

Before an hour had passed, even the worst rowdies were too embarrassed to continue. As soon as one left, they all did.

In a moment the attendants returned to prepare the bridal bed, which stood in the adjoining room concealed behind red curtains. Once more Glad Promise waited in the garden while Spring Moon remained seated, smiling to herself, pleased with him.

When the attendants had left, Fatso came in to unpack the bridal trunk and help the bride change out of her wedding gown. Spring Moon seized her chance. "Quickly! Quickly! Tell me what you have learned from the servants."

Fatso moved from trunk to chest and back again as she talked. "Your mother-in-law is not of a happy nature. Be careful always to please her."

Spring Moon shook her head impatiently. "No, no. What have you learned about *him?*"

"The Hanlin is a kind person but quite afraid of her."

"No, no, you infuriating dolt, not him! What of my husband?"

"Oh!" Fatso hesitated. "But you have seen him for yourself. And anyway, how much can he matter?"

She turned away to place the combs upon the dressing table, but Spring Moon grabbed her sleeve. "You know something. You must tell me!"

"It is not important."

"What?"

"It is nothing. Not now, not when you are already married."

"But how can I be a good wife to him if others know things that I do not?"

Fatso relented. "The servants say that the young master did not wish to be married."

"Do they say why?"

"It has nothing to do with you, my precious. They say that he is infected by foreign ideas, that he did not wish for a traditional wedding. He wanted to marry someone whom he had seen, found sympathetic, and chosen."

"Who was she?"

"No one. There was no such person. So the Hanlin had his way. Come now, it is time to change."

Spring Moon did not speak again while the many layers of red silk and brocade were removed and replaced with the long gown of pink silk that revealed her slender body. But the more she thought about what Fatso had said, the less she worried. Eldest Uncle would not have married her to a man who would not care for her.

When Fatso was satisfied with every detail, she embraced the girl warmly and whispered, "Remember what I have told you. Do not forget the white silk!" Spring Moon blushed. Amitabha! She was grateful to the old servant for explaining. If Fatso had not, she would still be puzzling over her mother's talk of this and that tree.

A moment more and the bride stood alone in the middle of the bedroom.

Before her was the bridal bed of carved rosewood, with its elaborately embroidered canopy and red curtains. The red satin coverlet was strewn with rose petals and baby shoes of every color. Nearby, on a stand, was the tray containing the small square of white silk. With this she must supply in the morning the proof of her purity and of her true acceptance as a daughter of the House of Woo.

She heard footsteps and turned to find Glad Promise standing in the doorway. It seemed to her that he looked all around the room, at the bed littered with the traditional symbols of fertility, at the tray with the white silk square, before he saw her standing there. She could not read his face.

For a long time he did not move. Then, quite deliberately, he stepped to the stand and kicked it over. He retrieved the white silk square and flung it as far as he could. It floated gently to the floor at his feet. Furiously he picked up the cloth and threw it again and again until he was panting with frustration.

At first she wondered if he were displeased with her. Then, No, she thought. He acts like a small boy. Fatso was right. He did not wish to be married to a stranger.

Neither her mother nor Fatso had said anything about such a

possibility as this. But somehow, as the silence lengthened between them, broken only by the harsh sound of his breathing, she knew what to do. As deliberately as he had done, she marched to the bed, picked up a red baby shoe, and flung it wildly into space. One, then another, and another.

Later, neither could remember who had laughed first. They laughed and laughed until they crumpled to the floor. Finally, he asked, "Why did you do that?"

"Why did you?"

"I asked first."

"I did not think you liked tradition."

"Do you, Little Sister?"

She did not know how to answer.

He continued. "You are right. I do not like tradition . . . to wed a stranger."

Her hand reached out as if to touch his lips. "Older Brother, we are married. We cannot undo what our families have done. But we need not be strangers forever. Strangers may come to know one another."

"That takes time."

"We have a lifetime, my brother."

"You will not mind waiting?"

She blushed and shook her head. So much had happened already for the first time. She could wait: happily, now that she had seen him, now that she knew she could make him smile.

"Little Sister, do you truly understand?"

She searched his eyes. They were rounder than hers, the eyes of a Northerner. They were like no other's, the eyes of her husband. She remembered what he had asked and whispered, "Yes." For a moment neither spoke, or moved, or even breathed. Then the spell was broken, and she began to search among the shoes that covered the floor, crawling here and there, tossing one to the left, another to the right.

"What are you doing?"

She put a finger to her lips. "Shhh!"

At last she found what she was looking for—the square of white silk. Before he could stop her, she bit the inside of her cheek and spit out the blood to stain the silk with red.

When it was done, she smiled despite the pain and tossed the square to him. "This will be the first of our many secrets, my husband."

It was almost dawn when they had restored some semblance of order to their bedroom, but neither bride nor groom admitted to being tired. Glad Promise suggested an early breakfast. She agreed. He went to notify the servants, who in no time returned with the meal.

When the table was set and the servants had gone, they sat down once more. She ate carefully, chewing on the right side of her mouth.

"These pastries are delicious. I have never tasted better." She helped herself to another.

"Can you cook?"

She shook her head, sighing mournfully. There was a silence. Then, "Do you think Por Por will scold me if the fish is not absolutely in one piece?" she asked.

"What are you talking about?"

"Did they not tell you anything?"

"I guess not."

"First, you and I must remain in seclusion for three days and three nights. On the following morning, I must clean and cook a carp for the family."

"Why?"

She blushed. How could she say that it was a test of her skill and a symbol of the clan's hope for many sons? She shrugged. "More tradition." She frowned and put her chopsticks down. "Will you eat a lot of it, even if it is terrible?"

"Why on earth—"

"Oh, please, you must. I will tell Por Por that it is a Soochow specialty and not everyone is expected to like it the first time. But will you pretend and say that you do? Ask for seconds and thirds. No one else will want it." She made a face.

"Do you expect me to lie to my own mother?"

"Oh, no! You do not have to say anything, just eat!" She smiled. "Please?"

He nodded, almost smiling himself. "I suppose that will be our second secret."

They laughed, but she avoided his eyes.

She had never felt like this before. It was not unpleasant. Definitely not unpleasant. She began to eat again. He was staring at her, his chopsticks in midair.

"Little Sister, you must sew beautifully."

"I sew like a bear."

"I know now that you are being extremely polite."

"No." Once more Spring Moon sighed. "No, it is the truth. I do not like sewing."

"Then you paint fans—flowers, mountains lost in mists?"

"I do not like painting either."

"It must be that you prefer to garden."

"No." She drank the bean curd milk.

"You sing, or strum the lute, perhaps?"

She put down her bowl and bowed her head. "I am lacking."

He stared at her.

Oh, what have I done? she thought. He thinks me a rice bin! Abruptly, she asked, "Do you?"

"Do I what?"

"Cook, sew, paint, garden, sing, or strum?"

"No."

"Good!" She clapped her hands. "We have a lot in common."

He nodded uncertainly. Silence.

"Shall I send for a set of tiles?"

"No. I do not play mah jong."

"Oh," he said, at a loss.

"Do you play chess?" Spring Moon looked up demurely and met his eyes.

"I? Yes, of course."

"Ah!" She tapped her temples. "That is a difficult game."

"It is not easy."

"Do you have a set here?"

"Yes."

"Well, set up the board."

"Do you play?"

"A little."

He called to the servants to clear the table, and when that was done he went to his desk and took out an antique ivory chess set. She watched him put the pieces in place. Without a word, she made the first move.

She pretended not to notice his bewilderment as she countered his attack. Finally, when her cannon made a strategic hit, he stopped looking at the board and, leaning back in his chair with his arms folded across his chest, studied her instead. She kept her eyes lowered. Suddenly he asked, "Can you read?"

"A little."

"As you play chess—a little?"

She tried not to respond, then hid her laughter behind her hands and nodded.

By the time the watchman had intoned the hour of the dog, they were yawning and fighting sleep. Neither wanted to be the one to suggest going to bed. They dozed in their chairs. At the hour of the pig, the clapper of the night watchman woke them. Both were stiff and weary. He said, "We cannot sit in chairs every night. Do you not think we had better go to bed?"

She nodded and then, her eyes on her hands in her lap, asked, "May I go into the room first, alone? I shall call you when you may enter."

"Please do. Take all the time you need, Little Sister."

She went into their bedroom and changed. When she was ready she rolled up a quilt and, climbing up onto the bed, placed it as a barrier between them. For a moment she lay without moving. Then, drawing up the coverlet, she called, "My brother, you may enter."

In the fifth moon of the Year of the Dog, 1898, during the thirteenth year of the reign of Kuang Hsu, the Emperor issued an edict which said:

"In promoting reforms, we have adopted certain European methods, because, while China and Europe are alike in holding that the first object of good government should be the welfare of the people, Europe has traveled farther on this road than we have, so that by the introduction of European methods, we simply make good China's deficiencies.

"Unless we learn and adopt the sources of their strength, our plight cannot be remedied. The cause of my anxiety is not fully appreciated by my people, because the reactionary element deliberately misrepresents my objects, spreading baseless rumors to disturb the minds of men. . . .

"Let this Decree be exhibited in the front hall of every public office in the Empire so that all men may see it."

But after one hundred days of Reform the Concubine acted, aided by the ambitious Yuan Shi-k'ai, leader of China's only modern army, who betrayed his Emperor, and by her lover, Jung-lu, the senior Manchu military commander.

—*Chinese history*

SPRING MOON STOOD, as she did every morning for as long as she dared, at the threshold of her mother-in-law's quarters, postponing the start of her daily trial. Lotus Delight, seated at her dressing table, was preoccupied, trying on earrings. Someday, Spring Moon thought, someday storytellers will sing my praises and I shall be known as the twenty-fifth paragon of filial piety. More beloved than Tong Yung, who sold himself into slavery to pay for his father's burial, more praised than Lady Tang, who fed her toothless grandmother with milk from her own breasts.

Sighing, she stepped softly inside.

The room had none of the spare elegance she had always associated with her elders but was cluttered with all the fancies Lotus Delight spent her days buying. Enamel, jade, cloisonné, ivory, and gold knickknacks covered every tabletop like the odd buttons in the tray in Fatso's sewing box. Layers of embroidered silk were draped over the screens, hiding the designs the artists had painted. Chests of value were stacked with worthless boxes. There was no harmony.

"Good morning, Por Por." She bowed.

"Where have you been?" Lotus Delight asked, dismissing the servant. Her eyes never left the mirror. "I was awake hours ago."

"I came earlier but was informed that you did not wish to be disturbed."

"That was then; now is now. Did not your people teach you respect for your seniors?"

Spring Moon bowed her head.

"I asked a question."

"I was well taught. I apologize if I have displeased you."

One of the earrings fell from the older woman's hand. Spring Moon quickly knelt to pick it up. "Por Por, the pearl has rolled under your chair out of my reach."

Lotus Delight pushed her chair back from the table. The earring was crushed. "Look what you have made me do! How do you plan to make amends for such clumsiness?"

Spring Moon did not know what to say.

"I asked a question. Must I always repeat everything I say to you?"

"Please accept a pair of my pearls."

"And?"

"Please select any others that please you as well." Spring Moon removed the pearls in her ears and offered them to her mother-in-law.

"How dare you insult me by the back door! Do you think that I do not have jewelry of my own? Do I look as if I cannot afford to buy another insignificant pair of pearls?"

"I stand rebuked, Por Por."

Lotus Delight threaded a pair of jade pendants into her ears. As she studied her profile in the mirror, she caught her daughter-in-law's eye and spun around. "Why are you staring? Am I so curious to look at?"

Once more Spring Moon bowed her head. "I was just thinking how beautiful you are, Por Por."

The older woman blinked, then turned back to the mirror, dipping a finger in the rouge pot and carefully applying the cream to her lips. When she was satisfied, she spoke again. "Do not think that beauty means much in life," was all she said.

As Spring Moon waited for her to complete her toilette, there was a tap on the open door. Glad Promise had come, as he came every day, to pay his respects. He approached and bowed to his mother. "Good morning, my mother."

She answered his greeting, and waved Spring Moon away. "You may go. I wish to speak to my son of things that do not concern you."

Silently the daughter-in-law bowed to her mother-in-law and to her husband, and walked from the room.

It was the hour when the women of the household gathered around the peddlers who came every day to the kitchen yard to sell vegetables, housewares, pins, and thread. Today the fruit peddler was there, with baskets of pale green melons, orange persimmons, and golden pears for sale.

"Good morning, Aunties." Spring Moon bowed to the wives of the Hanlin's two brothers and to the Hanlin's concubine. Busy selecting fruit, they did not answer her greeting. She turned to the twin daughters of the Hanlin and the concubine, girls her age who resembled their dimpled, round-faced mother. "Good morning, Sisters."

The twins nodded, not coldly but with reserve. She thought

there was the hint of a smile on the lips of the livelier one, but it faded before she was sure.

What could she expect? As the newest addition to the family, the bride was not entitled to consideration, not until years had passed and sons been born. Besides, yesterday she had been indiscreet. Their neighbor Lin Tai Tai and her daughters-in-law had come for an afternoon visit, and she, instead of maintaining a respectful silence, had blurted out that the flowers of Soochow were more varied than any she had seen in Peking. She would have to learn to guard her tongue and try to make amends. She spoke again. "The fruit looks delicious. I have never seen such melons in the South."

"Ah!" The robust peddler woman seized her opening. "This beautiful mistress is most observant. She will tell you that my fruit is worth twice the price I ask."

Another mistake! She should have known better than to say anything at all. As the women turned their backs on her and started haggling, she slipped quietly away to the small court where she and Glad Promise lived with Fatso and Old Hawk. Fatso was in the bedroom, putting away the washing, but when she saw Spring Moon she dropped the stockings back into the basket and took her by the hand. "What happened? Why the long face?"

"Nothing unusual." Spring Moon sighed as she sat on the bed, the servant beside her. "It is just ... oh, why can I never please anyone? Especially her. If the tea is too hot today, tomorrow it is too cold. If my steps are too loud when I leave her room, they are too secretive upon my return. If I smile, I am too old to grin; if I do not, I am being temperamental. What am I to do?"

"Nothing." Tenderly Fatso patted Spring Moon's hand. "There is nothing anyone can do, Young Mistress. It has always been this way. You are a woman now."

"But it is not always this way," Spring Moon argued. "It was not this way in Soochow."

"You were a daughter there, not a daughter-in-law." Heaving herself to her feet again, Fatso pulled a rag from her pocket and started dusting.

"It's no use anyway to think of Soochow. This is your home

now. You must try to understand. Who knows what Woo Tai Tai was like before she came here as a bride?"

"I think she must always have been the same. What could have happened to change her? These courts are not nearly as grand as ours, but no one here is in want. And you yourself told me it was Por Por who insisted that the Hanlin take a concubine."

Fatso opened a lattice window to shake out the cloth. "Young Mistress, did you not think the fried rolls especially delicious this morning?"

In spite of her woes, Spring Moon almost laughed out loud. When the servant wanted to change the subject, she was not overly subtle. But she did not intend to let her escape so easily.

"Old Friend," she said, "it was you who told me that she insisted. I know it was."

Fatso tucked the cloth back in her pocket with a sigh and gave Spring Moon her full attention. "My innocent, there are many ways to swallow bitterness. It is true that Woo Tai Tai was the one who arranged for a concubine. Have you thought that she might have preferred doing so to receiving the Hanlin's attentions?"

"But, Fatso—"

The old servant covered her ears. "No more! I do not want to hear another word. You must take care or you will be feasting on the northwest wind. Even the walls whisper tales. Take care, or your mother-in-law will send you away."

Spring Moon gasped; she had never thought of that possibility.

"Do you not see that you are vinegar in her tea, Young Mistress?" Fatso's voice was suddenly gentle. "Be patient. After all, you have only to wait. Soon, everything will be different, everyone will be kinder." She patted her stomach and broke into a wide grin. "Soon you will bear him a son."

Tears jumped into Spring Moon's eyes. Fortunately, Fatso was at that moment distracted by a dust turtle under the bookcase and did not see them. The servant must not suspect.

Willing herself to be calm, Spring Moon stood up and said formally, "You are wise. I shall take your advice to heart. Now I must go. I have things to do."

Slowly she walked into the courtyard, to the bench that was hers beside the stone chess table Glad Promise had installed for them. The fall air smelled of roasted chestnuts, and she breathed slowly, watching the Tang horse, which stood in a small embrasure nearby, fade from sunlight into shadow. Of all she had brought with her from Soochow, Glad Promise liked Young Uncle's present best. She must never again complain, never give Lotus Delight a reason to send her away. For she would die if she never saw her husband again.

At the thought of him she could not help smiling. There was no one as sincere, whether complimenting Old Hawk on the Peking duck, or advising his father on national policy, or teaching her English. He gave each his best effort. Once in a while she would deliberately mispronounce a word just to hear him laugh.

She had tried to write a poem about how she felt, to explain the way he walked into a room, the way he whispered good night. But no words had come. She only knew that her heart ached with pleasure and pride whenever he was with her, and when they were apart it was the same.

Now and then, however, he frightened her. A silence would descend upon him like a shroud and he would sit staring at the painted silk lantern that hung from the rafters of the library, twisting the ring she had learned came from the school in America.

At first she had interrupted these reveries. He had always answered her questions, patiently trying to explain why he was so preoccupied. Politics, the young Emperor's reforms, seemed to trouble him.

"I thought that you approved, my brother."

"I do. But I worry that with each edict the Emperor makes more powerful enemies."

"But he is Emperor."

"He is nevertheless vulnerable. Especially if his enemies convince the Dowager that the reforms are not in her interest."

The air at the Reform Society was filled with rumors of assassinations, coups, and foreign intervention. In their eagerness to convert the Emperor, the reformers had underestimated the bureaucracy. And, he explained, it was in the nature of officials to see change, especially sudden change, as a mortal threat. "If any of the rumors are true, I fear for our country and perhaps even for our lives. Our success with the Emperor may be our undoing."

"How could you have anticipated such a thing?"

"We should have. It has always been so."

Lately she had sat quietly as he brooded, wishing she could be unhappy in his stead, wishing he could know the joy in her heart.

The voice of Lotus Delight's maidservant roused her. "Young Mistress, come quickly! You are wanted."

Por Por. Always Por Por. At once Spring Moon hurried off to serve her mother-in-law.

In the evening, after dinner, Spring Moon waited alone in the garden for her husband, idly playing chess against herself until suddenly a droplet fell, turning the pink embroidered flower on her sleeve to red. In the distance, thunder. She went inside. By the hour of the rat, the storm was over, but he had not come.

It was very late when she finally slept. In the morning, the bed on his side of the blanket roll was undisturbed.

Like the curse of an enemy the thought came: I have lost my husband without being a wife.

As suddenly as it had come she disguised it, afraid that such an idea would presage the event. To fool the gods, she scolded herself aloud. "Silly girl, you see a droplet and imagine a flood. Silly fool."

Quickly she pulled aside the coverlet and lay where he should have been, tossing as he did when he slept. Then, as she did every morning, she hid the blanket roll from view and summoned Fatso to prepare the tea.

Throughout the day, she tried to act as if nothing were wrong, grateful for once that the rains kept her mother-in-law at home and, thus, the daughter-in-law busy. But when evening came and he still had not returned, she confided in Fatso. The old servant turned pale and would not meet her eyes.

"What is the matter?" Spring Moon cried.

"I thought he left for the society early—"

"But what is the matter, Fatso?" She tugged urgently at her

sleeve. "Tell me! Tell me!" It was the first time she had ever seen the old servant frightened.

"The peddlers have been talking about it all day. There are soldiers everywhere, and the city gates are closed."

They have killed him, Spring Moon thought. Then: No, he is well. If he were dead, I would know it. Nothing has happened. Nothing!

"Young Mistress, should I send Old Hawk to investigate?"

A nightmare. She could not think. She must.

Fatso asked again.

"No, you must not leave the court. He will be home soon, I am sure." She must not lose control.

"Do you wish me to stay with you?"

She shook her head and sent the servant to her quarters.

The rain left a chill in the air, and she added coals to the brazier before getting into bed. She remembered his talk of political enemies. Over and over she prayed, Let me sleep and wake to find him here.

But sleep did not come. The watch intoned the hour of the rat and of the ox. There was no other sound except the wind that stirred the willows. The hour of the tiger passed, the hour of the rabbit. The wind was rising now, and the willows moaned. Suddenly Spring Moon sat up. The sound was that of footsteps on the gallery. "Older Brother?"

There was no response. Quickly she turned up the oil lamp in the niche on her side of the headboard. Glad Promise stood in the doorway. His clothes were wet and splattered with mud, and his slim frame heaved with sobbing.

She scrambled out of bed to help him. "What happened? Where have you been?"

He gave no answer.

He does not know me, she thought. She reached out and took his hand. It was burning hot.

"What happened? Where have you been?"

Again he gave no answer. She led him like a child to the washstand and poured water into the basin to wipe the grime from his face. He stood unresisting as she removed his wet clothing and put on him dry inner garments from the wardrobe and wrapped him in coverlets. While she poured tea from the pot by the brazier he sat on the side of the bed, motionless except for the shudders that still wracked him. She coaxed him to drink. His teeth chattered on the porcelain cup.

"What happened? Please tell me!"

Still he gave no sign that he understood. She put her arms around him and laid him down and climbed in alongside to warm him. After a long time he quieted and seemed to fall asleep. She dared not move. Merciful Kwan Yin, please help him, she prayed. Merciful Buddha—

Suddenly he broke free of her embrace and sat up. He screamed. "No, no!" He was sobbing again. "No!"

"It is all right. It is all right, all right." She tried to soothe him as Plum Blossom had soothed her when she was a child, holding his head to her heart, rocking. "Shhh. It was just a dream. You are home. Nothing can harm you here." Her words seemed to comfort him, for he grew calm and returned her embrace, but briefly, then leaned back against the headboard. He held fast to her hands. She saw that he wanted to tell her, and she waited, very still.

"It was no dream." He spoke with difficulty.

"What do you mean?"

"I did nothing. I let it happen. I stood and watched."

"What? You must tell me what happened."

He did not respond but continued to answer his own questions. "I knew. I knew and I ran. I knew that she had taken him prisoner. I knew they would be coming. I did nothing."

"Please, I do not understand. Where were you?"

Again he did not answer her, pulling her to him instead. His unshaven face was rough against her cheek.

"My wife," he whispered. "My wife."

Keeping her close then, he told her, staring as he spoke at the far curtain of the bed, as if the scene he described were depicted there.

"Yesterday, at the carnival grounds near the stone Bridge of Heaven, a crowd gathered, though the rain pelted the earth. They had come to be amused. But there were no dancing bears, no wrestlers, no acrobats on bamboo poles.

"Instead, there were my friends: five who were in the movement; the sixth, the brother of K'ang Yu-wei. He was the cat they captured to frighten the monkey.

"I stood among the curious. I remember a boy with sores on his head who tugged at my gown and then crawled through for a better look.

"The rain plastered the black hood to the face of the executioner. His sword—" He stopped.

She did not move, and after a few minutes he continued. "A magistrate read the sentence of the Vermilion Pencil. My friends knelt. A guard pulled each queue forward to expose the nape.

"The bodies still knelt while the heads rolled in the mud."

Glad Promise's fever did not break until the eighth day. Slowly, he recovered his strength.

At the time, it never occurred to Spring Moon to wonder how it was that great sorrow and great happiness could exist as one; that only after her husband had seen ugliness and evil did they know the beauty and goodness of being truly man and wife.

At the time, she merely penned a poem the morning after their first night of love, while he slept.

> Strangers no more, but stranger still
> > the one who mocks me
> > in the bronze mirror.
> So unlike that frail shadow
> > I thought myself.
> Long exiled,
> Home at last.

❦ 8 ❧

Silent Waiting

On September 22, 1898, the Concubine proclaimed: "The Emperor being ill, the Empress Dowager resumes the regency." The twenty-six-year-old Emperor was imprisoned in an island paradise and his Edicts made null and void.

—Chinese history

WHILE GLAD PROMISE's association with the outlaw K'ang Yu-wei had not gone unnoticed, his role had been too minor and his father's position was too honored for him to suffer reprisal. With the Reform Society gone, he worked at home, translating political news from English-language publications into Chinese for the bureaucracy, and court pronouncements into English for the Diplomatic Corps.

Spring Moon eagerly volunteered to assist him.

"What of your duties to my mother?"

"Por Por would consent, I am sure she would, if you were to suggest it. She has never denied you anything. Remind her that I do not need to be paid."

When the proposal was made, however, Lotus Delight refused. "My son, that would be the perfect solution for you. If I could, I would consent. But who would serve me?" The honey on her tongue was unable to conceal the dagger in her belly. Having no choice, Spring Moon swallowed disappointment and attended her mother-in-law as before.

It was soon after the New Year when she first noticed things missing—nothing of value, but one day a handful of sweets, the next a teacup and some of the tea that she had left in the pot on the brazier. Fatso, suspecting a rat, reported the disappearance of a dumpling that had been put aside for Old Hawk's breakfast.

Then, on a bitterly cold morning, Spring Moon heard a sound coming from an empty rain barrel. Peering inside, she saw the upturned face of a girl and recognized the mute who had first come to the house with an old peddler woman selling thread "so fine that the eunuchs could not buy better for the Dowager."

Even as she ordered her to come out, Spring Moon's heart was touched. The child was very thin and clearly almost frozen, but she had stolen only food and little of that. The trunkful of fur-lined capes in the dressing room had been undisturbed. "Come out of there," she said again. There was no choice but to take her to her mother-in-law, who was consulting with a vendor of fine brass in the kitchen court.

Though the peddlers' gate was open, the waif made no move to run away as Lotus Delight sent the women to check the household's drawers and chests. She stood straight, with her arms at her sides, despite the wind that whipped through her thin, faded trousers and blouse. So had Plum Blossom stood, Spring Moon thought suddenly, outside the sickroom of the Venerable.

When the last report confirmed that nothing was missing, Lotus Delight announced her decision. "Let her go," she said.

"On your way!" shouted the concubine. The girl took a step toward the gate.

"No!" Spring Moon cried. Hearing herself, she forced an apologetic smile. "May she not remain? In this weather, she will surely die if we turn her out."

"And so?" retorted the concubine. "The dummy is no relation of ours. Lots of people are hungry. Do you expect to feed each one?"

The others warned that the dummy would bring bad luck.

"The gods are punishing her for the sins of another life!"

"Do not interfere!"

"But, Por Por," Spring Moon pleaded, "unhappy fates are not always the punishments of the gods."

The mother-in-law hesitated.

Spring Moon went on. "The girl is tiny and will not eat much. She is mute and will make no noise. She is abandoned and will cost us not a cent."

"She is a peasant and will be useless!"

"I will train her, Por Por. It will take no time at all, I am sure."

"Meanwhile, who will wait on me? I can barely walk these days, my legs ache so."

Fatso spoke up. "Let the dummy stay for a trial, Mistress. Let me serve you. These magic fingers"—she kneaded the air as if giving a massage—"will have you back at the mah jong table for forty-eight rounds at one sitting. Guaranteed!"

Lotus Delight played for a moment with the lapis lazuli bracelet on her wrist, then said airily, as if the matter were of no consequence. "My daughter-in-law's company was beginning to bore me. The girl may stay!"

Scrubbed, dressed, and fed, Dummy, as all the household called her, proved to be quite pretty, her angular northern face graced by flawless skin and large brown eyes. In time, she became a most efficient personal maid. And in time, Spring Moon's daily routine became more like what she had known in Soochow, though now she worked across the study from her husband instead of her uncle—a woman, not a child.

The affection that had followed marriage, the love that followed intimacy, the understanding that followed time together filled her life. Often without a word or a gesture, each knew what the other was thinking. Their joy was never displayed—that would have been vulgar—yet all who knew them felt it. The servants concluded that "Young Master and Young Mistress must have been married before, in another incarnation. And Dummy must have been their puppy dog."

Yet for all her happiness Spring Moon dared to tempt the capricious gods and prayed that two more of her wishes be granted.

Although she had traveled more than two thousand *li* and had lived in the capital for over a year, the bride had yet to see what lay beyond garden walls. Every request to join an outing, whether it was a visit to the neighboring Lin family, an expedition to the Convent of Our Lady of Good Eyesight, or a party at the American Embassy, was denied by her mother-in-law. No one, not even Glad Promise, dared appeal, for doing so would risk the privileges Spring Moon had. Besides, she told herself, now it was truly only a matter of time.

Thus the second wish was the more fervent one. As the weeks passed she found herself filled alternately with hope and, when each month brought the same result, with regret. What use the bliss she and Glad Promise knew in the bridal chamber if there were to be no sons? How long would the House of Woo wait? One year, at most two. After that, she would have to kneel before him and plead with all her heart for him to discharge his filial duty by taking a second wife.

It was soon after the second New Year's celebration in her mother-in-law's house that the faceless woman walked into Spring Moon's dreams and removed the books from the library to install a bed on which Glad Promise embraced her with the same ardor, the same tenderness, Spring Moon had known. With each coupling her husband and the faceless woman seemed to journey deeper and deeper into a secret world of their own, a world apart from her. Sometimes, in her dream, she would call after them, but her voice was lost in the great distance, and they never seemed to hear. Finally the couple had journeyed so far that even their shadows disappeared, and Spring Moon stared at the horizon, waiting. As she watched, someone came toward her . . . not more than a speck, then a blur. At last she saw that it was Glad Promise. Or was it? She saw that it was her husband as a man-child. The House of Woo bowed before him, bowed to the grandson of the Hanlin.

Over and over, night after night, the same dream. She longed to confide in someone, but the letter she wrote each month to her mother contained only news that cheered. And though she and Glad Promise shared much, this she must not tell him. Knowing how he felt about "barbaric customs," she did not wish to add her own despair to the sorrow he would feel when they would have no choice but to yield. She could not forget the look on his face when she had shown him Fragrant Snow's letter telling of the birth of Grand Vista to Bold Talent and Golden Virtue.

In the end, she turned to Fatso. "How is it, Old Friend," she began casually, "that you and Old Hawk never had children? He must have wanted a dozen. He worships you like a Buddha, everyone says so."

"It is true!" Fatso smiled, almost purred, as she reminisced. "It is true. Before I married that skinny thing, I was slim as a reed. It is hard to believe, I know. We lived with his family on two mous of land. The stupid one treated me like a rich man's wife, made me sit and eat sweets all day while he toiled in the fields. Soon I was as big as the rice merchant. But he told everyone I was beautiful. Imagine! What nonsense, saying something like that about his own wife! Even the matchmaker laughed.

"After a year passed without expectant happiness, I drank no cold water, never ate watermelon, wore three layers, and hugged the stove in the hottest weather. I went to the temple and paid the priests to let me touch the member of the bronze mule." Fatso paused, taking out a handkerchief to blow her nose.

"I got fatter and fatter, but not with child. Eventually we got used to being alone, and when his parents died, we came to work for your clan. Amitabha! If we had stayed on the farm, I would be as wide as the Great Wall."

"Was there nothing else you could have done?"

"I could have done many other things, but none would have given me a child. All the fortune-tellers agreed a son was not written in my palms."

Spring Moon sighed, examining her hand.

Quickly Fatso displayed her own palm. "See, they are not at all alike. You will have many sons!"

"Do you really think so, my friend?"

"As surely as there is an Emperor, I do."

❧ 9 ❧

Harmonious Fists

*In the Year of the Rat, 1900, the stalks and branches were bared
by flood and drought, and famine struck. By the season of wood,
when in good years winter wheat swells with grain and cherries
are ripening, children were sold by their parents for 50 coppers
a head.*

*Peking was especially gay, for appearances had to be kept up
by rich and poor alike, to break the chain of natural disaster
and national misfortune. Open-air theaters, temple fairs, and
flower shows flourished, and attendants in formal attire crisscrossed the hutungs of the capital, delivering coveted invitations
to lavish banquets, and baskets of boiled eggs dyed red for happiness.*

*It was rumored that sixty Jesus worshipers had been slaughtered
less than 200 li from Peking, but most foreigners in Legation
Quarters discounted the talk. Had not the Dowager pronounced
that "All within the four seas are brothers"?*

—Chinese history

WHEN DUKE LAN invited the House of Woo to a grand party to
be held on the fifteenth day of the fourth moon, His Excellency
specifically mentioned his wish for the presence of the son of the
Hanlin and his young wife. Such honor for a man so young! Such
honor for a bride so new! From the moment the red envelope
was opened, the women were kinder to Spring Moon, returning
her greetings, complimenting her on the loss of her Soochow

accent, happily discussing what hairstyle and gown and jewels each would wear. Even Glad Promise, who thought the Duke a reactionary fool and potential enemy, pretended enthusiasm for her sake.

Now, on the appointed day, as the hour of the monkey approached, she sat at her dressing table in her camisole and fanned furiously. She knew that Por Por had been ready since the hour of the horse, but for the first time in her life she could not make up her mind. The pendant of sapphires? Of rubies? What fan? The ivory or the silk? The crown of pearls or the headdress of silver filigree? Or flowers? An orchid, a camellia, a rose? Perhaps only jade combs. No! She shook her head. The gown, first the gown. Helplessly she looked at the dresses that were draped over the bed, the camphor trunks, the dragon couch, and the lohan chairs. What was wrong with her? Surely not only excitement at the prospect of seeing Peking and being seen.

Dummy, already dressed in her new turquoise silk blouse and pants, raised her hands in mock prayer.

"Yes, I know, it is late. But I cannot decide. . . ." The royal blue or the scarlet? The peach or the yellow?

Finally, she pointed her fan at the servant girl. "You choose."

At once Dummy, with one of her rare smiles, went to the emerald gown trimmed with gold phoenixes.

"You are right. Of course, that is the one!" It should no longer surprise her. Dummy had impeccable taste. Who would have thought it of a peasant? When her feet did not show, no one could tell that she was a mere country girl.

She felt a tug. It was Dummy straightening the hem. Now the jewelry. She reached for the box, caught her own eye in the mirror. No, still the hair.

At last she was ready. Slowly she walked into the next room. Glad Promise looked up. Their eyes met. Do I please you, my husband? she asked silently, and saw that it was so.

At once they joined the others in the receiving court, where hired sedans waited to carry family and servants to the House of Lan.

Through a slit in the curtain, Spring Moon stole her first glimpses of the capital. *Li* after *li* of gray walls, an occasional peddler, dust and more dust. Nothing to see, she thought. Nothing at all. But then the narrow hutungs gave way to an open expanse which boasted a great bazaar. Row upon row of colored silks shimmering in the setting sun. Hawkers. Beggars. Buyers and sellers bargaining. Stop! she wanted to say, but of course she could not. Numberless stalls piled high with furs—sables and mink, ermine and squirrel, white fox and goat skins. A camel! No, three. It was said that they were common in the North, but until now she had known them only from the picture in Bold Talent's copy of *The Great Silk Road.*

The dust made her cough and she leaned back, breathing through her handkerchief. When she peered out again, it was upon a narrow street lined with shops and beckoning signboards painted gold and vermilion and black. Benevolent Pills. Leaping Tiger Tonics. Snake Potions to Cleanse the Bowels. Now and then the giant gilded coin of a money changer.

Another corner turned. Another lane. She recognized the one Glad Promise loved, Booksellers' Street, with its shops offering brushes, ancient rubbings, inksticks, books: wares for the scholar.

Then once more, gray walls. Just as well. The dust and the swaying had made her queasy. She leaned back again.

Suddenly the sedan stopped. Shielding her eyes from the last rays of the sun, she saw lanterns bobbing along the top of a great wall. Bannermen on horseback, wearing brilliant green capes, guarded a huge portal over which hung pennants of black and violet, the colors of the Duke Lan.

She watched as one by one the male members of the Woo clan descended from their chairs. The Hanlin was first to present his calling card to the attendant at the gate, who then held it high overhead and announced the arrival of the Honored Guest. The voice was strangely familiar. Had he been the master of ceremonies at her wedding?

Her sedan stirred. According to tradition she and the female guests would not alight at the main entrance but would be conveyed directly to the inner courts, descending only when they were safely beyond the view of the men. Quickly, she pulled the curtain shut, hoping Por Por would not hear that she had been bold enough to peek. She straightened her skirts and smoothed her hair. The chair was lowered. The door opened. Dummy waited to help her alight, every step as they had practiced it.

The courtyard in which she stood was bigger even than the Great Court of her *lao chia*, but there was little opportunity to linger on its magnificence, for Lotus Delight led the Woo women at once into the presence of the Duchess. After Por Por and her handmaiden went the concubine and her servant, then Spring Moon with Dummy, and then the other female relatives, as was the custom.

Not until the concubine lowered herself on bended knee did Spring Moon catch a glimpse of their hostess. Why, she had the face of a horse! And it was true, Manchu women did not bind their feet but wore tall pedestal shoes painted to look like golden lilies. Amitabha! She was glad to be a Han!

When it was her turn to curtsy, her knees shook. Bad enough to have to pay allegiance to a Manchu; she must not embarrass herself by falling. Carefully she recited the greeting she had rehearsed. "How kind of you to invite your humble servants to such an august occasion, Your Graciousness."

The Duchess's smile changed her face. Her eyes were friendly. "So you are the one who has caused so many to drink vinegar. Now I see why!"

Spring Moon blushed, then blurted out, "I am so pleased to be here. I have never seen a palace or even Peking before."

"This is a most unremarkable evening," said the Duchess with a wave of her hand. "Just a foolish idea to amuse the inconsequential father of my insignificant children."

She eyed the next in line. It was time for Spring Moon and Dummy to follow the concubine. What a fool she had been, chattering like a magpie! Her mother-in-law waited at the foot of the stairs to the ladies' gallery, her long cerise fingernails tapping the rail.

Looking up, Spring Moon prayed that she would not get dizzy! There were nine steps at least. In the courtyards, every room touched the ground. She felt Dummy reaching for her hand. The girl's anxiety made her forget her own, and she whispered, "You are doing well. No reason to fret. Did you not see that the Duchess has even bigger feet than you?"

In the doorway of the anteroom at the top of the stairs, Dummy resumed her place behind, and they waited for the Lan maidservants, dressed in purple and black silk, to show them to one of the many round tables at which sat the ladies of Peking, Manchu and Han, attended by their personal slave girls.

"Kindly move your jade steps this way." Dummy close behind her, Spring Moon followed the attendant, walking slowly lest she trip over the fringes of the orchid silk rug. She felt as if each of the guests already seated knew the exact number of stitches in her gown, the exact weight of the gold in her jewelry, the exact location of the mole on her left shoulder. In their wake, tittering and whispers sputtered like damp firecrackers. What had she forgotten? An earring? A smudge on her nose? She smiled with difficulty, lifting her head high, hoping Dummy did the same.

Let them look! She could see with her own eyes that what people said was true. Soochow women were the most beautiful. Any afternoon at the Hall of Womanly Virtues one could see more beautiful ladies than these. Third Cousin would have a hard time finding even a second-class beauty among them, except for Por Por.

She took her seat between the daughters-in-law of Lin Tai Tai and, after the amenities, turned to peer through the wood lattice screen directly behind her chair. She could see the huge garden perfectly—the gentlemen dressed in silks of every hue, the servants running from table to table, the lights that flickered in the breeze, rivaling the stars overhead. She drew back, and the view was altered as if by magic, a giant kaleidoscope of shifting shapes and colors. Delighted, she leaned forward and drew back again, leaned forward and drew back, until Sister Lin asked what she was doing.

"The chair was not quite comfortable. It is better now." How could she say that it was all new to her, that she felt like a country girl? Soberly she leaned forward again, searching for Glad Promise.

It was a few minutes before she spotted him, seated directly below her. He seemed distracted, absently twisting his ring, and for a moment she wondered if something were wrong. But then he reached for a shrimp, and the elegant man seated beside him engaged him in conversation. She smiled and turned again to the ladies.

The Duchess had arrived at the center table. As she raised her gown of purple silk brocade, embroidered with the medallions of the Duke, four slave girls quickly eased the high-backed chair beneath her.

It was the signal for the festivities to begin. While servers darted among the tables, the ladies forgot their formal manners and chatted noisily, greeting friends across the room, exchanging seats and gossip. Handmaidens waved fans, set and removed dishes, fetched handkerchiefs. Spring Moon, too, paid and received compliments, noting who was who and where sat the richest, the most honored, the most literate. Proudly she pointed out the Hanlin and Glad Promise. "There is my illustrious father-in-law. And there is the man who married this foolish self." Even Dummy, serving her mistress, seemed at ease. In all the excitement, no one had noticed that she was mute.

When the crucian carp in red pepper sauce was on the table, the elder daughter-in-law of the House of Lin tugged at Spring Moon's sleeve. "Look, the Duke has crossed the entire courtyard to toast your husband."

Spring Moon turned back to the screen. The Duke was of ample girth, dressed in a deep purple gown and a black vest with buttons of fei ts'ui jade. His eyes were little black peas, the kind that see everything without seeming to move. At first she could only make out snatches of conversation, but as the men nearby stopped eating and talking to listen, she heard the Duke say, "You are impressionable like the Emperor—putting your faith in foreign magic. You are too young to realize that a man's will is everything. Will is what gives the Empress Dowager strength, power. . . ."

So that is why the Duke asked for our presence tonight, Spring Moon thought. He wished to point at the mulberry and curse the ash! Suddenly, pleasure was gone; in its place, fear.

The Duke glanced around, as if to see who among them was paying attention, and went on: "Once, the Empress Dowager was only one of hundreds of beautiful Manchu virgins residing in the Forbidden City. What set her apart? Will. Even the Emperor fell to his knees when she confronted him with his lack of filial piety. Yet she has never ridden in a steam coffin or fired a gun. She commands through moral authority. I have seen her call wild birds from the skies to perch on her fan and sing. The Dowager and the Empire will triumph over their enemies."

Spring Moon sighed with relief at Glad Promise's reply. "As you say, Noble Host. I only wish I were as optimistic."

She had no more desire for chatter, merely pretending enthusiasm until finally the dinner was over and it was time for the entertainment to begin. As the lanterns on the stage were being lit, she sent Dummy to help with the tea. No reason for the girl to share her fears. "Go look around, enjoy yourself. The Duke will probably speak before the play begins." Dummy touched her mistress's shoulder and walked away, swaying as gracefully as the other handmaidens, though her feet barely qualified as golden lilies.

Soon after, the men below clapped and shouted, "Hao! Hao!" and the ladies rose and scurried across the room toward the screen, trailed by a wave of slave girls carrying their chairs. Spring Moon had only to hitch hers around to see.

Duke Lan was onstage, nodding to the audience, acknowledging their thanks for his hospitality. A large temple altar stood directly behind him, dominated by a life-sized painting of Kwan-ti, the red-faced God of War, eyes popping, nostrils flaring. On the altar, incense burned in sacrificial bowls, and against the red brocade backdrop hung yellow scrolls with incantations in bold calligraphy.

The Duke cleared his throat. Silence was handed from table to table like a message.

"For your entertainment tonight, ladies and gentlemen, something different. This opera does not take place during the Period of the Three Kingdoms or at the foothills of the Great Wall. It is unorthodox. But we are living in unorthodox times.

"We live in times of danger, within and without, of war and betrayal. In the last year, the northern provinces have suffered from floods and famine, from locusts and drought. Appearing as they do on the heels of the most humiliating concessions to the foreigner, these disasters are an unmistakable sign that the gods are not pleased. Hardly a square mou of Chinese territory remains which is not already claimed, or about to be claimed, by one of the big-nosed peoples or the Brown Dwarfs. The Germans are in Shantung and eye the Northwest Provinces. The Russians are in Manchuria and eye Mongolia. The British dream of the Yangtze Valley. The French are counting on Yunan, Kwangsi, and the greater part of Kwantung. The Japanese are not satisfied with Korea, Formosa, Liaotung, and the Pescadores but want Fukien. There is not a harbor on all of China's nine thousand *li* of coast that can be armed without the consent of the foreigner.

"We must no longer simply stand by and allow the Barbarians to disturb the winds and waters of our beloved country. But we are men of learning who abhor violence and love peace, while the Barbarians value profit and power. How then can we be rid of them?"

"How then? How then?" chanted the men.

"The answer is here tonight. Honored guests, meet those who have received Heaven's blessing and the means to speak to foreigners in their common language—the language of brute force.

"May I present the true patriots of the Empire, the Society of Righteous and Harmonious Fists."

Gongs sounded. Cymbals clashed. From all sides of the hall men, women, and boys charged. To the roll of drums, they dashed up on the stage. The women, their hair in topknots, wore red jackets and trousers and carried red lanterns. The men and boys had red turbans on their heads, with their queues wrapped around once and looped over an ear. The colors of their short coats differed, but on each a black medallion naming their society was painted front and back. Around each waist was a long red sash, and in each hand a spear or sword trailing red streamers.

When all were assembled on stage, an eerie silence fell. There was no sound, no stirring. The moment seemed to last forever. Then one after another, the women and boys began to move, twisting and turning in a violent ballet of lightning kicks and blows punctuated by ferocious yells. "Sha! Sha! Sha! Kill! Kill! Kill!" The stage rocked with their fury.

With their swords and spears the men feigned battle, crying,

142

> "Strike Heavenward, and its gates will open,
> Strike Earthward, and its gates will sway,
> Support the Ch'ing,
> Exterminate the Barbarian!"

As suddenly as it had begun, the dance ended. One large, brown woman remained in the center of the platform, standing squarely on her ugly man-sized feet. The others crouched on the periphery.

Raising her arms above her head, the woman spoke . Her voice was deep and cast a spell. "The men of the West overreach the gods in their behavior," she intoned. "Being insolent and extinguishing sanctity, they enrage both Heaven and Earth until rain clouds no longer visit us. Missionaries bewitch those who listen to their blasphemies, and whoever sips tea at the parsonage dies, for his brains explode from his skull. The Jesus-worshiping nuns extract the eyes, marrow, and heart of the dead to concoct medicine, and tear the intestines from children to change lead into gold."

The audience gasped, and there was murmuring.

"Take heart and heed! Soon eight million spirit soldiers will storm out of the skies and sweep the Empire clean of the foreign plague. Only then will the Heavenly showers once more seed our land."

As she stepped back, the others on stage sprang up, shouting in unison. The sound echoed through the court.

"Hasten, hasten! Spread the news far and wide. Swords and spears break upon the back of the soldier of the Righteous and Harmonious Fists, defender of the glorious Empire. Bullets will not penetrate his sacred body. Fear not! Join us! Support the Ch'ing! Kill the Barbarians! Support the Ch'ing! Kill the Barbarians!"

Suddenly, again there was silence. Most turned and moved toward the altar, leaving only the three smallest boys downstage. Drawing three imaginary circles in the air, the boys wrote a character in each. Then, eyes shut, their palms pressed to their foreheads, they recited an unintelligible sentence and, foaming at the mouth, toppled backward like fallen trees. The audience cried aloud, thinking they were dead, but others propped them up again, and they stood unaided, though not a muscle moved.

With a spear, the large woman ran toward them. She thrust it into one, then another. Their skin was not pierced. She took a sword and hacked at them. Her blows were swift but no more harmful than a gentle breeze. Not a drop of blood was shed. Finally, she took a revolver, spun its cylinder and fired at a brass urn on the altar. The bullet sent it tumbling to the ground. She walked to the edge of the stage and aimed at one of the boys. She fired. Again and again the pistol cracked. The boys did not blink.

As the bullets rolled at their feet, around them the other players, triumphant, resumed the ballet: "Sha! Sha! Sha! Kill! Kill! Kill!"

Soon even the ladies took up the chant.

Spring Moon wished that she had not come. The face of Sister Lin had grown as fierce as those of the peasants on stage, her eyes bulging in their sockets like the eyes of cooked fish. So too the others at her table and nearby. Even her mother-in-law looked ugly. And the sound! "Sha! Sha! Sha!"

"Mother!" The piercing cry rose above the cacophony. "Mother!" It came from somewhere behind her. She turned, and saw Dummy. "Mother!" the girl cried once more, and then stood still, her face ashen, her eyes blank. Quickly Spring Moon looked around. Was she the only one who had heard? No, a few others. But they were already turning back to the screen. What matter an overwrought handmaiden, after all? Spring Moon glanced toward her mother-in-law. Por Por appeared to be still transfixed by the play, as were the others at her own table. She slipped away and hurried to Dummy's side.

Tears coursed down the girl's cheeks, staining the new silk blouse. Spring Moon embraced her and ushered her quickly to the anteroom, out of sight.

She left a message for Lotus Delight with the servants at the bottom of the stairs and called for the sedan chairs. But when they came, Dummy clung to her until Spring Moon whispered, "I will go with you." They mounted together and squeezed into one seat. The cries of "Sha! Sha! Sha!" followed them into the night, fading slowly as the sedan swayed through the moonlit streets.

When they reached the receiving court of the House of Woo, Spring Moon sent the hired porters home at once, and the gate-keeper to fetch Fatso.

The servant came running, her hair undone.

"What happened? Why are you alone?" She opened the door of the sedan and stood staring in surprise.

"Help me! I had to bring her home. She spoke. Three times I heard her call 'mother.' She holds on to me as if she were a child."

Gently they coaxed her until Dummy let go and descended from the chair. But as soon as Spring Moon alighted, she locked her arms around her mistress again, clinging like a limpet even after they had reached the tiny chamber that once was a storage room. There, while Fatso boiled the water for tea, Spring Moon cradled her servant in her arms, rocking her back and forth, whispering soothing words.

When the tea was done, the two women succeeded in forcing the cup between the girl's teeth, but after a few sips she pushed the drink away. Suddenly, without warning, she began to speak. The sound that issued from her lips seemed to come from far away, and was without color, like the distant chanting of priests. Spring Moon and Fatso strained to hear, not daring to move, afraid that any noise or gesture would end the recitation.

"How could we know what would happen? We were so hungry. The floods washed away the millet. Mother cooked with more and more water and less and less grain. Her breasts were dry, and Small Brother cried with hunger. We pawned what we could to buy food in the village. Everyone in Learned Cinders gleaned for roots and wild mushrooms. I hated gleaning. I never found enough to share with another family, and so I had to go alone. There was a pack of dogs. When most were killed for food, these escaped. They ate human flesh. No coolie dared sleep in the road.

"One day we heard that someone was giving away food in the village. We all went to see, bringing bowls, just in case. It was true. Out by the main crossing next to the temple, the villagers stood in one line, each with a bowl in hand. At the head of the line was a Hairy One. He wore a long gown like the tax collector. His queue was the color of straw, and his teeth were the size of a donkey's. He waved us into line. I was afraid, but I could smell cabbage soup. I pushed my toes to the heels of my father's feet.

"Finally, I stood before the devil. He thrust his dipper into the cauldron. He filled my bowl. There was a piece of cabbage in it, and the soup tasted of fat. When the bowl was empty I ran to the end of the line to try my luck again. The devil filled my bowl three times.

"When the cauldron was emptied, the devil told us stories. No one wanted to appear ungrateful, so we stayed. He said that he was a churchman, come to tell us of the carpenter god. We understood little, but everyone nodded. After all, what harm in a carpenter god? All gods are useful at one time or another.

"When he finished, he handed out printed papers. We each took one. He promised to come back with more food and stories the next day. We went home and used the three pieces of paper to cover a torn window.

"In the evening strangers came to our house. We thought they were bandits. Mother and I hid in the back room.

"The chief said that they were looking for traitors and spies called Jesus worshipers. Father laughed. 'Then you are looking for bones in an egg. There are no such people here. See for yourself.'

"They upturned everything. When they found the hand mirror that was part of my mother's dowry, they smashed it, saying it was foreign.

"Suddenly my mother thrust the baby into my arms. 'Run and hide!' she whispered. 'Do not come back until I call you. Hurry!'

"I opened my mouth to ask why. She slapped me hard across the face. 'Go, run, hide. Mind your brother.'

"I ran out the back door and away into the fields. I never looked back. I found a ditch and crawled in. I held the baby close. He was laughing, for he liked bouncing and running and his belly was full. Soon he slept.

"I heard a dog bark. There was no other sound until night came. Then I heard chanting. 'Sha! Sha! Sha!' And the screaming began. It sounded like pigs. But no one had pigs anymore. I wanted to get farther away, but it was dark. And I did not want to go too far to hear my mother call. So I waited.

"The chanting became louder and louder. 'Sha! Sha! Sha!'

"Suddenly the bandits were very near. They held lanterns high above their heads. I did not know what to do. I heard my mother whisper. 'Shh. Do not come out! Stay hidden, no matter what!' Then she screamed, 'Help! Help!' and jumped up and ran away from me. I had not seen her behind the clump of grass. The men with lanterns shouted 'There she goes' and 'Kill her' and ran after her.

"Their shouts woke Small Brother. What could I do? I scooped up a handful of mud to seal his mouth.

"I heard them thrashing in the bushes. One of them shouted, 'I have her.' They called her 'lying offspring of a turtle.' They said she was a Secondary Hairy, a spy, a woman who swallowed the devil's words.

"My mother begged. 'I am Chinese,' she cried. 'I spit on foreigners!'

"One of them asked, 'If you are not a Secondary Hairy, why did you put their paper in your window?'

" 'To keep out the wind,' my mother explained.

"They called her a liar. They said that she got the paper from the devil. They had seen him give it to her. They had seen her drink his soup.

"Then my mother screamed and screamed. After a while she stopped. The bandits marched away toward the village.

"I was too frightened to move. I waited until I could no longer hear them. Then I remembered Small Brother. He had been very quiet. I pulled the blanket from his face.

"He was cold. His mouth and nose were caked with mud. He was dead.

"I tried to stand up but my legs were limp noodles. So I crawled, dragging his body.

"Dawn came. In the mud I saw my mother's head.

"I left the baby beside it and ran toward our house. I saw someone standing in a clump of tall reeds. I thought it was one of them. I fell down. The man stood still, as if he were hiding too. I crawled nearer. It was the head of my father on a stake among the reeds. His body lay on the ground, covered with flies . . . so many flies.

"I dragged his body by the feet to where I had left the baby and my mother. Then I returned for his head. I tried to lift it off the stake gently but I could not, so I took hold of his queue and jerked it free.

"I dug with my hands. When the hole was big enough, I dragged Father's body into it. I straightened him and put his head where it belonged and sealed it to the body with mud.

"To his right, I laid the baby.

"I fetched Mother's head and placed it to his left. I searched for her body. I found the trunk, then the legs, her left and right arms. I carried them to the ditch and pieced her together. Her right foot was missing. I could not let her go into the other life without it. How could she walk if she had only one foot? I looked and looked. Finally, I found it, almost buried. I pushed up the leg of her *chang koo* and fitted the foot to the ankle.

"Quickly I heaped the mud over them, more and more, until they were buried too deep for the dogs to find.

"The next day, I walked away. I walked and walked. All along the road, the dogs were fat."

As she had begun, Dummy stopped, and silence filled the room. The flame of the oil lamp slowly died, and the walls and the ceiling faded.

Suddenly, she screamed. The sound rose in pitch and died away and began again in the age-old ritual. The eyes that had been so empty filled with the tears of mourning.

"Oh, my father! Oh, my mother! Oh, my brother!

"Oh, my heart! Oh, my liver! Oh, my spleen! Why have you gone from me?"

By the hour of the rat, she was asleep. While Fatso sat with her Spring Moon stood in the shadows of the receiving court waiting, her hands threaded through the sleeves of her tunic. The wind had risen suddenly, shaking the shutters, bending the bamboos. Dust curled beneath doors.

She strained for the sound of footsteps in the hutung on the other side of the garden wall. She heard only the rustling of trees and the scraping of wood against wood.

She had decided to apologize immediately for her behavior at the party but say no more. Glad Promise must decide whether the story of Learned Cinders should be told to the others.

At the thought of it, Dummy's words sounded again in her ears and bloody phantoms filled the empty court. She closed her eyes, put her hands over her ears, but she could not shut them out any more than she could keep the wind from entering.

When she looked again, the gatekeeper was bowing to the Hanlin's chair. Silently, one by one, the members of the clan alighted from their sedans and, silently, one after the other, they walked away in the direction of their quarters. No one spoke. Each footstep was soundless, carefully made.

Instinctively she knew it was no time for apologies. Even in the moonlight, she recognized the fear on everyone's face and stayed hidden until all had passed.

Then she hurried to overtake Glad Promise. "What is it? Why is everyone acting so strangely?"

"Were you not there?" he asked. "Did you not hear and see?"

Of course, he would not know that she had left early. Quickly she explained. Throughout, her husband merely nodded as if he had heard someone else tell the story before. When she had finished, all he said was, "That poor child. That poor child."

"Please now, my husband, you must tell me what happened after we left."

He shrugged. "It is not important. It was nothing."

It must have been something beyond imagining, she thought. "My husband, I am your wife. You must tell me."

He nodded, but said no more until they had reached their chamber. Then he took her hand. "You saw most of it. But after the theatrics were over, the Duke took the stage again. He gave another of his talks. When he spoke of the enemy, he pointed a finger at me."

At dawn, Spring Moon dressed and went at once to check on Dummy. But the girl still slept, and she proceeded toward the kitchen. Even on this morning she must see to the setting of the dishes of rice and water before the Kitchen God. The servants' court was empty except for the hens, and she shooed them away impatiently.

As she spoke, there was a knock at the peddler's gate. A woman called, "Please, I must see the young mistress of the House of Woo."

"What do you want?" Spring Moon approached but did not open the door.

"I have something for her."

"I am she, but there is nothing I wish to buy."

"Please, I am not here to sell. I must see you. It is urgent."

Spring Moon hesitated a moment more, then quickly slid back the bolt. A dirty hag pushed past her. Sitting down in the dirt she took from between the two cloth soles of her shoe a paper that was hidden there and thrust it into Spring Moon's hands. In a moment she was gone.

The paper was not addressed or signed, but there was no mistaking the calligraphy. Only Noble Talent wrote with such sharp, stiff strokes. Only a soldier, knowing of impending danger, would act so decisively upon the knowledge.

No one but the family must know who I am or suspect that I am here. Leave Peking! The Concubine is about to give her support to the so-called Harmonious Fists, who are already infiltrating the capital. No one with any foreign connection is safe. Go without delay!

In three days' time, traveling in eight closed mule carts, the Woo family left Peking. The story was put about that Lotus Delight had been suddenly taken ill, and hence an early start for the mountain retreat in which the family spent the summer must be made. Fatso, Old Hawk, and Dummy, who could be trusted, accompanied them. The other servants were left behind, to finish closing the house, it was said.

❧ 10 ❧
The Parting

On the twenty-fourth day of the fourth moon, in the Year of the Rat, 1900, the British Legation held a grand reception, celebrating Queen Victoria's eighty-first birthday with music, dancing, and champagne.

Four days later, as the Boxers were destroying the foreigners' railroad from Tientsin to Peking, the first drops of rain fell. The coincidence was proof of the Blessing of Heaven.

On the twentieth day of the fifth moon, the Dowager publicly announced her support and the Boxers overran the capital. Imperial troops were ordered to join the fight against the foreigners. The Legation Quarters came under siege.

—Chinese history

AT A LOOKOUT where pilgrims had placed a stone bench, Spring Moon sat waiting for Glad Promise, as she had waited every evening since they had taken refuge in the Monastery of Benevolent Climes one month before. The crimson sun was setting behind the eaves of the mountain temple, but for another hour luminous clouds would cast a mauve cape of twilight over the Western Hills. The air was cool, with the fragrance of pine. Below, nature's tapestry stretched as far as she could see, until the earth melted into the skies. Faint wisps of smoke spiraled upward from unseen chimneys. Now and then a breeze drifted by, trailing the melancholy vespers of the monks like the ribbon tail of a kite.

One of the temple deer paused in its drinking to watch the path that wound among mossy boulders and gnarled trees beside the small stream. Alerted, Spring Moon went to meet her husband.

Together they strolled in the rock garden, planted centuries ago by a Taoist who had seen its landscape in a dream of immortality. She hummed a tune. He slipped his hand around hers. She quickly freed herself, for this evening they were not alone. In the Pavilion of Worthy Contemplation sat a lone monk reading, his bald head glistening in the candle glow.

"Is it so strange to find a monk in a monastery?"

"Have you gone mad? Walking and talking in public is shameful enough! Now you want to compound the scandal by taking my hand for all the world to see. Have you no consideration for your family's good name?"

"Does it not please you to be with me?"

"That is not the point."

"On an evening like this, what do I care for the world?"

"The Woo clan cares. Your mother cares."

She turned as if to run away, but he took hold of her sleeve and whispered, "Checkmate!"

She smiled in spite of herself. He grinned like a small boy.

"Look!" He pointed to the pavilion. "The monk is leaving. We can hide there until dark and no one will see what a brazen woman you are."

The night was still. Soon only moonlight stirred, unveiling cliffs and the giant reclining Buddha, smiling for eternity. They sat for a while in silence, and then Glad Promise spoke.

"We have been happy, you and I—despite it all—have we not, my wife?"

She squeezed his hand. "I have never known such happiness."

"And if it could not last, would you regret becoming my wife?"

She did not understand. Soon they would have a son and then happiness would be theirs forever. Smiling up at him, she saw that he was serious. "My husband, why do you ask if I would regret our marriage? Why do you ask such a thing?"

He took her face in his hands and kissed her gently on the lips. "Because . . ."

"Because, my husband?"

"Because you should never have regrets. You should never change."

"Why would I change?"

"Ours is a time of change," he said gravely, looking toward the Buddha.

"The world, perhaps, but not us, not you and I," she insisted. "How could we change? We are husband and wife."

"No, that will not change." His tone was forlorn, as if what might be already was.

Quickly she put her hand to his lips.

"Please let us not talk anymore. Not tonight."

He nodded, holding her close. She tried to recall the tune she had been humming, but the song was gone. In its place, a line by Yuan Chen: "A magician closed you in his hand and opened it, suddenly empty."

She must have trembled, for he stood up and removed his vest and wrapped it gently about her shoulders. Then he took her hands in his and brought them to his lips as if to warm them with his breath before folding her in his arms once more.

But it was not the cold that troubled her, and at last she broke free of his embrace and put her thought into words. "You are going back to Peking, are you not, my husband?"

He nodded imperceptibly. "I must go. Even if I cannot do anything, I must try. Join my friends. Help the people in Legation Quarters. I must try."

He waited for her to say something, but she could think of nothing, and after a moment he continued.

"I wish I could stay, but I cannot. I cannot stand and watch again as I watched at the carnival grounds, doing nothing."

Spring Moon found her voice. "What can you do down there? Where will you go? Whom will you see?" She hid her face in her hands. "You will die, I know it, and all for nothing."

"For honor, perhaps. I cannot hide in a monastery with the women and children, can I?"

She looked up, shivering again. "But, my husband, you are not a soldier. You are not even certain which side is your side. You have told me that if the Harmonious Fists win, it will mean the slaughter of innocents. If the foreigners win, more concessions and humiliation. If the Imperial troops win, more power to the Manchus. There is no way for you to win!"

He did not argue. He only took her in his arms once more, gently rocking.

Not so very long ago she had held him thus, a grief-stricken stranger in a mud-spattered gown. Now he was her beloved and he was going to die. This time it was she who would go mad with grief.

She broke away, openly, shamefully, weeping now. "Please, my husband, please. The boundaries of my universe have always been the courtyards. Within them, I have known great contentment. Why must your world be any larger? Can we not be happy and live for one another? Is there anything out there worth dying for?"

"I do not know," he said, and then, again, "honor, perhaps."

Seizing upon his doubt, she forced herself to think, to undo the tangled strands of his thoughts, to pull them homeward again. "Let us be the grass at the foot of the tallest tree, and leave heroism to those like Young Uncle who crave greatness because love has not fulfilled their dreams." She held his hand to her womb. "You and I, my husband, have dreamed of our son. He is here. I am sure, now, that he is here." She waited. When he did not respond, she pleaded. "Promise us that you will not go. Promise us!"

He started to speak but then shut his eyes and slipped to his knees, his head in her lap. She pulled him urgently to her body and held her breath. Listen! She begged silently. Listen to your son's plea.

There was no sound, only the scuttling of pinecones chased by a sudden wind.

Alone in their room, they took off their outer garments in silence. She, in her camisole, climbed first into the bed, a stone k'ang covered with a braided mat of soft bamboo.

She could not swallow the tears. Glad Promise held her, gently caressing her cheek, wiping them away one by one. "My wife, you have given me more happiness than I can ever find the words to tell you. You know that, do you not?"

Spring Moon whispered hoarsely, "Yes."

"But a man without character can find no pleasure even in such happiness as ours. Ever since I wore my first vest, I have believed with people like your uncles that China can never be the Middle Kingdom again and thrive in isolation. China must become part of the world. So then must all Chinese. So then must I. If I tried to fit the world into one courtyard, I would be a man without character."

He waited for her answer. She said nothing.

"Say you understand." He was pleading now. "Spring Moon, I cannot live without taking part in this struggle. And I cannot risk death without your understanding."

For a moment more, she lay very still, already traveling from this life to another, envious of the water that skips in the stream, the rock that stands upon the mountain, the wildflowers that bloom this and every season, just outside the door. All would still be, when he was gone.

At twilight, nothing can delay the setting sun. Old Venerable had been right.

She lifted herself up and studied the face of her husband in the moonlight. She must not forget the smallest detail. She wanted to relive the two years, recalling each day, each night of their married life. Instead, she only whispered softly, "I understand, my husband," and bent to kiss his lips.

Sometime between the next dawn and dusk, while she attended her mother-in-law, Glad Promise left. He did not say good-bye and she did not see him go. Upon returning to their room in the evening, she saw that he had set up the chess board and moved his soldier into battle.

Weeks passed and there was no word from Glad Promise. Refugees from the capital, stopping to pray at the monastery before continuing south, spoke of unholy silences followed by the blasts of cannon and the clang of tower bells, cries of battle and of grief. They told of the execution of ministers who denounced the Harmonious Fists.

Spring Moon dreamed of the public humiliation of her husband.

At the end of the fifth moon the flow of refugees slowed. Those who did get through reported that only looters now dared walk the streets of Peking. Foreign goods were piled high in the squares and set afire. On the third day of the sixth moon spreading flames destroyed the Hanlin Yuan, Forest of Ten Thousand Pencils, the oldest library in the world. The heads of "Second and Third Hairys" were strung across intersections like lanterns.

Spring Moon imagined his among them.

Before the beginning of the seventh moon, the battle turned. Foreign reinforcements had landed at Tientsin and were burning their way to Peking. The Dowager and the Court fled to Sian. A new wave of refugees went from the city, carrying the news to the monastery in the hills. By the end of the eighth moon, the capital was all but deserted. Half the houses were leveled, shops picked clean. Now and again, a home-made sign said: *Most noble foreign sir: Do not kill us. We are all good men here.*

Spring Moon saw his body riddled with foreign bullets.

Through the fall and winter, foreign troops punished the North. Every town in their path was looted and thousands of innocents killed. Wells were fouled by the bodies of women who sought death in the bowels of the earth, to safeguard honor. The crops rotted in the fields.

Spring Moon watched helplessly as Glad Promise grew thinner and thinner, dying a pitiful death.

Many nights she screamed in her sleep. Dummy, who now slept in her husband's place, whispered, "Mistress, do not cry. You must be strong. Think of the baby. You must think of the baby."

Spring Moon tried, but how could she without also thinking of the father?

Finally, on the first day of the Fortnight of Great Cold, she gave birth to a baby girl. The Hanlin named his granddaughter Lustrous Jade, for jade was the fairest of stones and possessed five virtues: charity, for its lustre; rectitude, for its translucence; wisdom, for its purity of sound when struck; equity, for its sharp edges that injure none; courage, for it can be broken but not bent.

Not long after the child was born, when the great rains had stopped and the roads dried, the Woo household returned to Peking.

The walls of the Ancient City were festooned with chamber pots and bloody rags, useless charms hung to ward off the foreigners. Chien Men Gate had fallen. On Willow street, what had been a corridor of identical garden walls was a wasteland partitioned now and then by jagged enclosures.

Suddenly, Old Hawk halted the cart he drove. The others, behind, creaked to a stop. As the family looked on, he climbed down and disappeared through a broken gate. He was gone for some time. When he returned he looked as if his heart had been plucked from him. "This is it," he cried, wiping away the tears with his sleeve.

"No, it is not." Lotus Delight shook an accusing finger. "You are a blind old fool."

"Are you quite certain?" asked Spring Moon.

He nodded.

"How can you be, you silly man!" Lotus Delight sputtered. "All the houses along this hutung were much alike!"

"I will go and look," said Spring Moon, handing the baby to Fatso. Dummy helped her mistress down and supported her as they walked carefully through the debris from one court to another. Each looked the same—heaps of charred wood, broken brick, and earth. Occasionally, pieces of blue roof tile. Any intact ones must have been removed, along with everything else of use or value. Spring Moon recognized a corner of the stone chess table and crouched beside it, sifting the sherds for a piece of the Tang horse. The search was foolish, of course. The horse was certain to have been one of the first objects looted or crushed.

When they reached what must have been the court of Lotus Delight and the Hanlin, they found not a knickknack, not a volume. In a ray of sunlight, something glittered, but it was only a sliver of mirror. Por Por's treasures, too, were gone.

Slowly, Spring Moon turned away and started toward the carts. She was near the gate when she stumbled over a portion of the plaque that had for thirty years announced to the world, *Within lives a great family, one that nurtures a Hanlin Scholar to grace the Empire.*

❧ 11 ❧
Farewell

The grass may wither, but the roots die not
and when spring comes it renews its full life;
Only grief, so long as its roots remain,
Even without spring, is of itself reborn.
            —*Ch'en Shan-Min, Sung Dynasty*

THE HANLIN'S BROTHERS and their wives chose to return to the ancestral courts in Reed Village, a week's journey west of Peking. Though the garden walls were damaged, the land was still there and they could hope to begin anew. But no matter what the Hanlin said, Lotus Delight refused to leave the capital for the home of her mother-in-law, and so he sought refuge for his immediate family in the house of Scholar Yen, which had escaped harm. Their accommodations were two adjoining rooms. In the smaller slept the Hanlin and Old Hawk; in the larger, all the women.

They had been there a week when, at the hour of the cock Old Hawk announced that the third son of the House of Chang waited in a sedan to pay a call.

For what seemed a long time no one moved. Then the Hanlin said quietly, "Please show our honored guest in."

"No!" cried Lotus Delight. "Not yet. This room is not ready.

We must have time. Please go and beg our guest for a few minutes, so that we may prepare for the visit."

Old Hawk turned back to the Hanlin. The scholar nodded slowly. "Your mistress is right. We must have time."

Lotus Delight kept Noble Talent waiting an hour while she instructed Fatso and Dummy to make some order in the rooms. "What will he think?" she asked over and over.

"It will not matter, my wife," the Hanlin said kindly. "He will surely understand." She seemed not to hear and commanded that books and bundles already moved be moved again.

Holding the baby, Spring Moon sat rigidly in a chair while blankets and foodstuffs were crammed under the beds. Finally, screens were borrowed to enclose a small area where the guest could be properly received and served tea. Even after that was done, Lotus Delight was not satisfied until the Hanlin, Spring Moon, and she had changed into their finest. She shooed everyone else into the smaller room and told them to stay there until the visitor had left. Fatso alone would be allowed in, to serve tea. At last, she bid Old Hawk bring in their guest.

There were shadows under Young Uncle's eyes and, Spring Moon thought, a sadness in them that had not been there when he had left Soochow to live in the South.

The men exchanged formal greetings, the Hanlin's phrases more elaborate than those normally accorded someone so young.

"Please, illustrious son of my old friend, do sit down and join us for tea."

"You are most kind," Noble Talent said, avoiding the eyes of his niece.

"I have sent our inefficient staff to buy some cakes," said Lotus Delight, smiling. "There is an itinerant restauranteur who sells in this neighborhood. He has sesame squares that are quite good. Oh, nothing, of course, to compare with those made in Soochow. Everyone knows that the cakes from your honorable city are the best in the Kingdom. While I myself have never had the good fortune to taste one, that is what everyone says. . . . Is that not so, my husband?"

She babbled on, the most charming of pleasantries. For the first time, Spring Moon noticed threads of gray in her mother-in-law's hair.

There was a tap at the door and Fatso entered, carrying the tea tray. She bowed, then served them, starting with the guest. When she handed him the cup, he took it in both hands. At once Spring Moon knew why he had come. Young Uncle wore the foreign ring.

She dug her nails into her palms, for a moment denying truth. The ring could not mean what it did mean. She closed her eyes. When she opened them Young Uncle was still there, the ring on his finger as before. She looked at the Hanlin and Lotus Delight. Their frozen smiles confirmed what she had feared—had known all along. Her husband was dead.

Carefully, very carefully, she took the porcelain teacup from the old servant, certain that if it was dropped, Spring Moon would shatter into a thousand pieces.

They waited for the guest to take the first sip. As he did, the door closed, and once again the four were alone.

"I do hope you will be staying for dinner, son of my friend," said the Hanlin. "We cannot offer you much, but you will not go hungry."

"Please do," said Lotus Delight. "Of course, he will. Why, your father, Old Venerable, was a frequent guest. I remember well the many times he came to our home on Willow Street, how he always spoiled the children. . . . Yes, he always did. So many red envelopes. . . ."

In the hour that followed, Lotus Delight and the Hanlin inquired politely about the various members of the House of Chang. And although Noble Talent had not been home for more than a year, he answered as best he could, clearing his throat often, while all eyes focused on the blue and white pot that stood at the center of the round tea table.

Carefully, very carefully, Spring Moon listened, afraid to let a whisper slip by without her attention, afraid to think of Glad Promise.

When the pot was empty, she started to take it to the kitchen for more, but Noble Talent begged her to stay. "It is late. I must be off." He stood to go.

The Hanlin stood also. "Son—" He faltered, cleared his throat. "Son of my friend, please. Do not go . . . just yet." He looked at Lotus Delight and then at Spring Moon. The women nodded their heads, assenting. The Hanlin turned again to the guest. "Please, tell us. We wish to hear."

They sat down. Noble Talent removed the ring and put it on the table. "How shall I tell you?"

"My son left the monastery soon after the drought ended. Start there."

Noble Talent nodded, paused a moment, then began. "Glad Promise found me through parties known to both of us. He asked how he could help. I told him to return to the monastery. He would not listen. He insisted. So together we tried to do what we could, warning converts in peril, assisting them to leave the North. Later we tried to aid those trapped in the Legation Quarters, to reason with Chinese of responsibility. We smuggled in food and information. We sought out officers in the regular Chinese units who were worried about the implications of a victory by the Harmonious Fists and might be persuaded to withhold their fire. Many did. Others went through the motions of attacking, shooting into the air for the ears of the Dowager. We could have been killed at any time, by anyone." He stopped suddenly, as if there were nothing more to tell.

"Go on," said the Hanlin. "Please go on."

Noble Talent stole a glance at his niece. For an instant their eyes met, and she nodded. He went on. "It was the sixth day of the fifth moon. He came to see me disguised as a coolie. This time I did not know his mission. We exchanged only the usual greetings, but he took this ring from his pocket and asked me to hold it for safekeeping. . . ." He reached for his cup. "It happened that day."

"How do you know? How can you be sure?" the Hanlin asked.

Noble Talent took a sip from the empty cup and then whispered, "I know."

"Then we must know too," said the Hanlin.

Clearing his throat once more, the soldier went on. "We found him with three comrades outside a secret entrance to the foreign compound just before the wagon came and took him away with the others. There was nothing we could do. There was no time. There never is in battle."

There were no more questions. Spring Moon sat very still.

When finally Noble Talent rose, they all did, bowing several times to their guest. The women remained by the door, while the Hanlin accompanied him to his sedan. As the two men disappeared into the next court, Lotus Delight cried, "Come again! It was so kind of you, so kind of you to call."

Only then did Spring Moon realize that she had not said a word. No one had even told him that she had given her husband a daughter and her name was Lustrous Jade.

Slowly she turned away from the door and walked to the table, passing her palm over its wooden surface like someone unable to see, until she came upon the ring. It was still in her hand when she went to bed, but sometime during the night she let go and it fell on the tile floor, waking her. Only then did tears flow.

At first light the next day, Lotus Delight rose and walked deliberately to the k'ang where Spring Moon and the baby lay with Dummy. She shook her daughter-in-law. Tears streamed from her eyes. "It is her fault!" She pointed at Dummy. "My sister warned me that she was bad luck. Tell her to go at once!"

This time Spring Moon knew she could do nothing. If hate, though misdirected and undeserved, could ease the pain the mother felt upon losing her only son, she must not protest.

"How will you get along?" she asked as she embraced the girl. "Where can you go?"

"I shall return home, to Learned Cinders. For me, too, the land is still there. And the graves need tending."

❧ 12 ❧
The Widow

Thirty thousand Chinese were killed during the period known as the Boxer Rebellion.

Forty-five thousand foreign soldiers—Japanese, Russian, German, British, French, American—under the command of the German, Von Waldersee, occupied the northern provinces to avenge the death of three hundred foreigners.

In the Year of the Tiger, 1902, the Court returned to Peking and the Vermilion Pencil signed the Allied Protocol, thereby avowing that the Middle Kingdom had warred not only against other nations but against civilization itself. Many members of the Imperial family and those advisers who had supported the Boxers and thus led the Dowager astray received silken cords, a gesture of Imperial clemency. Each secured the cord to the roof-beam of his house and took his own life, as honor and duty demanded.

Her flight to Sian and her return to the capital were proof to the Concubine of the Middle Kingdom's poverty and the need for change. Without delay she instituted a series of sweeping reforms to remedy the education of the people and to develop the economic and military strength of the country. Fourteen divisions were recruited and trained under foreign instructors, thousands of able students were sent abroad to study at government expense, and the old examination system was abolished.

During the three years that followed, these reforms achieved many successes, but they had come too late. For none could compare with the victories of island Japan over the vast Russian Empire in the Year of the Snake, 1905. None could renew national pride. And so, even as the Imperial Edict prepared for constitu-

*tional government, insurrections and the suppression of insurrec-
tions continued.*

*In 1907, the Year of the Sheep, the revolutionary heroine Ch'iu
Chin was tortured, to no avail, and then beheaded and her flesh
left to rot. Her voice was heard throughout the land.*

> *The sun is setting with no road ahead,
> In vain I weep for loss of country . . .
> Although I die yet I still live,
> Through sacrifice I have fulfilled my duty. . . .*

*In 1908, the Year of the Monkey, the Emperor Kuang Hsu
died at the hour of the cock. So too the Dowager Empress, at
the hour of the goat the very next day. He was thirty-seven,
she exactly twice that. Some say that the Dowager had soaked
his face towel with pox so he would not outlive his aunt and
dig up her bones. How could she know that she would so soon
succumb to a fatal upset, after dining on crabapples and cream?*

*The new emperor, Hsuan T'ung, was a child of two. The new
Regent, Prince Ch'un, returned the Conservatives to power.*

—*Chinese history*

THE WOO CLAN decided not to rebuild the house on Willow Street
but to sell the land instead. Out of friendship, the wealthy Lins
purchased the property. Some of the proceeds were used for the
dowries and wedding expenses of the twins, who were married
to the sons of family friends in Reed Village. What was left belonged to the clan, which thenceforth provided an allowance to
those few family members remaining in Peking. Their circumstances thus reduced, the Hanlin, his wife and concubine, and his
daughter-in-law and granddaughter moved from Scholar Yen's to
a small rented house near the East Gate. There were no inner and
outer courts, only one courtyard and three roofs.

With the Hanlin Forest of Pencils gone, Fierce Rectitude retired,
working on a dictionary of ancient script for his own pleasure.
Spring Moon became his assistant, annotating his entries, while
Lustrous Jade amused herself in a corner. As time passed the scholar

and his daughter-in-law came to accept their new circumstances with grace and little rancor.

Lotus Delight and the concubine could not. Nothing had turned out as they had hoped and they had little to do and nowhere to go. Certainly they could not show their faces in the select circles they had once known. And how could they sip tea with the neighborhood women, the vulgar wives of rude pawnbrokers and petty clerks? Bored, they bickered incessantly and complained often to the Hanlin and Spring Moon about their conduct: "It is enough that we are poor, but you create talk with your disgraceful behavior. In any upright house, the father and daughter-in-law are seldom together. In this house, they are seldom apart."

Lotus Delight also dwelled on the failure of Spring Moon to give her a grandson. From the start she had called the baby Worthless Jewel, and loving her thereafter did not keep her from continually bemoaning her sex. Her tenderness and her disappointment were inseparable. "My precious good-for-nothing, what use are you? Will you care for me in my old age? Will you perform the rites to secure my comfort in the afterlife? You will only fatten at our table, grow more beautiful, gather a costly dowry, and disappear forever to your husband's home. Worthless Jewel, if only you were a boy!"

By the time Lustrous Jade was three, the lament was as familiar as a nursery rhyme and the child would join in the chorus, chanting, "Aye ya! Aye ya! A daughter with the virtues of eighteen Lohans is not equal to a splay-footed dimwit of a son."

By the autumn of the Year of the Snake, the Hanlin was dying. His reason and speech were not impaired, but he confused people and dates. With the end approaching, no one wished to correct him. It seemed only kind to allow him to be with whomever he summoned and do exactly as he pleased. Often, he asked for Lustrous Jade. The little girl seemed not to fear his pallor, or the pungent smell of illness and its cures, or the perplexing games he played. She would sit solemnly for hours in a small chair listening to him talk, somehow sensing that she must not laugh and break the spell when he asked the priest to shave his face and the barber to pray for him.

She was there on the eve of his death, when Fierce Rectitude dictated to Spring Moon a last petition to the Imperial Throne:

"Ever since the foreigner inflicted sorrow upon Your Sacred Person, You have sought the advice of us, Your humble servants, in Your anxious desire that a policy be devised whereby peace should be restored to the shrines of Your Ancestors and to the Chinese people. But we have failed thus far to avert calamity and to bring comfort to our Sovereigns; grievous indeed are our shortcomings, which fill us with shame and dismay.

"I humbly submit that the lesson of the war between the Polar Bear and the Brown Monkey be heeded. Once the Islanders of the Rising Sun also preferred no intercourse with the West, to continue in the ways of the old. Then they saw that their isolation would not be respected, and decided to seek new ways to direct their own destiny. Now we have seen the success of this enterprise.

"Woe that their war was fought for Chinese land. Woe that their cannons bombarded the Chinese coast. Woe that they battled for eighteen months upon Chinese soil. Woe that our neutrality was not respected and our countrymen were slain.

"However, in these latest insults lie the hope and proof of our eventual vindication.

"I, Your memorialist, now humbly desire to point out that if the entire Empire will learn what these other Orientals have already learned from the foreigner, we also shall be successful in preventing further catastrophe and restoring right in the designs of the mighty.

"War will then give way to peace, and the altars of our gods will remain inviolate. In the spirit of uncontrollable indignation at our plight, I present this memorial with tears and beg that Your Majesties may deign to peruse it."

Throughout the night, the old scholar dictated the same letter over and over and ordered it to be sent at once, each time calling Spring Moon back as if it had yet to be written. Finally, he fell asleep.

In the morning there was no sun, and all day the geese flew south. At the hour of the horse, the Hanlin opened his eyes and announced, "My summons has come. Let me be prepared!"

Fatso and Old Hawk moved him immediately to the atrium of

the house and placed him on a bed of boards with his feet toward
the door. Then they bathed him with water boiled with the fragrant
leaves of the pomelo tree and dressed him in his finest robes, of
midnight blue sewn with flying cranes and beads of red coral.
When all was done and the tapers lit, the household gathered
with Lotus Delight in the spot closest to her husband's heart. The
Hanlin murmured his gratitude. Family and servants burst into
tears. Lustrous Jade broke away from her mother and seized the
hand of the dying man.

"Grandfather! Grandfather!"

The Hanlin stirred but could not open his eyes. He gave a weak
smile. "My son. My son."

"Yes, Grandfather."

"Remember your duty to our family. Do not forget the sorrows
of our people. Promise, my son. Promise!"

Lustrous Jade bowed solemnly. "I hear my father and obey."

"Then I am ready." The Hanlin held the small hand tight for
a moment more and then let go.

For many weeks, as Spring Moon knelt by the old man's coffin,
grieving with the widows, she wondered what claims that promise
would make on her daughter's life, even as she wept for the claims
the dead made on her own. In the years since her husband had
left, the Hanlin and she had never spoken of Glad Promise to
one another. Perhaps it was because both had felt his presence
so keenly in the room that they found it unfitting to speak of
him as if he were not there.

Now the old man, too, had gone, and she could not sustain
the illusion alone. Before the Hanlin's death, Glad Promise had
always been with her, watching her, listening to her, following
her from place to place. Now he was somewhere else, and only
when she closed her eyes deliberately to summon him did he still
appear. It could not be that he was fading from her memory, she
told herself. It could not be. Perhaps his father needed him more
and somehow in the other world they were together, as she was
with her daughter in this one.

On the forty-ninth day, Fierce Rectitude was buried with his ancestors in the foothills near Reed Village. Spring Moon contributed her wedding gold toward a funeral worthy of the Hanlin, while a poor but talented cousin was adopted and performed the rites as the son of the deceased. When the ceremonies were completed, Second Promise accompanied his new family to the capital. There, in accordance with the agreement, he pursued further studies through the kind tutelage of the Hanlin's scholarly friends.

Lotus Delight nurtured her one hope for renewed riches and honor with the same care she gave to hiding the fishtails that now marked the corners of her eyes. "Just as soon as Second Promise is known in scholarly circles, we will buy a bigger house, in our old neighborhood, and then you will see the women of the Court calling on me again. Have I not always said that a son is worth more than gold? Now I will prove it!"

Spring Moon never mentioned to her what most already knew—that the old studies meant little in the new century, that the ancient system of sinecures was finished, that the modern breed of officials studied in Japan. Why destroy her illusions to no purpose? Second Promise was an unassuming sort who did his best to please, but he had no talent for the quick-footed, lucrative careers in trade which now opened a second, though still decidedly less desirable, route to influence.

As the widow of Glad Promise, it was Spring Moon's duty to serve her mother-in-law as loyally as the son would have, had he lived. But the Hanlin, in calling Lustrous Jade his son, had willed that she be educated as if she were a boy. Thus it became also the duty of Spring Moon to teach her daughter to read and write. Before long, one neighbor, then another, asked the Widow Woo to come to their homes to give lessons to their children. Lotus Delight consented, the income, however small, helping to overcome her distaste for such unseemly conduct.

Often at night Spring Moon would close her eyes and speak to Glad Promise. My husband, did you hear how well our daughter recited today? Were you not proud? She is very tall; now even Fatso says that she should have been a boy.

If only Por Por did not call her Worthless Jewel. If only you could speak to your mother, she would stop, I am sure. If only you were here. . . .

Now and then she succumbed to her loneliness and wept.

Later, when Spring Moon looked back upon the years that followed the birth of her daughter, the time seemed to flow seamlessly, marked only by death: the death of Glad Promise, of the Hanlin, of Old Hawk in his sleep. Finally, in the Year of the Monkey, there was the passing of Sterling Talent, after many months of poor health. When the Dowager abolished the old examination system, he had begun to fade. "The honor your father pursued was more precious to him than his life," Fragrant Snow wrote. Spring Moon read that letter again and again, and grieved. How strange that her husband and her father, so unlike in every way, should have surrendered to the same fatal sickness.

GOLDEN
ASHES

❧ 13 ❧
Homecoming

Southeast the peacock flies,
Every five li he whirls around. . . .
When the crowing of the cock came, I went on with my weaving.
Night after night I ceaselessly awaited you—
In three days I could finish five strips of cloth,
But the Great One found me too slow.
It was not at all that I was too slow,
But among your family—how hard to be a wife. . . .
So I beg you to ask your old parents
In a proper time to return me to my home. . . .

          —Han Dynasty ballad

SPRING MOON WONDERED if the children would ever stop taunting Lustrous Jade. It happened each time they walked to and from the neighbors' houses in which she taught. It was happening now in their own home.

> "Big feet, big feet,
>   feet so big
>   they block the street!"

Knowing that, had he lived, Glad Promise would have forbidden the binding of his daughter's feet, Spring Moon had lied in good conscience to Lotus Delight. "It was my husband's fervent wish. He made me promise many times." Her mother-in-law had had

173

no choice but to accept the will of her son. But now Spring Moon sometimes doubted whether she had been right. Although some converts, she had heard, no longer had golden lilies, not one of the neighbors' daughters had escaped.

Fatso's words were like arrows. "That girl of yours runs as wild as any boy in the street." She could not deny it. Indeed, Lustrous Jade wore her distinction, along with her unusual schooling, like armor against the cruelty of the young and the sympathy of their elders for the strange orphan girl.

From the garden now came her scornful retort:

> "Tiny feet, lily feet,
> freeze in cold,
> smell in heat."

Spring Moon sighed and got up to shut the door. She had no time today to be distracted.

Ever since the New Year, Lotus Delight, having spared no wiles or means to further Second Promise's career with little result, had seemed more desperate. When the festivities ended she had ordered the concubine back to Reed Village to serve the elderly aunts and had begun entertaining a succession of matchmakers every afternoon. She sent Fatso to buy dumplings and cakes for these women; at dinner she silently counted every mouthful that Spring Moon and her daughter ate.

Finally, almost one month ago, on the fourth day of the eighth moon, Fatso had told them that the negotiations for Second Promise's bride and dowry were complete. Within the hour her mother-in-law's hints had begun. "How many courts did you have in Soochow? Many must be empty today!"

At first, Spring Moon had not taken her talk seriously. Only wives who committed flagrant adultery were ever sent back to their families; private life, no matter how difficult, was always preferred to public loss of face. But then last week, Lotus Delight had forbidden her to continue tutoring. "I will not have you a hired servant in other people's courts. I will not—"

Suddenly the door opened, and Spring Moon glanced up, expecting to see one of the children looking for a place to hide or something to eat. Instead, Lotus Delight stood on the threshold.

"Por Por? How may I be of service?"

Without so much as a greeting, the woman began to shout angrily. "Bad enough that she is a girl. Bad enough that she has big feet. She must not be allowed continually to soil my name by associating with those ragamuffins. From now on, she must be confined to these rooms."

As suddenly as she had come, the mother-in-law left. Not once in her tirade had she been able to say her beloved granddaughter's name.

The raindrops that fell on the roof sounded like the tapping of a *hu chin* player's bow before the opera begins. The two women sat across from one another, about to enact the scene they had known would have to be played.

The daughter-in-law, having served the tea, spoke first. "Por Por, please forgive my unfilial request, but may I ask you kindly to release me from my duties to you so that I may return to Soochow?"

Lotus Delight raised her cup to her lips. When she replied it was without triumph. "This is most irregular, but perhaps not inopportune. . . . It is time for Second Promise to be married. Without a new alliance, there is little hope for me. With one, perhaps honor will return again to the family of the Hanlin. No doubt you understand. No doubt you agree. And that is why we sit here and consider such an unthinkable thing. Is it not so, my daughter?"

"Yes, Por Por," Spring Moon whispered.

"Then what can I do but accede, as you have? There is for both of us no choice but to think of the greater harmony of this house. And so I, the widow of the Hanlin, give you permission to return to your *lao chia.*"

For a few minutes, they sat together in silence, listening to the rain, allowing their tea to become cold.

Then Spring Moon spoke again, as was expected. "Por Por, please forgive a second unfilial request, but may I ask you kindly to permit your granddaughter, who belongs at your heartside in her father's house, to return with me?"

There was no answer. Merciful Kwan Yin, Spring Moon prayed, grant me this wish. I must not lose another.

When Lotus Delight finally spoke, it was with a gentleness her daughter-in-law had never known; nor were her words those that had been foreseen. "Once I told you that beauty means little in life. Now you see that it is true." She paused, her eyes wide, as if remembering. Before Spring Moon could decide what to say, she asked wonderingly, "How could beauty possibly allay the pain that I shall feel when I call my Jewel to me and see that she too is gone?"

She paused again. Again the only sound was the autumn rain.

At last, sitting very straight, the mother-in-law said what must be said. "I, the mother of your husband, give you permission to take my granddaughter with you."

Within the week, Spring Moon, Lustrous Jade, and Fatso were ready. When they left, even after their cart was far from the gate, Lotus Delight's lament could be heard. "How different it could have been, my granddaughter. How different, if only you had been a son!"

From a seat on the Nanking Express, Spring Moon saw for the first time what she had only dreamed of when she passed this way before, sealed within her bridal chariot—the land of her native Kiangsu. Was it the same now as it had been then? She did not know. Through the window, mile after mile of neat vegetable gardens and rice paddies, a different country from the dusty, yellow plains of the North. There were no towns of any size, only clusters of mud-walled, straw-thatched hamlets. Every inch was cultivated except for the narrowest of toe paths and the scattered mounds of earth around which the plows detoured. Thus the dead in their graves extracted their share from the land of the living.

Mile after mile, it was the same. As the iron snake wound through the fields, brown-faced men dressed in blue, their sinewy bodies bent slightly forward and to the left from the years of carrying twin buckets of night soil to nourish the crops, stopped working a moment to watch.

Mile after mile, Lustrous Jade's nose was pressed flat against the window. "How much longer? How much longer?" the girl cried. Spring Moon smiled at her daughter's excitement but said nothing. Lustrous Jade shook the dozing servant.

Fatso started. "What is the matter?"

"Tell me how much longer our journey will be."

"You itch for a spanking, Shameless Thing, robbing a faithful retainer of her sleep this way." She gave herself a good scratch across the belly.

"But how much longer?"

"If there are no bandits, suicides, or sleeping coolies along the track, we will be in Soochow in about an hour."

"An hour? That is too long, Amah! Much too long!" Lustrous Jade pouted.

"Pull in that lower lip or someone will use it for a table," said the old servant, yawning and nestling deeper in her corner for another nap, a possessive arm wrapped around the bundles beside her.

After a short silence, Lustrous Jade spoke up again. "Mother?" She tugged Spring Moon's sleeve.

"Yes?"

"Why did Amah mention suicides? Why would people kill themselves on the train?"

"Not on the train, near the train. The end of the year approaches, debts must be paid, accounts settled. But many poor people cannot pay their debts. They cannot live with the disgrace of not paying, but they cannot afford to die decently. So they kill themselves beside the tracks, knowing that the railroad companies will provide coffins and burials rather than let their bodies decay where all who pass can see."

The girl hesitated only a second. "Mother," she argued, "if the companies will pay for all that, why do they not just give the money to the people? Then they could pay their debts and no one would have to die."

"It is not so simple, Lustrous Jade."

"You always say that," the daughter complained. "You always say that about everything!"

"I suppose I do," Spring Moon agreed. It was true. There was so much that could never be explained or even understood. Perhaps it was fate, after all.

"But why, Mother?"

"Because it is so, my daughter. Ever since men first lived on earth, some have had more than others. Some lend and some borrow, and so it will be for all time to come. It was the Sage himself who taught that it is easier to move mountains than to change the hearts of men."

Lustrous Jade thought for a moment. Then, standing very straight, she announced, "Mother, it may be difficult, but I shall do both. I will!" Without waiting for a response, she went back to the window.

Spring Moon sighed. Why is it that my daughter never learns the lessons I teach? she asked herself. This was not the first time the child had made such vows. It was as if there were too many spirits within her, driving her this way and that. She will never learn to yield, Spring Moon thought, and prayed that she would not be broken.

After a while the train began to slow down. Lustrous Jade turned again to her mother. "Is it Soochow? Is it, Mother?"

Was it? So soon? Spring Moon looked out the window, then smiled to herself. She could not answer. Having never seen the city, how could she recognize it?

Suddenly, a shrill whistle sounded and the train screeched to a halt. Passengers lurched forward. Fatso slipped with her bundles to the floor and awoke with a howl.

"Merciful Kwan Yin!" The old woman in the seat across the aisle was screaming. "Bandits! It must be bandits!"

"Bandits! Bandits!" shouted Lustrous Jade.

Fatso picked herself up with difficulty, brushing the dust from her clothes. "Maybe one will kidnap you, Galling Mule. Maybe then I will get some rest."

"I am not afraid of them," Lustrous Jade boasted. "Not even if they pour chili sauce down my nostrils. Where are they, anyway? Mother, should I swallow my ring?"

"No bandits! No bandits!" called the conductor from his place at the end of the coach. "Just a short delay. We are less than a *li* from the station of Soochow. Patience! No trouble! No bandits!"

"It is not fair," wailed the girl, whose favorite story was that of Mu Lan, the daughter who took her father's place in battle. "I would have hooked out an eye. I would have—"

"Stop that now," demanded Fatso. "Everyone is staring."

Suddenly, Spring Moon was on her feet. Suddenly, she could not wait to see the city of her birth, as new to her as it had been on the day twenty-eight years ago when she first drew breath.

"Help me, Old Friend, help me with the window!" When it was open, all three leaned out to see what lay ahead. The city was not yet in view, but the station could be seen. Between the train and its sunlit roof, a great crowd had gathered, blocking the way. All were dressed in the short loose coat and faded blue cotton pants of the peasants except for one, who wore a gentleman's gown. Spring Moon was too far away to make out his face, but she was struck by the idea that she knew him. It was not just his dress that distinguished him from the others. While they ranted, he stood perfectly still, hands clasped behind him, looking off into the distance like a poet in a painting. It was Bold Talent.

"Who are those men, my mother?"

"I do not know. But the gentleman in the long gown is your eldest granduncle." She turned and nodded happily at the astonished Fatso, who immediately pushed the child aside and inched forward, squinting for a better look. Just as quickly, Lustrous Jade squirmed back into her place between the two adults.

"Eldest granduncle? The one who knew Father in America?"

"Yes, he is the one."

"But what is he doing there? Can we go to him?"

"No, we cannot. But I shall send him a note." Spring Moon wrote quickly and handed the paper and a coin to one of the sedan carriers who were stationed near the tracks.

As they waited, the other passengers disembarked, preferring to hire sedan chairs to carry them the last hundred *ma* into the station. Fatso gathered their belongings, while Lustrous Jade hung out the window, reporting on the progress of their messenger.

Spring Moon sat down to compose herself. This was not at all as she had planned. She had not written of her return, postponing the difficult explanation, knowing that hidden behind all the words of welcome in Soochow would be the nagging thought that she had been found lacking. Certainly she had never expected to see Eldest Uncle first. For a moment she wished that it were not too late to call the messenger back. What could she say, here on the train, in front of the world?

In no time, he was entering the car. Spring Moon stood up slowly, holding Lustrous Jade before her. He had stopped at the door, breathing heavily from the effort of walking at such a quick pace. Then his eyes met hers and he smiled, approaching deliberately, without haste.

"It is you, my niece!" He nodded. The three travelers from Peking bowed solemnly.

Turning quickly from Spring Moon, he exchanged greetings with Fatso and then looked down at Lustrous Jade.

"Can you be the daughter of my good friend?"

"Yes, Granduncle. I am Lustrous Jade."

He studied her face a moment, then touched her cheek lightly. "You resemble him, I think, more than your mother," he said. Once more he faced Spring Moon. "Why did you not tell us you were coming?"

Her eyes focused on the green ribbon in Lustrous Jade's hair. She hoped that her voice would be steady. "My uncle, it would seem that I am as troublesome as ever." She paused. "I—that is, we . . ."

"Troublesome?" repeated the daughter, twisting about to look up at her. "Mother, were you not always good?"

"Your mother was always good," Bold Talent said. Spring Moon blushed. The girl looked from one to the other and laughed.

A sudden roar from the crowd outside served dignity, for Bold Talent went quickly to the window. "I think it is best for you to take sedan chairs from here. There may be more trouble than anticipated."

"What trouble, Eldest Uncle? Is it dangerous?"

"It could be. The stationmaster took a bribe and sent another shipment ahead of our farmers' pigs. The pigs, packed in the railroad cars, died. We are here to do what we can."

Lustrous Jade tugged at his sleeve. "I know what you should do, Granduncle. Lock up the manager with the pigs! Then—"

Fatso grabbed the child and shook her. "You talk too much, Little Brat!"

"Then he will smell rotten and—"

Spring Moon felt her apprehension grow. What would become of so ill-mannered a girl in the courtyards? Eldest Uncle, however, did not seem to mind, for he smiled and gave Lustrous Jade a friendly pat on the shoulder. "I do not think we need such drastic measures, Grandniece," he said kindly. "We hope for a just compromise. After all, we cannot afford to antagonize the stationmaster. We have need of the railroads."

"But the man is no better than a pig!"

"The farmers will be satisfied with compensation. Besides, there is nothing more treacherous than a cornered foe. You should remember that."

The girl opened her mouth to say more but then saw the warning in her mother's eyes and nodded instead.

"I apologize for my daughter," Spring Moon said. "She speaks too freely."

"I like her spirit." Bold Talent's eyes suddenly crinkled. "It reminds me of you."

Fatso and Lustrous Jade left first, trailed by the cart with the baggage. Bold Talent motioned to the porters of the third sedan to wait. He looked up. "Welcome home, my niece."

"It is good to be home, my uncle."

Spring Moon closed the curtains of the sedan. Only a while ago she had strained for a glimpse of her native city. Now, surprisingly, it mattered little. Lao Tzu taught that the farther one travels, the less one knows, and so it seemed to her, after the encounter with Bold Talent.

Her thoughts returned to him. Would the women be as happy to see her? Never before in her memory had anyone been sent home by her mother-in-law, not even a slave girl. Now she was returning, a widow with a child.

Suddenly the sedan halted. She opened the curtains and saw for the first time the gate of her *lao chia*. She knew it by the lions, whose likeness had been painted on the porcelain plates that were used on special occasions. In a moment the chair had passed around the spirit screen into the receiving court.

According to the plan, carefully worked out before they left Peking, Fatso paid the porters and ran ahead to prepare the women for the shock of their return, while Spring Moon waited, holding the hand of her daughter.

Catching her eye, the watchman, too young to know her, bowed politely again.

By the entrance to the Great Court, an old man sat on a stool dozing. His face was hidden in his arms and a birdcage rested on his lap. Still holding Lustrous Jade's hand, Spring Moon approached him. Could Old Gardener possibly have survived all these winters of his life?

As they neared him, Lustrous Jade asked, much too loudly, "Does your bird sing?"

The man stirred but did not lift his head.

Before her mother could restrain her, the girl tapped on the cage. "Sing, bird. Why do you not sing?"

Now certain, Spring Moon spoke. "Old Gardener, it is I, daughter of the second son of the Venerable."

At her words he looked up, blinking slowly. When he saw Lustrous Jade, he broke into a grin. "Where have you been, Young Mistress? Your slave girl has been looking for you everywhere."

Lustrous Jade peered into the old man's eyes as if trying to discover whether he could see. "What do you mean? I am Lustrous Jade. I have never been here before, and I do not have a slave girl."

"I know, I know." He slowly turned toward Spring Moon. "I have known everyone in this illustrious family for five generations."

He looks more like a baby than an old man, thought Spring Moon. She bent toward him. "I am truly delighted to see you again, Old Retainer."

"Thought I would be on the other side of the Yellow Springs, did you? Well, not so, not so."

He put the cage aside, then leaned against the wall and slowly pulled himself to his feet, drawing himself up as straight as the years would allow. He bowed. "Welcome home, Young Mistress."

"Thank you. It is indeed good to be here again."

There was no time to say more, for Fatso appeared at the Bottle Gate and beckoned. When Spring Moon reached her, she whispered, "I have told them everything. They are waiting."

Holding the hand of the child, the servant led the way along a path her mistress did not know to the marble screen. On the other side, Spring Moon stopped. The Cypress Garden was as it had been on the day she stood in the Clover Gate, clad in rose for her Maiden's Feast. Nothing had changed, except perhaps to become more beautiful. Old Gardener's chrysanthemums had grown more varied, the aged pomegranate tree more gnarled, the bamboos even more luxuriant.

How did it go, the poem by Yuan Mei, the first one she had ever recited for Bold Talent?

> I had long had it in mind to make a boat
> that should skim the waves quick as any bird
> Yet never carry people away from their friends
> But only carry people back to their homes.

When they had crossed the Bridge of Coming and Going, and the red columns of the Hall of Womanly Virtues were just ahead, Spring Moon paused once more.

Merciful Kwan Yin, she prayed, let me find home. "It is all right," the servant said softly. And, again, "They are waiting."

Fatso and Lustrous Jade behind her, Spring Moon crossed the threshold.

All the women of the clan were assembled in their rightful places. No one moved. She did not know what to do, for there was no tradition to guide her, and their faces betrayed nothing.

As if her eyes willed it, one by one she looked at them, the Grandaunts and the Aunts, and the servants. Gone, of course, were the cousins of her age; in their stead the young wives of the bachelors who had serenaded her. Near the middle of the room, according to their rank, stood a gentlewoman not much older than herself who must be Golden Virtue; next to her Silken Dawn, the third wife of the Venerable; and then Fragrant Snow, the widow of his second son, in plum silk embroidered with narcissus.

Finally, reluctantly, her gaze moved to the one who sat apart, in the precise center of the hall.

Was the chair new? It seemed more imposing than the one she remembered.

Slowly she walked forward, then stopped and waited, her eyes lowered. For how long was the only sound the beating of her heart? Then, "My granddaughter! My heart! You are home!" Spring Moon looked up. The Matriarch smiled.

"Oh, Grandmother!" Spring Moon fell to her knees. She kowtowed.

"Flesh of my body, let me embrace you." It was Fragrant Snow. Again Spring Moon kowtowed. Her mother pulled her up and held her.

Tears blinded them both as relatives and servants pressed around, sobbing, trying to say the proper words of welcome, fussing over the child.

When the hubbub had subsided, the Matriarch took Spring Moon's hand. "Granddaughter, you must pay your respects to the wife of the Patriarch."

Golden Virtue's demeanor was so contained that she seemed to stand alone, but her smile was warm. Quickly, Spring Moon dropped to her knees. Before her forehead touched the floor, the young woman spoke, her gentle words touched lightly by the accent of the South. "No, no, you must not. I do not deserve such an honor. Please, my dear niece, do get up."

Suddenly, Fatso blew her nose, sounding like the goose that caught the butcher's eye, and laughter filled the hall.

Spring Moon thought, I am home.

Later, after tea, Lustrous Jade was introduced to the children of the house. "Our school is the envy of Soochow," the Matriarch boasted. "Every day I must turn away friends who plead with me to permit their children to attend."

"Children?" asked Spring Moon. "You mean that ours is a school for boys *and* girls?"

The Matriarch sniffed. "Of course. Ours is an enlightened family."

So. Spring Moon smiled to herself. Eldest Uncle had been right. It was just a question of time.

The pupils stood in line with their teacher in the Cypress Garden, ready to be presented according to their standing. First, the tutor, a young man whose round spectacles gave him a startled look. Then the boys. Each bowed in turn, beginning with the two sons of the Patriarch, proceeding through the great-grandsons of the Venerable's brothers, and ending with August Winds, an orphaned son of poor and distant relations. He was chubbier than the others and appeared to be munching on something. The Matriarch glared at him, but he pretended to be unaware of it and openly studied Lustrous Jade's big feet while the girls gave their names. They too noticed the feet and tittered shyly behind their hands.

Lustrous Jade, quick as always, lifted her skirts and stuck out a shoe, for their convenience.

The Matriarch coughed. There was silence. The girls curtsied in unison and walked swiftly toward the inner courts. The boys bowed and withdrew behind the marble screen, led by Grand Vista, elder son of the Patriarch. The chubby one brought up the rear.

Lustrous Jade started after him, but Spring Moon caught her hand. "Daughter, in Soochow you will learn many new things. The first is that you may not go where you do not belong. And you do not belong in the outer courts. Henceforth, you will remain here with the women. Except for school, you must never go beyond that marble screen."

"But why?"

"It is tradition."

"I do not like tradition."

"You must not say so again, my daughter. It is forbidden."

A few weeks after Spring Moon's return, on the first day of the Fortnight of Great Cold, Bold Talent sat at his desk in the Ming study clicking the abacus, jotting down the figures on paper. As they had the day before and the day before that, the various columns challenged him like a layout of solitaire.

At the forthcoming clan meeting the year-end accounting would be expected, and there was no way to conceal the deficits. What could he say? That they were not his fault, that all of China suffered? Undeniable, of course. But it was the monies he had invested in the iron foundries and spinning factories that were lost. And while he still hoped these funds, spent to further the modernization of China, would ultimately also serve the clan, he now feared that the clan would not survive its near-term difficulties with strength enough to enjoy any long-range benefits. For years he had salved his conscience with the fact that the single largest contribution to the clan treasury since he became Patriarch had been his wife's dowry. Now that was gone, and there was nothing to take its place.

Most troublesome of all were the sums he gave to Noble Talent. Young Brother's requests were increasingly frequent, urgent, and always sizable. Yet no one must ever suspect that the Chang treasury served the revolutionaries, whatever they guessed about Noble Talent's business in the South.

Bold Talent returned to the abacus, dividing up these contributions and adding the results to the columns representing the expenditures of the seven branches of the Chang household. He tore up the paper he was writing on. It was ridiculous. No one would believe the calculations.

And yet, two years ago, it had seemed to him that there was no choice.

"Reform is dead, my brother," Noble Talent had said then. "It died with the Dowager and the Emperor."

Why in the name of reason, Bold Talent thought, had the Old Concubine waited until after the Harmonious Fists did their damage to see the light? And why, once she saw it, could she not have lived long enough to push the belated reforms through?

"You must agree," Noble Talent had said. "You must agree that the new Regent is an ass with eyes for a tail."

It was true. Even the Dowager had not been as incompetent.

"What more proof do you need than his firing of Yuan Shi-kai?" Noble Talent's voice had risen with fervor. "He plans to replace all Chinese holding office with Manchus. How many Manchus are qualified to govern? Answer me that!"

"Not many. A handful." His reply had lacked the proper enthusiasm.

"Older Brother, you have been patient for sixteen years. This would not be a rash move. Despite a Child Emperor, an ignorant Regent, effete garrisons, corrupt officials, stagnation, floods, famines, bandits, and foreign enclaves, four million Manchus still rule over four hundred million Han. Nothing short of revolution will do. You must join us."

And he had agreed. Now he no longer knew how many taels of silver had been spent.

Abruptly he stood up, pushing the papers aside. What was the use of it all? There had been no revolution, just a lot of talk, some sabotage, the assassination of a Manchu official on the road to Canton. The results were not reform but oppression, censorship, and higher taxes to pay for local militia and Imperial troops.

He walked slowly to his writing table. Usually there was magic in gripping the brush, spreading the ink, sculpting the characters. Every swirl, line, and dot done properly revealed the beauty of balance, the power of imbalance, the restraint in freedom and the freedom in restraint. When the essence of a character was captured, it wedded idea, symbol, and tone. There was then harmony of opposites—of yin and yang. There were no contradictions, and intuition reigned.

This evening, it eluded him. He put away his brush and walked across the courtyard through the Patriarch's quarters, to his wife's room.

Ever since her return, he had hoped that Spring Moon would be around the next corner. She never was. Instead, Golden Virtue was there.

"You have called early," she said.

"I am too tired to work. Will you have tea with me in the receiving room?"

She bowed her head and put aside her sewing.

"And ask Spring Moon to join us."

❦ 14 ❧
The Good Wife

He threw me a quince,
I gave him a jade pendant;
No, not just as requital
But to make our love lasting.

He threw me a peach
I gave him an emerald;
No, not just as requital
But to make our love endure.

He threw me a plum,
I gave him a black jade;
No, not just as requital
But to make our love abide.
　　　　　—The Book of Songs

GOLDEN VIRTUE LIFTED the lid of the porcelain pot to see if the tea had completely settled. It was Dragon Well tea, known for its delicate flavor. A few leaves still floated on the steaming water. She looked again at Bold Talent.

His gaze followed Spring Moon, who wandered from cabinet to cabinet, now and then taking down a book to flip through its pages. Golden Virtue quickly lowered her eyes, not wanting to intrude on the longing in his. Then she, too, watched Spring Moon.

She was very beautiful, though she did not study beauty's arts. Neither she nor anyone else ever noticed if her dress were new or her cheeks rouged. One only noticed the sparkling eyes, infectious laughter, liveliness even when she was still. Since her return, the courtyards had seemed a much gayer place.

Golden Virtue poured tea into the cups and offered the first with both hands to Bold Talent. "My husband?"

"Thank you, my wife."

She took the second cup and held it out to Spring Moon, who was still looking at books. Her hands burned. Finally she said, "Come, my niece, sit and drink your tea before it is cold."

Spring Moon started, quickly replaced a large leatherbound volume. "Forgive me, Eldest Aunt. I forgot myself. There are so many new books." She took her tea and sat down. "Eldest Uncle, may I borrow some?"

"As many as you like. We would welcome you here any time, would we not, my wife?"

Golden Virtue nodded, offering each of them in turn a choice of pecan, almond, or sesame cake.

"I have already made my first selection—the new translation by Lin Shu of *A Tale of Two Cities*."

"Of course. But why the translation? Glad Promise wrote that you were learning English. You should read the original, not Lin's stories. He reads no foreign languages and so must write his Chinese version after oral reports. Very good stories they may be, but they are not Charles Dickens."

Spring Moon was suddenly laughing. "Oh, Eldest Uncle, you sound as if you were my teacher still."

He laughed too, arguing that what he had said was true, even so.

"No doubt you are right, my uncle." Spring Moon took another sip of tea. "But I was never the student in Peking that I was in Soochow. Besides, it has been years since I read English."

How easily they talk to one another, the wife thought, offering again the plate of cakes. As if they had been milk friends.

Bold Talent waved his hand. "No problem, my niece. Just jot down what you do not understand, and we will discuss it."

"You would waste many hours, my uncle."

"No, no, not at all. You must not lose any more of your English."

Spring Moon turned toward Golden Virtue. "Would you mind, my aunt? I will have so many questions."

Golden Virtue smiled and nodded. "My husband would enjoy discussing his books with you."

Impulsively, Spring Moon reached over and took the other woman's hand. "How can I thank you, my aunt? I have had little to do since my return, only to go once in a while to the convent to pray for my husband. My daughter no longer needs my tutoring, and the household is managed so beautifully by you that all is done for us."

Golden Virtue lowered her eyes with becoming modesty. She thought, Shall I treasure her too?

Bold Talent broke the silence. "Tell me, my niece, which English writers you are already familiar with."

As they talked about the mysteries that existed only in the foreign books, Golden Virtue ate an almond cake. She had nothing to add. Bold Talent had tried to teach her to read when she first came to him, but mere boys memorized more characters overnight than she had managed in weeks. Her head had exploded like firecrackers each time her husband tested her. He had never said one unkind word, but after a while he no longer inquired. She had felt such relief! Now she thought, If only he had insisted.

Suddenly, Bold Talent and Spring Moon were laughing. The wife laughed along. They stopped . . . and she was still laughing.

There was an awkward moment. Golden Virtue did not know if Bold Talent expected her to speak. Her throat felt parched, like cotton. She could not meet his eyes.

Spring Moon touched her hand again. "Auntie, these cakes are delicious. You must tell me how they are made."

Gratefully, Golden Virtue turned to her. "I am happy to. First, you must select the finest rice flour, then—"

Bold Talent coughed. "My wife, the secrets of your art cannot be so easily explained. May I suggest that you invite our niece to the kitchen the next time the cakes are made." His voice was gentle. The words were like new wine.

But he was right, of course. Recipes for tea cakes could not interest him. She bowed her head.

"My husband, you honor my small efforts." She forced the words to come. "But I shall certainly invite our niece to see how ridiculously easy it is to turn out cakes."

"I would enjoy that immensely." Spring Moon reached for another piece.

"To return to what we were saying, my niece. . . ."

Golden Virtue watched him. He had sipped only tea, but acted as if he had been drinking wine, so animated was he, gesturing with abandon as he talked, often finishing a thought for Spring Moon.

With his wife, he was always correct, always considerate, and as far away as a dream upon awakening.

From the moment he had lifted her wedding veil, she had worshiped him, and there were still times when she awoke with a chill in her heart, afraid it had never happened. Hers was a lowly merchant's family whose sudden wealth glared from the minting, and whose ancestral graves spanned only two generations. She had no right to call this learned man husband, to be the wife of the Patriarch of such an illustrious family. Yet he had never said one thoughtless word and treated her with the utmost respect. So did the clan. There had never been any tittering behind her back. He would not have tolerated it! She was grateful.

And the gods had been kind. Grand Vista was born the first year, Bright Vista two years later, and she had somehow survived the stillbirth of the girl two years after that. When she had recovered, he had come to her and said, "My wife, your life is most precious to me. You have already given me two strong sons, and it is only wise not to tempt the fates. I shall have my couch placed again in the alcove of the Ming study. You will not need to fear anymore." Of course, she had asked him to take a concubine, but he had only smiled gently and said, "The mother of my sons is all the wife I need."

She served her mother-in-law, helped him resolve courtyard problems and squabbles, was there whenever anyone in the household needed her, cooked his favorite foods, nursed his colds, saved his money, raised his sons, worshiped his ancestors. She learned to control the yearnings she could not master or understand, so out of place were they between a man and the mother of his children. She was not unhappy and he did not seem discontent.

Until now. Her heart ached for all three—the widow yet unaware, the husband who could not forget, the worthy wife.

After Spring Moon had gone, Golden Virtue asked her husband's permission to invite her niece to drink tea with them again.

❧ 15 ❧

The New Year

The ancients who wished to demonstrate illustrious virtue throughout the Empire first ordered well their own states. Wishing to order well their own states, they first regulated their families. Wishing to regulate their families, they first cultivated their persons. Wishing to cultivate their persons, they first rectified their hearts. Wishing to rectify their hearts, they first sought to be sincere in their thoughts. Wishing to be sincere in their thoughts, they first extended to the utmost their knowledge. Such extension of knowledge lay in the investigation of things.

Things being investigated, knowledge became complete. Their knowledge being complete, their thoughts were sincere. Their thoughts being sincere, their hearts were then rectified. Their hearts being rectified, their persons were cultivated. Their persons being cultivated, their families were regulated. Their families being regulated, their states were rightly governed. Their states being rightly governed, the whole Empire was made tranquil and happy.
—Confucius, The Great Learning

ON THE EVE OF THE Year of the Boar, 1911, the courtyards had been transformed overnight by snow, barren earth sheathed in white velvet. In the morning the sun, which for days had glimmered faintly in an iron bowl, shone in heavens of blue porcelain. Icicles sparkled on rain pipes. The green tile roofs, varnished with frost, gleamed like the finest jade.

For weeks the courtyards had been bustling. Fatso had supervised the thorough cleaning of the homestead for the Matriarch's inspection. "There must not be a speck of dirt. The house must begin the New Year in purity." The women of the clan had made and wrapped presents for friends. They had selected, sorted, diced, mixed, dipped, sliced, counted, and boxed. They had preserved apricots, apples, pears, and dates. They had pickled cabbage, ginger, and lotus roots. They had smoked hams and carp and had baked rice and almond cakes.

Now the House was in readiness, and the air keen with anticipation. All day visitors came and went bearing gifts, and red envelopes for the children and servants. All day porters swept drifting snow from garden walks.

At dusk there was a hush, a waiting. Wicks flickered in colored lanterns hanging along the galleries, and kerosene lamps made by the foreigner cast a glow like moonlight through papered windows. Spring Moon paused for a moment on the Bridge of Coming and Going, watching the lights dance among the icicles. Snow was rare in Soochow. She could recall seeing it in these courtyards only once before, when she was seven. Her cousins had frolicked from court to court, drawing faces in the drifts. How she had envied them! But her feet, bound only that month, had ached even more than her young spirits.

This time she knew only pleasure, as the gentle winds put the finishing touch to a scroll in chiaroscuro.

From the Cypress Garden, where the clansmen were gathering, came a muted chorus of voices. Still Spring Moon lingered. She wondered whether her happiness was as visible as the air she exhaled, and then thought that it must be so. This night was the best of all nights, when old debts have been paid and new ones have yet to be incurred, when transgressions are overlooked and exceptions are the rule. It had been so when she was a child. It was so now. Smiling, she hurried to join the others.

All had bathed and put on new clothes for the evening. The men wore black skullcaps and fur-lined satin gowns in vibrant hues, the women and children fur-lined silk jackets and red embroidered skirts. Many of the ladies had velvet headbands encrusted with pearls and jade over their ears. Each carried a small brass firebox filled with glowing coals to warm icy fingers and toes.

Everyone had come. Cousins appointed to far provinces. Distant relatives who had never before seen their *lao chia*. Even Noble Talent had returned from Canton. He stood between Silken Dawn and the Matriarch, besieged by the grandaunts and their slave girls. From the pained expression on his face, no interrogation by the Brown Dwarfs could have been more thorough or more embarrassing.

Not far from that group, beside the stone turtle, was Lustrous Jade, holding fast to Fatso's hand. When her eyes met Spring Moon's, she lowered them respectfully and waited for her elder to notice her.

For a moment Spring Moon studied her daughter, surprised that the girl had not simply called from afar and come running, her big feet menacing golden lilies along the way. Since their arrival three months ago hardly a day had passed when Lustrous Jade had not created some disturbance, boldly trespassing in forbidden courts, carelessly breaking heirlooms, loudly speaking her mind when silence was called for. Spring Moon had assumed that each incident was deliberate, an act of defiance. Until tonight.

Tonight the child's dress was impeccable, every pleat in accord, every hair upswept from her radiant face. Tonight, Lustrous Jade did not offend harmony.

The mother gestured for her daughter to come. Lustrous Jade hesitated a moment more, then, letting go of the servant's hand, hastened to clasp Spring Moon's, as if untethered she would fly away.

"Am I pleasing, my mother?" she asked shyly. "My hair? Is it right? Exactly like the others'?"

Exactly like theirs, my daughter, only more beautiful, much more beautiful, the mother thought but should not say. No other words came to mind.

"Am I pleasing, my mother?"

Spring Moon nodded solemnly. Together they went to pay their respects to Fragrant Snow, who had just arrived, an elegant orchid among the poppies. "My daughter," she whispered, "Tell me what miracle has transpired? My granddaughter looks almost civilized!"

Spring Moon smiled to herself, but before she could answer, the three generations were surrounded by the younger women, all chatting and exchanging greetings as if most of them did not see each other every day, as if the new faces were not strangers but sisters long awaited.

Then, at a moment when the men's talk of fortunes and the ladies' gossip were unaccountably stilled, through the Clover Gate came Bold Talent and Golden Virtue. Both wore coats of crimson damask lined with ermine, his plain, trimmed only with a border of gold, hers embroidered like fine tapestry. He went immediately to rescue his brother, and joined the men. She took her place beside the Matriarch, gently taking hold of the old woman's arm.

The Matriarch clapped her hands. Quickly, the women moved in behind her. Like the capricious tail of a dragon, their procession snaked through the Clover Gate and down the garden paths to the main kitchen. There the Matriarch sweetened the lips of the portrait of the kitchen god with honey and sent it to heaven in flames to ensure a favorable year-end report. When the old god was gone, she hung in its place the new portrait, and the women, each in turn, lit the incense in a bronze tripod censer and made offerings of dumplings, sweetmeats, and rice.

As Spring Moon raised the bowl of rice in both hands to honor the god, her thoughts suddenly were far away, in Peking at the House of Woo. There had been only two New Years with Glad Promise, and tonight was the tenth without him. Oh my husband, she cried silently, you must know that I served your mother dutifully for as long as she would have me. . . .

A whiff of incense brought her back. Others waited. This is not the time, she told herself. My debts are paid. She set the bowl upon the table and took her place again beside Lustrous Jade.

After the newest bride had performed the rite, the women returned to the Cypress Garden and together with the men walked leisurely, in no apparent formation, from court to court, filling each with warm gladness and much noise. At every gate the Patriarch pasted up scrolls of red paper on which the men of the clan had penned poems and couplets in their finest calligraphy, welcoming prosperity, harmony, scholarship, piety, and peace.

Now and again, as Spring Moon exchanged good wishes with elders and answered Lustrous Jade's queries, she sensed someone watching and instinctively lowered her eyes. It was not the scrutiny of old women, nor the curiosity of children. The gaze was kind. Tender. Without looking, she knew.

Am I pleasing, Eldest Uncle?

At last they came to the Great Court and the Hall of Ancestors. There, while the men watched, the women removed the old brocade from the altar and spread out the new one. All had worked on it together for months, embroidering in gold on crimson silk the Eight Immortals and their emblems. Upon it they placed bowls of vegetables, fish, meat, cakes, rice, and fruits, for the pleasure of the departed.

When all was in readiness, there was silence, broken almost immediately by the sound of a bronze bell. Three times Old Gardener struck the ancient treasure, a gift to their beloved ancestor from a fellow Senior Wrangler. Slowly the Patriarch knelt before the ancestral tablets. Three times he kowtowed. Then, standing reverently before the altar, he reported in a loud voice the good news of the clan.

"O illustrious ancestors, in the first moon of the Year of the Dog, the House of Chang was blessed with indescribable happiness, for one who still lives within our garden walls celebrated her ninety-fifth birthday. In the second . . ."

When the Patriarch's recital was done, he sat on the rosewood settee placed beside the altar, and one by one, as the women watched, the male members of the clan knelt and kowtowed according to their rank in the family hierarchy.

The ceremony was well underway before Spring Moon realized that Lustrous Jade was quietly reciting the rightful name of each kinsman as he knelt at the altar. "Maternal Granduncle Number Three . . . Maternal Uncle Number Four . . . Maternal Cousin Number One . . ."

She had not known that her daughter cared so deeply, indeed at all, for her mother's *lao chia.* To think her child so filial! Perhaps, she thought, the thought almost a prayer, perhaps in the new year Lustrous Jade will find a rightful place here.

Finally the youngest boy made his obeisance and resumed his place. At once Bold Talent stood. "On to the fireworks!" he shouted and strode to the door.

"On to the fireworks!" the company echoed, as all rushed outside to watch the dazzling display.

One rocket leaped toward the moon and, halfway there, burst into a peach tree in full bloom; then, bang-bang-bang, a pot of lotus, a vase of chrysanthemums, a basket of plum blossoms. A garden of flowers for each season was followed by sizzling cannon-balls that raced into the night until sparks broke away and etched the Eight Immortals one after another in colored lights.

The show ended when the Old Longevity God walked in the sky, driving the stars before him with his cane.

"Mother!" It was Lustrous Jade, her voice clear in the silence that followed the last explosion, before the applause could begin. "Mother, it is more wonderful than anything. I am so happy, so happy to be here!"

Thus it was that when the applause came it seemed to be for Lustrous Jade too, as if indeed she were a Chang.

As they re-entered the Hall of Ancestors, transformed by servants into a banquet room while the clansmen watched the pyrotechnics, Spring Moon bent down to whisper to her daughter, "You may sit anywhere you please tonight, my child. On this evening each year, all distinctions are forgotten and everyone is equal. But do not take the last empty seat at any table. Places must be reserved for our ancestors."

She left Lustrous Jade undecided, surveying the tables, and went to take a seat next to Fatso. They were exchanging holiday wishes when Fatso stopped in the midst of the third "Happy New Year."

"Look at that shameless girl!" she whispered through clenched teeth.

Lustrous Jade had chosen a chair beside the youth, August Winds.

Table by table the silence spread, as the assembled clan stared at the Woo girl and the orphan boy. The welcome of a few minutes before was gone as if it had never been.

"You see, my brother," said Lustrous Jade clearly, "I won. Here I am sitting next to you, just as I said I could." Her laughter clattered through the hall like the *p'ungs* of an unwanted mah jong player.

Everyone in the room looked Spring Moon's way, silently demanding that the mother deal with her charge. Unable to move, Spring Moon bowed her head. She wanted to explain, The child did not know, I told her to sit where she pleased, I never dreamed she would sit beside a boy. I never dreamed—

She heard a silk gown whispering, and looked up. Bold Talent walked over and took the seat next to Lustrous Jade.

The room buzzed with talk. Heads turned from the boy and the girl to Spring Moon and back to the Patriarch.

Oh, Eldest Uncle, Spring Moon thought. Eldest Uncle, you must not use wood to put out the fire.

As clear as the notes of the pi-pa came the soft jingle of gold bracelets. In a moment, Golden Virtue had taken the chair on the other side of August Winds.

At once neighbor greeted neighbor, and the spirit of the holiday returned.

"Happy New Year, my niece." Startled, she turned to see Noble Talent seated beside her with his wine cup raised. "Happy New Year," he said again.

He knows, she thought, what it means to be set apart.

Once more she found herself in Peking, on the day the soldier had come to call at Scholar Yen's. The teacups had been blue. Quickly she dismissed the memory. Not today. This evening must be filled with the happiest of thoughts.

"Happy New Year, my uncle," she replied to his greeting and, raising her cup to meet his, proposed, "Empty cup?"

"Empty cup it is."

At every table the celebrants toasted one another by drinking to the last drop, and the sounds of raucous good-will reverberated throughout the hall.

Deliberately Spring Moon's eyes swept the room, lingering upon each of the clansmen who belonged to the House of Chang. None were truly alike, many were as different as only brothers can be, one was separated from another by generations. Yet among them there existed a kinship that bound them irrevocably, so that whatever path and however far they traveled, each would continue to live in the shadow of his ancestors and on New Year's hear the echo of young laughter and bronze bells.

Her gaze fell last upon the Matriarch, who sat at a corner table. The old woman took notice of her granddaughter and waved, bestowing one of her rare toothless smiles.

Three hours later Bold Talent rose to signal the end of the banquet. All stood. In each bowl a few grains of rice remained, symbol of the hope that the clan would have surpluses in the year to come.

Following the Patriarch, men and women proceeded to the huge *mei-loo* that glowed in the Great Court outside the hall. There, each according to his rank, the adults filled their fireboxes with new coals, and then, together with the children, they marched throughout the homestead, depositing a few coals in the braziers of each of the thirty courts until all within the garden walls were warmed by the treasure of the ancestors.

At last, when this ritual was completed, the clansmen returned to the Hall of Ancestors to enjoy games, storytelling, and theatricals. Every member was present, even the smallest baby, for on this special night no one dared sleep, lest he dream an unlucky dream and it be an omen of things to come.

Only at midnight was the gaiety briefly interrupted, when the Patriarch led the male members of the clan to the main gate to perform the rite of turning the key, locking happiness and riches within.

⚜ 16 ⚜

The Conspirators

Tens of thousands took the revolutionary oath: "I swear under heaven that I will do my utmost to work for the overthrow of the Manchu Dynasty, the establishment of the republic, and the solution of the land question on the basis of a fair redistribution. I solemnly undertake to be faithful to those principles. If I betray them, I am willing to be punished in the most severe way."

Throughout the Empire men asked, "What are you?" and were told, "We are the Chinese."

"What is the thing?" And were told, "This is the Chinese thing."

"What is the matter?" And were told, "The universal matter."
—Chinese history

IT WAS THE FIRST night of summer, and the unseasonably humid air was filled with the sound of frogs croaking like dying men gasping for breath. Golden Virtue had moved her chair nearer the window and in the evening light worked on her embroidery, stitching a willow leaf on a vest for her elder son. Bold Talent and Spring Moon still sat at the tea table, an opened book between them. All three were silent, as if part of a tableau, watching Fatso gather up the teacups they had pushed aside.

The old servant normally did not serve the Patriarch. She had been pressed into duty because the other servants refused to conceal their outrage at the daily meetings of Bold Talent, his wife, and his niece.

Nothing, of course, could prevent gossip. "Why, the virtuous widow of the Venerable's father never entered the presence of another man after his death! Why, the virtuous widow of the Venerable's uncle never touched an object that had been held by a man! What is the clan coming to?"

Publicly, the clansmen boasted of Spring Moon's learning. "Did the Soongs not send their daughters as well as their sons to study in Japan? This is a new century. The House of Chang must not be backward!" Privately, they believed they had been manipulated by the Patriarch. It was true that, with the government and missionaries opening new schools everywhere, qualified modern teachers for the clan school were no sooner hired than they left for better positions; thus when the Patriarch suggested Spring Moon for a vacancy, they had not objected. But they never imagined they were consenting to private English lessons as well. And if the wife's presence at the lessons shamed those who thrived on stirring vats of vinegar, it did not prevent their resenting the unseemly intimacy between the Patriarch and the widow.

When Fatso left, Spring Moon cleared her throat and resumed her reading aloud. The book was *Oliver Twist*, and whenever the hero was named, she hesitated. Oliver was difficult to pronounce properly.

Bold Talent did not listen for long, although he nodded from time to time, pretending. All week he had played his part as if nothing were wrong, when in fact everything was at stake.

Once, when very young, he had boasted that he could at the same time draw a square with his left hand and a circle with his right. Then, in front of his cousins, he had tried again and again and failed. Finally, he had run as fast as possible away from their laughter and stumbled, hitting his head. One week ago the same pain had returned. Squares and circles, circles and squares. Looking at his hands, he saw that they were trembling. Silently he cursed his brother.

"Is anything the matter, my uncle?" Spring Moon asked in Chinese.

He started. Their eyes met. Perhaps if she had not asked he would never have thought to tell her, tell anyone. Now, irrationally, he decided to share his secret.

"Is anything the matter?" she asked again.

He shook his head, glancing at Golden Virtue. "No, nothing. I was listening to the frogs, that is all. Come, give me the book. I shall read for a while."

She looked perplexed but moved the book toward him.

"My niece," he said, in English. Again, their eyes met. "I have something to tell you. I shall pretend to read, but my words will not be those of Dickens."

He paused, but she showed no surprise, merely nodding, as if she had played this game before.

"Good. Speak English. My wife must not suspect and become alarmed. Do you understand?"

Again, she nodded. Together they bent over the book, and, tracing the lines with his finger as if to show her the words, he began. "My brother is a sworn member of a revolutionary group and has been one for years." He paused, expecting almost any reaction but the one she gave. She spoke as if she discussed a point of grammar, nothing more.

"I know. I have suspected since the time of the Boxers. It was he who warned my husband's family."

So Young Brother had, then at least, understood his obligations. Bold Talent nodded and turned back to the text. "Some weeks ago a shipment of guns he purchased proved defective, and he is now under suspicion. Many have distrusted him since the beginning because he is not Cantonese. Now they demand that he prove his loyalty by carrying out a special assignment."

He glanced up. Spring Moon stared fixedly at the text. He continued.

Having begun, he found that he had no trouble controlling his voice, acting his part, and line by line, page by page, he told her Noble Talent's story. His brother had agreed to assassinate a certain Manchu, an Imperial adviser on transportation, who had dipped his hands into treasury funds and amassed a fortune in bribes. A ruthless man, he had also caused the death of many innocents.

Once, when he paused, he felt the eyes of Golden Virtue upon them and looked up, forcing a smile.

"Is the story very sad?" she asked.

It was Spring Moon who answered. "Yes, my auntie."

"Perhaps, then, you will tell it to the ladies when you are finished?"

Spring Moon promised that she would.

He turned the page and went on. "My brother confided this to me when he came here last week, even the method he planned to use. 'A bomb is sure,' he said. 'By attacking at the Yamen we guarantee that no one will mistake our cause.'

"When I tried to stop him, he left the courts. I have failed to find him—"

She placed her hand on the page and turned it back, as if she sought some clarification of the text. "My uncle, you must stop him. If he is captured, all who share his blood will die."

For a moment, there was silence. This time his wife did not rush in with nervous chatter.

"I pleaded with him, but he did not listen. He said that he has not implicated the clan and never will. The fool! Now time is short. The official arrives next Wednesday for a stay at the Convent of Sedate Quest. He will be attending meetings at the government house on Thursday. I cannot even make inquiries, lest people suspect."

"Tell the official not to come!" She pointed to a line in the middle of the page.

"On what pretext?" Even if he, as Patriarch of the House of Chang, joined the Manchu's party, there was no guarantee that Noble Talent would recognize him in time to stop the attack. There was no way to protect the Manchu without revealing the plot, no way to save his brother without calling attention to his treason, no way unless the official died in his sleep. But he was not old and enjoyed excellent health. There was no way to save the clan, no way at all.

"There is no way," he said aloud, "unless the villain dies in his sleep." He stopped reading and looked up, feeling foolish and defeated. "I should not have told you, my niece. It serves no purpose, and I do not know what made me—"

"My husband, should I fetch more tea?"

He started. "No, no," he said, too loudly. He recovered quickly.

"I am fine, my wife. But it grows dark. Will you light the lamps?"

Spring Moon said nothing, and when Golden Virtue had returned to her embroidery, he turned the page and began to read in earnest. He had read a chapter without understanding or interruption when Spring Moon suddenly put her palm over the book. "Wait, my uncle. You said something interesting before."

He could not think what.

She flipped a page, then another. "You said something about him dying in his sleep. That is our answer."

"Logical, but impossible to carry out."

"Let me think," Spring Moon said. "Read on."

He had read several more pages mechanically as before when suddenly Dickens was speaking to him, to his brother . . . "'Unworthy son, coward, liar—you, who hold your councils with thieves and murderers in dark rooms at night,—you, whose plots and wiles have brought a violent death upon the head of one . . .'" He faltered, went on. "'. . . gall and bitterness to your own father's heart—'"

"Eldest Uncle?" Spring Moon captured his attention. He glanced at Golden Virtue. Apparently she had noticed nothing.

"Eldest Uncle?" Spring Moon said again. "Did you not say that the official has been accused of wrongdoing?"

"Yes. Everyone knows that if it were not for his close ties at Court, he would have been punished years ago."

"Then, my uncle, I think I know a way. We can send him a sign of Imperial clemency. A silken cord."

A silken cord. A silken cord. . . . Slowly, he nodded. It might work. It just might.

It would have to be at the convent, before the Manchu reached Soochow. And since Spring Moon went there periodically, it would be not unlikely that at the right moment she. . . . He turned the pages back to an earlier, happier chapter, and pushed the book toward her.

"You read now, my niece."

His mind was engaged, testing all possibilities against the probable, refining the circumstances, adjusting each facet until it fitted the next and the next so that everything was designed to lead to the desired event. Then he worked backward, going over and over each stage as in a chess game, one in which his opponent must never be allowed to make an unpredicted move.

Now and then, Spring Moon glanced up from her reading. Once she turned up the wick in the lamp on the table.

❦ 17 ❧

The Silken Cord

Once there was built a Buddhist convent, the lofty temples set among majestic pines only a day's journey from an ancient city. For centuries, the refuge prospered. Then bad times and mounting debts threatened to shut its hobnailed gates and cast its women out into the world.

But the Mother Superior had been the scorned widow of a grand house, and losing her home a second time was unthinkable. A woman of great resourcefulness, she took drastic though not unprecedented steps. No longer would the younger, more comely nuns shave their heads. Instead she taught them to paint their faces and saw that they donned gowns of silk and learned the arts of conversation, of the solicitation and return of favors, of sexual pleasure.

These special nuns were then assigned to overnight guests and to the many cultivated patrons who made regular contributions to the convent's treasury. And while most ladies of the gentry continued to visit the retreat to pray, a few, for a certain sum, found it suitable as well for the conduct of more worldly affairs.

Thus was the business of mortals conducted together with that of the gods, without any conflict of interest or violation of propriety, and the home of the homeless preserved.

—Chinese tale

IT WAS ALREADY HOT when Spring Moon's sedan chair left the House of Chang, turning down Pagoda Street toward the northwest footgate. Before dawn, gentle rains had fallen, so that in the morning light Soochow shimmered, a city of jade. Along the canals, fisher-men in brown straw capes slipped through rising mists like phan-toms, seen, then unseen.

The porters jogged rhythmically, across the crescent moon bridge, on which ancients sunned their singing birds, then beside the main canal, where flower boats anchored. Spring Moon's heart raced faster than the patter of their sandals upon the cobblestones.

Suddenly the chair lurched to a stop. She gripped the rails, grate-ful that she had not slid off the seat. Opening the speaking window, she asked the head porter what had happened.

"It is a fire, Young Mistress. We cannot get through."

"Are you certain?"

"Yes. Shall we turn back?"

"No! There must be another route."

"Only a most unfortunate one. Young Mistress, let us go back. The other route would not be fitting."

"The route is of no importance."

The porter shrugged and returned to his task. They detoured left, down a narrow side street lined with silk shops. Afterward she could not remember when she began to hear the sound. It was low at first, like the sound of locusts, but as the sedan moved on it grew until it seemed like the wailing of a hundred widows, the roar of dragons. Suddenly there was the stench of offal and of fear, more powerful even than it had been on the day she had returned to Peking from the hills.

She parted the curtains. The sedan had entered a broad expanse that she had never seen before. It was the site of official punishment, where criminals were flogged, pilloried, branded, racked, or be-headed according to ancient tradition and Imperial justice. From poles along the edge of the square blood-clotted heads, black with flies, stood watch.

A young thief sat in the dirt, pleading with the crowd and the gods to swat the flies that covered his swollen and sweaty face. His own arms were useless; he could not reach around the three-foot-square cangue that weighed upon his spindly neck. Surround-ing him, four or five children played a game, pretending to tiptoe to his aid, only to scramble away, howling with glee.

Nearby, a merchant in expensive clothing knelt beside his confession of larceny, painted in large bold characters and posted for all to see. The sound of a gong recorded each stroke of the whip.

In the center of the square, the sedan came to a halt, the way blocked by a crowd of shirtless coolies. Three men in tatters sat upon the ground, joking as they selected vegetables and pork from the dishes before them, smacking their lips with noisy satisfaction. Standing by, the executioner, hooded in black, waited patiently for them to finish eating.

"Make way! Make way! Honored citizens, make way!" The chair surged through the spectators only to halt again beside a robber of graves. This man's head was locked outside the top of a tall cage, while his body hung stretching inside with only his toes resting on a pile of stones. As Spring Moon watched, the guard removed one stone, then another. A different man, perhaps one who loved life less, would have sought death quickly with a single kick at the precarious pile. The wretch's eyes, opened wide, met hers before the sedan moved on.

When she reached the convent, the setting sun had cast a rippling net of light over the temple of vermilion and gold and was slowly retrieving it across the forest floor. Birds sang those evening songs which warn that all light is passing and will soon disappear.

She went directly to the great burner that stood at the center of the courtyard and threw in the spirit money, standing back to watch it catch fire and curl into ash. As usual the small nun with the pockmarked face was there before it was gone, her dark sackcloth gown exhaling dust which glittered as she moved in and out of the light.

"Amitabha!" She bowed deeply. "Honored Patroness, should I take you to your prayers?"

"Not today. I have urgent business with the Mother Superior."

Without a sign of surprise or curiosity, the nun bowed again. "Please come with me."

Spring Moon followed her up the scarred stone steps and down a long and winding gallery to a small room tucked away so far from the sun that it was already dark. It contained only two stools and an oak table, upon which a small lamp flickered. "Please wait here," said the nun, and closed the door behind her. Spring Moon shivered, surprised that the dirt floor was dry, that water was not seeping through it. She sat down to wait, tucking her skirt about her, motionless as a stone held fast by creeping moss.

A moth circled the lighted wick, its flight recorded on the walls in the shape of creatures that seemed to pursue it, chasing it round and round, ever closer to the wick, until it was captured and fell into the bean oil in the shallow dish. It fluttered briefly before its pale wings were still.

Outside a woodpecker tapped, stopped, then tapped again.

At last the ancient Mother Superior glided in, her voluminous ecru robe billowing. Spring Moon had never met her, indeed had only seen her at a distance, for she did not concern herself with women not her charges, unless they required one of the convent's special services. Inclining her head, she sat down without a word. Without a word, Spring Moon removed the two gold bracelets from her wrist and laid them on the table.

The old nun's watery eyes were nearly blind, but she calculated the value of the jewelry with a glance. Then she closed her lids slowly and, drawing a deep breath, held it, hunched on her perch like the vulture that sleeps yet does not sleep.

Abruptly she cleared her throat. "Things are dear these days." Her voice was gruff, as if she dined on bones. "What do you require?" She did not commit herself to the proposal Spring Moon put to her until a gold ring and two jade combs were added to the bracelets on the table. "Most irregular, but agreed. Amitabha!" She stood to go. "Follow me!"

Spring Moon was barely able to keep up the brisk pace the old woman set as they made their way out of the temple, through the Garden of Silence to the other side of the wisteria arbor, and down a winding path covered with pine needles to a long structure hidden in the woods. Its smooth facade was broken only by a line of tiny windows and doors closely set, one after the other.

The Mother Superior opened one of the doors. "Everything you need will be in the cupboard."

Before Spring Moon could thank her, she was gone.

The cell, lit by a taper on the wall, contained only a bed, a washstand, and the cupboard. From it Spring Moon took a black gown with long, full sleeves and the snug black bonnet of the novice. It did not take her long to change.

She slipped out the door and walked swiftly along the path through the pines back to the main compound. The sky was darkening now, muting vermilion, stealing gold, and the Great Hall of Worship loomed before her, only its eaves still caught in the net of the setting sun. She waited a moment to catch her breath, then bowed her head and climbed the steep steps with great care, using her hands to steady herself.

Tonight the two giant idols that guarded the entry at the top of the stairs seemed to challenge her, and she lowered her eyes to the earthen floor as she slipped past them. Inside, she paused again, willing the pounding in her ears to stop. She reached for her handkerchief. None was there. She took a deep breath. The air was pungent, thick with incense, and gave no relief.

The vaulted wood ceiling was higher than she remembered, transformed into the roof of a cavernous mouth, and the elderly widows praying at the feet of the idols seemed to her like ghosts, their prayers the wailing of ghosts. The flickering candles they had lit cast more shadow than light. None noticed her as she hurried past them toward the screen that filled the far end of the hall, concealing the gods.

As she approached it, the painting of the Seventh Hell seemed to come to life. In the flickering light the whips wielded by mad demons and wild beasts fell again and again upon the backs of the condemned grave robbers and eaters of human flesh, driving them into the river of fire. Their eyes were opened wide in terror, like those of the robber of graves in the square.

At last she forced herself to move on, edging slowly toward the corner and around the screen into the Hall of the Three Buddhas. Representing the Past, the Present, and the Future, the gods stood behind the long altar table laden with the paraphernalia necessary to propitiate them and to reveal the future. She saw no one, but it seemed to her that the drowned

spirits on the screen had filed into the hall behind her, and she
shrank from their unseen presence, hurrying to the dark recess
at the far end of the room where Bold Talent was to be waiting.

He was not there. Frantically, she looked into all the recesses,
but there was no one. At last she paused before the Buddha Present
and tried to fill her lungs completely, to breathe evenly. What
could have gone wrong? A most unfortunate route, the porter had
said. Not fitting. Yet what else could she have done? What could
she do now but wait? Wait, Merciful Kwan Yin, but not too long.

Slowly she walked to an obscure corner near the feet of the
Buddha Past and knelt. The dirt floor was damp. She closed her
eyes. "Merciful Buddha, please. . . ." She tried to pray silently,
but the voice within her chanted instead, over and over, a line
from a poem she could not place.

> So dim, so dark,
> so dense, so dull,
> so damp, so dank,
> so dead.

Over and over, the words reverberated in her head until she
thought it would burst. Minute after minute she waited, until her
legs were numb. Darker and darker, the hall. So dead.

Suddenly, the deserted room echoed with an infernal din. A
stench assaulted her. The smell of burning flesh? She got to her
feet and pressed her back to the wall, staring at the screen, which
glowed with some infernal light. Slowly the light moved around
the screen and into the hall itself, making a path on the dirt floor.
She covered her mouth to hold back the scream—then, weak with
relief, stifled laughter instead as a parade of chanting nuns carrying
tapers burst into the hall. The nuns were followed by novices shooing along scores of chickens, three goats, two mules, a cow, and
numerous ducklings and rabbits. Behind them came a flock of widows, giggling and gushing, pushing past one another for a good
look. Amitabha! The entire convent was there. Quickly she sought
the shadows behind the massive Buddhas.

Last the Mother Superior entered, her bald head glowing in the
tapers' light. Waving the widows to the side, the animals to the

center, she made way for a portly gentleman in a green silk gown who proceeded with bowed head and hands clasped in prayer through the skittish congregation to the center of the altar table before the Buddha Present. Following him, a dozen porters bore two large boxes draped in red brocade.

Solemnly, the gentleman lit a stick of incense and kowtowed three times. Then he knelt in silent prayer while the nuns muttered, the widows chattered, and the animals clamored in unholy chorus.

When the Mother Superior struck a gong the gentleman rose and, with his clasped hands held high in supplication, intoned "I release you from earthly toil so that you may serve my honorable mother in the other world!"

The gong sounded again. With a flourish the servants removed one of the brocade coverings. A hundred pure white doves scattered into the air, flying high and low, frantically seeking a way out of the hall.

Once more the gong sounded. "You also I release from earthly toil so that you may serve my honorable mother in the other world," the gentleman intoned again, as the servants removed the other brocade and unlatched the sides of the box. A hundred snakes slithered to every corner of the room.

Although she knew they were harmless, Spring Moon drew her skirt tight. Mercifully, none came near, and in a few minutes all had vanished into the earth.

The doves escaped less easily, darting about overhead, until one by one they found the spaces under the eaves and fled. When only an exhausted few were left, still flying from perch to perch among the rafters, the filial son shouted, "Amitabha! Amitabha! Amitabha!" The others echoed his cry, and then the entire party turned and made its way to the other side of the screen.

Once more, Spring Moon was alone.

She must move. Her legs were as numb as sticks of wood, yet stung by a thousand bees. Slowly she put one foot in front of the other until she reached the altar. She lit a candle and incense and again knelt down to pray. The flapping of wings seemed to fill the hall and the air was rank with the odors of alarm.

and flight. Merciful Buddha, she begged, lead the birds out. Lead the last birds out.

Suddenly she heard footsteps. Bold Talent's steps. In a moment he fell to his knees beside her. "Merciful Buddha . . ." he cried without a pause, then whispered quickly, "I have seen him. He is here."

Without turning, Spring Moon asked softly, "Are you certain?"

"Keep us from harm . . ." he intoned. "Yes. He left this hall a few moments ago."

"But no one has been here since the Mass for Releasing Life."

"The Manchu Pu Hsiao, himself, released the animals for his mother."

"It is not true!" Spring Moon cried aloud.

"Careful," warned Bold Talent.

"How could that filial son be the corrupt man you described?" she whispered desperately.

"A worthy son may be an unworthy official. And we are not here to judge him. Our duty lies with the clan. I will send him to you after dinner tonight." He stood to go.

"Wait, please. . . ." She looked toward him, words trailing off as she saw his face, as calm, as empty of expression as a stranger's face, as if the gods had already granted him absolution. Had there been no omens for him? He had not traveled the same route as she. Perhaps he did not know. Or was it only that he knew they must go on, that there was no other way?

"Take care!" He walked swiftly from the hall.

The temple bell tolled the coming of night. Spring Moon wanted to run after him but did not. In a few minutes he would reach the dining room, where he was to befriend Pu Hsiao, ply him with wine, win his confidence, and arouse his greed. There was no going back. Once more she prayed. "Merciful Buddha, keep us from harm." But she felt no peace.

At last she rose and slipped from the hall, taking a taper to light the way back through the wood to her cell.

A dinner tray had been left on the bed. She took a bite of the bread, but her throat was too dry to swallow. She drank the tea.

It was cold. She put the tray outside the door and lay down, trying to think their plan through, step by step, all over again, exactly as they had rehearsed it during her English lessons.

When the bell tolled the hour of the boar, the nun rose and slowly retraced the path to the Great Hall of Worship. The lighted wicks of the lamps flickered and slithered in the shallow bowls of oil and the room was alive with spirits and ghosts, leaping from the ceiling, crouching in crevices, stalking the shadows that clawed the walls. The Buddhas were painted with blood, their breath tinged with flame and frost. Their eyes followed her as she took her place, and the gowns they wore seemed to rustle in a breeze that touched her cheeks but did not cool them. Faintly, from a far corner of the convent, came the chanting of sutras, the clapping of *mu* on *mu,* the beating of an ancient drum.

A dove lay on the floor. The nun laid it upon the altar. Its soul had already gone.

In the obscure chapel behind the Buddha Past she knelt down to wait.

Two gentlemen came into the hall.

"It is too late. She is gone. Let us go back and finish the wine," said one, a Han.

"Do not be in such a rush, my new friend. We have not looked in any of the chapels," replied the other, who was a Manchu.

"No one is there."

"How can you be sure? Stop dragging me away."

"Tomorrow. I promise to introduce you tomorrow."

"Why not now?"

"Well . . ."

"I do not blame you." The Manchu smiled compassionately. "If she is all that you claim, no wonder you want to keep her for yourself. But you have boasted all evening. It is time for me to judge for myself."

The two men pushed and pulled drunkenly at each other until the Manchu managed to get away. He ran at once to the far chapel, where the nun recited her beads.

"Is that she?"

"No!" The reply was sharp. "No, that is not she."

"Take a good look, my friend. I insist."

"Perhaps it is she." And then, soberly, "It is she."

"Introduce me. I am anxious to lose the wager we have made. If she can foresee the future you win my stallion. Go ahead."

As the gentleman approached the kneeling nun, she looked up. "Excuse me, Holy Sister. It is your unworthy servant, once your neighbor."

"What has happened? The hour is late."

"It is unforgivable of me to disturb your prayers, but a most powerful official insisted on meeting you tonight. How could someone of my lowly station refuse? May I present the honorable Pu Hsiao now?"

"Even nuns need friends in high places. Amitabha!" She rose and turned to clasp her hands and bow. "May I be of service? I shall be happy to say prayers for your ancestors."

"Thank you, Holy Sister. My ancestors' needs have all been attended to. But if you will grant me another request, I would be most grateful."

"I am honored. You need only speak."

"My friend here has informed me of your unique gifts."

The nun frowned and looked at the gentleman, who hung his head. "I am drunk. I was boasting."

"How could you reveal my secret? I became a nun to escape the worldly ones who plagued me with questions about the future."

"Now, now, do not fret." Pu Hsiao soothed her, his manner most reasonable. "Since I know, and you know that I know, and we three are here alone, will you not honor my request?"

The nun bowed her head, then looked at the Han. "I will not retrieve my promise. But, my neighbor, you cannot be a party to this. You must go."

The gentleman bowed obsequiously as he backed out of sight.

"Shall we proceed?" the nun asked.

They knelt together before the Buddha Present.

Pu Hsiao recited the details of his horoscope, the names of the great seers he had consulted.

The nun then began her calculations, bending and straightening her fingers, counting the ten celestial stems, the five elements, and the twelve branches, as well as the solar animals, revealing the details of his character and life.

As she spoke, the man nodded eagerly. When she had finished, he was astonished. "Holy Sister, you have not erred. Everything you have mentioned is indeed true."

"Is there anything about the future you wish to discuss? The hour is late."

He smiled beseechingly. "Please," he begged. "Tell me only the number of years that are left to me."

The Holy Sister did some rapid calculations. "Would you kindly shake out a joss stick? I need further signs."

Pu Hsiao removed the container from the altar and shook it until one of the wooden sticks fell out upon the ground. The nun read the symbols on the stick. "Kindly shake out another."

"What is the matter?"

"Nothing. . . . There is some confusion. I wish to be absolutely certain."

This time Pu Hsiao shook the joss sticks longer than before. Finally one fell out. The nun read it.

Thoughtfully she ran a finger over the symbols, then asked, "What have the other seers told you?"

"That I will live to see great-grandchildren."

"Ah, they must be right. You will live to see many great-grandchildren!"

"Holy Sister, you are not sincere with me."

"Sir, you are mistaken."

"Then why the confusion?"

"Sometimes it is best not to know too much."

"Let me judge."

The nun was quiet, not moving except to finger the beads she held in her left hand. Finally, she spoke again. "May I suggest further clarification through meditation? I do not wish to speak in haste."

Pu Hsiao agreed. When the incense was ready, burning slowly in its brass holder, the nun began to beat a hypnotic rhythm on the wooden fish. Pu Hsiao fussed with his gown, picking lint from the hem that lay folded across his knees.

After the incense had burned a while, the holy sister abruptly stopped the drumming and went limp. In a voice like a mother calling a child, she cried. "Bald Tiger! . . . Bald Tiger! . . ."

"That is my milk name. That is what my mother called me."

"Bald Tiger . . ."

"Is that you, Honorable Mother?"

The nun did not answer but continued to call his name.

Pu Hsiao watched helplessly, his forehead glistening with perspiration.

Suddenly, the nun was silent. For a moment she sat unmoving, as still as the air in the room. Then she picked up the stick and began beating the drum as before. "Did I say anything?" she asked.

Pu Hsiao was ashen, his voice hoarse. "Do you not remember, Holy Sister?"

"No, I never remember."

He took the handkerchief from his sleeve and wiped his forehead. Then, determined, he asked her, "What have you learned? Will I enjoy longevity?"

She nodded slowly. "Indeed, the others were right. I do not understand how I could have been so confused."

He grabbed her arm, then released it as if her flesh burned. "You lie. I do not believe you."

"I have exhausted my powers. It is late. It is time to retire."

"You did not tell me the truth!"

"Please accept my apologies. I bid you good night." She rose and moved away from him, toward the door.

"You are not leaving!" Pu Hsiao shouted. And then, with more control, "I command you to be seated again!"

She hesitated.

"Holy Sister, you will not leave this hall until you have told me everything."

"But nothing will come of it."

"Let me be the judge."

She lowered her eyes. "I am afraid."

"Of what?"

"Of your power."

"On my honor, I shall not be angry. Tell me!"

Cupping her hands around her beads and holding them to her breast, she spoke gently, as if to a child. "The others were not wrong. You were allotted over seventy years. But tonight I detected strong and unexpected interference from an unknown source. It was not illness or accident or infirmity. My intuition tells me that you yourself will determine the moment of your death."

"When?"

"Your life will end this night."

"What do you mean?" The perspiration dripped into his eyes, and he blinked but did not look away from her.

"I am surely mistaken, sir. In fact, I do not see how I could possibly be right. Therefore, I must be wrong."

"No, wait. . . . What did you see?"

"I saw an old woman with alabaster skin and silver hair. She was in great distress, wailing and crying. I cannot be certain who she is, but surely a member of your family—perhaps a grandmother or an aunt?"

"No, it was my mother. What else?"

"She kept calling for Bald Tiger. She said that only he could prevent her from becoming a hungry ghost, a soul living alone in silent darkness through all eternity."

He shook his head. "But I do not understand. My mother has no reason to be afraid. She is buried in a magnificent tomb, at a site chosen by six geomancers. I observed three years of mourning. I render to the gods all the proper offerings and prayers. How could they punish a soul who lived a virtuous life on earth and whose son thus enhances her spiritual credit in the other world?" He searched the nun's face for a clue.

She lowered her eyes and mumbled a short prayer, then looked up at him once more. "Your mother, sir, fears that her grave will be defiled. She said that angry men would scatter her bones upon the earth unless Bald Tiger placates them."

She paused.

"Unless Bald Tiger placates them," she said again, "his mother will endure a hell more terrible than the river of fire, the sea of scorpions."

"But what can I do?" Pu Hsiao's voice was weak, barely audible. "Who are these angry men? And if it is tonight, where are they now?"

"I have no idea; that is why I think I must be wrong."

Pu Hsiao hid his face in his hands and cried like a child. "Mother," he begged. "Tell me what to do. I will do it. I swear. Mother, your son begs you to tell him what to do!"

As he knelt, the nun turned and walked quickly from the hall.

It was the hour of the rabbit when Pu Hsiao reached his quarters. He hardly noticed that his sentry was sleeping, and opened the door himself. Once inside, he fell into the nearest chair, unaware that he was shivering, his clothing rain-soaked. He reached for the bottle of wine.

A glimmer of light shone through the shutters. He laughed out loud. He was saved. He glanced toward the bed and thought of the woman he had planned to meet. She must have come and gone before he returned.

For the first time, he noticed the package. It had been placed on the pillows. The yellow wrapping used only by the Imperial Family was so encrusted with dirt that he could barely make out his name.

His hands trembled as he untied the silk and opened the lid of the ivory box. Carefully, he lifted from it the long silken cord.

He stared at it a moment before he quite understood. Who had betrayed his secrets to the Regent? His third wife? Or the Eunuch? What had they said to incriminate him? He groaned. What did it matter? It was the appointed hour.

As if playing a role he had played many times, he wound the cord around a rafter just behind the closed door, adjusted the loop, and set a carved stool directly beneath it. Then he returned to his chair. He finished the last of the bottle, all the time staring at the silken noose. How innocent it looked, like the string of his favorite kite, an orange carp his mother had bought for him. It had become tangled in the branches of the peach tree in the Great Court of his *lao chia,* and the tatters had fluttered in the breeze throughout the winter.

Gratefully he surrendered to the alcohol. His body became an alien weight that encumbered but was no longer a part of him. He touched his face and felt nothing. He rose unsteadily but then thought better of it. If his shaky legs made him topple accidentally, the sentry might come in before he was ready. Slowly he eased himself to his knees. On all fours, he crawled across the room. He touched the redwood claws that were the feet of the stool, pulled himself up, and slipped the noose around his neck.

He braced himself on the wall and shut his eyes. "Mother, I will be with you shortly. . . ."

But he did not have the courage to kick the stool from beneath him. He forced a bitter smile. He understood himself well and was prepared.

With an anguished effort he called out, "Guard!" At once the sentry threw open the door, overturning the stool, snapping the neck.

❦ 18 ❧

The Assassins

Force is followed by loss of strength.
This is not the way of Tao.
That which goes against the Tao
Comes to an early end.
— *Lao Tzu*

IT WAS ALMOST DAWN. Mist hovered above the canal, thickening to fog, hiding the eyes painted upon the bows of the flotilla of flower boats. The laughter and song of the pleasure seekers had long been stilled, as the ladies known as flowers and their customers disappeared below. The scent of opium lingered.

In a sampan moored by the crumbling stones of the Lazy Camel Bridge, Noble Talent stood watch while Resolute Spirit slept, huddled against the hull of the boat. He lit another cigarette. Let the boy sleep some more, he thought. Let him dream for the two of us. He inhaled deeply, savoring the harsh smoke. His own eyes had not closed for several nights, and his hands shook with fatigue. Luckily, the plan he had chosen did not demand precision.

A sudden noise made him turn, but it was nothing. A rat, or their hostess snoring in the cabin. He smiled grimly. The converted canal boat, though hardly the battleship he had once dreamed of commanding, had turned out to be the perfect hiding place.

In fact, he had grown quite fond of it: the fragrance of fish being smoked, the swaying lanterns, the rhythms of the river, the small cabin where the farmer's wife entertained her clients, with its garish quilts and painted bamboo shades and, incongruously, a western violin. The girl, flashing her gold tooth and dimples in greeting, had almost swooned when he offered her 25 strings of *cash* for two weeks' exclusive rights.

After the first week, however, she had grown impatient with them—the gentleman for not responding to her charms, the peasant for availing himself of her services all too frequently. In the last few days she had avoided both, playing cards instead with her old woman servant, whose tattling could destroy her reputation. Noble Talent suspected that if she had not counted on buying a piglet for her husband and new shoes for the children with the money they had paid, she would have ordered them to leave.

Sleep well, he thought. In a few hours they would be gone and her professional standing secure.

He sighed, wishing he too could sleep and stop thinking.

It seemed to him that he had been cursed from the beginning, was cursed now, perhaps, until the end. Only a curse could explain why the rebellions had failed. There had been so many of them he had forgotten the number. Twelve? Fourteen?

If the Tung Meng Hui planned for the weather, they erred on the weapon. If they equipped the men, a crucial two or three failed to identify themselves. If the men recognized one another, some did not understand the others' dialect and might as well have been Russians trying to talk to aborigines. The latest attempt, when 120 Dare-to-Dies stormed the Yamen in Canton, had buried 72 martyrs beneath the Yellow-Flowered Mound.

Perhaps Bold Talent was right and the people were not ready for change. And yet, if the moment was not ripe for an uprising, when would it ever be so?

He threw his cigarette into the water and struck a match to light another.

He had given half his years to revolution, to an oath that demanded absolute loyalty. Others might doubt his dedication; he did not, and so would carry out the order he had been given.

The order. Now, after all the weeks of planning, it was just that, although when the garlic eaters from Canton had first hinted at their baseless suspicions he had known such fury that both murder and laughter had filled his heart. But he had forbidden himself to react, to be driven from the battlefield by stupidity or slander. Factions divided the country. Factions must not divide their society. For the cause that united them, he would continue working, even with the Cantonese.

More than once in fifteen years he had willed himself to turn anger safely to the insignificant, to the hideous dialect of Kwangtung, for example. He smiled grimly. How had he borne it, the sound that shatters eardrums and shreds composure? People said that Cantonese speaking of love did not sound as sweet as a troop of beggars from Soochow fighting over a purse of gold, and it was true. Still, perhaps it was the very clatter of their dialect that made them so restless, and their restlessness that made them so much more likely to voyage, to change, to be true revolutionaries.

While people who cultivate the old arts resist, he thought. Like Bold Talent.

But Eldest Brother was right on one point. For all their efforts, the revolutionaries were no closer to overthrowing the Manchus, no closer to expelling the foreigner, than they had been the year the Brown Dwarfs sank the navy. Indeed, China marched backward.

Why, then, did they—did he—go on? Sometimes he wondered, but never for long. Revolution had become a way of life, the only one he knew. There would be no returning.

Suddenly, Resolute Spirit moved, pulling his knees to his chin, smiling in his sleep.

What an unlikely pair of assassins they were! At forty, he was twice Resolute Spirit's age; the youth two heads taller and half again as wide. He had had all the advantages of birth; the other was the illiterate son of that Farmer Lee who had supported Bold Talent's ill-fated efforts at modernization so long ago. He was a soldier who craved order; Resolute Spirit aspired to knight-errantry.

At twelve he had left the mou of land to his brothers and gone to pull freight barges on the canals, joining one of the *bee mi tzu shr* which flourished among laborers, providing mutual aid Through some of its members he had been introduced to another more active, group. That, simply, was the story he had told the night they met in the labyrinth of secret societies where improbable friends pledged to be blood brothers. Only after they had drawn this assignment together as men of Soochow had they discovered their true names and earlier connection. Now they were to share a common destiny.

He roused himself. The sky lightened in the east. It was time to wake his companion.

Resolute Spirit stepped ashore first. No one noticed. Just another farmer on his way to market, twin baskets of fruit swaying gently from his shoulder pole. He grinned to himself. He had already committed an irrevocable act of treason that morning by cutting off his queue, although no one knew it, for the braid was still affixed by a bandanna. He did not want even Noble Talent to know. The gentleman worried too much already.

It was a short walk from the bridge to the marketplace at the Yamen, and he trotted through the crowd quickly enough, his size, the laden baskets, and his cries of "Aye ho! Aye ho!" giving him the right of way. Crossing Horse Street, he followed the high walls of the compound toward the gate, stopping to glance at the posted notices. He supposed one of them announced the visit of the Manchu, but he could not read. He spat.

As he approached the gate the popping eyes of the gods that decorated the arch seemed to seek him out, and a shiver ran down his back, despite the heat. What if the ghost of the Manchu returned to haunt him? Of course, that was up to the Fates, just as it was the Fates who had sent him here to do their bidding. He spat again, this time with less authority. Better not think so much. For a moment he paused to ease the yoke on his shoulders. Then he walked through the gate, ignoring the high-and-mighty sentries dressed in black, each with a lance of gleaming steel. They were only men and easily overpowered.

"Hey, you son of a turtle, where do you think you're going?"

The gatekeeper's shout stopped him. He turned, nodded respectfully.

"Honorable sir, I have an aged mother to support. If you would kindly let me pass inside to sell fruit to the petitioners, you would earn rewards in Heaven."

"And what about the here and now?"

"That too, sir." He stuffed some coins into the man's pocket.

Once inside the outer court, he surveyed the scene carefully, searching for just the right spot. The yard was full of petitioners who had arrived early and would stay late, squatting, pacing to and fro, gossiping, quarreling, wailing and weeping until they were called. He hitched up the baskets and headed for a niche in the far wall, where he would be inconspicuous and could, he hoped, await Noble Talent undisturbed.

The plan called for the peddler to sell a certain melon to a gentleman who would arrive shortly after the Manchu, a gentleman in a long beige gown, sporting a mustache, eyeglasses, and a Japanese Panama. Resolute Spirit grinned to himself. He had laughed more than once before Noble Talent had gotten the mustache on straight and the angle of the hat just right. People like the Changs, who knew so many more words than people like him, never needed one to express their disapproval. From the merest quiver of the lips, Noble Talent had made it plain how much he hated putting on that Japanese hat. But as a gentleman from Soochow, he dared not risk recognition. And only a gentleman could gain easy access to the building where Pu Hsiao was to have lunch that day.

His last lunch, if all went well. Resolute Spirit set his burden down most carefully, for the smallest melon in his front basket contained a tin can filled with gunpowder and a tiny vial of nitroglycerin.

Before he could plant himself on the ground as well one of the Yamen servants approached. "It has been weeks since I have tasted a good plum," he said, fingering the fruit in the near basket.

Resolute Spirit bent down and quickly picked one out, handing it to the man with a flourish. "Please, sir, have one on me."

"Only if you insist."

"I insist, I insist," said the peasant, bowing.

The man pocketed the plum and fixed his gaze on an orange. "Sir, have a taste of my oranges, too!"

The lackey selected one. "Naturally, if they are any good, I shall return to buy some a little later."

"It will be my pleasure, sir."

That one had barely left when another came along. "I see you are giving away samples!"

"Only to you. Only to you."

Resolute Spirit wondered what he would do if his wares were all sold or given away before the crucial hour. Even he had not foreseen the greedy eyes of the servants, who had little to do but look important. To leave with one unsold melon would invite suspicion. To refuse to part with it would be disastrous.

As the sun rose, he discouraged sales by pretending to be asleep, his arm around the basket with the melon. Most potential customers sought out other, more aggressive peddlers. Unfortunately, however, the cuckolds in uniform did not hesitate to kick him awake whenever they pleased, and if he sold little, he made many gifts. As his supplies dwindled, he cursed the unlucky demon that had tricked him into bringing first pick instead of fruit with bruised skins.

An hour passed, and another. Where was the Manchu? There had certainly been no salutes of any kind. The eight musicians by the gate had not played a note all morning. The gunpowder still lay in the iron dish at their feet. Soon the sun would be directly overhead, and the Yamen closed for the meal hour. The Manchu must have changed his plans. Must have spent five minutes with a sunflower and wilted! Resolute Spirit sat up and spat again, this time in disgust. What did he expect? The man was a Manchu, wasn't he?

Suddenly he was alert, though careful not to show it. Noble Talent had arrived. He stood talking to the guard but looking his way. When their eyes met, the gentleman said a few more words, then bowed to the guard and left.

That did it! Something had gone wrong. There was nothing more to wait for.

Resolute Spirit stood up and gathered his things. But as he headed toward the gate one of the sentries left his post and confronted him. When he tried to go around, the guard stuck out his foot, so that he tripped and almost fell.

"Don't be in such a hurry, stupid. I come to buy." More likely to die, Resolute Spirit thought as he placed the baskets carefully on the ground again. Very carefully. He wiped his palms on his trousers. That lucky gold-toothed flower had come all too close to never knowing bliss again.

The sentry began pawing through the fruit. Quickly Resolute Spirit offered him a plum, hoping to discourage his interest, if any, in melons. But the soldier was a meticulous man. Saying nothing, he continued to fondle oranges, giving each fruit his undivided attention. Clearly he would not be satisfied until he had fingered all that was left in the baskets.

Resolute Spirit almost laughed aloud. From the first he, the peasant, had had a plan of his own. Now was his opportunity, even if it was to play the fool!

Clutching his stomach, he doubled over and moaned. "Honored sir!" He groaned more loudly and gingerly backed away toward the gate. "Please excuse me. Too many plums. Urgent business! Big business!" To the whoops and howls of the onlookers, he turned, dashed past the guard, and sprinted through the gate, tripping over a beggar who lay in the dirt. He had almost reached the safety of the busy market when a thousand firecrackers burst behind him. He swiveled around. In the Yamen court, smoke and billowing dust. People running, screaming. A few writhed on the ground. One or two lay still. As he stood there staring, one by one the sentries took up the cry, "The peddler! After the peddler!"

Resolute Spirit turned again and ran, making for the warren of streets on the other side of the square, jumping the obstacles in his way, twisting out of the hands that reached for him. He had almost made it when he fell over a bucket of eels and sprawled in the dirt. The crowd closed in. One of them reached down to haul him up. The others drew back, and he saw that the man was Noble Talent. He scrambled to his feet.

"I have him!" shouted Noble Talent, waving the others away. The crowd, deferring respectfully to the gentleman, cleared a path.

The two fugitives dashed through the opening. They had almost reached the alley when out of nowhere a boy pounced on Resolute Spirit's shoulders. The monkey held on by the neck. By the queue. Tumbled off. "No queue! No queue!" he shouted from the dirt, waving the black braid at the guards pushing through the crowd in hot pursuit. "The big one has no queue! The other is a gentleman! The big one has no queue!"

Resolute Spirit took the lead as they scrambled down narrow side streets and dark alleys where doors and shutters slammed shut at the sound of the hue and cry.

When they reached the Horse Street canal, they were slowing down, almost winded. Without a pause, the peasant headed for the water. He held his nose and bent his knees. The gentleman hesitated. A dead rat floated in the offal. Resolute Spirit grabbed his arm. "Hold your nose!" he cried and pulled Noble Talent in.

They went under and came up beneath the ruins of an ancient bridge, neglected beyond repair. Resolute Spirit braced himself against the crumbling wall, supporting the other, who vomited and coughed convulsively. Soldiers clattered by, shouting. Noble Talent covered his mouth to stifle sound.

Even when the soldiers had gone, the two men did not move, as if blinking would call them back. Minutes passed. They dared not look at one another, but watched in opposite directions for the slightest movement their way. There was none. Apparently this stretch of canal was without boats and washerwomen.

After a while the usual traffic returned to the street. All who passed talked of nothing except the huge peddler, the gentleman with the Japanese hat.

When it was dark, and the only sound the distant cry of a blacksmith cursing a mule that refused to be shod, Resolute Spirit whispered, "What happened?"

"Pu Hsiao is dead."

"What?"

Noble Talent nodded. "I read it on the wall poster."

So that was it! Blind bat! Resolute Spirit knocked his head against the bridge in anger. "We may get killed now because of this thick head."

"It is no one's fault."

"It is mine. If I were not an ignorant blind man, we would not be trapped now."

"No use wasting words. The battle has begun. We must get to safety!"

"Master, let me go alone. It is me they are after."

"Quiet. Let me think!"

When the moon rose the plotters swam to the canal bank and clambered out. Cautiously they made their way down streets empty except for the watchmen, who announced their passing in time for the fugitives to take cover.

At last they reached the peddler's gate of the House of Chang.

"Open up! Open up!" Noble Talent whispered hoarsely.

No one came. He picked up a pebble and threw it over the wall. They waited. He threw another, and another.

Finally, an angry voice hissed, "Go away! I'll call the guard!"

"Fatso, open up. It is the third son of the Venerable!"

The gate opened, and they hurried past her into the servants' court. "What are you doing here? And who is that?" She backed away. "Phew!" She held her nose. "Get away from me."

"Close the door, faithful servant, and go to bed. Tell no one that you saw us!"

"I'm going. I'm going. Don't worry. No one would believe me!"

The two men crept silently through the shadows of the moonlit courts until they reached the Ming Study. In the alcove the Patriarch lay in bed, asleep.

Noble Talent put out a hand to waken him, but withdrew it without touching the silk coverlet. His hands were foul with the waters of the canal.

"Eldest Brother, wake up! Wake up," he whispered.

Bold Talent opened his eyes. "What? Who is there?"

"It is your brother. We must talk."

Awake now, Bold Talent sprang out of bed. "What are you doing here? You smell like the canal." He reached for the lamp on the night table, turned up the wick. "Come with me!" He marched past them and, placing the lamp carefully on his desk, spun around to face his brother. "Who is that with you?"

"Excuse me, Master," said Resolute Spirit, bowing. "Beg your pardon, sir. I am Resolute Spirit. Farmer Lee's son, the one with the pig. The black one, called Ham."

Bold Talent looked from one to the other. "I understand nothing! Explain, my brother, and quick!"

As Noble Talent spoke, the Patriarch never moved. His face was without expression, his eyes hard.

"You mean to say that soldiers are looking for him?" He pointed to Resolute Spirit. "And you led them straight home! Have you lost all your faculties? You should have drowned yourselves and been done with it!"

"I had no choice. The boy is my responsibility."

"And what of your responsibility to this household? To the clan? To the ancestors?" His voice shook with anger controlled.

"Be reasonable, my brother!" Noble Talent started toward him, but Bold Talent sent him back with an abrupt wave of the hand.

"Get away! You offend!"

"Where else could we go? Besides, no one saw us. No one." Noble Talent looked toward Resolute Spirit, who nodded sheepishly.

"What does that matter, you fools! They seek an oversized peasant without a queue and a gentleman. You think they will not dare come here? They will knock down the door of every gentleman's house. How long before they connect today's gentleman at the Yamen with yesterday's gentleman at the—"

There was a knock. The three whirled around to stare at the door. "It is Spring Moon," she whispered, entering. She looked from one to the other. "What Fatso said is true."

Noble Talent threw up his hands. "Aye ya! I should have known. No secret is safe here. Not in this household. Not for a single night!"

"Secret? What secret? There are no secrets, not now." Bold Talent stood now behind the desk, holding to the back of the chair with a grip so powerful it seemed that the wood must break. "How could you have brought that boy home? When they find him here it will be proof!"

"I have told you. There was no choice. I am responsible for him." The soldier cleared his throat, tasting venom. "My brother, you cannot possibly be so callous as to sacrifice a man's life to avert some imaginary or, at worst, improbable danger to the family."

There was no reply.

"Can you be so callous, my brother?"

Slowly Bold Talent shut his eyes and shook his head as if in pain. "The danger is not improbable," he said. "You do not know. You do not understand. . . ."

The others waited. On the roof, a cat mewed.

In the end it was Spring Moon who spoke. "It is time they understood, Eldest Uncle. Let me tell them what happened after Young Uncle left home. . . ."

✒ 19 ✑
Destiny Foretold

*Somewhere between Shanghai and Manila, the sea-faring junk
Joss was caught in a cyclone and all aboard were seized with
terror. When the storm was at its height, a god appeared and
in a fearsome voice demanded who among them were brothers.
Laughing with relief, the passengers pointed at two who stood
side by side. The god spoke again. "Deny your brother and you
may stay aboard. Claim your bond and jump into the sea!"*

*Without waiting a beat of the heart, the brothers, as if they
were one, plunged into the turbulent waters. Deeper and deeper
they sank until their feet touched the ocean floor. But as they
bowed to bid farewell, two giant turtles stopped before them.
In no time, they rode to the surface of the sea. One swam toward
the continent, the other toward the islands.*

*The great ship was gone. Nowhere to be seen were those who
had denied their bonds. The waters were without a ripple and
the skies a luminous blue.*

—Clan story

DURING THE Fortnight of Planting Rice Sprouts, the heat increased
until it was almost unbearable. Every bamboo blind was drawn
to keep out the relentless sun, and many never rose from their
straw mats, sleeping until nightfall while the servants cooled the
flagstones and flower beds with well water sprinkled from a broom.
Nothing helped, except perhaps an even hotter cup of tea. There
were rumors of a great storm coming.

Nevertheless, on the seventh day following Noble Talent's departure for Shanghai, the Matriarch rose early from her afternoon nap, for it was her inviolate custom once a year on this day to imbibe the elixir of pearls. By the hour of the sheep, she was seated at her dressing table supervising the preparation of the potion.

While the senior slave girl gently waved a fan, the other and more comely one ground the seed pearls that had been steamed with rice.

"Is this fine enough, Mistress?"

"Almost. Just a few more turns," the Matriarch replied.

"I hope my husband will buy me pearls someday," the girl ventured. "I would not drink them but would wear them in my ears."

"What good are pearls in your ears," the Matriarch asked, "if there is no gloss in your hair or gleam in your cheeks? Better to drink them."

The other slave girl shrugged. "Why talk of such things, Sister? You and I will never see pearls again once we leave here."

The Matriarch nodded. The older girl showed good sense. She must make a special effort to find her a hardworking husband.

When the pearls were ground as fine as ashes, the Matriarch herself mixed the powder into a glass of sugared rice water and drank it slowly, giving no sign of its foul taste.

She had not quite finished when there was a commotion at the door. The Matriarch's eyes narrowed, but before she could say anything Fatso hurtled in, strands of hair over her eyes, her apron askew. Gesticulating to the heavens, she wailed like a woman whose baby refuses to be born.

The Matriarch cut short the second crescendo. "Enough, Fatso! What is the matter? Has your husband come back to haunt you?" Old servants were indulged, but not even Fatso was privileged to interrupt the Matriarch's restorative rituals.

"It was terrible! Terrible! But thank the gods they did not penetrate the inner courts!"

"Who? What are you talking about, woman?"

"The Green Bannermen!" Fatso wiped the perspiration from her upper lip with a sleeve. "They had sabers. They poked them in

235

the bushes. They marched through all the rooms beyond the marble screen, tracking mud. They lined up the porters and went from one to the next, yanking on each queue. Old Mistress, they are searching every house in Soochow for the two madmen who bombed the Yamen."

The slave girls darted toward the door. Such a spectacle was not to be missed.

"Fools!" Fatso blocked the way. "Your duty is here. Besides, the soldiers are gone. The Patriarch paid a handsome bribe, or else they would be in this room now."

They would not dare, the Matriarch thought, not in the House of Chang! And yet . . . "Fatso, let the girls go. They have tried my patience. Out! Out!"

When they were alone, she turned on the servant. "What do you mean by crying and shouting like a beggar woman? Where is your dignity?"

Fatso bowed her head, tucking the stray strands of hair behind her ears.

"A thousand pardons, Old Mistress."

The Matriarch did not relent. "Go at once and send my son to me."

"I regret to inform you that the Patriarch has left the courts for the day."

So, as usual, he was not where he should be. Never mind. There was someone else who would know and could more easily be made to tell. "Go and bring Spring Moon instead."

Fatso apologized again and took her leave.

Alone, the Matriarch permitted her back to rest against the chair. Her head was aching; she put her hands to her temples and closed her eyes. Disaster, she thought, had been coming for months, ever since Spring Moon returned with that incorrigible grandchild of the Hanlin. How many times had the others complained about the Patriarch's partiality toward the two of them?

Now everyone grumbled about the allowances, each accusing the other of extravagance. The old generosity was gone, dissension spread, and soon she would not be here. . . .

A knock. "Grandmother? May I enter your presence?"

With an effort, she straightened and waved Spring Moon to a chair.

They sat for a long while in silence. The young woman bowed her head. Tiers of heat rose, stealing breath.

At last, the Matriarch spoke. "I may not be able to read books. However, I do read faces. For some time now, I have been suspicious of what has been happening in this household. It is not merely the heat of the sun that sends Third Granduncle and Second Cousin to the mountains. It is not merely the state of our stomachs that makes my daughter-in-law shuttle to and from the kitchens without rest. It is not merely the gaiety of Shanghai that causes my third son to arrive in the night and to leave without so much as a nod. It is not the location of our courtyards in Soochow that invites the attention of the Manchus."

The old woman paused, waiting to hear what the other had to say.

Spring Moon said nothing.

"Well? well?"

Still, nothing.

Angered, the Matriarch snatched the fan from her jacket and pointed it at Spring Moon. "My granddaughter, I command you to tell me everything! I do not wish to be the frog that sits at the bottom of the well."

"Times are uncertain, Grandmother. Our people are afraid," Spring Moon whispered, her head still bowed.

"Afraid of what?"

"Of the boy."

"What boy?"

"The new retainer that Eldest Uncle hired to help Old Gardener in the inner courts."

"Why?"

Spring Moon hesitated. Then, looking up, she touched her hand to her hair. "Because he is big and wears a towel around his head in this hot weather."

"Do not speak in riddles. Explain." The Matriarch snapped open her fan.

"They think he might be one the soldiers were looking for today—the peddler at the Yamen who hid a bomb in a melon and lost his queue."

"Why, then, does not Bold Talent dismiss him or give him up to the police?"

"He does not say. He merely refuses. So now everyone suspects that Eldest Uncle is the gentleman in the gown who helped the peddler get away."

"Ridiculous!" The Matriarch sniffed. "Have all my clansmen fever in the brain? Ridiculous!" She thought for a moment. "He is not, is he?"

"No, my grandmother."

"Exactly!"

"No, it was Young Uncle who was with the peddler."

The Matriarch's fan slowed and then stopped. She closed her eyes. Merciful Kwan Yin, she prayed, be kind and spare this house from *luan*. Aloud, she said, "How do you know this?"

Spring Moon did not answer immediately, and the Matriarch repeated her question. Reluctantly, the young widow explained.

As she listened, the old one felt herself withering, until it seemed that only the rice powder sealed her features in place. When the story was done, she could only whisper. "Amitabha! My sons and you have committed treason. The Manchus will stack all our heads together like duck eggs. They will overturn our ancestors' graves and scatter their bones to the winds. Amitabha!" Tears filled her eyes.

"Grandmother, please do not cry. All is going to be well. The peddler is already gone. Eldest Uncle is seeing him out of town right now."

The young see what they wish to see, the Matriarch thought. The old see what they do not wish. She was certain now. Her days of strength were gone.

"Grandmother, do not be grieved. Everything will be as before."

"How? Soon the authorities will connect you and my son with the Manchu, the Manchu with the bomb, the bomb with Noble Talent, Noble Talent with these courtyards. You are a fool if you

238

think it can be as before. So, too, is my son. It is only a matter of time . . . only a matter of time." She let go of her fan. It fell soundlessly on the rug.

Spring Moon knelt to retrieve it, laying it gently in the old woman's hand.

Long after her granddaughter had left the room, the Matriarch sat motionless. Never in her seventy-three years had she imagined that the whole would break into its parts, that the gates in her husband's homestead might close, parting kin from kindred. Even if only temporary separation was the intent, isolation would be the result. Yet never could there be true honor for one brother if the other tarnished the family name.

For the rest of the afternoon, she remained in her chair. When the slave girls came to escort her to dinner, she told them that she would eat in her quarters. And when the ladies went strolling through the gardens to take advantage of the night breeze, she did not join them. She had no wish to sit again by the lotus pond where the cypress had once stood.

After a sleepless night, she sent for her favorite fortune-teller.

It was the hour of the snake when the servant ushered Gifted Seer into her private quarters. As always the thin man's gray cotton gown was not quite clean. A black umbrella dangled from his left elbow; in his right hand, the bamboo cage painted red that housed his mynah bird. He bowed and they exchanged greetings before he took his seat at the round walnut table on which tea was normally served. As he reached into his cuff for the cards, the old woman swept the room with her eyes. "Out. Everybody out." The slave girls left without the usual protest.

"Shall we begin?" Gifted Seer asked.

The Matriarch stood up and went to the open window. There was no sound, but shadows melted away. She closed the shutter and returned to her seat. "Now let us begin!"

He shuffled the cards three times and laid them out in three rows of three. Then, addressing the bird, he chanted, "Spiritual bird! Spiritual bird. Examine the heart of this old woman. Divine the answers to her quest. Select what you must."

He opened the door of the cage. The mynah hopped out, bowed to the Matriarch, danced among the cards. He pecked a few, took one in his beak, and gave it to Gifted Seer, who rewarded his pet with a few grains of wheat from his other cuff.

There was an uneasy silence while the fortune-teller studied the card. "Great changes are coming," he said at last. "The end of old existences. The beginning of new orders. A time of decay and genesis."

"When will these changes take place?"

"Soon, perhaps within a fortnight. Be prepared."

"How many changes will there be?"

"Three. One is irreversible!"

"Death!" gasped the old woman.

The fortune-teller lowered his eyes and did not say no.

"And the other two?"

"Only one is irreversible. The others will follow the fury of the storm."

"What will become of the clan?"

"The cards do not say. Only that one among you today will live to see five generations under one roof."

"Who?" asked the Matriarch.

"One who basks in reflected glory and warms the snow."

"Is that all you can tell me?"

"That is all I have seen, old woman."

The Matriarch took a silver coin from the embroidered bag that hung from her waist. At once the bird hopped across the table to relieve her of it, clamping it tight in its beak as if to test its metal before hopping back to deposit it in the coin box inside the cage.

All that day and night, the Matriarch tried to decipher the riddles without success. Near dawn she slept.

Upon waking, she knew.

The irreversible change was her own death. The others were the "deaths" of her sons, who would disappear in the storm that was coming. When the clan donned the white hemp of mourning, then and only then would pursuit end.

As for the one who would live to see five generations:

The moon mirrors the splendors of the sun;
each spring melts the winter ice.

In late afternoon on the fifteenth day of the fifth moon, the
Patriarch of the House of Chang left the family courts for Shanghai.
On arriving in the city, he was to send a telegram, purportedly
from Lotus Delight, recalling Spring Moon to Peking and a message
to Noble Talent to inform him of their impending "death" by
typhoon. Then he was to find a mission school for Lustrous Jade
and a house in the international section for "Mr. and Mrs. Yang."

The next day, the summons came for Spring Moon. When they
heard the news, the women of the courtyards were quick to congrat-
ulate her, for she was returning to her husband's house, where
an honored widow should be.

They would weep at the gate, she knew, but sigh with relief
when the sedan turned the corner. She and her daughter had disturbed the harmony of the House of Chang. Only two would miss
them.

Before the sun had set, she was ready. She and Fatso closed
the last trunk, then sat together on the bed, hand in hand.

"I will send for you as soon as I am able."

Fatso nodded. Spring Moon was confident that the old servant
would ask no questions. She had seen enough to recognize danger
and had in fact anticipated their separation, justifying it in advance
to the others with loud complaints of being asked to travel again
at her advanced age.

"Do not worry, Old Friend. I will be well."

Suddenly, Fatso was sobbing.

It was no time for the mistress to falter. "Please, do not cry.
We will be together soon enough. I know. I promise." She offered
her own handkerchief.

Fatso wiped away the tears and blew her nose. After a moment,
she said, "Young Mistress?"

"Yes, old woman." Spring Moon smiled. "It is long since I have
been your Young Mistress, my friend. What is it you wish to
say?"

The servant cleared her throat. "If you promise not to laugh, Young Mistress, I will tell you a secret."

"I promise."

"Do you remember the day you came to my room and called me 'Old Friend' for the first time? Do you remember?"

"I remember well. You were doing laundry."

"That is true. That is true. Well, ever since then, I have pretended that you . . . that you were my daughter. Is that not the funniest thing you have ever heard?"

Before Spring Moon could answer, Fatso broke away and hurried toward the door. At the threshold she turned back. Her eyes were still wet but her voice was strong.

"Take care, Young Mistress. You need not worry about me. I would fart in the face of the devil himself!"

When the watchman intoned the hour of the pig, Spring Moon put on a fresh gown. She wanted to pay her respects to Golden Virtue, to thank her for the kindness that had made it possible for her big-footed daughter and herself to stay all these months in Soochow without tasting the bitter rice of charity.

Even as the days had grown hotter and hotter, her aunt had gone endlessly, tirelessly, from court to court, seeing to everyone's needs, as she always did. She picked fresh mint in the garden and offered it with dried chrysanthemum petals to refresh the family's tea. She made a cool custard of green beans for Lustrous Jade when the girl mentioned a fondness for it, despite a kitchen that was now a dark inferno.

She had sat by the window, embroidering in the light of the setting sun, while her husband and her niece conversed of things that meant nothing to her. Spring Moon had never asked herself if the other desired to be there, listening to words she could not possibly understand, waiting for the hour to pass, watching her husband teach his niece when he did not even read their sons' lessons. What would she say to her now?

Still uncertain, she was putting her fan into her tunic when there was a knock at the door and Golden Virtue, serene as always, stepped into the room. In her hands was a small box wrapped in red silk.

"My niece, I have come to wish you a fair wind and a peaceful journey home."

Spring Moon blushed. "My aunt, you do me an undeserved honor." She showed her guest to a chair. "I was in fact just on my way to your quarters," she added, fussing with the teapot and offering a cup that was tepid and quite undrinkable.

"I shall miss you, Spring Moon," Golden Virtue said simply when her hostess took her seat. Before Spring Moon could find an appropriate response, her aunt held out the red-silk box and smiled. "This is for you."

"Thank you, most gracious aunt." Spring Moon stood and accepted the package in both hands, bowing. She almost dropped it, for it was heavier than she had anticipated. Smiling she gave it a gentle shake. "Another undeserved honor, my aunt?"

She was about to put it away with the other gifts when Golden Virtue said, "Do not stand on ceremony, my niece. Please open it now."

"Could I?"

Golden Virtue nodded. "Please."

Sitting at the table once more, Spring Moon removed the wrapping, revealing a beautifully embroidered case. The scene, of Kiangsu's waters and mountains, of mists and the moon rising, had not been completed, but she recognized at once the exquisite hand of her aunt.

"I wish I had had time to finish it properly, but you are leaving tomorrow and I had no other gift."

"I treasure it as it is, my aunt. The void enhances the beauty of your art."

Golden Virtue blushed. "You are too kind, it is nothing. Please open it."

Curious but unsuspecting, Spring Moon removed the lid. Inside were coins of gold. She stared in amazement.

"There are fifty-two of them," Golden Virtue said. "My mother sewed one in each of the dresses in my trousseau, so that I would have good luck in my husband's home. But I have not needed them. What harm could come to me within these honored courts? You have been good to me and to my husband. You must have them." She bowed her head. "I, with more than I should have, would be so happy if you, who deserve more, would accept this unworthy gift."

For minutes Spring Moon studied the woman seated across from her. She who lived to serve Bold Talent, whose reward was his pleasure: what would happen to her when he was believed dead? It was not inconceivable that she would find life so wanting that she would swallow opium, seeking to join him in the other world. Spring Moon shook her head, but the thought would not leave her, nor the image of Golden Virtue's spirit wandering in the netherlands, calling, endlessly calling for her husband, who was not there.

"Do not shake your head, my niece. You will need the coins. If your mother-in-law had your welfare in mind, she would never have sent you . . ."

But Spring Moon was not listening. As clearly as if she had been there, she saw the Manchu dangling from the rafters, a holiday scarf around his neck.

"What is wrong, my niece? What is wrong?" Golden Virtue cried.

Together they reached across the table and held each other's hands.

"My aunt . . ."

"Yes?"

For a while Spring Moon could not speak.

At last, she began again. "My aunt, I have no gift for you except the story I tell, a story I solemnly vowed to Grandmother I would never repeat, a story known only to us and the Patriarch."

She went on slowly, pausing now and then, as if recounting a fable filled with people and places so strange that she feared the listener could not imagine it at all.

Golden Virtue did not move during the recital, and when it was over, there was no sound for many minutes except the song of a lark being aired in the garden.

Finally, the wife spoke. "I thank you for the gift which you alone deemed me worthy of receiving, which truly weds me to the House of Chang. Be assured that I shall keep your trust. No one will ever suspect that I know, not today, not ever."

Then she stood, and said most formally, as if performing a ritual, "Now I must ask that you do three things. First, that you take the coins, for your comfort in Shanghai. Second, that you see to the welfare of the men, for your exile may last many years. Third, that you arrange for a concubine who will please my husband while he is so far from home."

The next morning, by the hour of the dragon, Spring Moon and Lustrous Jade were on the train to Shanghai. When it arrived, they went directly to the appointed place beneath the station clock. After a few minutes a messenger approached and handed Spring Moon an envelope.

She opened it and read: *Mission School, 100 James Street. Travelers' Hotel, 780 Rue de la Paix.*

Taking her daughter's hand, she followed the porter to a hansom for hire, paid the man, and helped Lustrous Jade into the carriage. She gave the driver the first address.

"Where are we going, Mother?"

Spring Moon did not answer immediately. Instead she straightened the collar on her daughter's tunic.

"Where are we going?" the girl asked again.

"My child." She had rehearsed an explanation. Quickly, before will deserted her, she offered it. "I am taking you to a school. It is an excellent one. You will learn many things there, not just the traditional subjects but the languages and the ways of the foreigner."

Lustrous Jade said nothing but twisted her head away, to look out the window.

"Daughter?"

The girl folded her arms, seemingly intent on the people in the street.

"Look at me, child!"

When she did not, Spring Moon gently put her hands on the small shoulders and turned them toward her.

There were tears in Lustrous Jade's eyes. The mother could not remember the last time she had seen them. Certainly she had shed none upon leaving the House of Chang this morning, or the House of Woo nine months before.

"What is it, my daughter?"

"I do not want to go to a Barbarian school and learn foreign things. I want to be with you in Peking."

"My precious, you cannot come with me." Spring Moon smoothed the hair from her child's face. It felt feverish. She drew a deep breath, searching for the right thing to say. "Do you not remember the stories of your father? Of how he once traveled to the West and was many years away from home? He knew that he must go. Now you, too, must go."

At the mention of her father, the girl cocked her head, listening.

"I would not have wished that my daughter go from my care so soon, but both of us, you and I, must yield. It is the only way." She waited for a response.

Lustrous Jade nodded.

"This school will help you keep your promise to your grandfather. Remember?"

She nodded once more and asked, after a moment, "Will I be a hero?"

"Perhaps. Heroes are for history to name. But you will gain the knowledge to help you find the right path. Nowadays it can only be traveled by those who have mastered the ways of the West as well as the ways of China."

"How long will we be apart, my mother?"

"The school is a demanding one. The missionaries teach many things."

"How long, Mother? How long?"

"The school requires six years, without interruption."

"Six years? Will I not see you at all in those six years?" A tear started to fall. "Oh, Mother, it is so long, so long."

Spring Moon lowered her own eyes, lest she, too, weep.

"Will I not see you in all those years?" Lustrous Jade asked again.

"I hope so, my daughter. I pray. But I cannot promise." She pulled the child to her until the sobs quieted and she found the courage to resume the speech she had planned.

"My daughter, once your father said to me that he must be a man of character. It is your destiny to be your father's daughter. It is your destiny to be your grandfather's son."

Lustrous Jade seemed not to hear, for she asked, before her mother could continue, "Will you write, my mother?"

Spring Moon shook her head. "No, my child, not soon. To hear from me would only make your noble mission more difficult. Perhaps later, when you will have learned much."

Lustrous Jade opened her mouth to protest, then did not, and Spring Moon went on.

"My daughter, the lessons we studied together . . . do you remember what must happen before a caterpillar can become a butterfly?"

The child nodded.

"Then tell me. What must take place before the magic transformation?"

The girl's shoulders began to shake and tears again filled her eyes. But they did not fall, and her voice was clear and steady as she recited what she had learned. "The caterpillar must weave a cocoon, and live within it alone. It becomes a chrysalis, always changing, waiting until the proper time. Then the cocoon is broken."

"And . . ."

"The butterfly escapes."

"It is . . ."

"Beautiful."

"And it . . ."

"And it flies."

"Good. You have learned your lessons well, my daughter." Again the mother wiped away the tears.

"Mother?"

"Yes?"

Lustrous Jade swallowed hard. "I did not know that heroes must be unhappy!"

It was the truth. Spring Moon wanted to explain, and yet how could she? How could she show that great happiness and great unhappiness were one? She did not try, and said simply, "My daughter, you cannot have, without giving. That would be unworthy. You are a child. Someday you will be a person of character."

By the hour of twilight on that same day, Spring Moon sat alone in the city that flew fifteen flags, in a room that belonged to no one, in a chair so contrary that her feet dangled wearily above the floor.

Somehow, she must have enrolled Lustrous Jade in the mission school and bid her daughter farewell. Somehow, she must have registered in the hotel and unpacked. She could not remember.

Picking up the letter that rested on her lap, she broke the circle of red wax stamped with the Matriarch's seal.

For a while, the paper lay folded in her hands. Not yet, she thought, not just yet. The message was her last bond with the House of Chang. Once severed, how long the silence? She could not guess.

A sigh escaped, so forlorn that immediately she chastised herself. If she were not strong enough, how could she expect the child she had mothered to survive alone? She opened the letter.

My Sons and Granddaughter—

When these echoes of my thoughts reach you, I will have begun my passage beyond the Yellow Springs. Long before you left, I had heard the spirits calling. I am tired and yearn to sleep alongside our ancestors in the garden. Do not grieve. We are all pilgrims on a journey toward the same destination.

I am prepared. When news of the tragic death of my sons reaches Soochow, the world will think I have succumbed to sorrow. This accords with my plans and wishes.

Keep me in your hearts. Do not wail beside my coffin. For the same reason I sent you away, I forbid you to return to these courtyards to kneel at my side. Do not fail me. The clan would be lost if passions ruled.

But in a season when harmony reigns, on a day when the hills are green and the wind is mellow, gather your children and your children's children to sweep the thatches of our enduring abode. Thus the past is linked to the present and the present to the future. Do not neglect these rites, lest we be alone, without a rightful place or name, without home.

Life is a paradox the gods have fashioned for mortals to play at being gods. In his desire to conserve the old, the Venerable sent you, my sons, to learn the new. How could he have foreseen that, to reclaim the Empire, the clan must wither? I am glad that I will not live to see how the struggle will end. I suspect it will be when the old is new and the new is old.

My granddaughter, it has been foretold that you are blessed with the best of all possible fortunes. You shall live to see five generations. Cleave to your destiny, child. Heed the sages, uphold tradition, and secure our posterity under one roof.

Through you, my children, I live.

Mother, Grandmother

The typhoon that the heat forecast careened for three days along the China coast like a giant spinning top, sinking ships at sea but sparing the land. It was reported that the Chang brothers of Soochow were among the many drowned.

SUMMER
WINE

✂§ 20 §✂

Interlude

The Emperor of Heaven had a beautiful daughter who lived alone by the eastern shores of the River of Stars, weaving. Her diligence so moved him that when she came of age, he searched the universe for a man of good heart. After many moons he found such a man—a cowherd who lived on the western shores. And obeying the father's wish, the two were married.

After the wedding, the man and wife fell so in love that they had only time for one another. The loom was stilled. The cows strayed.

The Emperor was displeased and sent word by the magpie that the immoderate pair must immediately resume their duties on opposite banks of the river and meet but once a month.

Alas, the bird was forgetful and told them once a year.

Thus each year, on the seventh day of the seventh moon, the magpies soar to the heavens, stretching their wingtips until they span the River of Stars, paving a way for the reunion of the Weaving Maid and the Cowherd. Though the other 364 days of the year are barren, the happiness of the husband and wife on that one day is so great that the rain clouds must conceal it from the eyes of mortals by discreetly blanketing the heavens.
—Chinese tale

As she had every day since she came to the Travelers' Hotel, Spring Moon sat on the awkward chair by the window of her room. It seemed to her that she had been there forever, seeing and not seeing Shanghai. When had the storm passed? She had watched its progress, yet remembered little. Her thoughts returned again and again to the convent. Not to the Manchu, for that deed had been necessary and was done, but to the conspiracy that now bound her to her uncle. Night after night, there had been little rest. Phantoms she could not name pursued her along winding galleries through unfamiliar courts to strange heights where there was no escape. By morning she was exhausted, unable to forget.

The second day she had sent for a volume by the Sung poet Li Ch'ing-chao, whose fate was not unlike her own. She too had married young and happily the son of a famous scholar, been widowed, and then been forced by war to leave the North for the South.

> Lonely in my secluded chamber,
> A thousand sorrows fill every inch of my
>   sensitive being.
> Regretting that spring has so soon passed,
> That raindrops have hastened the falling
>   flowers,
> I lean over the balustrade,
> weary and forlorn.
> Where is my beloved?
> Only the fading grassland stretches endlessly
>   toward the horizon;
> Anxiously I watch the road for your return.

Again and again the same poem.

Now and then she would close her eyes to summon Glad Promise, and his face would appear as it had been on their wedding night, on the morning he left. How young he looked! She had already overtaken him by three years.

Why, my husband, did you leave me? Nothing I wish now could compare to the joy that would have been ours if you had stayed to stroll in the garden, your son's son in your arms. Nothing I feel now can compare with what we felt when we were young. Nothing I pledge hereafter will be as sincere, for in pledging I break my vow to you.

Once, she had been able to reconstruct entire days they had spent together. What he wore. The changing expression in his eyes.

How the air felt against her cheeks and if there had been leaves underfoot. She had hoarded every detail. When had she begun to forget? She no longer knew.

So much was lost to her now. Had the tiny scar been on his thumb or his index finger? It was the first of the memories that had strayed. She did remember that. And the fact that she had wept when she lost it. Thereafter, she had arbitrarily placed the scar on his thumb. After eleven years, it was difficult to know what had been and what she had assigned him.

Now and then, when she called him, the eyes in the photograph in the silver frame would stare back from a lifeless face, and then the image would fade and another return in his place.

"No," she would cry when this happened, "he is not the one I love. My husband was young. There was no gray in his hair."

But Eldest Uncle's presence lingered, and Golden Virtue's parting instructions.

Over and over, the questions. Where were her loyalties? To the past? To a vow made? To one? To many? To debts incurred? What to sacrifice? What to keep?

She turned away from the window, taking a cherry from the tray of food that had been left on the table untouched, and ate absently, swallowing the pit, hearing her own voice scolding Lustrous Jade for doing the same. Merciful Kwan Yin, she prayed, let our tender moments outlast the harsh words, and comfort my child in the years to come.

Restless, she took her folding fan from her tunic. It was made of ivory, but so intricately carved that it looked like white lace. A voice from the past whispered, "Are you certain, little girl, that the fan is red? Look again!" It was blue. "Look again!" said the magician. It was gold. What was true and what was trickery? Surely anticipation had colored it. Or was she bewitched?

And if not, why was she able to think of little else but what it would be like without clan, without name? Just the two of them, pretending.

Snapping the fan shut, she stood and went to the basin, twisting the knob that called the water forth. She washed her hands. When they were dried, the scent of roses lingered. She smiled. The scent was of summer evenings long past, when she had stood with her childish fingers outstretched as Third Cousin patiently rubbed each nail pink with rose petals. Had it been her fourth year when the honeysuckle had been so sweet and Plum Blossom had plucked the topmost flowers on the vine to tempt her?

What would it be like, just the two of them, pretending?

It was too early to sleep, but she lay down upon the bed and tried to arrange herself comfortably. The western mattress was too soft, the feather-filled pillow too formless. She felt like a caged bird that the family had misplaced on the way to a new house.

She forced herself to concentrate and count the days. Had it been seven or eight since she had come here? Still no word from Bold Talent. Before leaving Soochow he had warned her that it might take a week or more. A new life was not easily or quickly accomplished when secrets must be kept. But she feared that if he did not send for her soon, loneliness—or was it longing?—would overcome reason and she would betray them.

The hotel room was not small, but it was crowded with what had been and what would be. If only she could go for a walk, talk to someone.

What would it be like, just the—

There was a knock. She scrambled to her feet. "Who is it?"

"Letter for Woo Tai Tai."

She opened the door. The porter bowed, handing her the envelope. Asking him to wait, she tore it open. The message read: *Tonight, 333 Bubbling Well Road.*

At last! She thought she saw a knowing look on the face of the porter and quickly assumed the proper bearing. "Please prepare my account."

"It has already been settled, Mistress. And a hansom awaits your pleasure."

The trip, the driver said, would take about a half hour. Gratefully, she leaned back in her seat. The air was mild, even cool, but she had difficulty breathing. She closed her eyes, then, fearing visions, opened them and looked out the window. But it was night and they were going too fast for her to see much.

There would be one thing to remember. Not long after they turned away from the Bund, another carriage pulled alongside. It gleamed like a lacquered jewel box in the light from its two shining brass lamps, and inside, alone, was a man. Their eyes met for a moment before she could lower hers. Something about him puzzled her. His face was familiar. Where had they met before? Not in Soochow; Peking, perhaps. Then she knew. He was no one she had ever met. She had only seen a resemblance to Glad Promise.

Without being summoned, her husband appeared to her as he had been the first time she had seen him on the day they were married. His skin was smooth, his eyes like no other's. And all at once she found herself explaining what she had not yet understood. "I fought hard, my husband, so very hard to keep the season from changing. But spring has gone and summer now is here."

His image lingered just a moment more, and she thought she heard him say, as he had before, "Ours is a time of change."

When the hansom came to a halt at an intersection, she looked up again. The same carriage had pulled up beside hers, and the stranger was smiling warmly. Unthinking, she returned his smile. By the time she realized what she had done, his horses had galloped ahead and the carriage had disappeared.

She leaned back and closed her eyes.

"Mistress, we are here." The driver held open the hansom door. Spring Moon stepped out and watched him unstrap her bags, then led the way up the brick steps of the townhouse. She paid him and waited until the sound of hoofbeats could no longer be heard before ringing the bell.

The door opened. A man in a white linen suit and black bow tie stood before her.

"Eldest Uncle?"

He laughed and raised a hand to smooth his hair, cut short and shiny with pomade in the style of the Europeans. "It is quite a change. I cannot get used to it myself."

He looks younger, she thought, much younger.

"Come in, come in. I will take your bags. There are no servants yet. I thought it best if you chose them yourself. Until then, we are alone."

He shut the door behind them and showed her to a long, narrow room paneled with the kind of wide *mu-ban* she was accustomed to seeing on the floor. The effect was strange but not unpleasant.

"Please, sit here." He motioned toward one of the black leather chairs that flanked a mahogany table and resumed his seat in the other. The book that he had been reading lay open across the overstuffed arm.

Spring Moon could not think of anything to say. She looked around the room, at the massive fireplace, the oil paintings of men on horseback, sailing ships, and huge spotted dogs.

Bold Talent cleared his throat and in conversational tones reported on what he had been doing to establish himself as B. T. Yang, an overseas Chinese in Shanghai on business. She asked only a few appropriate questions. When that subject was done, he stood up, saying, "Well, how about some refreshments?"

"Refreshments?"

"Yes. I stopped by the bakery and bought some of your favorite almond cakes." He started to go into the next room.

She impulsively reached out, almost shouting. "No! Do not go. Do not bother."

"It is no bother."

"Please, Eldest Uncle, I ate at the hotel before leaving to come here."

"Then, perhaps just tea!"

"Tea?"

"Tea."

She shook her head. "No, I am not thirsty." As soon as she had refused, she regretted doing so. Tea would have given her something to do with her hands. Desperately she searched for conversation, finally blurting out, "Where is Young Uncle?"

"In the Philippines," he said, sitting down again. "He left here more than a week ago."

"How long will he be gone?"

"As long as necessary. His friends in the overseas Chinese community will help him." Their eyes met. "Do not worry, my niece. He is not alone. . . ."

She looked away, staring at the book between them, reading the title over and over without comprehending.

He hastened to fill the silence, but she did not hear what he said. Had there ever been a time when she did not have words to say to him? She could think of none, until tonight.

"My niece?"

"Yes?"

"I was saying that this room is a replica of certain sanctuaries you find in London." He explained the unnatural surroundings. "The adventuresome ones who come to China seeking their fortune often furnish their homes like this. Back in England they could never aspire to belong to the exclusive clubs that have such rooms."

"How sad."

"Do you really think so?" he asked, his tone the one he had used long ago to coax the right answer from his pupil. When she said nothing, he went on. "It does not seem sad to me. After all, who can realize every dream? For some an illusion, even for a little while, is enough." He waited, but she merely stared at the pattern in the rug.

"It would be sad," he continued, "only if there were no place, even in Shanghai, that exiles could make their own. . . ." Again he waited for a sign that she understood. Her eyes reluctantly met his. It was enough.

When he finally spoke again, there was a tenderness in his voice she had never heard before. "Spring Moon? I have so much to explain—"

No, she almost cried out, not now, not just yet. Abruptly she stood up. "Eldest Uncle, please excuse me. I am tired."

He rose also. "It is most understandable." He carried her bags to the front room on the second floor. She thanked him. He bid her good night. When he left, she stood in the doorway to watch him descend the stairs. She would know him anywhere, she thought, no matter what disguise he wore.

Alone, she unpacked, moving mechanically from suitcase to wardrobe to dressing table and back again.

When the bags were emptied, she sat down beside the photograph of Glad Promise that lay on the bed, studying it for a long time. He was tall and his skin was smooth. His eyes were like no other's.

She and her husband were strangers again.

Before leaving the room, she placed the silver frame carefully in a drawer.

Downstairs, all the lights had been extinguished except for the lamp on the hall table. The front door was wide open. Bold Talent stood just beyond the threshold with his back to her.

For a while, she watched him. Whether he was in motion or, as now, at rest, his demeanor called to mind the ideals of elegance and subtlety. His grace was true grace, strong, and whoever looked upon his harmonious features was immediately invited to become acquainted with his character.

She tapped lightly on the door.

He turned to face her without surprise.

"Why are you outside?" she asked. "Are you expecting someone?"

"No," he replied gravely. "No one else."

"Why do you wait then?"

"Ah, but I have been a fool for so long, Spring Moon, for so long."

"How have you been a fool?"

"Only another fool need ask."

Closing the distance between them, she pressed her face to his heart.

All that summer, the moon above Shanghai was translucent, a crystalline scale lost by a shimmering mermaid. The nights were soft. A perfumed breeze stirred the willows tenderly, without haste, and crickets chirruped to finish their song before the end of life's fleeting span.

Summer wine quickened desire.

✑ 21 ✑
Yielding

At nine o'clock on the evening of what would be known as Double Ten of the First Year of the Republic of China, a band of rebels captured Wuchang arsenal in Wuhan.

As the news spread, rebels rose throughout the land. They met little resistance. When an enemy cut off his queue, he was welcomed into the Republican ranks without prejudice.

On the sixth day before the first day of the Year of the Rat, 1912, the Vermilion Pencil issued its last decree:

> *The wishes of millions cannot be disregarded for the glory of one family. Accordingly, the Emperor will retire to contemplate at leisure the waning and waxing of many moons to come, the consummation of wise government.*

The Purple Dragon of the Ch'ing Dynasty had floated over the rooftops of China for more than two hundred and fifty years. Overnight, it was gone. On every shop and shanty in Shanghai the white flags of revolution flapped like laundered sheets hung to dry. At street corners, in trams and alleys, before dawn, after dark, anytime, everywhere, squadrons of scissors snipped the long black queues from unsuspecting and unwilling heads. Men laughed to see their neighbors shorn and were in turn deprived. The poor looked like porcupines without the restraining queue; the rich, who could afford Vaseline, like wet ducks. Sons wept as they begged their elders' forgiveness for disfiguring a gift of the ancestors. Wailing mothers caressed the severed braids.

—Chinese history

On the first day of the first moon, Spring Moon wrote to her mother-in-law, wishing her and the family a happy and prosperous Year of the Rat. According to tradition, she reported on how she had fared in the year past, keeping the lie as close to the truth as possible without revealing any secrets. "Lustrous Jade attends an excellent school nearby and I have found employment with the Yang family of Shanghai. . . ." She did not expect to receive Lotus Delight's greeting, for her mother-in-law had not written the year before.

Three weeks later, on a morning when horses breathed white smoke and the light made the front rooms seem much larger than on other days, she sat alone in the study, reading. Bold Talent was out, keeping appointments. As usual, she had sent one of the servants to return his latest gift before the noon hour, when he often came home for lunch.

She smiled to herself, touching the gold hairpin she wore. It was his first gift, the only one she had kept. Obviously it was the pleasure of giving he treasured, for he never noticed that his subsequent gifts were gone. His joy in her, and, since Wuhan, in the new Republic, was that of a young man with only hope and plans for the future. "Perhaps the world has changed," he said again and again. "Perhaps the struggle will achieve its ends. Perhaps we shall be free." He acted as if their happiness would last forever. Some nights, he laughed aloud in his sleep.

She was about to stir the logs in the fireplace when the bell rang. It was a messenger. Her hands shook as she received the telegram.

It was from Peking. Lotus Delight needed her daughter-in-law at her side.

There would be no weeping. From the start Spring Moon had known her happiness with Bold Talent must be an interlude. At first, she had thought there would be more time, years perhaps. But after Wuhan her heart had sunk with each setting sun, for once the Manchus were subdued and order restored, the revolutionaries would go home. The dead, like the Chang brothers, would come to life again. The rootless, like the Yangs, would die.

She must not be like a child without a care, without a wish

unfulfilled, as if she had saved her slave girl and altered fate. Over and over, she had repeated the Venerable's lesson, so that when the moment came she would be able to let go. But even as she had tried to prepare herself, she had wondered where she would live. Soochow was out of the question. How could she change from being his wife to being his niece overnight? She could not. He could not. Yet there was nowhere else.

Now the telegram gave her the answer. Without giving in to sorrow, she ascended the stairs to prepare for the journey.

It was the hour of the monkey when the servant announced that the Master had returned. Spring Moon entered the study to find him already engrossed in the newspapers that lay spread across the desk. She placed the telegram over the page he was reading and took the seat nearest the window without a word.

For a long time neither moved. Her back was taut, her composure flickering like a candle in the wind.

Suddenly, he laughed. The sound was hollow, like the laughter of marionettes that entertain children.

"It is ludicrous. These are the very words I used in the false message I sent to Soochow last summer. Quote—Spring Moon needed immediately. Signed, Mother-in-law—unquote. The gods haunt us with our own lies! Funny, is it not?"

She nodded woodenly.

"Then you should be laughing. Why are you not laughing?" He rose deliberately and tore the telegram into smaller and smaller pieces before throwing them into the fire. She watched the paper bits ignite, burn to ash, and gently float upward until they disappeared into the chimney.

Picking up the poker, he speared the flames.

No words came to her. It was as if the room were full and could not accommodate another thought, another cry.

Suddenly, he let the poker fall and came to her, raising her brusquely to her feet. "Do you regret our love?" He searched her eyes for an answer.

She did not reply, recalling that once her husband had asked the same question. Did happiness always end like this?

He held her tight and asked again, "Do you regret our love? I must know."

Why do they ask? she thought. Do they ask the sun if it regrets the light? "No, I do not," she answered tenderly. "I only regret that we must part today."

"Must it be today?"

"Today is easier than tomorrow," she replied. He did not deny the truth.

Silently, they clung to each other.

"It may only be for a little while," he whispered.

She broke away and walked to the globe that stood in the corner of the room. Idly spinning it, she said, "It will be forever." And then, "My mother-in-law blames me for all her misfortunes. If she had another choice, she would not have summoned me. Something must have happened to her adopted son. I am all she has left. It is my duty, my fate. In honor of my husband, I shall serve his mother as he would have served her if he had not died. Our ancestors, who gave us life, deny you and me a life together. We who have no rightful place with one another must yield. There is no other way." She looked down at the lines in her palm. Had it all been written there? Her fate? When she looked up, his eyes were bright with anger.

"No other way?" He was pleading. "There must be another way. The revolution has put an end to yielding. Do you not see?"

When she did not respond, he took the worry beads she had given him from his pocket and, fingering them, paced back and forth, back and forth, recalling the disappointments of decades. She did not interfere. The more vehement he was, the calmer she became.

"Do you not see what is wrong?" he cried. "What is wrong with you, me, us? With Golden Virtue? With all Chinese? With the Old Empire? With the old ways?

"Yielding! That is what is wrong. In the end, we always yield— to tradition, to foreigners, to family, to authority, to duty. To everything and everybody, living and dead—except our needs, our dreams, our passions! If we do live for ourselves, it is not for long.

A moment here, a month there. As long as no one knows. As long as nothing is truly changed. Then, once more we yield. Once more we live as others would have us live."

Abruptly, he stopped speaking and peered out the window, painted silver with frost, darkening now as the sun set. Only the sound of the wood sputtering in the fireplace could be heard. When he resumed, his voice was lifeless.

"Even as I protest, I know nothing will come of it. You will honor your dead husband. I will not dishonor the clan. So we will live apart, lives we did not choose."

She walked toward him, her arm outstretched. He would not look at her. She took his face in her hands. "We shall survive," she said. "We shall eventually think that our separation is a natural state. Yielding more, we shall desire less. So it is with us Chinese. So you have often said."

Gently, she kissed him on the lips. But he would not be comforted and broke away. With the poker, savagely he pushed the charred remains of the burned-out logs off the andirons, then tossed in two more from the bin. After working the fire for a while, he said, "What no other men will tolerate, I will endure, for I am Chinese. When foreigners walk, they dream of riding a cart, a horse, then a coach, a train, and one day a horseless carriage. When we Chinese walk, we consider ourselves fortunate to have the use of both legs. And should our legs be chopped from under us, we tame our tempers, ignore threats, accept insults, dispel savage thoughts. And if that is not possible, we hide them from the world and adjust to a cripple's fate, convinced that we are lucky to sit, saving money on shoes, while others less fortunate lie under the ground.

"We yield and we survive, Spring Moon, but to what end? To what end?"

"A life of sacrifice—of duty—of honor," she replied.

"It is not enough. . . ."

She could not bear the pain in his voice and put her hand to his lips. "Please, no more. No more."

He nodded slowly.

There was nothing more to say.

At the station, when it was time to part, he dared to touch her hand in farewell, and smiled in spite of himself at the familiar furrows that appeared on her brow. So had she looked as a girl, before he knew it was she who held that part of him the gods had fashioned but casually misplaced at the moment of his birth and then absently given to her when she was born.

On his return he found a letter from her on the bed. He set it on the night table, and for a while sat staring at the envelope, afraid to know what she had not had the courage to say. Finally, he opened it and read.

Dearest—

Once my life seemed no more confining to me than a cocoon seems to the silkworm. Then you gave me wings and I reveled in flight.

But the moon is never round for long, and our time is spent. My heart is full. I have no room for regrets.

The love we feel will endure. But the dreams we have dreamed must die.

Let us write but once a year on the first day of the first moon, as is the custom. Should we meet again, let us not journey to the beginning.

Your niece

⌒§ 22 §⌒

To Fool the Gods

Sons shall be born to him—
They will be put to sleep on couches;
They will be clothed in robes;
They will have scepters to play with;
Their cry will be loud.
They will be resplendent with red knee-covers,
The future princes of the land.

Daughters shall be born to him—
They will be put to sleep on the ground;
They will be clothed with wrappers;
They will have tiles to play with.
It will be theirs neither to do wrong nor to do good.
Only about the spirits and the food will they have to think,
And to cause no sorrow to their parents.
                                    —The Book of Odes

ON CERTAIN DAYS when the wind blows from the west, the sand
haunts the skies above the Forbidden City, tinting the air gold.
So it was when the daughter-in-law returned to Peking.

She arrived to find her mother-in-law alone with one half-witted
servant in a ruined house. The adopted son had been lost in the
fire, one of many that had burned after the Emperor's abdication.

His frail widow had returned to the countryside, but Lotus Delight had refused to go. Had she not been known as the Beauty

of the Northern Capital? She would rather die than kowtow to her nephew's wife.

Spring Moon sent at once for Fatso and began the search for a new home—smaller quarters than before, in an even less desirable neighborhood. Lotus Delight did little but stare into the distance, watching the fire that had long since burned out, asking of no one in particular, "What kind of dynasty is a Republic? What kind of Mandate of Heaven is the Will of the People? What kind of Chinese has no queue?"

When the first month passed, Spring Moon barely noticed.

When the second ended without reassurance, she began to remember stories: of the official who lost his office when his wife became pregnant during the nine months of national mourning . . . of Master Koo, who beheaded his wife and her lover and was pardoned . . . of the lascivious Widow Ling, buried alive for soiling the clan's name.

She had loved Bold Talent, and as long as her misconduct was secret, she felt no shame. After all, laws were arbitrary limits placed upon men by men to ensure harmony, not divine standards. But with the passage of the third month, she knew her affair must soon be known and the clans of Chang and Woo dishonored. Fear took hold. Neither potions of green ginger, orange peel, and ginseng nor scalding baths and fasting induced abortion.

It was Fatso who first spoke of the unspeakable.

"Mistress, I have known for many weeks, and for many weeks I have thought. At another time, the baby would have been brought into the courtyards through the back door, as my child. But I am too old. And so you must allow me to find Dummy and make arrangements for the birth. We will tell your mother-in-law that you have taken a tutoring assignment with a foreign family. She is not well and will not object. I shall serve her until your return."

No more was said. Fatso left the next morning. A week later, her mistress boarded the small canal boat that was to take her to Learned Cinders.

When she reached the village, she wore the green skirt of a concubine. No sedan chair was for hire, but the servant from the boat secured a mule cart for his master's only passenger.

As she rode past the clusters of adobe houses, adults gaped and children giggled and pointed, running after the cart, flashing palms and soles painted with flowers that would dissolve at once should they dare to play in the forbidden canal. A few beggars cried out for alms. Even the village dogs gathered, scenting a stranger. She bowed her head, pretending they were not there.

With a lurch, the cart stopped. At once the urchins surrounded her, fingering her skirt and her baggage. Uneasy, she looked about. The driver had left his place and was behind the cart, shoveling the dung dropped by his mule into the basket that hung from the rear of the vehicle, collecting it quickly for his own fields before it could be taken by another.

The crowd around the cart grew larger as the women of the village joined their children. Spring Moon peered into each face, hoping to recognize one.

Suddenly a voice cried, "Aye ya! Aye ya! It is you!" The women stepped aside and Dummy walked slowly forward.

"Who is she?" the women shouted. "Who is the pretty lady?"

Dummy did not answer but helped Spring Moon down from the cart. "Our house is just a few steps away," she whispered. Spring Moon paid the driver, asking him to help with the small trunk. He bowed, counted the coins, and then flashed a big smile. "Certainly, Mistress."

"Sister," the women shouted, "you give too much. You spoil the driver. Too much!"

Shooing away the children and the beggars and the dogs, they followed Spring Moon and Dummy unabashedly into the two-room house, touching the tunic, hair, and skin, ogling every aspect of the stranger.

"Just like the bottom of my grandchild," whispered one. "Feel, if you do not believe me!"

"Have you gifts from the city?" cried another. "Staying long?"

"Sister Hua, shall I fetch the master of the house?"

"How much did that comb in your hair cost?"

"Introduce us, Sister!"

Not now, please not now, Spring Moon prayed silently. Dummy steered her toward the stone k'ang, but the others had left no sitting room, and finally, with her arm around her guest, she said, "Alas, my house is too small to receive all my dear neighbors, and I have not prepared refreshments for this unexpected pleasure. Aunties, Sisters, Nieces of Learned Cinders, allow me face. Come back tomorrow when I have everything ready."

Trapped by these hospitable words, the women shuffled out reluctantly, one by one.

When they were gone Spring Moon, sitting next to Dummy on the quilt, spoke for the first time. "Sister . . . ?

"Yes, Mistress?"

Spring Moon bowed her head. "You are my sister," she whispered. And then, "Has Fatso not told you everything?"

"Everything." Dummy also whispered. "Do not worry. Your secrets are safe here in Learned Cinders. I have not even told my husband. He and everyone else will think you are a distant relative, a rich man's concubine who has been sent away by the jealous wife."

Spring Moon hid her face in her hands, ashamed.

"Do not worry," Dummy said again. "You are welcome. My husband is a good man."

Brother Hua was indeed a good man. He had begun as a laborer on the farm he now owned. Away gleaning when the Harmonious Fists had killed the Hua family, he had continued to work afterward as if nothing had changed, tilling the five mous just outside the north gate of Learned Cinders that had belonged to them. No one ever saw him drinking or gambling at the local tavern. His pigtail never hung down his back; it was always wound around his head, out of the way. He took no holidays. People forgot his name and called him Non Stop.

Soon the roof of the house was rebuilt and there were once again chicks and piglets in the yard, corn and onions hanging from the rafters. The graves were tended. Non Stop moved his sleeping mat onto the heated k'ang in the main room but assumed no other privileges.

When Dummy returned to the village, she was grateful. He immediately moved out of the house and asked One Hundred Percent Satisfaction to make the proper arrangements. After the wedding, he took her family's name, to perpetuate the Hua line. He must have been happy, for thenceforth he worked even harder.

Although Sister Hua never mentioned what their neighbors never forgot, that the farm had not always belonged to him, he also remembered, and so when Dummy told him that Spring Moon would be staying with them for a while, he had not complained. To him the land was still hers, as long as they did not have a son. But the first night, in the privacy of their k'ang, Non Stop said to his wife, "This is not a rich man's home. You cannot do your share and hers as well. She must do more than leave deposits in the night-soil bucket. She must work!"

Spring Moon overheard and vowed to do so.

She was as useless as a baby. Like all men and women of the gentry, she had never exerted herself physically except to lift a brush and occasionally a needle. A life of gentle repose was the ideal. She did not even know how to bind her own feet properly, much less how to start a fire, steal eggs from hens, or drive piglets from the house. She offered to prepare the meals, but her steamed bread was either raw or waterlogged, her vegetables limp and taste-less, and, worst of all, she was wasteful. After a week, Non Stop declared that he could not work all day and eat mush, and Dummy resumed the cooking.

By then it was the Fortnight of Sprouting Plants, when strawber-ries ripen and women go forth to gather the fruit. Spring Moon, despite her golden lilies, insisted on going along. The women en-joyed themselves thoroughly at her expense, but they did not send her away, and every evening, though her feet were raw, her hands scarred, her back sore, she stood proudly by her small pile of berries, giving them to Non Stop to sell at the market.

Even when her burden began to show, she joined the women in doing what work she could, and the women in turn grew fond of the runaway concubine who never acted as if she were better than they, though she had once belonged to a gentry house. When they called her "Greenhorn," she did not mind and laughed along. Some clucked that it was a shame her cheeks were becoming brown, her feet less shapely, her palms calloused. All loved the stories she told, of the Alchemist, of Cruelty Avenged, of the Wise Magistrate, and the Midget General. In return they told her the story of Learned Cinders, and how it got its name.

Over two thousand years before, at the time of the tyrant Emperor Ch'in Shih Hwang Ti, who first unified China, built the Great Wall, repudiated Confucius, and burned the books, there had lived in the town a brave and faithful scholar. When the Emperor ordered the words of the Master burned, the scholar tried to save his classical library by sealing his books within walls. Alas the scheme was discovered. The scholar was buried alive and plowed under, with no mound of earth to mark the place. The village was burned. But in less than twenty years, the Ch'in Dynasty fell and the Emperors of Han restored the teachings of the Sage. The town was rebuilt from the ashes and was thenceforth known as "Learned Cinders."

After she had heard this tale, whenever Spring Moon told a story she would begin by saying, "Naturally, the story that I am about to tell cannot compare with that of your most illustrious town."

"No matter! No matter!" the villagers would cry. "Sister Hua says that you have a story for every one of the sixty-three hundred steps to the summit of the Gate of Heaven."

Even Non Stop grew accustomed to having Spring Moon around. After her pregnancy became obvious, he declared that he had never cared much for eggs and insisted that she eat his share. Had not the old midwife said that someone with child must have thirty-six eggs?

When the millet had ripened, and Spring Moon was big and awkward, almost unable to walk or bend, Non Stop gave her a special assignment. "Until the grain is cut, tied, and brought safely within the town walls, we will have to watch night and day for poachers. I want you to sit in one of our fields."

"Certainly. That is the least I can do."

"Good. Take a straw mat with you."

Spring Moon prepared some food and the mat and was ready to follow Non Stop into the fields before she thought to ask, "But what if a poacher comes? What am I to do? Surely I cannot catch him!"

"Shout 'Get away, get away!' "

"Is that all?"

"Yes. There is no reason to punish a starving beggar. Just shout and chase him into somebody else's field."

It was the morning of the third day of the Fortnight of Small Snow when Spring Moon felt the first pain and took to bed. This time, unlike the first, the birth was an ordeal. *The child is ashamed,* she thought over and over as the hours passed. *He has no right, does not wish to be born.*

She heard the scream of a pig being slaughtered. No, it was she. She no longer knew how long she had labored, drifting in and out of agony, ashamed to have Dummy and the midwife look upon her face, upon the beast that was she. She fought to keep awake, to keep from calling out his name. Then she could hold on no longer and fell into blackness. She drowned.

Where was she? What was the noise? The scratching of dogs or a hoe? Slowly, for it was most painful, she turned her head toward the sound.

The midwife was digging the hole for the placenta in the earthen floor beside the k'ang. *It is a boy, then,* she thought. If the baby had been a girl, the afterbirth would have been buried outside the house, for one day she would belong to her husband's clan.

Dummy bent over her, shaking her head to contradict the words she shouted for the benefit of the jealous gods. "It is a girl baby! A worthless girl baby!" Then she whispered into the mother's ear, "A wonderful man-child!" and placed the bundle on the quilt beside her.

"Thank you, Sister Hua."

Embarrassed, Dummy smiled and left quickly, escorting the midwife to the gate.

Spring Moon stared after her, not wanting to look at the small creature that lay by her side. Tears welled. She blinked them away. The baby whimpered. Reluctantly, she turned toward him. She did not want to know him. She had no right to claim him. The pulsating soft membrane at the crown of the head was as vulnerable as a papered window in a storm.

Twice now the chair outside her door had stood empty throughout the length of her labors, empty when the door opened at long last and the announcement was made. And when the preparations were completed, no one entered and placed a gold hairpin of gratitude upon her pillow, attesting to her husband's esteem and her own fulfillment. No one took up her baby, neither the girl in red satin twelve years before nor this boy in quilted cotton, to kneel before the grandmothers, to parade with pomp through each court of the homestead, and finally to stand under the lamp of continuous life in the Hall of Ancestors. There was no one to light the incense, guiding the tiny hand with his large one, and announce the glad tidings to all forebears before returning the child to the mother's keeping for the three days of quietness.

Her hand moved to touch the baby's cheek, and the black down on his head. Suddenly she felt a rush of concern so strong that she tore open the quilted cloth and undressed her son, to see if he was really fit, not lame or lacking.

He awoke, kicking furiously, crying to be acknowledged.

This son of ours is beautiful, Spring Moon thought, and has the strength of ten tigers.

On the morning of the fourth day, Dummy stood by the bed of the new mother, nervously tugging the sleeves of her blue cloth jacket. Spring Moon lay with the baby beside her.

"What is it, Sister Hua?"

"If it would be possible, my useless husband, he is anxious. . . ."

Spring Moon nodded. "Yes, let him come."

Dummy ran to the door and called. He came at once, pausing at the threshold. He had washed.

"It is too early, Elder Sister. I shall return tomorrow."

"No, please come in." Spring Moon turned back the baby's red quilt.

In two large strides, he was beside the k'ang. The newborn was asleep, contentedly blowing bubbles. He reached toward the tiny face. Abruptly, he withdrew. His hand was as coarse as the bark on a stone pine.

"Ahhh," the man sighed. "What a man-child! What a man-child!" He stepped back and bowed. "How can we thank you? I never dreamed that such a thing would happen to us."

Spring Moon nodded, fighting tears, holding tight to the baby this man would call son.

23

Letters

The mist is deep, the waters are broad;
Tidings and letters have no way to reach her.
Only in the azure sky there is the moon beyond the clouds,
Minded to shine on the lovelorn pair so far apart.
All day things remind me and wound my heart;
My sad eyebrows are like a lock that is hard to open.
Night after night I ever keep for her the half of my quilt
In expectation of her spirit coming back to me in a dream.
—Li Po, Tang Dynasty

First day of the first moon
Year of the Ox, 1913

My niece:

Life here is quiet. Only the five widows, my wife and sons, and I remain in Soochow.

When I returned, many of the courtyards had already been sealed off and sold. The Matriarch had insisted on extravagant mourning for her two sons so that our "death by typhoon" would not be questioned. Then my wife made certain that my mother's own passing was marked with appropriate pomp.

When revolution came, the relatives feared for their share of what little was left in the treasury after the rites had been paid for. It was decided that the lands and monies should be divided equally among the various branches of the clan. The others have sold their property and moved to the coastal cities, where they hope to pursue their fortunes.

Even the orphan, August Winds, has gone. I offered to send him to school with my sons in Soochow or to recommend him as a clerk to friends. He politely refused. Then one morning he simply left, taking with him only a handful of red envelopes, gifts of money from the widows. He said that he had no plans, and he certainly did not look as if he had cares.

My wife has assumed the responsibility of managing the farmlands that remain in my hands. She does it better than I ever did. Perhaps she has inherited a talent for business. While she still has not learned to read, she has devised her own method of keeping account of all transactions. Into holes bored in the top of a large table, she inserts different-sized pegs and colored threads, representing the tenants and their obligations, the expenses and the incomes.

But the tenants who farm the lands are not mere pegs on that board to her; she knows them intimately: the size of their families, their habits, and their troubles. Unlike many of our friends, who send bailiffs to collect their rents and taxes for them, your aunt pays regular visits to those who still work for the family, resolving problems with a personal touch that gains the loyalty of all concerned. Her patience is endless, but she is also not afraid to say no. Instinctively she understands that favors extended too often and too generously would only be resented in the end.

If it would not embarrass us both, I would tell my wife how well she manages everything. But obligations among family members are deeper than those that can be expressed easily or discharged with mere words of appreciation.

As for me, I do what I must for the Republic but prefer my own company to that of the new breed of politicians. Sun should never have resigned in favor of Yuan Shih-k'ai. He should have known that the Northerner would break his pledge and move the capital from Nanking to Peking, where his soldiers are.

Sometimes I wonder if a republic can be made to work at all where old ties cannot be denied and new laws are not understood or respected. I fear that when change comes to ancient ways, no matter how long in the making, no matter how fervently wished for, chaos follows.

Within the courtyards, bricks now seal the gates that once connected the family courts, offending beauty. How many years must pass before the color of the new bricks will blend with the old, before the harsh will mellow? How long to restore solidarity?

A happy new year to all,
Your uncle

First day of the first moon
Year of the Ox, 1913

Eldest Uncle:

I have nothing extraordinary to report, except that Lustrous Jade has not joined me in Peking. I wrote that I was lonely and wished her by my side, but she had taken to heart the life of the mission school and asked to remain. How could I insist that she give up the very goals which I had set for her?

We live simply. My mother-in-law has never fully recovered from the shock of the fire. If only she could think less of the past and all that she once had, she would be better, but that, I know, is not easily accomplished.

For some months after my return, I taught Chinese to the wife of a foreign missionary in the interior. Her first tutor had become sick, and although she was soon to go on home leave, she did not want her lessons interrupted for longer than necessary. Now that she is gone, I miss the work and my mother-in-law misses the extra dividend. I hope for other employment soon. Meanwhile, I pass the hours reading and trying to remember my English.

A happy new year to all,
Your niece

My niece,

I write from Soochow because I am home for the holidays, but I now live in Shanghai, in the house once owned by the Yangs.

Quite unexpectedly, last summer, friends from the Self-Strengthening Society decided to finance a new venture, New China Publications. They stipulated two conditions: one, that I assume the responsibilities of publisher and, two, that the offices and press be located in the International Settlement, for greater freedom and security.

Soon we begin publishing books for the modern student in every grade; translations of western classics and contemporary works of interest; a weekly magazine devoted to reform.

This opportunity could not have come at a better time. I was languishing at home, and when the second revolution and Sun's efforts to consolidate the Kuomintang in opposition to Yuan failed, I was able to persuade Noble Talent to join me. He now lives with me on Bubbling Well Road, swallowing his bitterness as the foreign democracies continue to back Yuan with fancy excuses and loans that are more truly liens upon the sovereignty of China.

I have tried to introduce my brother to several families with eligible daughters. He says he is too old, that it is too late. I fear he resists for the same reason as always—that he is not through with a life of danger.

Your daughter, no doubt, has faithfully reported on my periodic visits to the school. She is a model student, champion debater, and badminton star.

My eldest finished middle school this year, and I asked him if he would like to continue his studies in Shanghai. I did not realize that he had already set his heart on going abroad to college and so would be leaving his mother all too soon. Thus he stays in Soochow. Will we ever have a chance to know one another?

I thought that my second son might come to Shanghai in his stead for a few years, before he too goes to America, as I suppose he will. But when I broached the subject to his mother, she looked as if the heavens were falling even as she whispered, "As my husband wishes." Needless to say, I shall not mention it again.

A happy new year to all,
Your uncle

First day of the first moon
Year of the Tiger, 1914

Eldest Uncle:

After a year of tutoring groups of foreign ladies in the art of communicating with their houseboys, I will at last be teaching in a school. My daughter is responsible for my new employment. She overheard her teachers talking about vacancies in the mission grammar school here in Peking and volunteered my credentials. For once I am thankful that she has such big ears.

Fatso wagers that my soul has already been pledged to Jesus in advance.

My unlucky daughter—fatherless, growing up among foreign women in a foreign compound. Another year is past and I have not seen her since I left her at the school.

Her letters are filled with admiration for the missionaries, who have traveled halfway around the world to dedicate their lives to China and who stay despite the risks to their safety and health. Two trekked thousands of *li* to Shanghai after their parents were killed by the Harmonious Fists. Lustrous Jade asked them directly why they remained in China after that. They answered that it was God's will. This seems now to be Lustrous Jade's answer as well, and sometimes I fear that she will be a missionary herself. Her favorite teacher, a Miss Clayton, also works at the Door of Hope, a home for the mistreated administered by the foreigners of the Concessions. Lustrous Jade has volunteered to tutor these girls at night.

I am proud of how well she seems to be doing, but I worry

too. She writes almost nothing of the girls in her class. It would not surprise me if she pronounced them all frivolous.

Think how my mother once worried about my lessons. The gods must be laughing now.

A happy new year to all,
Your niece

First day of the first moon
Year of the Rabbit, 1915

My niece,

I wish that I did not share the fears about your daughter you mentioned in last year's letter. If the girls of the inner courts are miniature versions of their mothers, Lustrous Jade is a Chinese version of the missionary—all good works and sturdy shoes. No foolishness, like yours. No romance, like her father's.

But enough. Perhaps my biases are showing.

New China Publications is now well under way. I enclose several of our books, which may be of help in your teaching.

Young Brother leaves Shanghai frequently. He will not tell me where he goes, but I am sure he plots and plans again. There is no use trying to stop him now that the Japanese have joined the Allies and taken Tsingtao while Yuan's so-called government in Peking merely stands by. My brother has always despised the Brown Dwarfs. He thinks that Tsingtao will whet their appetite for even more Chinese territory. I cannot disagree. But what can any of us do to stop them?

A happy new year to all,
Your uncle

First day of the first moon
Year of the Rabbit, 1915

Eldest Uncle:

Dear Fatso is gone, buried next to Old Hawk in Reed Village. It happened on the fourth day of the tenth moon. She worked all day, ate a huge meal, saw an opera, went to bed, and never woke up again. I would not put it beyond her powers to have arranged it that way.

She had certainly been explicit about the funeral, her favorite topic in recent months. "Do not waste your money, and you keep all that is mine," she said. "No use feeding silk to the worms or tempting the grave snatchers with the Matriarch's brooch of gold. Just my work clothes and a plain pine box. What good for a shrimp to don a dragon's tail?"

While she bravely eschewed the expensive trappings of a traditional burial, she nevertheless wanted a hedge against the remote possibility that the comforts of this life would be needed in the next. So she made me promise to arrange for "loom cer biz." Anything, anything, I promised, but what is that?

"The most wonderful thing," she said. "Ah Sing, the servant at the big house of the foreigners, saw it when she traveled in America with her foreign family. In every stacked-up house they stayed in, there was a talking box, and any time of day or night the Mistress could order whatever she desired by asking for 'loom cer biz.'"

How I do miss her! But what heavenly havoc she is surely wreaking with her telephone.

> Happy new year to all,
> Your niece

> First day of the first moon
> Year of the Dragon, 1916

My niece:

I write from the Convent of Sedate Quest, where I have come seeking solitude.

News of Yuan's acceptance of the Mandate of Heaven has driven me here and my brother to Peking to protest Japan's 21 Demands. You may have seen him by now.

What has happened to the revolution? Have we been dragging the lake for the moon all these years?

I do not know how long I shall stay here. With all that has befallen the country, there seems little reason to return at once to Shanghai after the holidays. I have taken a pavilion tucked into the woods. With five strides I can walk its length or breadth. A rude cot, a chair, a table, a few utensils, and a stove complete my home here. Outside the door, piled neatly to one side, are bundles of twigs and pinecones to feed the brazier. Beyond the eaves of the roof stand earthen jars to catch rainwater. I hear the temple bells but see only trees and hillocks. Silent nuns bring me my food. There is no meat, but the vegetables are cooked to resemble the choicest morsels of chicken, pork, and beef.

This morning began with blue skies and a drift of clouds. I put on five layers and sat by the door waiting for the snows to come. Inch by inch, gray coaxed the blue away and veiled the horizon. As the distant disappeared, the scene I saw edged closer and closer until finally there were only the flakes that floated down into the jars. I counted them. Then I scooped the snow into the kettle and brewed tea. Sheltering my cup's warmth in my hands, I savored the difference.

There is nothing more I may say.

Your uncle

First day of the first moon
Year of the Dragon, 1916

Eldest Uncle:

There is little news. My teaching goes well, but the household has not been the same since Fatso left. When she was here, her presence took the place of a clan. Now that she is gone, the house is full of ghosts.

Young Uncle came to see me a few days ago. I thought he looked older, suddenly middle-aged. He would tell me only that he was here to protest Japan's 21 Demands. I suspect that there is more.

Why should he risk arrest when the students are already marching in the streets? I hope that he has not so quickly forgotten the lesson of the Yamen. Yet who can deny that Yuan, by making himself Emperor, has made a mockery of the Republic?

Instead of politics we talked about home. Do you remember the redwood chairs along the walls of the Hall of Ancestors. Are they still there? Young Uncle thought they had been sold. The carp are gone, he told me. But not the dwarf trees in their shallow pots or the bronze lions at the gate. I take comfort in that.

A happy new year to all
Your niece

First day of the first moon
Year of the Snake, 191'

My niece,

Grand Vista studies at Harvard in America. Did he notice that I stood on the quay until his ship disappeared from view. So did the Venerable stand beside the lions, the day I began my journey to the West.

August Winds now lives in Shanghai. I do not know where he has been these five years; the story changes with each telling. Somewhere along the way, he has learned English.

When he wrote me of his job with M.S. & Company in the French Concession, I invited him to live with me, and though he declined, he often comes for dinner. He has brought laughter back into my life with his irrepressible and impudent ways.

This is not to say that I approve of him any more than did when he was a young devil cheating sedan carriers out of their tips at cards. But he has an undeniable charm. Last week he had me in his arms, teaching me to tango while he hummed. How he ever got me to take such an undignified position, I cannot reconstruct. But we escaped discovery, and now that I am safe in Soochow for the holidays, I rather think it was fun.

Although he is not so very much older than my eldest, he is not remotely like either of my sons. August Winds, despite his passion for all things foreign, would never think me as old as Confucius because I refused last year and again this year to substitute three reverent bows for the kowtows in the family ceremonies, as many have. The rite of kowtow fills me with both humility and pride. It is at once personal and abstract, affirming mortality and immortality. I shall not be the patriarch to change this tradition. If my son wishes to, in his time, so be it. Until then, it will continue.

There is too much uncertainty now. Yuan is dead, but the Republic was already lost. It seems that throughout the country, men of cunning, not culture, men of arms, not virtue, triumph. Thus, *luan*. North against South, East against West, leader against leader, interest against interest, generation against generation.

So ever more fervently do I wish a happy new year to all,

Your uncle

First Day of the first moon
Year of the Snake, 1917

Eldest Uncle:

My mother-in-law is gravely ill. I have left my teaching post to be with her day and night. It is a hard death, and I fear there is a painful journey ahead.

A happy new year to all,
Your niece

⊸§ 24 §⊸
Rightful Name

*The blind storytellers know thousands of tales and upon hearing
them the people often weep, for the strains of the pi-pa they
play are so sweet and the virtuous lives they praise are so upright.*

*One story tells of four who fled the scourge of the Barbarians
from the north. Soon the son and the nephew were too weak
to walk. The father could carry only one and asked the mother
to choose who should be left behind.*

*The virtuous mother said, "Let it be our son. We can have
another. But your brother is dead, and his only son must live
to feed his spirit in the other world."*

—Chinese tale

THE LAST LEAVES were falling from the trees like drowsy butterflies
when Lotus Delight became ill. From that day Spring Moon waited
on her mother-in-law, busying herself with chores, feeling more
useful when there was something, however unpleasant or trivial,
to be done. Each suggested remedy was pursued until the bedroom
was cluttered with bottles and pillboxes.

Nothing else was as effective as opium. Spring Moon learned
where to buy its purest form, how to twirl the pellet with a needle
above the flame, and when it was ready to insert into the pipe.
She performed this ritual at all hours, day after day, whenever
Lotus Delight nodded toward the tray where the implements were
kept. Only when the sweet odor had completely saturated the

oom would the daughter-in-law excuse herself to go outdoors
or fresh air.

Often while under the spell of the drug, Lotus Delight talked,
ecalling snatches of dreams and souvenirs of the past. At other
imes, Spring Moon filled the uneasy silence by reading from the
Dream of the Red Chamber or the *Book of Odes* or the Sutras. By the
nd of the Fortnight of Great Cold, she knew her mother-in-law
vould not live much longer. Through the months of her illness
he had wasted away until her chest was like a washboard and
ier hands and face were spotted black. The doctors had given
ip and came no more, lest she die in treatment and they be accused
if killing her.

Sometimes, Spring Moon wondered if death should not be hoped
or, wishing someone wiser were there to comfort them. She imag-
ned the bed emptied, its silk coverlet smooth, the dresses folded
ieatly in the wardrobe scented by the woman's perfume, a strand
if hair in a comb, a white film of mold beginning to stain the
:hoes. Nothing more, for the greedy earth would claim the rest.
The walls of the room were damp with dying.

She tried to recall the time when no one she knew had died,
when life was without limit and mortality but a word, when Grand-
'ather had coaxed his bird to sing for her in the garden and nothing
vas sadder than the sound of the rain that splattered the courtyards,
ending games.

Now thirty-five, she was seized with the idea that she was at
he midpoint of her life, as far from its beginning as its end. Soon,
with the death of Lotus Delight, she would have fulfilled her tradi-
ional responsibilities as wife and daughter-in-law. What then?
Golden Virtue had asked that she return to Soochow. Was that
where she belonged, with the widows? But then, what fate for
Lustrous Jade? It seemed unlikely that her daughter would stay
with the women for long. She would have her own plans. "Mother,
I would like to study in America, just like my cousins," she wrote.
"Mother, I shall be a doctor, for who can do more to heal mankind?"
Yes, Spring Moon had answered, but was it truly a suitable calling
for a young woman? "Mother," the reply came forthwith, "there
are no differences between men and women, not in the minds of

the truly enlightened. Did you not hear of the brigade of golden lilies who stormed Nanking during the outbreak of the revolution? The Manchu soldiers laughed, but fell before them just the same!' Spring Moon had not pursued the subject. Last year her daughter had wanted to be a scientist, the year before, a teacher.

One evening, when the wind wailed like an old woman in mourning as it swept the rooftops and hutungs of the Northern Capital, Lotus Delight, after many pipes, motioned for Spring Moon to come closer. "Daughter," the dying woman whispered hoarsely, "Daughter, bring me the boy."

She is delirious, Spring Moon thought, just as Fierce Rectitude was at the end. "There, Por Por, there," she said softly. From the bedside table she took the tarragon salve and gently moistened the parched lips.

Lotus Delight pushed her hand away but then reached for it and held it fast. "Listen to me, listen. . . ."

"Yes, Por Por, I am here." Spring Moon was alert now. Afraid. There was an urgency in her mother-in-law's voice quite apart from pain. Was it time? She bent closer. "I am here."

The woman's eyes were now opened wide. The effort she made to keep them from closing again seemed immeasurable, contrary to nature. Her breathing quickened. "Daughter?"

"Yes, Por Por."

"Daughter, go. Bring me the boy."

"Yes, of course. Of course." What madness was this? Was she young again and calling for her son?

"Your boy," she whispered. "Your boy."

Still Spring Moon dared not hope, dismissing the impossible. But Lotus Delight commanded her.

"Bring him home so that he may feed my spirit in the next world. He will be my adopted son. Say nothing more."

Spring Moon slipped to her knees, forcing back tears. She kowtowed. "Por Por, can you forgive me? Can you ever forgive me?"

Lotus Delight gave no answer, merely whispering, "Go quickly. I must see him before I die."

"Yes, Por Por, you shall see him."

There was no response, except that now the lids fell. Lotus Delight was asleep.

In the morning, the wind still had not subsided, but Spring Moon could not postpone the trip one day. She ordered clothing to be bought for a small boy, the windows sealed, and the sickroom attended without fail in her absence. Then, with her head covered and her trousers tied, she set off on her journey. It was dark when she entered the village where she had given birth to a son.

She did not say why she had come. They knew it the moment they unlatched the door. The boy was already asleep. She would wait until morning to see him. They sat and drank a cup of tea before retiring.

The boy in the red flowered shirt and green pants stood in the doorway of his home. Beside him, his mama and papa, who had always left a warm space for him to sleep between them; before him the cart and the beautiful stranger who called herself Sao Sao, Elder Sister-in-law. Eyes wide, he stared at her, biting his lips.

"Go, Little Treasure, we have fed you long enough. Go with Sao Sao where you belong!" Mama's voice was unnaturally shrill. When the boy did not move, she scolded. "What, will you shame me, boy? Have we not taught you manners? Behave and obey your elders. Go, Stupid One." She gave him a shove. "Go, we have had enough of you!"

Little Treasure looked up at the farmer. Papa's face was full of sorrow, but when he spoke his words held the same meaning as his mama's. "Go now, boy. Go!"

Papa never had much to say. What he said was always so. The boy turned and walked and then ran to the cart. He clambered in. The lady followed. "Please, driver, we can go now," she said.

As the springless cart lurched into motion, jerking along the ruts of the old road, Spring Moon, for the first time since he was a newborn, touched her son, pulling him to her. She stared ahead, striving for composure, ignoring the curious stares of the villagers, who stood motionless except to wipe the dust from their eyes. Only when the mule turned toward the canal where the boat was waiting did Spring Moon glance back. Dummy must have gone inside the house, for Non Stop stood alone in the doorway, staring after the cart. In the palm of his hand was the leather purse, on his face a look as desolate as the hard cracked fields of winter.

She fixed her eyes on the boy again, taming his cowlick with her hand. The gold coins would buy Brother Hua another son, many sons. This child was hers: her flesh, her blood. He was meant for a better life than theirs. A life of learning, not toil.

Throughout the journey to Peking, Little Treasure never spoke and Spring Moon respected his silence, allowing him time to grieve. They reached her mother-in-law's house at nightfall.

The two servants greeted them at the door, craning to get a good look at the strange boy. Spring Moon waved them away.

Food had been set out for the travelers, but neither ate.

She ordered a tub of warm water, and the child allowed her to bathe him. He stood in the water, letting himself be turned like a wooden doll, arms lifted, feet soaped, always his eyes on her face. Naked, shivering from the cold, he looked as vulnerable as he had been when she tore off his swaddling clothes. His back was straight, his knees knobby, his clear, ivory skin colored earth brown wherever the sun had touched. Scrubbing his legs, she noticed that the blue birthmark, where tradition said the City Magistrate of the other world had kicked the reluctant baby's bottom to send him into this one, was now gone without a trace.

She dried him in a large towel, putting her arms around him without attempting tenderness. He needs time, she thought, proud that her son was loyal. There was no reason to hurry, now that his name was Woo.

Once the boy was dressed in the quilted inner garment that had been laid out, she gently put him to bed in the alcove outside her room.

Was he frightened of the dark?

She did not know, and after turning down the wick until the

flame barely flickered, she retreated silently to her mother-in-law's room. Lotus Delight was asleep, but the sleep was not restful. Now and then, she snapped her head as if to say no. After a while, Spring Moon nodded to the servant on duty and retired to her quarters.

It had been a long journey, but sleep would not come. She lay awake watching the passage of the moonlight across the walls of the room, remembering Dummy: the terrified peasant girl huddled in the rain barrel. The beautiful young woman who was there, holding her hand, when each child was born. Most vividly the anguished cry of mourning for the family that had been taken.

"Oh, my heart! Oh, my liver! Why have you gone from me?"

Soon after the watchman had passed, intoning the hour of the rat, there was a noise. She turned to look at the door. A small shadow darted to her bed. "Sao Sao." The boy's voice quivered. "Are you asleep? At ho—at the village, I did not sleep alone."

Of course. There were no braziers in Learned Cinders, and it was always cold. She flipped open her quilt. "Come then, Little Treasure, there is room for you in my bed."

They slept late, and when she dressed him in the morning, she smiled shyly, pleased to be able to put on so many layers, until he was warm. For a moment she thought he returned her smile, but when she showed him the new shoes, he shook his head and padded into the alcove. Upon his return, he was wearing the tiger shoes he had worn in Learned Cinders.

Together, they ate a hearty breakfast of pancakes and pork. When they were done, Spring Moon took his hand and said, "Little Treasure, I know you are a good boy, for inside there is a hollow no bowls of rice can fill. Is that not so?"

Tears welled in his eyes. He nodded.

She took a deep breath and continued. "That is as it should be. You must talk to me of the people you know and the places you miss. It will help you. It will help me. Promise?"

"Yes, Sao Sao."

How strange the name he calls me sounds, she thought. Yet it was fine, for only he would ever call her by it. "Little Treasure, was there something in Learned Cinders that you had to do every day?"

"Oh, yes!" he said, nodding. "I gathered sticks for the fire. I swept the yard. I fed the pig—"

"Here, too, you will have something to do. It is more important than the tasks you have had. It is very difficult. Not many boys your age could do it." She paused as if waiting for a sign that he understood.

He looked puzzled but not frightened.

"Little Treasure, I think you can do this task that I give you. Will you tell me that you will try?"

"Yes. Yes, I want to try." His eagerness invited her, yet she must not embrace him. He was not ready.

She sat very straight. "Good. In a few minutes, I am going to take you to see your True Mother. She will be in bed. She is very sick, and her face is all bones. But you must not show it if you are afraid."

"Will you be there, Sao Sao?"

"Yes. Right beside you." She smiled. "When we enter you must kowtow three times and call her by her rightful name, which is True Mother, and announce that you are a son of the House of Woo. Can you remember?"

He nodded. "Yes." He nodded again, firmly. "Yes. She is my True Mother and I am a son of the House of Woo."

"Your mother may speak to you; if she does, you must do what she says. It will make her very happy at a very unhappy time."

"Is she going to die?"

"Yes."

The boy chewed his lips, his brow furrowed. "Will you hold my hand?"

She shook her head. "No. But I will be right beside you."

"Can I do it tomorrow?" he asked hopefully.

"No. You must do it now."

The two maidservants had prepared the room. The medicines were hidden, the smells masked with incense, and the dying woman propped up so that she appeared to be sitting. Her face was powdered, her cheeks and lips rouged. A perfect willow-leaf brow had been drawn over each eye and a turban hid her matted hair. Drooping from her ears, a pair of jade pendants made her face seem longer than it was. Her ringed fingers, withered and wrinkled like the claws of an old rooster, rested on top of her quilt.

When the door opened, the servants slipped out, wiping away their tears with their sleeves. Together Spring Moon and Little Treasure walked toward the bed. "Por Por, your son has come."

Lotus Delight lifted a hand.

At once, the boy fell to his knees and kowtowed, then scrambled to his feet and said, "True Mother, I am Woo, your son."

Opening her mouth slowly, as if it took all the strength she had, Lotus Delight whispered, "Son . . . good."

Little Treasure looked at Spring Moon, as if to ask what he was supposed to do next. Lotus Delight spoke again. "Come . . . take my . . . hand."

The boy obeyed. A tear crept down the dying woman's cheeks, drawing a sallow line in the powder.

That night, Lotus Delight died.

For three days and three nights, Spring Moon, the boy, and the servants wailed beside the coffin, and when it was sealed, they returned often to the room to pay their respects, waiting until spring for the journey to Reed Village.

Meanwhile, mother and son were never apart. She told him stories of the House of Woo—of his father, the Hanlin of the Forest of Pencils, and his brother Glad Promise, who traveled across the seas, and his mother Lotus Delight, who was once known as the Beauty of the Northern Capital. In return, he told her about his old home—about sleeping with the piglets when the canal froze, about Mama, who had sewn the tiger faces on the toes of his shoes, about Papa, who was strong and could carry him on his shoulders to the next town. Spring Moon recounted the adventures of the Monkey King who voyaged to the West. The child sang for her the songs of Learned Cinders. He kicked a shuttlecock, and together they played marbles and hide-and-seek. He laughed when she could not find him hiding behind a door, and laughed again when he found her easily.

He was very quick. It was not long before he no longer spoke the harsh, guttural dialect of Shantung but Mandarin, with a trace of the softer Soochow tones, imitating her. By the time of the funeral journey to Reed Village, he had learned thirty characters and never tired of grinding the inkstick upon the inkstone and tracing the words in the squares she drew on paper.

At the village of the Hanlin, the son performed the rites with deep solemnity. On the Day of Pure Brightness, he swept the graves and placed the offerings and kowtowed to the ancestors of the House of Woo as if he had been born to these duties. According to custom, he and Spring Moon then picnicked among the dead, so that the ancestors were associated also with happy times and the offerings were not wasted.

As expected, when the rites were completed the Patriarch of the Woo clan offered them a home in Reed Village, most graciously. As expected, Spring Moon declined, most regretfully.

She and Little Treasure returned to Peking. There she settled her mother-in-law's affairs, wrote Bold Talent that she would return for Lustrous Jade's graduation with the Hanlin's adopted boy, sold the furniture, packed, returned the key to the landlord, and dismissed the servants.

When they boarded the train for Shanghai on the ninth day of the fifth moon, Little Treasure had put away his tiger shoes and wore the new ones of leather.

As the train sped south, Little Treasure became increasingly excited, Spring Moon anxious. He could not take his eyes from the window, she her eyes from him. Neither spoke much.

How perverse the gods, she thought. They change yearning to dread and back again, as certainly as the seasons return, different as the years must be. Once again she was aboard a train with her child. As before, and yet not at all as before. Once again the child knew no father. Once again, she and Bold Talent would meet in Shanghai. His letters still invoked the past, a past she had put away like leaves gathered in autumn long ago and pressed between the pages of a book. Now she was coming back and he was waiting. Now the boy was more precious to her. What his father and she had known together could live only in him.

Deliberately she did not dwell upon her reunion with Lustrous Jade, telling herself it would be a most joyous one. How could it be otherwise? Mother and daughter together after so many years. And yet sometimes, watching Little Treasure, she wondered. Now that she was coming back, would her daughter be waiting? Or had their bond been packed away like the boy's tiger shoes?

When the trip was almost over, he turned to her. "Sao Sao, will everyone in Shanghai and Soochow call me by my milk name? Do you not think Little Treasure is a silly name for a boy who can read?"

"So that is what you have been thinking about all this way!" She smoothed down his cowlick. "Perhaps it *is* time for you to have a school name."

"What will it be?"

"I have been thinking about it too. It must have one character in common with the name of your elder brother, Glad Promise. As for the other . . . do you think you would like to be called Enduring Promise?"

The boy nodded. In a few minutes she had taught him how to write the characters, and for the rest of the journey he practiced them until he drew them perfectly. Every now and then he would look up at her and smile. His smile was her smile, his eyes Bold Talent's. Merciful Kwan Yin, she prayed, do not let him see.

In the crowded Shanghai station, Enduring Promise bobbed up and down, eyeing all who passed beneath the clock, where it had been agreed they were to wait. Spring Moon was no less impatient, holding fast to his hand, searching this way and that for Bold Talent and Lustrous Jade, describing them to the child. She saw no familiar face.

Just when she was about to inquire if there might be another clock elsewhere, a dapper young man in a white linen suit approached. He was flanked by two tall foreigners, magnificent in dark green uniforms and caps encrusted with gold braid—clearly a man of consequence. He bowed. "Welcome, Auntie."

Spring Moon's astonishment must have showed, for he laughed gleefully. "Auntie, it is I, August Winds."

What had happened to the chubby youth who seldom paid attention in class? The man who stood before her was not tall, but he was slim. His dress was impeccable, his gold watch chain as thick as Shanghai noodles. "August Winds, you have changed!"

"Do you really think so?" He laughed again, as at some secret. His dimpled smile was so infectious that Spring Moon found herself laughing, too, and did not notice until much later that his features were not remarkable at all.

Enduring Promise tugged at her sleeve. "Sao Sao, are they generals?" He was staring at the two foreigners.

August Winds looked most pleased. "Could be. Could be. For who can really know what any of the White Russians are?" He bent down until the tip of his nose was level with the boy's. "But I know exactly who you are. You are Little Treasure!"

"No, I have a school name." Puffing out his chest, he proclaimed, "I am Enduring Promise!"

"Indeed! What a fine name for my uncle!"

"No, no," the child insisted. "It is *my* name."

"Yes, I know. But you are also"—August Winds bowed even lower—"my esteemed uncle"—he bowed again—"my honorable uncle."

"Am I, Sao Sao, am I?" Enduring Promise clapped his hands with delight.

Spring Moon nodded, but her mind was suddenly far from their little game, and when August Winds straightened, she asked, "Where is Eldest Uncle? Where is Lustrous Jade?"

"He sends his apologies," August Winds replied. "He was called away at the last moment and asked me to meet you. I tried to persuade the school to allow Lustrous Jade to come with me, but the missionaries were most suspicious and thought it best that your reunion take place tomorrow at graduation." He shrugged, his eyes twinkling. "Perhaps . . ."

Spring Moon thought, Yes, tomorrow will be much better. And denied the thought at once.

". . . my fault." August Winds' voice claimed her attention again. "I told them I was her uncle too. They obviously did not believe me. Somehow I am cursed. It seems that no one ever believes me!" The pride in his voice betrayed him, and she could not help smiling to herself. The man was very much the boy after all.

But just as she had recognized him, he changed again, taking charge, sending one of his men to get the luggage and the other to fetch the automobile, graciously leading the way through the crowds, chatting all the while about how wonderful it was to see his teacher again. When they had passed through the main doorway to the street, he stopped.

"What is it, August Winds?" she asked.

He waved a diffident hand at a long, elegant chariot that gleamed like the surface of a lake at sunset. "Behold! My Pierce Arrow!"

Enduring Promise dropped her hand and ran to touch the splendid sight as if he could not quite believe it real. Satisfied, he grinned and turned to study the chauffeur, who stood by the opened door. "Look, Sao Sao, there are six of me!" He pointed to the six shining buttons on the coat. Before she could say anything, the bodyguard appeared. Together the two Russians lifted the boy into the air, conveying him to a seat in front. August Winds and Spring Moon followed his laughter inside.

Seated, Spring Moon shook her head, smiling to herself. August Winds nodded as if reading her thoughts. "Auntie, I cannot believe it either. But it is mine, truly it is!"

The bodyguard dashed to the crank at the front of the car. The Pierce Arrow shivered. In no time, they were moving. As the bodyguard leaped to the running board and folded himself into the seat beside Enduring Promise, the chauffeur honked the horn at the crowd of admirers. The sound startled the boy and he twisted around toward Spring Moon. But the chauffeur chuckled and took his hand and let him squeeze the bulb. *Honk! Honk!* The crowd scattered. Enduring Promise beamed, an emperor riding the fiercest dragon.

Along the route, August Winds pointed out the places of interest: his favorite restaurant, his watchmaker's, his tea shop, his tailor. Filling silences, banishing thought.

During dinner, he amused them with stories but immediately after the meal excused himself. "An urgent business matter!"

Spring Moon wished he could have stayed and distracted her,

for the house on Bubbling Well Road was as she remembered. Only the servants had been changed.

Enduring Promise was sleepy, but he would have to wait until Bold Talent came home. She must not be alone with him, not at first.

It was the hour of the dog when a carriage came to a halt outside. Spring Moon gently shook the boy, who was sleeping beside her in the chair. "Wake up, Little Brother," she whispered. "He is coming." Enduring Promise opened his eyes and closed them again. "No, you must wake up!" She shook him again.

"Spring Moon?" She rose. He stood at the threshold. She lowered her eyes, then looked at him again. He looks older, she thought. Or perhaps it is only that I have not seen him age.

He opened his arms and started to come toward her, then stopped, for she had raised a palm and stepped aside, revealing the boy. "Little Brother, stand up!" The child scrambled to his feet and, clinging to her skirt, rubbed the sleep from his eyes.

She felt Bold Talent's gaze, as tangible as an embrace. Quickly she maneuvered Enduring Promise between them and stood with her hands on his shoulders.

"Spring Moon?" he asked again.

She dared not speak. What could she say? He must understand. Each waited for the other to end the silence.

At last, the boy spoke. "Sao Sao, is the honorable gentleman our grandfather?"

Between tears and laughter, she could only shake her head, looking down at his son.

Bold Talent gave a rueful laugh and motioned for Enduring Promise to come closer. The child looked up at Spring Moon, wondering if he should. She nodded, tried to speak and could not, then gently pushed him away from her.

Taking the child by the hand, Bold Talent led him to the wing chair, where he seated himself with his usual grace, saving a place for the boy by his knee. Enduring Promise clambered up and sat solemnly, the toes of his new shoes pointing straight up.

"Who are you, sir?" he asked in his most courteous voice, looking up into his elder's face.

Bold Talent nodded, but said nothing, as if he had not heard the question. The boy kindly reminded him of it. Then, "I am certainly old enough to be your grandfather," he said gently. "But I am your Sao Sao's uncle, and therefore your uncle too."

The child frowned. "But Sao Sao told me that you had black hair."

Bold Talent stole a glance at Spring Moon. "Perhaps she meant your other uncle. . . ." His voice trailed off.

"Yes! That is exactly who I meant," she hastened to explain.

Satisfied, the child tugged at Bold Talent's sleeve. "Uncle, my name is Enduring Promise," he said proudly.

"But that is the name of a scholar! I would not think such a little boy could write the characters of a grand name like Enduring Promise."

"But I can! I can!" the boy cried delightedly. He seized Bold Talent's arm, pried open his hand, and, using his index finger, drew the various strokes.

"Who was your teacher?"

"Sao Sao!"

"Did Sao Sao tell you who taught her?"

Enduring Promise did not seem to hear. He was busy making the strokes and calling out the name of each of the characters he knew. "House! Horse! Sky!"

As they sat side by side before her, it seemed obvious to Spring Moon that man and boy were father and son. The high forehead and intent eyes, the gestures were transparently alike. During pauses in their conversation, each looked toward her, his head slightly cocked to one side. Surely Bold Talent would see it. He must. He must not. How could she have been so foolish as to think that they could meet and be strangers?

When the last dot of the character "write" was made, man and boy both laughed and looked to her for approval.

"Uncle, now write your honorable name for me, please," the boy demanded, thrusting his small palm forward.

"But I cannot." Bold Talent hung his head as if ashamed.

The child blushed. He had caused an elder to lose face by forcing him to reveal that he could not read or write.

"No, I cannot," repeated Bold Talent, shaking his head. Looking toward Spring Moon, he paused ever so slightly, then broke into a smile. She tried to return it, but could not and lowered her eyes. He does not see, she thought, he does not know, and wondered why she felt so alone.

Suddenly, Bold Talent laughed. "Enduring Promise, do not be embarrassed," he said. "I was only teasing you. I can write, but not on your tiny scrap of a palm. With one dash and a hook, it would be filled."

Once more he glanced at Spring Moon, his eyes veiled now, concealing pain. When she did not respond, he turned again to the boy. "Come with me," he said. "Come with me to the library and I shall teach you to write like a true calligrapher. You must practice at least once a day. . . ."

Spring Moon watched as they walked hand in hand into the next room, the man leaning down toward the child.

Slowly she followed them and sat in the chair farthest from the writing table to watch. Bold Talent busied himself with preparing the lesson. Only once did their eyes meet, when he removed the worry beads from his pocket and laid them aside on the table.

Yes, his temples were gray now and there were lines around his eyes. He looks his age, she thought suddenly: sixty-two. So many years had gone.

He twirled the hairs of the brush and showed the boy how to grind the ink, nodding at his progress.

Her eyes did not leave them. The father. The son. They were oblivious to her. She rose and started to join them but stopped when she saw that they were whispering to one another.

She cleared her throat. "I will tell the servants you are here. . . ."

The man and the boy burst into laughter.

She fled from the room.

While the table was being prepared, Spring Moon put the child to bed and then joined Bold Talent in the dining room.

"Will you not eat something, my niece?"

"No, we had dinner earlier with August Winds."

He was looking directly at her, yet did not seem to realize that she had answered his question, for he repeated it.

When she had answered the second time, he looked quickly away and asked another. "What do you think of our orphan boy?"

For a moment, she thought he was talking about Enduring Promise; then, blushing, she laughed. "August Winds tells so many tales, one more outlandish than the next, that it becomes impossible to think of him as anything but a rogue, yet . . ."

"Yes, I agree." He finished the sentence for her. "No one has a bigger heart."

There was a silence. Bold Talent absently picked the bones out of the fish.

Finally, Spring Moon asked, "How is my aunt?"

"My wife is well. She looks forward to having you in Soochow again."

"And I look forward to seeing her."

"You are such good friends." He looked at her. "One would not have thought it likely."

"Why? She is the kindest person I know."

"And the most understanding."

"Yes, the most understanding."

Another silence. Spring Moon poured herself a cup of tea and sipped it. The clock on the wall ticked loudly, and yet time did not seem to pass. The floorboards groaned with each step of the old servant who cleared the table. They watched him come and go, come and go, until only the tea service remained.

When they were alone again, both suddenly spoke at once and then gave way to the other. Neither could remember the interrupted thought. Finally, Spring Moon asked, "Where is Young Uncle now?"

"He is back with Sun, trying to establish Canton as a second capital."

"Will they succeed?"

"I do not think so, not as long as the foreigners continue to recognize Peking. I am not even certain that my brother thinks so anymore. He continues because he has nothing else."

She nodded.

Bold Talent cleared his throat and said, very softly, "You, at least, have not changed."

"But I have, my uncle."

"Not to me, not to me."

She reached out to touch him. His hand was trembling, and he quickly withdrew it from the table.

The father followed the muffled cries down the moonlit hall to the chamber of his son.

Enduring Promise was buried under the coverlet, shivering.

Why do children cry in the night? Bold Talent tried to remember. He asked softly, "What is the matter? Do not cry! Was it a bad dream?"

The child shook his head. Slowly the tears fell, like brave soldiers marching before the king.

"Was it a ghost?"

"I . . . " His words burst forth. "I do not want to die, I do not want to die like True Mother. Why do I have to die?"

Bold Talent put his arms around him, comforting him. "You see, if no one ever died, the world would be a terrible place. There would be too many people, no room to grow food or play. So it is better to have a season and live each minute until it is time to join our ancestors."

The boy nodded. "Tell me, what will death be like?"

"Do you remember what it was like before you were born?"

He shook his head.

"Did you feel anything bad?"

"No."

"Were you frightened?"

"No."

"I think that is what death will be like."

"Are you sure?"

"Yes. Now lie back and I will sit here until you are asleep."

JADE
PHOENIX

◆§ 25 §◆

The Graduation

In the time of the Liang Dynasty, there lived a loyal soldier, his good wife, and their most filial daughter, Mu Lan.

One day, the man fell gravely ill. Soon thereafter came an Imperial summons to war.

"Prepare my horse," the father said, but he could barely stand.

"How can you ride, my husband?"

"I shall! I must!" the soldier vowed, then fainted away.

To preserve honor, Mu Lan donned her father's garb and rode off to war in his stead.

For twelve years, she led men into battle. Never once did the general betray her sex.

—Chinese history

"SIX YEARS AGO, we left the courtyards of our ancestors and entered these halls of learning. Today, we step forth into the world to do God's work. . . ."

Spring Moon sat with August Winds, Enduring Promise, and Bold Talent in the third row of the chapel, barely listening while her daughter delivered the speech called a "valedictory."

Valedictory. She repeated the word, smiling to herself. She had not known it until today, until she saw it in the program, and beside it "Margaret Woo," the name the missionaries had given to her daughter. The honor did not surprise her. After all, the girl was descended from two houses of Senior Wranglers.

Fleetingly she thought of Sterling Talent, saw him vividly as he had always been, seated at his desk, open book in hand. Let Father be comforted, she prayed, that scholarship lives on in his descendants.

Lustrous Jade's voice rose, and Spring Moon looked again toward the platform, at the stranger who was her daughter.

". . . We shall not compromise with illiteracy. We shall not compromise with corruption. We shall not . . ."

She tried to concentrate on the English words but could not. The pride she felt in her daughter's achievements was overtaken by the embarrassment of seeing Lustrous Jade exhort her elders. Her gestures were so extravagant, like those of operatic warriors, and her tone so inhospitable. Spring Moon almost wished that the valedictory were over.

Even before the speech had begun, when all the graduates sat on the small stage side by side, all dressed in long black skirts and white overblouses, their big feet bigger in high-buttoned shoes, her daughter had stood out. She had, of course, her father's look of the North, of sculpted strength quite unlike the delicate almond faces of her classmates. Yet there was something else, something that had not been evident in any of the pictures she had sent during the years of their separation, something . . .

She let her eyes wander over the figures on the platform. The other graduates, she thought suddenly, despite their western dress, were not so different from the cousins in the courts. She could imagine them huddled together after the ceremony gossiping, assigning to their schoolmates the appropriate rank of pulchritude. The priest, too, was not unfamiliar. Except for his round eyes, he reminded her of Gifted Seer; indeed, she had half expected a mynah bird to appear on his shoulder when he first bowed his head to welcome them.

Her gaze passed from him to the missionary women who sat together beside him on the platform. One by one she studied them, these women to whom she had entrusted her daughter, who now commanded Lustrous Jade's allegiance. They did not resemble one another, even though they dressed alike in black and wore their hair of different colors swept up in identical puffs on top of their heads. But they shared something, something that made them seem very *like* one another, very like . . . Her eyes returned to Lustrous Jade. She finished her thought. Like Lustrous Jade.

A clatter startled her, and she glanced down. Enduring Promise had dropped the tiny car that August Winds had given him that morning. She flushed, hoping no one else had noticed. Perhaps she should have left him with the servants. No one else had brought a child so young. It was probably not done. The boy tugged at August Winds' sleeve, but the young man seemed mesmerized by the words of Lustrous Jade, and it was Bold Talent who retrieved the car and pocketed it, handing the boy his handkerchief to play with.

Their eyes met. For a moment they were no longer at this strange graduation but at her Maiden's Feast, almost twenty years ago. He looked so solemn. She was so young. Slowly they raised their wine cups.

"I drink to your happiness, daughter of my brother."

"I drink to yours, my uncle. . . ."

Just as suddenly, she found herself again in the huge rectangular space, with its endless pews of people who sat very still, listening. The great glass windows, the walls of unadorned white, the cross that seemed about to fall: it was so different from the temples she had known, where shadowed corners invited secret intimacy and magic. Had she been shown this room when she first brought Lustrous Jade to the school? She could not remember it; indeed, could not remember anything of that earlier visit. Seeing the school now, she thought she must not truly have seen it then—the high hedges, the straight paths, the huge buildings with many layered rooms under one roof that thrust themselves up into the sky instead of curving gracefully to meet the heavens. All unbending, as if built to challenge the elements, to confront nature, to separate rather than to harmonize. If she had seen it then, she could not have left Lustrous Jade.

" . . . And on behalf of my classmates, we thank you, our teachers, from the bottom of our hearts." Lustrous Jade stood tall, so very tall, and then bowed deeply.

August Winds led the applause, his efforts shaking the entire bench. Enduring Promise clapped too, copying him, until Spring

Moon, horrified at family lauding family, reached out to stop him. Again she caught Bold Talent's eye. He smiled and shook his head. Suddenly she smiled too. It was indeed difficult to restrain oneself when one's daughter was first in all.

Gradually, the applause ended and the Headmistress announced the presentation of diplomas.

As the girls, one by one, walked forward to receive their certificates and shake hands with their teachers, the applause broke out again. This time Spring Moon clapped too, for all the graduates.

When the last girl had resumed her place, the music from the organ sounded. The audience rose and burst into song. As she had on the first such occasion, at the beginning of the program, Spring Moon struggled to her feet, took the songbook from its niche in front of her, opened it, and stared blankly at the page. She caught very few of the words, something about Christian soldiers and the Cross of Jesus, going on before. August Winds, beside her, seemed to know the song well. His exuberant baritone soared in a most unlikely way, and she wondered for a moment where he had learned it before returning her attention to Lustrous Jade.

When the singing ended, she started to sit down, then rose again when she saw the others merely bow their heads.

The priest had stepped forward and was praying aloud. "... May the Lord bless thee and keep thee. ... Amen."

At last the formal ceremonies were over and the graduates were marching from the platform to greet their families, who stood in clusters along the aisles. Spring Moon waited for Lustrous Jade, watching her descend and come directly toward them. A moment later she was caught in an embrace. "Mother! How happy I am to see you." Spring Moon stood stiffly, her arms at her sides. Although others were displaying such intimate behavior in public, somehow she could not.

"My daughter," she said formally. "It has been a long time. Stand away, let me have a good look at you." For a moment their eyes met and the mother thought, my child, you are so grown up, so beautiful. She wanted to reach out, to put her hand upon her daughter's cheek. . . .

"Grandniece, it is good to see you again." Bold Talent's voice called her back.

"Granduncle," said Lustrous Jade, bowing.

"And I am Little Treasure," the boy shouted. "Sao Sao has written about me. No, I am Enduring Promise."

Laughing, Lustrous Jade stooped to give him a squeeze.

Only then did Spring Moon remember that August Winds waited. "Lustrous Jade, do you recognize our friend here?"

The girl shook her head tentatively, stealing a glance at the young man.

Before anyone could say a word, he stepped forward and offered his hand. Automatically, Lustrous Jade took it, then quickly let go, as if she realized that shaking hands with strange men was one foreign custom from which even the most westernized girl should refrain.

"Little Sister, I am August Winds!"

Lustrous Jade stared.

"Yes." He nodded. "Yes, I am August Winds. Remember?"

He smiled, and suddenly Lustrous Jade was laughing again.

"My brother," she said, and bowed.

"My sister."

There followed a tumult of greetings between Lustrous Jade and other guests and students, who congratulated her. Spring Moon nodded politely again and again but did not speak. Her daughter talked quickly, alternating between English and Chinese, introducing her friends and their relatives, the priest, her mathematics teacher. All of them seemed at home here. August Winds in his way was as deft as Lustrous Jade. Bold Talent had not forgotten the western forms he had learned. Even those women who spoke no English had come dressed in the slim sheaths that were now fashionable, and nodded and smiled as if they belonged.

"Shall we leave now, my daughter?" Spring Moon asked suddenly, during a lull. She wished to be among her own.

"Not yet. Not yet. There is tea in the garden, and I want you to meet Miss Clayton."

"If it is expected, then of course."

Lustrous Jade led the way, walking briskly alongside Bold Talent, matching his steps stride for stride, stopping now and then to shake hands or bow, to pay and receive compliments. It was August Winds who tarried behind with Spring Moon, picking up the boy for a ride on his shoulders, heedless alike of a disapproving stare from one of the older teachers and the possibility of a smudge on his white linen suit.

"No reason to hurry, Auntie. Let the big-footed ones go ahead. You and I will take our time."

She was touched that he had remembered her golden lilies.

The tea tables were set up in the badminton courts, which were surrounded by tall hedges. Each graduate played hostess at a table, pouring tea, passing the cucumber sandwiches cut in circles, the watercress in triangles.

After August Winds had seated Spring Moon, he took out his watch and put it down on the table in the adjacent place. Glancing at Enduring Promise, who had climbed into the chair next to Lustrous Jade, he slowly opened the lid. Suddenly, music escaped. Enduring Promise, his eyes big as a dragon's, climbed down from his seat and ran to the watch. Laughing, August Winds lifted him up so he could inspect it more closely, before slipping gracefully into the chair beside his childhood friend.

As Lustrous Jade poured tea, he paid her compliments, but she did not return his smiles. Spring Moon was relieved. At least in this one thing, it seemed, the little girl who once flaunted her preference for the chubby youth had grown up with proper modesty. But before long, Lustrous Jade was trying to recall the last time they had met. He insisted that they had seen each other the day she left the courts. She denied it, quite adamantly. He asked her if she remembered the New Year's when she had shocked the clan by sitting next to an orphan boy. She laughed and did not deny it, offering him the cucumber sandwiches.

Although August Winds stood barely as tall as Lustrous Jade, he seemed to have within his compact frame the energy and charm of several men, and there was an eagerness in his eyes that belied his casual manner, as if he had looked forward to this reunion for many years. Did he know her so well then, the mother wondered, despite the garden walls?

"What are your plans, Grandniece?" asked Bold Talent when everyone had been served.

"God's work." August Winds answered for her.

"God's work or not," said Spring Moon, "we are first going to Soochow. We need to have time together. . . ."

"Yes, Mother. Yes!"

"But you will return to Shanghai, will you not, Little Sister?" August Winds asked.

"I shall go where the Lord sends me."

"Ah, then it is certain. Shanghai is the city of sin. We sinners have need of thee." He winked, holding out his cup for a refill. But Lustrous Jade had turned away, her attention caught by a tall woman with hair the color of roosters who was coming toward their table. She walked mannishly, as did Lustrous Jade and the others with big feet. "Oh, Mother, it is Miss Clayton." For the first time, Lustrous Jade seemed unsure of herself. "You will like her. She has been like a . . . an auntie to me."

As Miss Clayton drew near, Spring Moon saw a lined face with a prominent nose, but it was the intelligent blue eyes that dominated. After the introductions were made, the missionary took the empty seat at the table and, speaking to no one in particular, said, "We are very fond of our Margaret!"

"Margaret?" asked August Winds, and then, laughing, "Of course, you mean my sister, Lustrous Jade."

Miss Clayton nodded. "Chinese names are so difficult. One or two would be manageable, but we have a hundred girls. For the young teachers, especially, memorizing a hundred Chinese names would be much too difficult."

"It is most understandable," offered Spring Moon politely, unable to suppress the idea that Lustrous Jade had managed to learn enough English to give an entire speech in that language. She herself had mastered . . . but Miss Clayton was speaking again.

"Yes, Margaret has surpassed all our expectations. We are most proud of her, most proud. She will be a shining example to Chinese women of what can be accomplished with schooling."

Spring Moon lowered her eyes, uneasy. A foreigner was boasting of her daughter. Was such praise the custom among foreigners?

"Are you not pleased with all she has accomplished in these six years, Mrs. Woo?"

"All *you* have accomplished, honorable teacher, for my backward daughter!" Spring Moon blurted.

Before Miss Clayton could respond, August Winds drew the teacher's attention, complimenting her on the ceremonies, cleverly turning the conversation to other subjects.

"Where is your old home, Miss Clayton?" he asked.

"Philadelphia."

"Wonderful place, just wonderful!" He nodded approvingly. "When did you pay your visit?"

"Never. But I think of Philadelphia rather as I think of Heaven—one need not go there to know that it is a fine place."

Momentarily speechless, the missionary offered an uncertain smile. August Winds did not seem to notice, going on to tell a story he had heard while cruising on a pleasure boat for his health.

"Were you sick?" asked Lustrous Jade.

"Ah, Sister, I see that you are concerned. You need not be. My voyage, like herbal medicine, was preventive. Why should one wait until one is sick to enjoy such a trip?"

There followed discussions of the merits of western and eastern medicine, the YWCA in China, and the rise of banditry. As Miss Clayton, August Winds, and Lustrous Jade chatted, the hour slowly passed. Spring Moon was silent, watching the shadows cast by the tall hedges fall across the table like a somber cloth. Bold Talent, too, said little, although he listened closely when the talk turned at last to politics. The child, by then sitting in his lap, had nodded off, and many tables were empty.

"What do you think, Mr. Chang?" Miss Clayton asked. "Will China join America and the Allies in this war?"

He nodded thoughtfully, pausing a while before he spoke. "I think Peking is on the brink of announcing its decision to join. If it were up to me, I would keep China neutral."

Lustrous Jade broke the silence which followed. "Why, Granduncle? Why are you opposed to China's entry?"

If Bold Talent was surprised by her forward manner, he did not show it, answering her quietly. "Because China has no special grievance against Germany, my niece, and Peking plans to join only to receive additional arms and loans from the Allies. I do not think our poor country can afford much more of the Allies' generosity." He shook his head.

"Perhaps," said Miss Clayton, "if China joins the Allies, she can partake later of the fruits of victory. Otherwise, she will have no say in the world of the future."

To Spring Moon's horror, her daughter spoke up again. "I think China should join in the fight. President Wilson has said that the world must be made safe for democracy. China would have everything to gain from such a principle. Can you deny that, Granduncle?"

Again Bold Talent answered as if he had not noticed her rudeness. "Principles have a way of yielding to power. Yuan Shih-k'ai once promised to uphold Republican principles—"

"But, Granduncle, President Wilson is not Yuan!"

Spring Moon cleared her throat, hoping to get her daughter's attention and put a stop to her insolence, although Bold Talent still did not seem to be offended. "Grandniece," he said gently, "he is only a man."

"He is a Christian."

At that, Spring Moon spoke—in Chinese. "How dare my daughter think herself equal to the Patriarch?"

To which her daughter replied in English, "Mother, everyone has a right to his opinions."

Had she no shame? Spring Moon spoke again in Chinese. "I forbid you to utter another word in that manner. Has it not occurred to you that the German King is also a Jesus Worshiper?"

There was an uncomfortable silence. So be it, thought Spring Moon. Elders were elders, even at a graduation.

August Winds recovered first. Clapping his hands together, he said with a burst of good cheer, "Ah, let me translate. You see, Miss Clayton, you are such a good friend that we forgot you do not speak our language. My honorable auntie was just saying how much tastier the round sandwiches were. But my young sister begged to differ, evidently preferring the triangular ones. As for me, I agree with my dear departed friend: 'De gustibus non disputandum est.' "

All thought what he said, whatever it meant, hilarious. Recovering from laughter, they bid Miss Clayton farewell and slowly made their way together to the main gates of the school. Lustrous Jade and August Winds each held a hand of the child.

As they passed the chapel steps, Bold Talent turned to Spring Moon and said softly, so that no one else could hear, "Her father would have been pleased today, of that I am sure."

"Her mother . . . " She paused, remembering. Then, slowly, she smiled. "Her mother as well," she said.

When they reached the gate and the Pierce Arrow, the child, suddenly wide awake, pulled on Lustrous Jade's hand. "Come, Niece, come and see!"

But Lustrous Jade had turned once more toward the foreign buildings. For a moment she stood there, very straight, very still, looking back. In her daughter's eyes, Spring Moon thought, were tears.

❧ 26 ❧
Gifts

Not so very long ago, in the province of Kiangsu, an orphan youth decided to seek his fortune and departed the house of his benefactors.

In Chinkiang, where the Grand Canal and the Yangtze River intersect, he listened to the talk in the teahouses, losing at cards on purpose, so that he would be welcome at any table. Thus he learned the name of the compradore who had made the most money in the shortest time with the least capital.

Joining that great man's game at the Drunken Whiskers Teahouse, the orphan hinted that he was, in fact, the delinquent heir of an important clan, and lost again. Unable to redeem his markers, he offered himself as an unpaid assistant, and the compradore, with nothing to lose and the patronage of a powerful clan to gain, accepted. The orphan learned sales methods, bookkeeping, and when to reduce inventory. After half a year the debt was paid and he departed for Yangchow, where, from another unwitting teacher, he learned of credit, foreign exchange, and the operation of factories.

His next step was to learn English, the language of money. In Nanking, he presented himself at the Baptist mission. He had vowed to his beloved mother, he said, only minutes before she journeyed through the Jade Gates of the Christian Heaven, that he too would swallow the foreign religion and spread the Good News among the people. The head of the mission himself undertook to teach him English. After a year, he begged leave to visit the grave of his mother and was soon on his way, singing lustily, "Praise God from Whom all blessings flow. . . ."

In Shanghai, he obtained a job as steward on the steamer Odys-

sey. *Faithfully he carried out his duties; diligently he studied the ways of the rich foreigners.*

Among the passengers, one voyaged alone. He was, the purser said, a rich Jew of Germany who lived in Shanghai and was traveling for his health.

When he disembarked, the Jew offered his steward a job as rent collector.

Before long, the orphan knew precisely which tenants were unreliable and who was likely to leave without paying. One by one they were replaced by money trees, prosperous and discreet women whose only customers were the most respected of Europeans.

Within a year, he was his patron's personal assistant, and a new rolltop desk was installed in the office beside the old.

After two years, there were rumors that the property of Germans would be confiscated, and so, as a precaution merely, the owner signed over his holdings to his Chinese assistant. Toasting their foresight with vintage sherry, neither imagined that anything had changed.

Then, one night after his protégé had left, the old man sat down to have a last look at the columns in the daily ledger. In the morning, the assistant found him sitting there still.

The youth gently took the body in his arms and laid it on the bed in the back room, where the old man had slept. Searching, he found nothing of family—only a faded photograph of a wood frame house, tucked into a corner of the mirror.

He ordered the most expensive coffin and a replica of the dead man's dark suit, an exact copy even to the cigarette burn on the sleeve. He commissioned a marble monument in the likeness of the house in the photograph.

On the forty-ninth day, unshaven and unkempt, the heir led a grand procession to the grave site. Following him were hired mourners with white hemp tied around their heads and waists, and the ladies of the night in dark-hued bombazine and stylish bonnets. The wailing of the multitude moved even the Heavens to tears while the band from the Astor Hotel played the "Waltz of the Blue Danube."

—*Clan story*

AUGUST WINDS ESCORTED the Woos to Soochow on one of his houseboats. The journey took three days and three nights. In the evenings the travelers lingered on deck, enveloped by darkness and the fragrance of jasmine. There was no moon, so that the shores vanished, and the lanterns flickering on the yuloh just ahead were as one with the lights of heaven. It was almost as if the houseboat were being towed through the River of Stars. Tilting her head skyward, Spring Moon dreamed, reveling in the happiness of homecoming, only now and then thinking of changes, thinking that her mother's hair would be gray.

Sometimes Spring Moon and August Winds took turns telling stories while the child sat on Lustrous Jade's lap and laughed as much as she. Once, in his excitement, Enduring Promise tripped, nearly falling into the water. After that August Winds tied a rope to the boy, with the other end around his own waist, pretending it was a game.

August Winds' tales were preposterous accounts of how he had acquired his wealth. "Not long ago," he would say, "I was introduced to the most successful businessman in the world and he immediately saw in me such promise that he begged me to be his partner." Or "I journeyed to Tibet, where the Dalai Lama showered me with diamonds and rubies, one for every bone in my body, for truly, he said, I was meant to be a maharaja!"

Sometimes, he would suddenly disappear below and emerge again in a moment dressed in new attire. Strutting before them, he solicited their opinions of "the Prince of Wales' tennis outfit," or "the Prince's riding habit." He and the Prince had the same tailor, he explained, and the same circle of friends. "How else," he asked, "can you account for my Pierce Arrow, my fleet of canalboats, my freight line?"

How else? Spring Moon thought, wondering if she wanted to know the truth.

Her stories were of the ancestors, and the myths, legends, and poems Lustrous Jade had never known or had forgotten. It was almost as if her daughter were her child again, as if the years had not been lost.

Occasionally Lustrous Jade would relate something of school or a tale from the Bible. But her stories were told with such earnestness of moral purpose that they made the others uncomfortable. Glad Promise had been as sincere, yet had been able to laugh at himself. His daughter laughed at the outrageous charades of August Winds but seemed to take herself very seriously indeed.

The skies were azure when the party alighted from the carriage beside the bronze lions, and from the distance came the singing of pagoda bells. It was a day to gladden spirits—or so it had seemed at first. But as she stood beside the spirit screen, Spring Moon felt a longing so swift it took her breath away. She had felt it once before when, many weeks after Glad Promise had left, she had walked past the pavilion in the Western Hills and thought that he was there. Today, although she knew that it was gone, for a moment she saw the Hall of Womanly Virtues as it once had been, and the tiny erect figure of her grandmother in the rosewood chair.

She had drawn upon the strength of this place as heedlessly as one draws upon youth. Now, both were spent.

Suddenly, fear overtook longing, erasing memories. Enduring Promise had run ahead. What if one of the sharp-eyed widows saw the resemblance? Quickly she walked over to take his hand, at the same time telling herself that what was done was done, that she must give no sign.

With an effort, she smiled at the guard. They were expected in the Hall of Ancestors, he said.

How would it be, she wondered, without all the women in their rightful place?

August Winds had taken charge, instructing the guard on the disposition of the caravan of gifts that would soon arrive. "Send them directly to the Hall. Then summon the household and see that they assemble. You as well, of course!"

The man's eyes were large with anticipation, and he bowed many times. "Welcome, welcome!"

"What *do* you have in all those boxes, August Winds?" Lustrous Jade asked.

"Soon, soon enough!" He grinned, adjusting the ascot of the Prince's walking outfit.

Enduring Promise tugged at Spring Moon's hand, pulling her through the entrance to the Great Court. Immediately she noticed that the Bottle Gate was gone, in its place a dark shadow made of new brick that blocked the view beyond. Gone: the Chess Garden, the schoolhouse, the boys' dormitory—and what else?

She shook her head. She must not dwell on all that had gone but think of all that remained. Before her was the Hall of Ancestors, its red columns freshly painted. Yet, she held back, postponing the moment when she would see the changes that had been made within: the new ancestral tablets behind the altar, the gaps left when some had been removed to other cities.

Suddenly there was a burst of excited chatter. "Welcome home! Welcome home!" All who still lived in the *lao chia* were there as if by magic, on the threshold of the Hall.

Spring Moon laughed through tears as she embraced each woman in turn and exchanged bows with the solemn youth Bright Vista had become.

They were the same: the Grandaunts, Silken Dawn, Fragrant Snow, whose hair was not gray but dyed ebony and arranged like a pearl-studded box at the nape of her neck. Only Golden Virtue seemed to have aged, her figure more matronly. But her smile was warm. "My niece," she cried, "how your presence cheers our hearts!"

All talked at once, telling one another how well they looked, how tall Lustrous Jade had grown. And thanks be to Buddha, the boy seemed healthy. No one recognized August Winds, who introduced himself with becoming modesty but was clearly pleased at their astonishment.

They entered the Hall of Ancestors together in one joyous wave of enthusiasm.

The once harmonious room was cluttered with the mah jong and dining tables, the embroidery rack, the rosewood chairs from the Hall of Womanly Virtues. A coromandel screen hid the altar and the ancestors' tablets from view.

For an instant it seemed to Spring Moon that the cheerful welcome had been affected, as if everyone were trying to ignore the melancholy difference. But then, there was Enduring Promise taking her hand, pulling her toward one of the tables, on which refreshments were arrayed. "Come, Sao Sao, come quickly!" he cried. "This is the most beautiful palace I have ever seen, even in books." And looking about, she thought, It is so.

"Lai! Lai!" the women called, each waving to the child, inviting him to climb up beside her as the travelers took seats around the table.

Enduring Promise looked to Spring Moon for a cue, then ran to the eldest. Second Grandaunt giggled. The others nodded approvingly.

The old woman squinted at the boy's face as he scrambled up onto her lap. "Your features are most refined. In truth, you resemble Grand Vista when he was your age. Do you not think so, Sister?" She turned to Silken Dawn.

Spring Moon's pulse quickened, but before anyone else could voice her opinion, Golden Virtue spoke. "Nonsense! Enduring Promise is nothing like my eldest. He is better looking, much better looking than Grand Vista. . . ."

There was a commotion at the door: the gifts had arrived! So, too, the household retainers, perhaps two dozen, many as old as the oldest widows. Though family might move to distant cities, those who had served the household were ensured a place until death.

Once more August Winds directed traffic, seating the servants on the floor along both sides of the family table, summoning the appropriate bearer as he presented the gifts one by one. Mysteriously, the man who had left the courtyards five years before had chosen the perfect gift for each. There were eyeglasses for the farsighted seamstress; perfumed soap for the scullery maid; a dog for the night watchman; foot basins and pith helmets for the sedan carriers; a squirrel coat for the thin-blooded amah, too old now to do much but sit in the yard and chat with the peddlers who came to the door; a year's supply of Lydia Pinkham's Tonic for the fearful cook, who had aches in each of the 367 points in his body that singularly eluded both the herbalist and the golden needles man; a spring scale for the keeper of the storeroom keys; a bicycle for the head porter; jade earrings for each of the servant women; a hot-water bottle for every bed.

With each munificent presentation came a squeal of delight that heightened expectations of the grand gift yet to come, the one he had brought for the family.

At last, he ducked his head out the door and called the bearers, six men carrying a heavy burden hidden under red brocade. As they made their way to the center of the room, the assembled burst into applause.

"What is it? What is it?" they shouted, bidding the porters not to drop it, guessing at what it could be.

"Three coffins!"

"An electric wagon!"

"Young master's bride!"

"Five years' supply of bean curd!"

"Gold! Gold! Gold!"

At each guess, August Winds, standing beside the gift, shook his head solemnly. When they began repeating themselves, he clapped his hands for silence. "Honored grandmothers, old friends and new."

No one breathed.

"I shall give you each one more guess!"

"Oh," wailed Second Grandaunt. "Please, no more guessing. Let this old woman see it before she ascends with the stork."

"As you will, my grand, grand, *grand,* grandauntie." He bowed again. Then, with a flourish, he whipped off the brocade cover. A vision of rosewood and mother-of-pearl, ivory and silver, stood revealed.

The household burst into cries of happiness, and even Spring Moon was so dazzled that it was a moment before she realized the gift was a piano.

The three old widows scurried forward, swaying on their golden lilies as they circled the object, reaching out with their hands but lacking quite the courage to touch it, while the servants pointed and slapped their thighs, shouting their approval. Silken Dawn and Golden Virtue maintained dignity, fanning furiously. Spring Moon restrained Enduring Promise.

A hush fell.

"What is it?" Second Grandaunt asked. "What is it?"

"Do you not know, Sister?" Third Grandaunt's tone was most superior.

"No. Do you?"

"Naturally, I know." Third Grandaunt paused as the gathering leaned closer to hear the answer. "But I shall leave it to August Winds to enlighten the rest of you." As the others wailed she burst into laughter, the jiggling of her body, as round as a summer gourd, belying the modest hand she raised to conceal unseemly glee and two missing teeth.

Enduring Promise could wait no longer. Breaking free of Spring Moon, he ran up and tugged at August Winds' pants. "Tell, tell!"

Now laughter echoed through the hall, mingling with chants of "Tell, tell!" led by the widows. Spring Moon could not help laughing too. My grandaunts, she thought, will live to be a hundred, if not two.

August Winds raised his hands in mock surrender, then tapped each of his many pockets until he found a handkerchief to wipe his brow. All eyes were upon him. He carefully folded the handkerchief and tucked it in the pocket of his suit. "Please, all be seated, for I am about to show you what this is."

The widows shook their heads as if to say, About time, about time, and helped one another back to their chairs. The servants took their places again on the floor.

August Winds grinned. "But first . . ."

The crowd moaned.

"But first, before I can demonstrate the magic herein, I need the assistance of a girl with big feet!"

Heads whipped around toward Lustrous Jade. "You! You! You!"

Spring Moon had almost forgotten Lustrous Jade in the excitement. She had not moved from the table, where she sat very erect in her missionary suit.

Lustrous Jade shook her head. My daughter, Spring Moon thought, looks as if she had judged something and found it wanting. Even August Winds' charm did not move her.

Spring Moon joined the chorus. "You, you, you!"

Finally Enduring Promise came and took her by the hand. "Please, my niece. Please?" No one could resist him. Everyone cheered when she sat down at the piano.

"Now, Sister, pay close attention." August Winds' voice boomed.

"Place your big left foot here." He pointed to the left pedal. "And your big right foot there."

Reluctantly, Lustrous Jade obeyed.

"Now, my sister, put your feet to good use. Push one, then the other."

The girl did as she was told. Suddenly, the hall was filled with music. No one except August Winds and Lustrous Jade recognized the melodies, but everyone applauded nonetheless when August Winds announced that they were written by that famous American, Stephen Foster.

For hours, the courtyards reverberated with song and the tapping of golden lilies and straw sandals as the entire household hummed the tunes of "Camptown Races" and "Jeannie with the Light Brown Hair." Again and again, Enduring Promise twirled across the floor, arms aloft, head back, laughing as Bright Vista and one porter after another followed to catch him should he fall. And Lustrous Jade, cheeks flushed, tirelessly pumped the piano, exchanging tender glances with the conductor as they sang.

It is almost as it used to be, Spring Moon thought. So much warmth, so much noise, so many people. Even the ancestors seemed near. She imagined her father, the Matriarch, and the Venerable sitting side by side in their rosewood chairs, nodding their heads with great dignity to the music. Old Gardener rested in the corner, and Fatso was everywhere, laughing.

The merriment lasted until nightfall, and even after breakfast the next day, snatches of the tunes could be heard in the courtyards as the servants went about their work.

Spring Moon was unpacking her books in her quarters in the Court of Wise Heart when one of the handmaidens came to request a private audience for August Winds.

She received him uneasily. He should have had the good sense to wait a while before approaching her about her daughter.

"Auntie, how good of you to see me."

She showed him to a seat. "It is only fitting for a teacher to receive her old pupil."

"I would prefer it if you could think of me in a better light. Despite your brilliant efforts, I was a most backward student."

"For some, life is a better teacher."

He drew his chair closer. "May I ask a favor of you, my aunt?"

"I cannot imagine what favor I can give you at this time, August Winds." She drew out her fan and snapped it open.

He smiled, apparently unaffected by her formal tone. "As you can see, I have come into many business opportunities."

"Do not speak of business to me. I know nothing of such things."

He smiled again. "Please, bear with me. I wish to ask a great favor, a favor only you can grant me, my aunt."

She nodded.

"My proposal involves a property I own and wish to hold for future use, when a factory or a railroad junction may be needed in that location. I do not want my competitors to know of my plans to buy the surrounding properties. To allay suspicions, I need someone I can trust to inhabit the house. It is furnished with all the necessities, including a staff. If I move in, people will suspect. But if you move in, no one could possibly guess my intentions." He paused, as if awaiting a reaction.

Spring Moon put the fan away but said nothing.

He continued. "You would be doing me the kindest favor if you would agree to live there. Naturally, I would defray all expenses."

Spring Moon shook her head.

"Auntie, I know this is a great imposition, but you must not say no until you have seen the house."

"August Winds, where is the house located?"

"In Shanghai, in the French sector, on Rue Flaubert."

And conveniently near your M.S. & Company, she thought. Yet she could not be angry with him. Did he not realize that the prize he so artfully plotted to attain was not hers to give? There would be no go-betweens for Lustrous Jade.

"August Winds, we have just come home!"

"Please, Auntie, forgive me for speaking to you of my business problems so soon after your return. I should have refrained. But do not say no now. Give it some thought during the months to come. There is no hurry." He hesitated, seeming to consider whether he should go on, and then said softly, "I have waited this long, I can surely wait some more. Despite what you may think, my teacher, I am a most persuasive man."

❦ 27 ❧

A Person of Character

Once there was a wife who wished to please her husband, to make him smile, to make him content.

Hearing that he admired big feet, she vowed to unbind hers. For the first month, she faithfully bathed her golden lilies in medicinal waters until the calluses and bones were soft again. During the second, little by little she straightened the crippled toes. During the third, she learned to walk again, a step at a time. Every month, she shed a cistern of tears.

When the unbinding was done, her feet were still too short and she stuffed the toes of the new high-heeled shoes with cotton and a wooden cone. Proudly she walked to the Moon Gate to surprise her husband on his return from a stay in another city.

He did not notice the change until she almost fell.

The wife cried silently, "My husband, I only wanted to please you, to do what none other in our house has done. I wanted you to be able to say that you were proud of your wife, a modern Chinese with big feet."

—Clan story

IT WAS TWILIGHT on the third day of the Fortnight of the Small Snow. Lustrous Jade sat in the room she shared with Enduring Promise turning one by one the pages of her Testament, while outside on the gallery, the boy played with a broom, singing a song she did not know.

At the hour of the snake the widows and Golden Virtue, escorted by Bright Vista, had left for a week's visit to the Convent of Sedate Quest. She had enjoyed the hours without their company, and the fact troubled her. Was it a sign of weakness, of a lack of devotion to the duty that was hers? She was meant to do God's work. It should not matter that they thought her behavior indecent and uncivilized.

There was no denying that in the four months since her return she had become sand in the eyes of all the household. After she took down the Kitchen God from his place of honor and gave the offerings to the beggars who waited at the peddlers' gate, the elders had scolded for a week and her mother had had to beg their forgiveness many times. When she removed the earrings and hair ribbons from the only son of the head porter, who had managed to father one after six girls, the man actually wept! "Now the jealous gods will steal my boy!" he had cried over and over, no matter what she said, until she returned what she had taken. The old retainers to a man had threatened to resign if she did not stop interfering, and Golden Virtue had had to placate them with gifts.

She had soon stopped reading about Noah and the Flood and Moses and the Plagues, even the parables of Jesus. The women enjoyed the tales too much, and missed the truth. Now she read only from the less diverting passages and sermons, at once edifying and unlike the traditional stories they told each other every day. But they laughed at the Beatitudes and went back to chatting, sewing, and drinking tea before she had reached the last of them.

The worst was her grandmother, Fragrant Snow, who seemed to spend all morning doing nothing but fixing her hair and painting her eyebrows. What vanity!

Her mother was not at all vain, but neither was she of any help. She had taught in a Christian school, but here, in the court-yards, one would never know it. Their last confrontation had been only yesterday, a reprise of all the others.

"But Mother—"

"My daughter, I do not wish to debate the merits of every rain-drop. I talk about the storm—the storm you create everywhere you go, preaching this, lecturing that. You must not insult elders.

You must not act as if you are wiser than they. I should have listened to Por Por and taught you how to read faces instead of sending you to learn English."

"But Mother, can you not understand that their ignorance keeps them from a more productive and godly life? You say I should stop. But if you saw a person drink from a poisoned cup, would you not try to stop him? Especially if that person were as helpless as one who cannot hear or speak or see?"

"Enough! To talk of the people who make a home for us in such a fashion is . . . sinful! I fear, Lustrous Jade, that in broadening your mind, you have narrowed your heart."

At least Golden Virtue did something besides play mah jong and embroider altar cloths, although she too seemed impervious to Jesus, calmly setting the Kitchen God back in his place upon the wall. Still, she alone had not been angry when the cook did not work for a day after being told that the fires of Hell were hotter than his stove. And she had truly heard the good news about the thousands unbinding their feet, while the widows merely clamored for a sketch of the fashionable new high-heeled shoes.

"Grandauntie," she had said, "young men of good families all over China have sworn never to marry anyone with golden lilies."

When the widows claimed that she lied, she resolutely read them names from a newspaper clipping.

Still the women did not believe, until Golden Virtue herself spoke up. "It is true. I have heard my husband speak of such things. I have heard him say that he would urge our sons to marry girls with big feet."

"If that is his wish, why do you not unbind yours?" asked Second Grandaunt, triumphant, as if she had just scored a p'ung.

"You could! You could!" Lustrous Jade urged.

"It would be too painful," Spring Moon argued. "Can anyone forget the tears we all shed during the first months when our feet were bound?"

The women were silent.

"Would you ask anyone to go through that pain again, even if doing so would let her capture the wind?"

"Oh, no!" cried the women, all but Golden Virtue. "Oh, no!"

"Only someone like my daughter, who never knew the agony, would even suggest such a thing! What is done is done!"

They nodded. Lustrous Jade bit her tongue to stifle the retort that lodged like a fishbone in her throat.

When autumn came, she had begun accompanying Golden Virtue on her rounds of the few tenant farms that still belonged to the House of Chang. Everywhere they visited, the tenants were hollow-eyed and thin, bone weary. Many who had pawned their winter clothes and did not have the money to redeem them shivered as well. But when she mentioned their plight, Golden Virtue did not encourage sympathy, merely saying in a most matter-of-fact way, "Too little rain. Bad harvest."

"Grandauntie, you must do something to help!"

Golden Virtue did not respond to this, but, unable to ignore her niece's questions, she tried to explain.

While crops were still equally shared between the owner and the tenant, as had been the custom for centuries, life was becoming increasingly difficult for those who worked the land. Because sons were prized as living purses, more precious than gold to parents in their old age, many were born, and when they became adults, they too wished for sons, until there were too many mouths to feed with the tenants' share. Once, before Soochow had become a treaty port, the peasants had supplemented their portions by selling handicrafts; now not even they preferred the native goods to the cheaper and better manufactured ones of the foreigner. In recent years, many men had left the land to seek jobs in the cities, but few succeeded and most became liabilities to their families.

It was a list of reasons with not a word to suggest a remedy, and Lustrous Jade persisted.

"Can we not at least reduce the rents, my grandaunt?"

Golden Virtue pretended not to hear and spoke of other things.

But Lustrous Jade would not be daunted and asked again and again. Finally, Golden Virtue said, "The House of Chang has many responsibilities. There are many in the courtyards who cannot farm, many who have served the family for generations, many who cannot change, one who studies abroad, others who count on our help, the hospital, the beggars' guild. . . ."

"But Grandauntie." Lustrous Jade did not so much interrupt as take advantage of a pause. "Grandauntie, what will happen to them? Some will not have enough to eat. Will they sell their children? It is not right. We must do something."

The Patriarch's wife said only, "It is fate," and then repeated a phrase that Lustrous Jade herself had used: "God's will be done." Lustrous Jade said no more.

Even so, she could not accept what she saw. Certainly, she had known that China was poor; the missionaries had taught her that it was so, and she had heard the tales of horror told by the girls at the Door of Hope. Yet she had never really *seen* until now.

At one farm they visited, a mou of land worked by two brothers named Lee, she asked Golden Virtue how old the tenants were. The adults were tens of years younger than she would have guessed. They looked beaten, despite their ready smiles, and the smallest children, clinging to their mothers' hips, had sores on their legs and running noses.

She was troubled, too, by the many times the tenants bowed, by the way grown men pleaded for the smallest favors. Few dared speak at all, though the mistress was never unkind. The older children hid until she left.

Endlessly her thoughts chased one another. She must do something to help, must not waste any more time. . . . Perhaps she would not go to America, after all . . . perhaps she should enroll in a provincial college and be less indebted to the clan. . . .

Finally she had made up her mind to volunteer at the hospital. How could she be a doctor if she had never seen the sick?

The reaction from the old widows had been predictable. "Merciful Kwan Yin," they exhorted Spring Moon. "Is it not enough that the House of Chang has never failed to contribute monies to cure the sick? What could a girl like her do among strangers with even stranger diseases? Nothing but bring their ills home. You must forbid it!"

For once, her mother did not take up their cause. "Let my daughter go to the hospital," she suggested calmly. "Let her inquire if there might be work for her to do."

Elated, Lustrous Jade wanted to go immediately but was told

that the carriage was engaged. "Tomorrow," her mother had said. "Wait until tomorrow."

That night she had been unable to sleep, so excited was she by the prospect of accomplishing something at last.

In the morning, the wife of the mission doctor received her most cordially and spoke at length over tea about the importance of community relations and the great need for the continued support of influential families such as the Changs.

"I too would like to help. I could—"

"Yes, I understand that you plan to attend medical school. Please do think of us, Margaret, when you are ready to practice. We are always in search of doctors. But we do not need volunteers."

On the way home, she had wept silently. Margaret was not important, only the clan.

Lustrous Jade closed the Bible. It was almost dark, and she turned up the wick. Bedtime. She opened the shutters and looked out the window for a moment, watching the boy. Plump as the First Immortal in his many layers, he was pretending to gather things into a make-believe basket, chanting to himself.

> "Snatch an egg, snatch an egg,
> If you drop it, break a leg.
> Pick a twig, pick a twig,
> If you drop it, lose a pig."

It sounded like a peasant rhyme, and she wondered where he had learned it. But the north wind stirred her hair. "Enduring Promise!" she called, shivering. "It is late. Bedtime!"

She smiled when he came running. The boy, at least, never balked at her suggestions, never retreated to cold silence, never told her that she was foreign.

"Shall I help you get undressed?" she asked.

He shook his head solemnly. His eyes were wide open, as innocent as . . . as those of the Lamb of God. Clear evidence of his intent to prolong the ritual. She smiled again. Somehow, seeing through him gave her courage, and as his head disappeared into the chest that held his night clothes she put away the Bible and took up a pencil and her notebook. She would set specific goals just as she had done in school, when crossing an item off the list gave her a feeling of great accomplishment. With one eye on him she scribbled down what she must do after the women returned from their retreat.

It was not easy. At the thought of them kneeling before idols blind anger overcame her and she crumpled the page, only to start all over again when calm returned. A sprinkling of paper balls soon lay here and there about the room. Still, the list grew. Must try again to convince the cook that opium cures nothing. Must try to volunteer again, this time at the orphanage. Must explain that gourds under beds do not keep ghosts from choking the sleeper. Must . . . suddenly, she ran to the bed and looked underneath. Nothing was there, no gourd, no clump of garlic, not even a dust turtle. She returned to her chair.

Must prove the fortune-teller's prediction wrong. Must . . .

Enduring Promise skipped in from the bathing room, his face still wet after washing. "A game! A game!" he shouted, running to pick up a paper ball.

Again she could not help smiling. "What game?"

"In the paper ball? A surprise for me?" he asked hopefully. "If I find it, can I keep it?"

"No surprise," she said, quickly gathering up the papers. "It is time for bed."

"One story?"

"No, it is late."

"One song?"

"No," she said with finality. "Just time enough for your prayers."

He did not protest but got quickly down on his knees by the bed and, assuming the proper position, repeated the prayer she had taught him. He said it perfectly. In closing he added, "God bless Sao Sao. God bless my niece, Lustrous Jade. God bless my nephew, August Winds. God bless all the House of Chang—" Suddenly he looked up at Lustrous Jade, on her knees beside him. "May I ask God to bless anyone I wish?"

Suspicious, she hesitated. But there was real anxiety in his eyes. "Of course."

He bowed his head again and said, "God bless Mama, God bless Papa. Amen." Then he quickly clambered into bed.

It was the first time she had heard them mentioned, and she asked, "Are Mama and Papa from the village?"

He nodded. "Learned Cinders."

"You mean Reed Village."

"No." He sat up and shook his head.

"Are you sure?"

"Yes!" he insisted. "Sao Sao took me to Reed Village but I did not live there. Only in Learned Cinders."

"With Mama and Papa?"

"Of course! Papa took me to the fields every day. Mama sewed my tiger shoes!"

She must have said aloud that she did not believe, for the boy slipped out of bed and scampered into the dressing alcove, returning with a pair of old shoes. "See! See! I told you so!"

"What was your name before?" she asked. Could it be that this boy was not a member of the Woo clan?

"Little Treasure. But I do not like that name anymore. It is a baby name. I can read!"

She was not listening. Learned Cinders . . . Learned . . . She had heard the name before. Long ago. When she was a child. Something in one of her mother's stories, perhaps.

Then she remembered. Learned Cinders was Dummy's village. Dummy, who had comforted her mother when she was born, whose family had been butchered, whose suffering her mother had recounted over and over. Enduring Promise must be her son.

She had never seen the handmaiden, but she imagined her now, tattered, bloated with hunger, carrying the son she loved above all else to her former mistress, her friend, seeking help. Instead of giving, her mother, whose gold hairpin would have fed a family for a year, had exchanged goods for goods, accepted the unacceptable.

"What is it, my niece? Why are you sad?" Anxiously, Enduring Promise reached up to touch her cheek, reclaiming her attention.

But even as she soothed him, tucking in the quilt, the image persisted, becoming more and more vivid until she was sure of its truth. Her mother was no different from all Chinese who lived within garden walls, locking their hearts against those without. Her mother had taken a son, perhaps the only son, from the most wretched of souls, one who had buried her mother, her father, her baby brother. Her mother had taken a son . . . had bought a child . . . had taken a son . . . had bought—

Enduring Promise stirred in his sleep and again she reached out to soothe him. She had not risen from her knees, and now she prayed, whispering lest she disturb the child. "Our Father, who art in heaven . . ."

The next morning, she awoke wearing the same clothes she had worn the night before, unable to remember when she had fallen asleep, the boy in her arms.

All that week, except for necessary attentions to Enduring Promise, she remained in her room, wondering what to do, reading over and over the same passage from First Corinthians: "And now abideth faith, hope, charity, these three; but the greatest of these is charity."

The decision was made during the night before the eighth day of the Fortnight of Small Snow, when the women were to return from their retreat.

She dreamed she was playing badminton at school, only this time a crowd watched. Everyone, even the Hanlin and her father, in a silver frame, was there. Then, somehow, the game changed. The shuttlecock became a bird, the net a spirit screen. The racquet was a stone she pitched at the bird. She missed. The crowd surrounded the court. Each held a stone. The bird was gone. In its place, her mother. In Lustrous Jade's hand, another stone. Now everyone was shouting, "You, you, you!" Spring Moon smiled, opening her arms wide. She too took up the chant. "You, you, you!" Lustrous Jade did as she was told and heaved the stone. Her mother fell, and she awoke.

Her cheeks were wet with tears.

Had the dream been a message from the Lord, or something else? She did not know. She only knew that she could not accuse her mother, would never confront her with what she knew.

The last day of the Fortnight of Great Snow was unusually cold, o that the pots in which the yellow chrysanthemums bloomed racked and rainwater caught in a footprint in the garden congealed.

Spring Moon worked, as she had done all week, glazing the chestnuts and ginger for New Year's gifts while the other women sat around the embroidery rack, hurrying to finish the altar cloth, chatting about who might return for the celebration, who had done well in the port cities, whom they missed, and whom they were glad to be rid of. Only Golden Virtue and Bright Vista were absent, busy with the New Year's accounts and the preparation of red envelopes for the household.

At the mah jong table in the corner, Enduring Promise and Lustrous Jade decorated the small Christmas tree that August Winds had sent, along with an elaborate crèche made in France. From time to time she heard the boy's piping voice rise above the din the others made. "Cow! . . . Goat!" Lustrous Jade was teaching him English. "Virgin Mary!"

Spring Moon looked from one group to the other, savoring the contentment within that seemed to glow as warmly as the brazier in the center of the room near the Matriarch's empty chair. Was it because the holidays were almost here? Because each woman, even Lustrous Jade, took such pleasure in her task? The scene was so familiar, so like that of her childhood, and yet . . . and yet, not at all like it. Self-consciously she studied Silken Dawn's graceful hands, the serenity of Third Grandaunt's face and Second Grandaunt's squint. Why was she so intent upon etching them in her memory? Her eyes lingered on her mother, who had combed the strands of hair at the temples to resemble the wings of a dove.

All at once, Spring Moon knew that she would be leaving soon.

No one had suggested such a thing. But the less said, the more heartfelt the strain. It was time to withdraw, without a confrontation, so that no one would regret words better left unspoken, no one would lose face.

She would say nothing until after the festivities, then mention schooling for the boy as an excuse. She would accept August Winds' offer, which he still made, in a different way, in every letter. The latest had asked her not to think of the house as largesse but as a small payment against the debt he owed the House of Chang.

Accepting his house meant accepting him as a suitor for her daughter, but Spring Moon had seen enough of Lustrous Jade during the last few months to know that the girl would never consent to an arranged marriage. These were new times, and modern young people made up their own minds. If Lustrous Jade chose him, the elders would have to acquiesce, as clans throughout China had acquiesced.

She decided that, once settled in Shanghai, she would ask Bold Talent's help in obtaining a teaching post. He would not misunderstand her reasons for returning to the city where they had once been lovers, of this she was certain. For although he had seemed expectant on the first evening of her return, nothing he had said or done thereafter had suggested that they were anything but uncle and niece again. Perhaps even those hours had been shaped, for him as well as for her, more by memory than by longing.

Her decision had been the only one possible. To have been a fool once was human. He had been her teacher, her lifelong friend, her second love. But to be a fool twice would be unworthy, without dignity or grace. Exiles might live for themselves, but not clansmen. Now he, too, had yielded, as both knew they must even before they had parted. It had to be. It was so.

During his most recent visits to Soochow, when the talk was of politics, increasingly he had spoken of the passage of centuries; when reminiscing, he dwelt upon the beauties of a single bud, a certain dawn. While he still lived in the city and only occasionally visited the courtyards, he seemed far removed from both. She remembered that once he had spoken of wandering free in the mountain mists as the ideal way to pass the last days of his life. He had not grown a wispy beard, yet it seemed to her that he had already begun to lose himself in hills which took form in his mind. The man she had known was gone.

The glazing was finished. Spring Moon went to join the other women, choosing a seat beside Fragrant Snow.

❦ 28 ❧

The Courtship

A tiger came upon a fox and was about to devour him when his meal shouted in a most regal manner, "Take care, my friend, do you not realize that I have been appointed the King of the Beasts by the gods? Should you touch even a hair of mine, they will punish you!"

The tiger roared with laughter. "You could not be more mistaken, for I am the King of the Beasts!"

"Then follow me into the woods and see if all the animals there do not flee from me."

The tiger agreed and trailed the fox. When he saw for himself that all the animals fled at the sight of the puny fellow, he bowed his head and slunk into the underbrush.

So sure was the fox that he continued on his way without a backward glance.

—Chinese tale

IT WAS DUSK when the travelers reached 42 Rue Flaubert. The two-storied red brick house seemed to glow in the fading light, resembling, Spring Moon decided, nothing so much as a giant wedding trunk. Its interior confirmed the impression. Their new home was a gift of love, containing everything August Winds imagined anyone could ever desire. That it was vulgar, that it was cluttered, that it made her feel as if her eyes had no place to rest was not important.

"It is beautiful," she said with genuine emotion.

August Winds beamed with pleasure, more like the student she remembered from her class than the shrewd businessman he had become. "Look, Auntie, did you ever see a better telephone?"

"No!" Enduring Promise answered for her, picking it up and shouting, "Wei? Wei? Wei?" Lustrous Jade quickly stopped that game, but the irrepressible boy was soon off, gleefully fingering the velvet drapes, the flowered wallpaper, the Tiffany lamps.

"Look, Auntie, books, books, and more books!" August Winds pushed open the double doors leading to the library.

"Have you read even one?" asked Lustrous Jade, pulling a fat volume down at random, then another.

"Your question, Sister Margaret, shows that you have no idea what an entrepreneur does! Have you not heard? Time is money, and money is what my business is all about."

Lustrous Jade paid him no attention and sat down in the nearest chair to read.

"Is this my chair?" asked the boy, pointing to a footstool on which the antics of Scotty dogs had been worked in petit-point.

"It is yours, if you want it!" August Winds gestured magnanimously. "If you like, my uncle, I shall buy you one for each room."

"No," Spring Moon cried out. "We have more than enough chairs now!" To herself, she counted those in the parlor alone—seven that seated one, two that seated two, and one that looked as if it could seat a dozen.

"Auntie, what is wrong?" August Winds asked. "Everything you see is an exact replica of what you would find at Buckingham Palace."

Perhaps, but did they keep it all in one room? she wondered.

"Everything is fine," she said, smiling.

"What pleases you most, my auntie?" he asked, hoisting Enduring Promise to his shoulder so that the boy could pat the nose of the boar's head on the wall.

"I will tell you, August Winds, only if you promise not to obtain another."

He laughed, nodding. "I promise, but you must tell!"

Spring Moon walked slowly around the parlor, frowning as if

making a difficult decision. August Winds and Enduring Promise followed, a step behind.

Many items were quite beautiful, though more to Por Por's taste than her own. What could she say? The grand tour was coming to an end at the library door when she saw what she was looking for. The globe. It was just like another that stood in the study of the house on Bubbling Well Road. She pointed to it. "I like that best!"

"The globe?" he asked.

She nodded emphatically.

He heaved a sigh. "Oh, Auntie, if I could, I would gladly give you the world!"

"I do not doubt it for a minute, August Winds." She smiled. "You are most kind, most kind."

The stay in Shanghai began thus auspiciously, and within the first month each member of the household knew in the morning what he would do that day. Spring Moon and Enduring Promise went together to the Modern School, where she taught fifth grade and he attended the first. Lustrous Jade worked at New China on a translation project for Bold Talent, waiting to start Shanghai College in the fall. When they had first returned to the city, she had gone at once to the mission, hoping that Miss Clayton would give her a more demanding project. But the missionary had been away on one of her regular visits to the interior, and before long the girl had become interested in the political questions that dominated conversation at the press.

In the evening, August Winds, who lived in the back room at M.S. & Company with no amenities or even servants except for the Russian chauffeur and bodyguard, joined them for dinner. On Sundays, Bold Talent dined with them, purposely avoiding serious topics of conversation, preferring to play games with the boy. "Lustrous Jade, kindly permit me my day of rest," he would say when the girl asked his opinions on the latest news.

Whenever Noble Talent came to town, he joined them as well. The soldier would sit stiffly in his chair, speaking only when questions were put to him and then complaining bitterly of the cliques that divided the country, of old reformers like K'ang Yu-wei, who had supported the short-lived restoration of the Manchus, of China's entry into the war. When Lustrous Jade tried to counter his pessimism with talk of President Wilson's Fourteen Points for peace, he retreated into silence. Spring Moon thought that life had been kinder to the women of the clan. They, at least, had a home and many diversions. Young Uncle had neither.

From the first, not surprisingly, August Winds developed a deep interest in Christianity. Lustrous Jade was suspicious but could not refuse to give him Bible lessons, and when her pupil proved to be most diligent, she told her mother that Miss Clayton had always said God works in mysterious ways.

Spring Moon watched August Winds' courtship of her daughter with a mixture of anxiety and amusement. What an unlikely pair they made! Not even the blindest of marriage brokers would have dared such a match. He was like a panda, insouciant; she, a panther, anything but carefree. Yet whenever he was there, Spring Moon felt more at ease with Lustrous Jade, and worried that it should be so. Often in the quiet of those evenings at Rue Flaubert, she would look up from her students' papers and catch August Winds watching the girl write furiously in a notebook. Sometimes, he reached across and brushed a stray strand of hair from her eyes. The gesture was so unaffected, almost solemn, that the mother ignored the impropriety.

❧ 29 ❧

The Dragon Boat

In the time of the Warring States, the poet-statesman Ch'u Yuan was falsely accused by rivals at Court and lost the favor of the King. Banished, he wandered the countryside, collecting legends and penning tragic appeals, until one day, upon completion of his most beautiful poem, he drowned himself in the Mi Lo River.

The King, realizing the sincerity of his ex-minister and his own errors, sent out a party to search for Ch'u Yuan's remains. But the river would not yield the corpse. And so the boaters threw rice into the waters to appease the devils of the deep and to feed the virtuous poet's spirit in the next world. Since that time, on the fifth day of the fifth moon of every year, Chinese, who love poets and honor noble officials, have flocked to the rivers and lakes to remember Ch'u Yuan.

—Chinese history

BORED BY THE POLITICAL talk that seemed to engage the others, August Winds took the champagne bottle from the waiter and stood up to serve his guests personally.

"No more! No more!" insisted Bold Talent, covering the crystal goblet.

"Nonsense!" August Winds laughed, removing the scholar's hand, pouring the wine.

"More! More!" shouted Enduring Promise, next in line.

"Absolutely not!" Spring Moon appropriated his glass and

handed it to the nearest attendant, brushing a crumb from the protesting boy's trousers. "Now be good, Small Brother. Tell your nephew more about what you have learned in school."

August Winds sighed. If the conversation was not of the boy's geography lesson, it concerned the Brown Dwarfs sending troops to Mongolia or the Chinese students returning from Japan in protest. And this was supposed to be a party!

When he poured the wine for Lustrous Jade and Noble Talent, they took no notice of him, though the soldier, following tradition, downed the contents of his glass at once and had it filled again. August Winds liked Noble Talent better when he did not drink. Sober, he seldom spoke. Today he was recounting his life story to Lustrous Jade, who found it so compelling that she had forgotten not to drink the champagne.

Now that the warlords of Kwangtung had driven Sun out of Canton again and he was living in Shanghai, Noble Talent would be visiting more frequently. Already he and Lustrous Jade worked together at the press, collaborating on pamphlets supporting the Republic. "*Must* keep him away from her! *Must* keep her away from him!" August Winds muttered to himself, mimicking Lustrous Jade's style. After filling his own glass, he tossed the bottle to the waiter and sat down to sulk in earnest, elbows on the table, chin in his hands.

Not a cloud in the sky, and a perfect view of the river, but no one even looked. Perhaps when the races started, they would remember why he had invited them. The canvas pavilion that shielded them from the sun and the rent of the godown roof on which they perched had cost him the price of a house! He gulped his champagne.

Holiday crowds lined the shores of Soochow Creek. Along its banks flew dazzling red pennants, marking the course of the boat races. Here and there, long craft as slender as a man's waist, with the head of the dragon thrusting into the wind and the tail jutting upward at the stern, jounced in the water as if preparing for flight. In some, as many as a hundred men sat poised waiting for the gong, eyes upon the flowing sleeves of the "general" at the bow.

When he waved the paddling would begin, to the beat of the fat drums.

Suddenly, the gong sounded and the crowd roared. As suddenly, August Winds' guests, even his missionary and her mentor, stood up and cheered. To his surprise, Bold Talent hoisted the boy onto the table, and when Spring Moon objected, the scholar laughed and put a protective arm around the little monkey.

The dragons were off! August Winds motioned to the waiter for another bottle of champagne.

"Ho lo! Ho lo lo lo!" All afternoon the rowers' chants rose above the clang of cymbals and the boom of drums, the popping of firecrackers, and the cheering of the spectators. The boats careened through the water, darting from pennant to pennant, the generals reaching for the prize. Now and then one of them, splendid in the brightest purple or yellow or green, would tumble overboard. Popping up like a cork, with a toss of his head and a wet grin, flailing his arms, he would make his way toward shore while another took his place.

All afternoon Enduring Promise kept count on his fingers of generals lost and replaced, while the rest of the party ate and drank and laughed as if they lived in the sumptuous courts of Yang Kwei-fei, whose lavish ways had broken an earlier empire. When it was time to go home, one by one his guests rose and, according to custom, toasted August Winds. Solemnly he clinked his glass with that of each in turn, saying, "Today has been the most memorable dragon-boat race in all of twenty-two centuries because you have honored my unworthy table with your illustrious presence."

When the Woos and August Winds reached the house on Rue Flaubert, the amah took Enduring Promise straight to bed. Spring Moon was also tired and soon excused herself.

"Mother, I am much too excited to sleep. May we stay here a little longer?" Lustrous Jade smiled one of her rare smiles.

Spring Moon hesitated, then nodded. "Not much longer."

"I promise."

When they were alone in the parlor, August Winds sat on the piano bench, playing a note now and then, marveling at the sight of Lustrous Jade, heady with wine, dancing about the room. She hummed to herself as she danced, the tune of "Jeannie with the Light Brown Hair." He smiled, thinking he had never seen her dance before, wishing, but not quite daring, to take her in his arms. It must be the champagne, he said to himself, and almost laughed. Praise be to the Lord for champagne!

Sitting down beside him, she said, "I have never had such a wonderful time. I do not think I ever will again."

"It is my purpose in life to see that you do, again and again and again!" He played a chord each time for emphasis.

"Shhh!" she said, leaning close. "Shhh!" Even closer.

He was certain that she did not wear perfume and yet . . .

"What is the matter?" she asked, tilting her head to one side.

He merely brushed the stray strand of her hair into place, for he could not speak.

Her hand hovered over the keys, as if searching for a tune to play. "How well the dragons raced! It was glorious." She closed her eyes and leaned her head on his shoulder. "My friend."

"Dearest friend?" Tomorrow, he must buy a vineyard.

"Dearest friend!"

"Will you marry me?" He expected no answer. He liked saying the familiar words. He had said them often these past months.

"Shhhhh! I am dreaming!" Her eyes were still closed.

He dared not move, afraid to break the spell. Softly he whispered, "What are you dreaming of, Little Sister? Let me make the dream come true!"

She seemed to give the idea some thought, then said in a wistful voice, "I dream I ride in a golden dragon."

"Someday, I promise. Someday."

Abruptly, she straightened. "I want to do it now!"

"Now?"

"Now!" She stood up and started to pull him by the hand toward the door.

"What will your mother say?"

"She will never know."

He hesitated, but there was no sound upstairs and she was holding his hand. They raced to the door.

"No car! A hansom!" she said.

"Shhh." He nodded, stealing with her down the street.

There was one for hire on the next block. He helped her in and told the driver to take them to the creek.

But when he sat down next to her, she shook her head and pointed to the seat opposite. "It is too hot."

He moved and asked the driver for his fan and waved it in her direction.

She was as bewitching as a fox spirit in her pale yellow cotton sheath, her arms stretched along the width of the seat, her head upturned toward the sky. He waved the fan rhythmically.

"What are you thinking of, Lustrous Jade?"

"Snow and the icy wind of the north."

"Ask me what I am thinking of?"

"Shhh. It is too hot to talk."

"I will tell you anyway." He stopped fanning and leaned toward her.

"Lustrous Jade, will you marry me?"

She only smiled.

At the creek, he helped her with great care into one of the golden dragons that tossed against the wharf, until she lay safely prone in its bottom. To sit upright was to risk overturning the slim craft. He climbed in after her, stretching out so that they were head to head, their hands under their chins, their noses almost touching.

"Will you?" he asked.

"Perhaps." She closed her eyes.

So they lay until almost dawn. While she slept, he kept watch, dreaming of another dragon-boat race when he would stand with his arms around their son.

✥ 30 ✥

Riding the Tiger

If along the highroad
I caught hold of your sleeve,
Do not hate me;
Old ways take time to overcome.
        —The Book of Songs

THERE WERE MANY hansom rides after the first, but the magic of the night of the festival never returned.

The city suffered from remorseless heat. Torpor spread. Flies buzzed over dung, frantic for a turn to alight. Day after day people mistakenly said that the heat wave had reached its zenith and tomorrow must subside.

In the streets of baked mud, indigents died. Their bodies were carted away with others not yet dead but too weak to survive the hopelessness that stretched before them like an endless corridor.

On the Sunday when Lustrous Jade finally agreed to take August Winds to tea with Miss Clayton, their carriage passed such a cart. At once, she joined her hands in prayer. At once, he cursed his driver for choosing this route and not another.

A few minutes later, seated between them with cup in hand, he swallowed his disappointment and nodded politely as Lustrous Jade vented her anger at the sight she had just seen. It was no good trying to divert the conversation. How could his pain possibly compete with that of the poor, the orphaned, the sick?

When it was time to leave, Miss Clayton led them through her office to the garden walk. On a small table behind the teacher's desk were brown-tinted photographs, each in a gilt frame, each face with the missionary's intense pale eyes.

"Your family?" he asked.

Miss Clayton nodded, taking the opportunity to explain who was who.

He never would have believed that any person with so many relatives, even a foreigner, would go halfway across the world to live among strangers. Miss Clayton had even donated to the school the passage money sent her by her sister after the death of their parents. "Mother and Father would have approved," she explained gently, when he could not conceal his astonishment. "They were already with God. The money was put to better use here in China."

How sad, he thought, to have had a clan so large and yet no room in her life even for one of them. But riding home, he could not push away the thought that though one's complexion was as fine as porcelain and the other's as coarse as lemon rind, the lithe young beauty and her favorite teacher were kin. Like the missionary, Lustrous Jade would spend her life caring for strangers.

"August Winds, you are not listening," she charged. She was looking at one of the beggars, called chrysanthemums because their clothes were so tattered.

"I do not have to. Your lectures are always the same."

She glared at him.

"Please, let us not quarrel again." He reached across to take her hand.

She withdrew it.

"Be my wife," he begged

"August Winds, there is so much pain around us."

"But you give me only pleasure."

She shook her head. "Now you are laughing at me again. Ever since we were children, you have laughed at me."

"But I do not. I just do not want to live as if high purpose—"

347

He broke off, then began again. "Ever since Miss Clayton's return, good works have been all your life. Beggars and orphans. There are other things just as important."

"For me, they are everything."

He got up and took the seat beside her, whispering, "Lustrous Jade, you are everything to me."

"There, you are doing it again. Laughing at me."

"No, not at you. At us. Fate has set you and me upon the same tiger. We cannot ride it and we cannot get off. I, who desire you above all things, can never be the person you esteem. And perhaps if you became more like me, I would find you less desirable."

She did not disagree, and for a long time the only sound was the hoofbeats of the horse on the cobblestones. Such a hollow sound, he thought, wondering what had made him tell the truth. It served no purpose. It never did.

She asked, "Will you not even try to see things more my way, August Winds?"

He nodded.

"Will you come with me one day to the Door of Hope?"

"Sure, sure."

She took his hand. "And will you contribute to our cause?"

"Sure, sure."

When autumn came and Lustrous Jade began her classes at Shanghai College, August Winds saw even less of her. At Noble Talent's suggestion she had joined the Students Society for National Salvation and no longer had time for rides. If there was no schoolwork, or orphans to attend, there were political meetings. Far into the night she wrote and distributed pamphlets proclaiming all that must be done to save China, urging the patriotic to organize before the war ended, before the Allies gave back what belonged to the Chinese. "Only in a strong China can be found solutions to the ills of society," she explained.

Noble Talent worked with her. "We cannot afford any more rump Parliaments," he wrote, "any more cabinet shuffles, any more warlords. It is time to form a government that will keep what is China's." Meanwhile, he and Sun's followers waited for the right moment to make another try at establishing a southern government, one that would not be overturned by a clique.

One wintry morning, Lustrous Jade called on August Winds at M.S. & Company. It had been raining since nightfall and he had worked late, trying to close his books. He must have fallen asleep over the abacus, for he was at his desk when he was awakened by a loud knocking and her familiar voice. "August Winds, open up. I must talk with you. It is urgent."

The sun blinded him as he let her in. He winced and held his head.

"Are you drunk?" she asked, following him into the back room, where he took a swallow of cold tea from a half-emptied cup. "Are you drunk?" she asked again.

"I must be, if you are here." They sat down at the small marble-top table where his patron had once eaten his meals.

"I must talk to you, August Winds."

"Do not tell me." He put up his hand. "Let me guess. One hundred? Five thousand?"

She shook her head impatiently. "Have you read the newspapers lately?"

He yawned, rubbing the sleep from his eyes. "I do not need to. Nothing has changed. Famine in the North. Floods in the South. Warlords fighting all around. Politicians calling for justice. Students striking. Foreigners foreclosing. Teachers demanding more discipline. The Soviets are our allies. The Americans are unreliable. Japan is the enemy. Sun is mounting another campaign. Confucius is confused. And you, my little sister, my Margaret, my Lustrous Jade, need money for another one of your dire emergencies."

He shrugged, then went behind the screen on the other side of the room to wash his face. Stuck in the corner of the mirror above the basin was a picture of Lustrous Jade he had cut out of the church newsletter.

When he returned to the table, she sat in the same position, hands folded in her lap, straining one against the other.

"Remember when we were children, Sister?" he asked softly. "How we used to hide behind the rockery and study aloud? You could never get the answer because I made you laugh. You would stuff your fingers in your ears, but nothing worked. And you could only recite the multiplication tables if you plowed straight through." He smiled.

For a moment, her look softened, as if she did indeed remember, and he went on.

"I do not know why everyone thought you were so bright. I wager you cannot get through the times table even now."

She was not amused. "I have no time for this nonsense!"

"Sister, say your seven times table, please."

She ignored him.

"Please?"

"No! This is nonsense!"

He tried to take her hands. She hid them behind her back.

"Say the seven times table, or else I will not listen to what you came to say."

She gritted her teeth. "Seven, fourteen, twenty-one—"

He interrupted. "Twenty-one, twenty-eight."

"Seven, fourteen, twenty—"

"Sister, let us start over—"

"Seven, fourteen, twenty-one, twenty—"

"Please, a new start."

She stood up. "My brother, you have had a new start. China has not. You must help. There is so much to be done for our country, our countrymen."

He too rose. Why did he care? She was so . . . missionary. "I will not help strangers," he whispered hoarsely. "I will help you."

On the Sunday before they were all to go once more to Soochow for the New Year, August Winds came as usual to the house on Rue Flaubert.

Lustrous Jade sat in the library writing, her notebook on the arm of the chesterfield sofa. Pieces of paper, crumpled pages from the book, littered the floor.

"Have you forgotten, my dear Margaret? It is Sunday."

She glanced up. Her eyes were red, as if she had been crying.

"I am not going to church today."

"What is the matter? Are you not feeling well?" He placed his hand solicitously on her forehead.

She brushed it aside. "I am well."

"What is it then? The bells are already ringing."

"I *said* I am not going to church today!"

"But why? What has happened?" he asked, although he knew the answer. Like any man who succeeded by his wits, he had his own sources of information. He had already moved to protect his investments.

She pointed an accusing finger at the newspaper on the floor. "Woodrow Wilson lied!" Her despair was charged with anger. "The Allies lied! All the God-fearing Christians lied!"

The headline read: "Treachery at Versailles." The Allies were not going to return the German holdings in Shantung as they had promised. A secret treaty, signed months before China entered the war on their side, had promised the lands to Japan.

Could it be, he asked himself, that she had never suspected? It was politics, nothing important, just politics. He held out his hand. "Come, let us go to church. It will make you feel better."

She stared at him in disbelief. "I will never understand you! You never really believed. You only went to church because I did. Now you insist that I go!"

There was something in her voice he had never heard before. Contempt? "Is it so difficult to understand, my sister?" She did not answer and after a moment he said, "You must not turn your back on old loyalties, my Margaret, lest you get into the habit of doing so."

"What loyalties?" she asked bitterly. "Can you not see that China has been betrayed? Elder Granduncle was right. All the talk about Christian principles and the Fourteen Points was nothing but a trick to lull us to sleep so that foreigners could plunder us until there was nothing left. From now on, I will put no trust in their promises."

He was driven to argument. "But Lustrous Jade, such promises are always made by those who are at war to entice others to join them. So it has always been. It will never be different."

"You . . . you sound just like my mother." She tugged at his tie angrily. "Look at you. You dress just like one of them! You would have lied too! You do not care! You never have!" Her voice rose.

Suddenly, Spring Moon was at the threshold. She clapped her hands once. "That is enough, my daughter. You scream like a street peddler. Have you no self-control?"

August Winds stood up to put on his coat. "Please, my aunt, it was my fault. Perhaps I should go now." He looked toward Lustrous Jade.

She said nothing.

It was Spring Moon who spoke. "Yes. Perhaps that would be best." She accompanied him to the door. He bowed and hesitated, looking back, hoping to see Lustrous Jade at the end of the hall. She was not there.

Spring Moon smiled. "I shall expect you for dinner, August Winds."

He bowed. The church bells had stopped ringing. He walked slowly to the waiting car.

❧ 31 ❧
Games

Once there was a peasant boy from Soochow who journeyed far from home, until one day he came to a village in Hunan where a troupe of entertainers had stopped. The fair was a wonder to him, with attractions as many as the pebbles on a go-board. There were stilt walks, dragon dances, shaolin boxers, a panda, a camel, and a monkey that smoked a pipe.

A smiling barker called out to him, "Hey, Big One, want to double your money?"

"How?" asked the peasant.

"Pick up the cow, as does this little fellow here." At his signal a hooded man as wide as he was tall squatted beneath the drooling cow, then straightened, lifting the beast off the ground.

"I can do that," the boy boasted, and draped the cow around his shoulders like a straw cloak.

In the morning, as he ate his black beans and noodles by the roadside, twenty men appeared, each with a gleaming sword. The barker was among them. "Give me your money," he said to the boy, "if you value your life."

The boy shrugged. "Here are my winnings," he said. "The rest was mine."

The barker brandished his sword. "The rest, or I shall scoop out your liver and my friends will feed you piecemeal to the pigs."

The youth stood slowly, the smile of one prepared to fight unto death upon his lips. But before anyone had been sent beyond the Yellow Springs, a short, husky man appeared, the same who had lifted the cow. With a wave of his hand, he vanquished the foe.

"Who are you? A bandit chieftain?" asked the boy.

"My name," said the man, grinning, *"is Mountain Pirate. But you must come with me and decide if I am a bandit."*

And so the boy went into the hills.

Mountain Pirate, as a child, had snatched a squalling baby from the jaws of a tiger; as a youth, he had disarmed a hundred men with a look; as a man he brought peace to the villages, charging only what was reasonable. He and his men lived simply, sharing all they had equally, taking only what had been agreed upon, doing all that had to be done.

Thus, the peasant from Soochow learned that justice is not necessarily garbed in long gowns, and the defiant are not always the enemy.

—Clan story

IT WAS EVENING on the second Sunday of the Fortnight of Pure Brightness, and for the first time in many days Lustrous Jade was content. That morning Miss Clayton had convinced her to go to church. "Did you think, Margaret, that being a Christian was easy? In the life of every believer, there is testing. Not once, but many times."

So she had gone. And that very afternoon the Lord had shown her His grace, for she had been able to persuade twenty more merchants to send telegrams to Paris urging the walkout from Versailles of both the Northern and Southern Chinese Delegations, should Shantung be given to Japan.

Now she was talking to a true hero, someone who was a pioneer, not just a student. He was the tallest man that she had ever seen, with broad shoulders and an open face. His name was Resolute Spirit. Noble Talent had brought him to dinner, introducing him as the son of tenant farmer Lee, an old friend from revolutionary days who had just returned from France. Immediately she had asked for details of their exploits. And when Young Granduncle said no more and her mother merely fussed about eating the fish before it was cold, she had turned to the hero himself. He had made light of his role by laughing. Only after much prompting on her part had he mumbled something about being an errand boy who supplied melons.

This man is different, she thought. So unlike August Winds, who needs to boast to make himself tall.

"Young Lee," she said, "tell me, then, about your experiences in France. What did you see there, and what did you do?"

"I saw little. I dug graves for the Frenchmen who died fighting the war."

"Did you meet any of our students there?"

"I met some. They taught me to read a little and that we should learn from someone called Marx. One of them, T. J. Hu, became my friend. It was he who helped me and others return . . ." He stopped, as if remembering, then said abruptly, "I did not much like France."

"But why?" She would have given anything to have been in France.

"Once the war was over, the French no longer wanted us."

"How could that be? You were there to help them with the war."

He shrugged. "Not all were unkind. I did not like it most because it was not home."

For a moment she did not know what to say. She remembered the Lee hovel, the sickly children who must be his nephews, the smell of night soil. Finally she blurted, "I saw the land your people farm, when I was staying in Soochow. I did not think they had enough to eat."

Resolute Spirit blushed.

"Let our guest enjoy his meal, my daughter. You talk too much." Spring Moon served him another helping of chicken.

"But I am interested."

"Perhaps," Bold Talent said quietly, "the tenant does not wish to discuss such things in front of landlords."

"Oh, no, sir. Your clan has always been good to us. Master saved my life." Resolute Spirit smiled in Noble Talent's direction.

"An exaggeration! An exaggeration!" replied the soldier, filling the younger man's glass with hot rice wine.

Before Lustrous Jade could think of a way to resume the discussion, August Winds tapped his glass with a chopstick, a grin on his face. "I think, my friends, it is time for a game!"

Oh no, she thought.

"Yes! Yes! Yes!" cried Enduring Promise.

"Settled, then!"

"How about a round of antithetical couplets?" suggested Bold Talent. "Shall I start by stating the head?"

"I want to be first. Can I be first? Oh, please?" Enduring Promise clapped his hands, upsetting his glass.

"Fine, you start," said Bold Talent.

Silence.

"Well?" said Spring Moon, removing the porcelain cups from danger. "Well?"

The boy's face reddened and he covered his eyes, as if not seeing meant being unseen. "I do not know how." Everyone laughed. Enduring Promise turned to Resolute Spirit, who was the only one still eating, and tugged at his shirt. "Can you explain the game to me?"

Resolute Spirit peered over the rim of his rice bowl and said nothing. August Winds coughed into his handkerchief.

Bold Talent recovered first. "I will explain, my nephew. You start by making up the first line of a poem. Then one of us must match it with an antithesis and a parallel."

"Yes, Uncle. But can someone explain the game to me?"

Even Bold Talent joined in the laughter.

When it had subsided Spring Moon took the lead. "What is the opposite of earth?"

"Heaven," the boy shouted.

"Moon?"

"Sun."

"Walk?"

"Run."

"Night?"

"Day!" called out Resolute Spirit, catching on.

He looked apologetically at the child. Enduring Promise smiled up at him, as if to say he did not mind, then asked, "May I start now?"

"Careful," cautioned Spring Moon. "We have just begun. Green trees?"

"Red trees."

Spring Moon shook her head.

"But why, Sao Sao?"

"A word that is opposite of green, and a word that is the same family as tree."

"Red flowers."

"Correct." Spring Moon smiled. "Now, yellow birds sing."

Enduring Promise took a deep breath. "Green frogs talk."

"Almost; better if 'green frogs croak.'"

Lustrous Jade saw that Resolute Spirit had resumed eating, as if the bowl were a screen behind which he could hide. He does not understand the game, she thought. Why should he? The game was not important, a pastime for book bags. If only they could go into the parlor and talk!

Spring Moon was coming to the end of her explanations. "The first line, Enduring Promise, is called the head; the reply, the tail. Now you may begin."

The boy buried his head in his arms to think. The adults waited. He popped up, opened his mouth. Nothing came. He frowned, then buried his head in his arms again.

The only sound was that of Resolute Spirit slurping soup.

August Winds spoke up. "My friend from France," he said, "why do we not show the boy how to play the game?" He smiled innocently. "You, beautiful girl, are sublime, fragrant as spring water, learned and good."

Resolute Spirit grinned, shrugging his shoulders.

"Take your time, my friend. We have not had dessert yet!"

Still the peasant did not reply.

It was the boy who answered, tugging at his shirt again. "He tricked you, Older Brother! Now you must say, 'I, ugly boy, am ridiculous, smelly as mud, stupid and bad.' He tricked you!"

Resolute Spirit did not know where to look.

Quickly Lustrous Jade filled in the silence. "No, Enduring Promise, you said it. My new friend is much too smart to be taken in by such a trick."

As the laughter faded, August Winds lifted his glass to Lustrous Jade. His smile was bitter. She did not care. Nothing he could do would stop her from seeing more of the farmer's son.

When the meal was over, Resolute Spirit stood and bowed most respectfully. "My ancestors and I thank you for this honor. Tonight is the happiest day of my life."

❧ 32 ❧
The Vanguard

*What would later be known as the May Fourth Movement
began when, on that date, in The Year of the Sheep, 1919, thousands of boys and girls marched through Peking toward Legation
Quarters to protest the infamy of the allies and to plead China's
case. The police turned them away. Angered, the students burned
the house of one pro-Japanese minister and abused another.*

Many were arrested.

*The public was outraged. Merchants, workers, intellectuals, cit-
izens in all the major cities joined in a patriotic strike against
continued injustices and national humiliation.*

—Chinese history

THE SUN HAD ALREADY disappeared behind the domes and spires of
Shanghai. Still August Winds did not come. Lustrous Jade tapped
her foot impatiently, paced the width of the offices of New China
Publications, looked again up and down Nanking Road for the
familiar Pierce Arrow. Why today, of all days, was he late? She
fingered the swatch of material hidden in the pocket of her skirt.
Over and over, she rubbed its surface, unable to stop, as if it were
a sore tooth.

At last the car appeared. She gathered the pamphlets headlined
"Peking under Martial Law" and hurried out, giving the address
to the chauffeur before sliding into the seat next to August Winds.
"You are late!" She spoke sharply, without greeting.

"The streets are clogged with demonstrators. We had to detour several times." He paused. "Were you worried about me?"

She lied and said, "Yes."

He smiled. "How good to see you, my sister. It has been a long time, and I have missed you."

She avoided his gaze, staring at the flyers she had stowed on the floor of the car, but he seemed not to notice. "Have you missed me? Even a little?"

Must he look at her that way? Quickly she launched into the speech she had prepared. "This morning Resolute Spirit and I went to ask a certain Mr. Ling to forfeit his Japanese goods for the cause. No matter how much we appealed to his patriotism, he refused. He accused me of being a hypocrite and a convenience patriot."

"How dare he?" August Winds sounded angry.

"Exactly what I said. He claimed that I was calling for the burning of Japanese goods so that my relatives could profit from the new scarcity."

"That is ridiculous!"

"I asked him for the names of these so-called relatives of mine." She paused, looking into his eyes for the first time, hoping that he would say something. He did not. She continued. "The man named you." She paused again, but August Winds again said nothing. "He said that you only pretended to sacrifice profit for patriotism. He claimed that you had not burned your Japanese goods, that you had burned only the few yards you needed to cover the fake bolts which you threw into the fire. When the show was over, he said, you changed the markings on the goods and sold them as Chinese. I defended you. I asked him for one shred of proof. He challenged me to ask you."

August Winds reached for her hands, but she withdrew them. He shrugged and laughed. "That Ling has an imagination. Can you not see that he has cut my foot to fit his shoe? Do you really believe that I would do such a thing?"

"I do not know," Lustrous Jade answered. "Do you deny it then?"

"I deny it."

"The truth," she said slowly, softly. "The truth this time, August Winds. It is most important to me."

He shook his head sadly. "But I have told the truth. Ling is the liar."

"August Winds, you are the liar!"

She took the scrap of cloth from her pocket and spread it on the seat between them. The markings had clearly been altered.

"You should have told me the truth!" she cried. "I begged you for the truth."

She gathered the flyers and opened the window behind the chauffeur. "Stop at once, please. I am getting out."

The car pulled over to the curb. She did not wait for the Russian to open the door.

Ahead, gathered around a bonfire at the intersection, was a group of young people. Some chanted rhythmically, "China awake! China awake!" while others fed the fire with confiscated Japanese goods. One who towered over the rest turned toward the car, as if he had been expecting it. The stench of burning combs, rubber tires, soap, silks, perfumes, umbrellas, tooth powders, toys, books, clocks, medicines, thermos bottles, was overpowering.

"Sir," Lustrous Jade heard the chauffeur ask, "shall we wait?"

She looked back. August Winds was staring at the fire. There was the sound of an explosion. He held out his hand. She turned away and walked, then ran to join Resolute Spirit and the others at the intersection.

Four days later, Lustrous Jade woke at dawn. There was still time, and she lingered in bed rehearsing the speech she had written, changing a word here, a phrase there. It must be the best speech. It must move even the most reluctant to action. When she was satisfied, she prayed that her voice would be strong, as forceful as the whirlwind. Please God. . . .

She washed quickly. For the first time she pulled on the loose blue cotton trousers and short-sleeved peasant shirt and slipped into the straw sandals she had bought from a street vendor in the Chinese sector. Carefully she checked the contents of her satchel for all that would be needed if she could not return home that night. When she was satisfied, she slipped the shoulder strap over her head and inspected herself in the mirror. Yes, that was right. Almost. For a moment she could not decide what was missing. Then she remembered. Since early May the students had been wearing white cotton caps—white for mourning—in place of the once popular straw Panamas from Japan. She took hers from the bedpost and tried to secure it in place with pins. Her hair proved unruly, slipping out of its topknot. The cap fell to the floor.

She tried again.

Then, disgusted, she gave up and rummaged through her drawers for the scissors. She brushed her hair free. It fell to her waist. Holding it with her left hand, she cut it straight across, just below the ears. When she set the cap on her head again, it stayed where it belonged. Once more she looked in the mirror, smiling at the coolie who smiled back.

Outside, several other students were waiting with Resolute Spirit and his friend Hu. Mei Mei too had cut her braids, and they all laughed when the peasant pronounced their haircuts a doubly good omen. Lustrous Jade looked up at him and nodded approvingly. He blushed.

Side by side, they started down the rue Flaubert. At each street corner, more young people waited to join them. Throughout the International Settlement they marched, gathering forces. All was as had been planned. None of the stores, save a few foreign ones, had opened. Even the beggars were gone from their usual locations. They, too, had joined the strike. At intersections, piles of Japanese goods burned while onlookers cheered. Girls in school uniforms directed traffic.

Only on Lantern Lane did they stop. In front of a rice shop stood a Chinese merchant, shouting at a group of angry pickets. "Go away! Never have I closed this shop! Never have I suffered losses! Never will I do so!"

One of the youths recognized Lustrous Jade and pulled her toward the front. "Only you can persuade him. You must! He is the only one who refuses in this entire section."

What could she say? She glanced toward Hu, half expecting him to come to her rescue with some tactic of Lenin's. Hu shrugged helplessly. The merchant shouted even louder. "Never did my ancestors close this shop. Never will I, and break the chain of fortune. Go away!"

Ancestors . . . the chain of . . . Suddenly Lustrous Jade almost smiled. It was so simple, after all. She would not badger him or call him names but would venerate him publicly, making it impossible for him not to act more worthily.

She raised her hand, asking for quiet. Even the merchant stood still, watching her.

Without a word, she fell to her knees and kowtowed. The crowd gasped. Three times her forehead touched the ground. Then, "O friend, honor your ancestors by honoring your country," she implored him.

She looked up. The merchant was very pale. She kowtowed again.

"If you do not do your duty, I shall leave my head on your threshold until you seek the path of virtue!"

Again she looked up. At last the outraged merchant spoke, his voice quivering. "I shall join the strike. Now go!"

The crowd cheered. Smiling triumphantly, Lustrous Jade rose and, linking arms with Resolute Spirit and Hu, led the parade once again. Behind her, faintly, came the sound of shutters closing.

Hundreds were already gathered in front of Wing-on Department Store in the British Concession when Lustrous Jade and Resolute Spirit led their group up Nanking Road. Girls were passing out bundles of leaflets. Boys unfurled white banners painted with red characters: "Free Student Demonstrators," "Boycott Japanese Goods," "Impeach Traitors," "Down with Imperialism," "Citizens Awake."

The cart was in place, along with the megaphone and the flower drum. It was hot, and Lustrous Jade was glad when Resolute Spirit gave her a boost onto the makeshift platform. He smiled up at her. "Do not worry about anything. I shall be right here."

"I am fine. Go and mingle. People know you and will feel confident when they see you among them."

She watched as he made his way through the crowd and then turned to tell Hu to start the drumming. But the marchers were oblivious to the call to order, talking, whispering among themselves, occasionally laughing.

"Give the drum to me," said Lustrous Jade.

When the only sound was the boom of the drum, she put it aside and began. "Citizens of Shanghai! Peoples of the world! Listen, and heed what we say!

"China awakes. China is united. China speaks with one voice. Students, scholars, farmers, merchants, workers, artisans—men, women, and children—all speak with one voice!"

The crowd cheered.

Let them cheer, she thought. Let the people be heard. Her eyes swept the audience. Here and there among those gathered, she recognized a face.

"Citizens of Shanghai! Peoples of the world. We gather here to demand sovereignty, to protest promises solemnly made and treacherously broken. Those who subject us, enslave us, degrade us, to them we say, Beware! Beware!"

The crowd repeated her cry. "Beware!"

"Heed our one voice. Where many pursued different paths, now there is one people. We strike for justice. Justice at Versailles. Justice at home. Justice in the high councils of the government.

"We shall be heard. You who would stand in our righteous path, beware! You who wrote the Magna Carta, the Declaration of Independence; you who once cried Liberty, Equality, Fraternity; you who call yourselves democrats and ministers of the people, beware!

"China awakes. So long as there are those who dishonor us, patriots will march! Students will not study, workers will not work, merchants will not trade, until justice is done.

"If the country is paralyzed, so be it!

"China awakes! Beware! Soon will come a new tide, a renaissance, a cultural revolution! Beware! Beware!"

Now the cheering was an endless wave that filled her with pure joy. She had done her job, and she had done it well.

She descended from the cart and slowly, buffeted by the aroused students, made her way to the edge of the crowd. Then, raising the drum high, she struck it in measured cadence and stepped forward. The others followed. Up one street, down another. The thoroughfares of the European town echoed. "China awake!"

Suddenly the marchers stopped; before them was a solid wall of police. At their head, the European captain brandished his sword. He ordered the students to disperse or face arrest.

"Arrest us! Arrest us!" Lustrous Jade cried. "All patriots to jail!"

The crowd took up the chant.

Our voices have the strength of a whirlwind, she thought. The police started to encircle the vanguard.

Out of nowhere, Resolute Spirit appeared and took her arm. "Come, I can get you out of here."

She shook him off. "But I do not want to go!"

"I promised your uncle I would see that nothing happened to you. You must come with me."

"I will not." She smiled. "Are you not a patriot? Are you not going to jail?"

"But I promised—"

"Are we not both leaders of this march? We of all people must go to jail."

For an instant, he was still undecided. Then he threw back his head, laughing, and took up the chant. "To jail, all patriots to jail."

The jail was an empty room on the ground floor of the Nanking school. When they were locked inside, the patriots cheered.

Seated on the floor, they chatted and took turns telling stories, singing songs.

The next morning, the doors were unlocked. The students were told to go home.

Lustrous Jade immediately stood up. "I will not go until the traitors in Peking are punished!"

Resolute Spirit stood up. "I will not go until the traitors in Peking are punished."

One by one, all stood up and took the pledge. Throughout China, the answer was the same.

❦ 33 ❧
Mother and Daughter

Wherever there is repression of the individual, wherever there are acts contrary to the nature of the individual, there can be no greater crime. That is why our country's three familial bonds— between prince and subject, father and son, husband and wife— must go, and constitute, with religion, capitalists, and autocracy, the four evil demons of the empire.
—Mao Tse-tung, New People's Study Society, 1918

SPRING MOON PEERED out the opened window at the dusty street, waiting. With the dismissal of the pro-Japanese ministers, the student demonstrators had triumphed. Lustrous Jade, after nearly a week in jail, would be coming home.

For a moment she wished Gifted Seer were beside her, although the mynah bird could tell her nothing she did not already know; prophecies do not alter fate, only confirm it. No other sign would have been more telling than Lustrous Jade's refusal to leave the school the second day after her arrest, when all had been arranged by Noble Talent and August Winds. She had said no as easily as if she were declining another cup of tea.

Now, looking back, it seemed to Spring Moon that there had been so many signs. Born outside the courts, at a time when ladies saved honor by seeking death in wells and the Hanlin library burned. Sent away first from her home in Peking, then from the Altar of the Ancestors in Soochow. How could she expect her daughter to care for her *lao chia* when the girl had never known the shade of the old Cypress, or heard the calling of faithful companions?

The telephone rang. Enduring Promise was in the room at once. "Wei, wei, wei?" he shouted into the apparatus. There was a pause. Then, "I am fine, my nephew! Are you fine too?" Still shouting. Another pause. "Yes, Sao Sao is here."

Spring Moon stood up, smiling at the boy. In the weeks before the demonstrations began, Lustrous Jade had neglected even him, so infrequently was she at home. Last night, he had not asked for the girl to hear him say his prayers.

She took the telephone and waved the child upstairs to take a nap.

"August Winds, any news?"

"Yes. We were right. Your daughter will be home today."

She sighed with relief.

"She is fine, I am sure. Do not make yourself sick over her. She is a good girl at heart. Once home she will listen to reason, you will see!" His voice was tender, like that of a filial son.

Suddenly she thought she would cry, seeing a vision of her daughter in short hair, remembering how grown men had wept as they begged their elders' forgiveness, though their queues had been forcibly severed. She had not seen Lustrous Jade the day she had left the house, nor two days later, when she and Bold Talent had waited in vain outside the school. But she had retrieved the cuttings and put them away in a box. It had seemed the thing to do.

"Auntie, are you all right?" When she could not speak, he said, "Auntie, I will come at once." The line went dead.

In minutes, he was at the door. Concentrating on each word, each gesture, she led him into the parlor. "You see, I am fine." She smiled gratefully.

He studied her, chatting kindly about matters of no consequence, until she offered him refreshments. Then he said, "I should be going, before Sister returns."

"Please, a few minutes more, August Winds." She paused, collecting the thoughts she had planned to voice at dinner, before she knew her daughter was coming home.

"August Winds, has there been any change in your plans for this house? It has been over a year since we moved in, surely long enough for you to decide if the investment will be a profitable one. Recently I have been offered a teaching post in Soochow and could easily return to the courtyards. Lustrous Jade is always welcome to stay at the mission. Do not be afraid to inconvenience us."

He stared past her. "Nothing has changed. My plans are as they were."

"But for some time now I have suspected that no railroad station or factory will ever be located here. You should sell this house and start over."

August Winds shook his head slowly as if he did not wish even to hear her words, much less consider them.

"Please," she urged gently. "Listen to what I am saying."

"Auntie, a good businessman always sees opportunities no one else sees. I shall turn a good profit yet. This is not an affair that can be decided in a year or two or three. I have no other plans. I can afford to wait."

"Are you certain that it is wise?"

"Yes." His voice was low, as if he were talking to himself. "This is what I want to do. I plan to wait, wait as long as I must." He lit a cigarette. After a few puffs he put it out. "Auntie, you must help me!"

"I can help by leaving, by forcing you to sell. . . . August Winds, I see no sign that anything will change. I fear you have been dreaming."

"What harm is there in dreaming, my aunt? When I showed up at the gate of the House of Chang, a ragged orphan with a letter of introduction from my dead mother, I dreamed that someday I would be rich. That dream has come true. No one would have believed it then. No one would deny it now."

"And so it is, but this time—"

"It is the same."

There was a long pause. When she spoke again, the words were meant for herself as well. "One dream come true in a lifetime is already a bounty from the gods. Dream on, and you will be disappointed. I am older. I know there are things even the gods cannot change—"

"They cannot change the hearts of men." He finished for her.

In the distance she heard the popping of firecrackers, like laughter remembered when happiness is gone.

Two hours after the demonstrators left the school, Lustrous Jade stood at the intersection and watched Resolute Spirit and Hu march away toward the Teahouse of the Lost Flute, where strike leaders were to discuss a literacy program for workers. Every few steps, the peasant turned to wave, smiling as if to assure her that all would be well. She had wanted to go with them, but Resolute Spirit had insisted that she should not. "A mother's heart is a fragile thing. Besides, I am responsible for your absence from home this week. Do not make your family think me entirely untrustworthy, entirely disloyal. Please?"

She had agreed. Now she was uncertain, watching her friends go off without her. What difference would an afternoon make? Her mother would be angry just the same. Slowly she turned and walked up Rue Flaubert, each step a trial.

When she opened the front door, Spring Moon was sitting by the window, staring at her, staring through her. Mother does not know me, she thought. She approached cautiously and bowed.

Spring Moon rose. "Are you well?"

"I am fine, Mother. I have never felt so well."

"You are too thin. What have you had to eat? Never mind, I have had the cook prepare a few things. . . ."

How could she eat? "Mother, I am not hungry. I—"

Spring Moon wrinkled her nose. "What is it you smell of?"

"Mother, you are imagining things. Perhaps it is the firecrackers you smell. We lit many in celebration."

Her mother was not listening, but reached up and removed the cap she still wore. Smoothing down the short hair, Spring Moon said as if talking to herself. "So carelessly done, yet it suits you. You look—"

"Never mind my hair." Lustrous Jade slipped out of her reach. "Do you not know that the whole country is awakening? There is a new spirit of unity, a new resolve. The march was just the beginning. Today, three ministers disgraced. Tomorrow—"

"Daughter!" Spring Moon's tone commanded. "Daughter, do you not understand how I have worried?"

Lustrous Jade shook her head impatiently. "I told you I am fine. My speech was a great success." She paused a moment. When her mother did not respond she hurried on. "Even before the speech, I proved myself. A merchant on Lantern Lane refused to join the strike, said it would be bad luck. *Hwen tan!* But even he joined when I kowtowed—"

Her mother stiffened as if slapped by an icy hand. "You what?"

She hesitated. Why had she told her? She had not meant to. Now it was too late. "I said that I kowtowed. . . ." Spring Moon's face was expressionless; in her eyes no light, no recognition. The cap in her hand fell to the floor. Lustrous Jade stooped to pick it up and set it upon the table.

Although she towered above her elder, she felt as if she were shrinking, had shrunk until she was as tiny as the reflection in her mother's eye. The silence between them gripped her like a fist. She dared not move.

And when Spring Moon spoke at last, it was not her mother's voice that she heard.

"Never, my daughter," she said slowly, "never again will you kneel and knock your head at the feet of a stranger. By such deeds, you have humiliated our clan. By such deeds, you soil the very name the ancestors have bequeathed us."

"I meant no disrespect."

"You lie! How dare you lie to me!"

Lustrous Jade had never before seen her mother lose control. Even now, anger lasted no longer than a flash of lightning. Visibly Spring Moon asserted her will, and when she spoke again she was calm. Too calm.

"Daughter, we kneel only to our elders and our ancestors, out of deep reverence and respect. Did you not once write an essay on the evil of kneeling before idols? Now you kneel before mere merchants. Surely any god, to those who worship him, is more worthy."

"But I did not kneel to worship, Mother," she argued. "I knelt to show my sincerity."

"You knelt to háve your way, knowing full well that to kowtow before strangers is a shocking act, knowing full well that kneeling is submission. How dare you flaunt your disregard for those we honor? What has happened to your sense of filial piety? When that is gone, what is left?"

Lustrous Jade said nothing.

"What is left, Daughter?"

Again, she said nothing.

A third time her mother demanded, "Answer me. When filial piety is gone, what is left?"

The injustice welled up, choking her. It could be swallowed no longer. Deliberately, she began, "When filial piety is gone, what is left is"—she paused, taking aim, using the very words her mother had once used in a hansom cab, long ago—"what is left is a 'person of character'!"

Spring Moon did not move. The silence in the room weighed as heavily as the night weighs before a battle at dawn.

Finally, the mother said, "When filial piety is gone, there can be no family. When family is gone, there can be no civilization. When civilization is gone, men are no better than beasts." She drew herself up and stood very straight. "And I, who gave you life, shall not have a beast as a daughter. Kneel, child, kneel!"

No! Lustrous Jade cried silently. You must not. You must not make me do such a thing. For a moment, she thought she would turn and run out the door. Then, unexpectedly, her legs failed and she sank like a broken kite to her knees.

Even as she knelt, she made a vow. This would be her last act of obedience, the last time she would be a child. No more would she kneel: to her mother, to her elders, to her ancestors.

The eyes of the two women met. Spring Moon looked weary, as if she had not slept for days. It did not matter. Within Lustrous

Jade was the hardness of anger grown cold, as strong as steel.

The mother reached out to help the daughter stand. Without a word they climbed the stairs.

That night Lustrous Jade awoke to the sound of weeping and hurried to Enduring Promise's small chamber. The child was asleep. Softly closing his door, she walked to the next. For a long time she stood there, remembering. It had been a beautiful hansom, almost new, with leather seats and a white horse.

"Where are we going, Mother?"

"To school."

"How long?"

"Six years."

It is so long, she had thought then, so long. Without father, without mother. Like the orphan, August Winds.

Gently her mother had brushed away the tears.

Tapping lightly, she entered the room.

⊸§ 34 ⧉⊱

The Proposal

Who could guess, who could guess,
A poor man's cart
filled with tears . . .
Truly, a hatred born in a day
Takes a thousand years to die!
                    —T'ien Chien, about 1950

IT WAS THE FIRST day of the Fortnight of Rainwater and a month before the forsythia blooms, but there was a hint of spring in the breeze off the water as Lustrous Jade made her way quickly along the Woosung docks toward the riverboat. She used the two empty baskets she carried as shields, pushing her way among the peddlers and rickshaws, the crates of chickens and pigs that crowded the wharf. Every now and then, forced to pause by the milling crowds, she watched the beggar women who battered the sides of newly arrived foreign steamers with baskets at the ends of bamboo poles, crying for coppers. Strapped to their backs and chests, the hungry children of China.

On one dock, where a ship from the Philippines was pulling in, coolies fought among themselves for space, each wanting to be first to leap up and cling to the deck, to scramble aboard, perhaps to secure a job. The passengers lined the rail and watched as if it were a sport, cheering for one or the other. The young and agile made the leap easily, but not long ago she had seen an older man plunge to his death. He had dived from the top of some crates, missed, slipped, caught himself on the lip of the deck. Hands weakened by hunger would not hold. In a moment he was gone. Another had taken his place.

No member of the family knew of Lustrous Jade's journeys on the river, or anything about the activities that brought her to Woosung. Ever since she had defied them to stay in the school prison, she had kept some of her political work secret even from Young Granduncle. Had he not tried to obtain her release before their objectives were achieved, saying, "You are, after all, a girl"? And later, when strikes threatened to engulf the Concessions and even the foreigners imposed censorship, had he not refused to print her essay on the compradores, saying the merchants would be offended?

Secretly she had bought a mimeograph machine, with money obtained from August Winds, and had hidden it in the back room of the godown where Resolute Spirit worked as night watchman. There they and Hu now printed the views of the Student Union as well as her own essays and Hu's translations of Marx. Every two days she carried the forbidden pamphlets to Woosung, to a young student who met her at the fish stand in the local market. He in turn passed them to others, and they to still others, until copies reached schools all along the coast.

Today the student had not been there when she arrived, and she had been delayed. Now, stepping aboard the riverboat, she asked that they depart right away. She must not be late for the Student Union meeting.

The deaf old boatman, who always ferried her back and forth, evidently did not hear her, for he merely bowed, saying, "Your visit went well, Young Mistress? Too bad so crowded. Too bad."

Impatiently she repeated the order, louder this time, and walked forward to take her seat before he could speak again.

The old man said the same things each time. Each time they passed the Japanese mills, he spat into the water and cursed, "Aye ya! Nothing but a herd of buffaloes farting smoke and soot!" Each time they sailed through floating refuse, he scooped it up, saying, "Aye ya! Nothing but banana peels for my dinner."

She had no time for his idle chatter. Her thoughts were on her list of things still to be done. Must see Miss Clayton at once about a doctor for Sister Su, who, fearing the child would cost her her job, had jammed a chopstick into her womb. Must start a drive to recruit more student volunteers to teach the women of the silk factories to read. Must update the list of unpatriotic merchants and publish it. Resolute Spirit and his friends could not picket all the offending establishments at once. Publishing the list might aid the boycott of those who continued to deal in Japanese goods.

"Mistress, hold on tight!" The old boatman shouted. "Foreign steamer coming close."

She nodded and braced herself as the small craft tossed in the wake of the bigger boat. Resentment welled.

Would nothing ever change? Had she merely been spitting into the water like the old boatman? Perhaps Young Granduncle was right. "Your schoolgirl demonstrations accomplish nothing!" he increasingly complained. "Nothing matters as long as there are unequal treaties, as long as warlords carry on like bandits, fighting among themselves like the foreigners for another slice of China. We need the merchants' support to fight the foreigners. Force the Chinese out of business and the business goes to the Japanese. Priorities, Grandniece. One step at a time. I have been at revolution longer than you!"

But that was exactly Hu's point. "What revolution? Sun is a clown! What difference have his yearly revolutions made to those without a rice bowl? Lie down with merchants and you are no better than the warlords!"

"Mistress?" called the boatman, pointing toward the old fortifications on the shore. "Mistress?"

She sighed. "Yes, yes, I see. . . ."

"You may not believe it, Mistress, but once I wore a gown and marched along the ramparts. . . ."

She nodded absently and returned to her own thoughts. Only Resolute Spirit never belittled her efforts. Nor was anything she suggested too difficult for him. If she needed twenty men, he produced them. If she needed information, he obtained it. Though he was a big man, others seemed to feel protective of him.

They care for him as he does for them, she thought. Suddenly she was smiling. Her first impression had not been wrong. Together, the peasant and the granddaughter of the Hanlin were inspired. No one could deny his warmth and her zeal.

The sun was low in the western sky when the riverboat reached Shanghai. Lustrous Jade disembarked even before it was secured and made her way quickly through the crowds on the Bund to the intersection at Nanking Road.

Suddenly there was the squeal of brakes, a scream. She looked back. Passersby ran to the scene of an accident. Despite the lateness of the hour, something drew her there as well.

By the time she had pushed her way to the front of the crowd, several Sikh policemen had arrived to hold back the curious. A black coupe had swerved onto the walk. Beside it stood a foreigner with a thick mustache, mopping his brow.

One of the Sikhs, a sergeant, saluted. "I saw it all, sir. The fool ran across your path." He spoke in English.

"I did not see him!" cried the driver. "I did not see him!"

An American, she thought. She forced her way to the other side of the car and broke through. The old boatman was sprawled on the cobblestones like a stain. Her two baskets, unbroken, lay beside him.

The two men approached the body. "Who was he?" asked the foreigner, turning quickly away, his face very pale. He leaned against the car.

"No one," said the Sikh. "Just a coolie."

"Poor yellow bastard." The foreigner shook his head. "What should I do?"

"We will take care of it. From the looks of him, you did him a favor."

The other reached into his coat for his wallet, took out a handful of bills. "Maybe this will help."

"Keep it, Sahib. It happens every day. You should go now."

He motioned to one of his subordinates. "Ride along with the gentleman. See that he gets to his destination safely."

With his men the Sikh forced the people back, clearing a path in front of the car. For a while they stared after it, muttering, then began slowly to drift away.

The baskets! She darted toward them. Others did too. She wrested one of them from an urchin. "It is mine!" she cried, not knowing why. "It is mine!" The child let go and ran, disappearing in a moment.

The other basket was already gone. The other worthless basket. Worthless to her, but not to the boatman. He had given his life for it, for her. She clung to the basket as if, by seizing it, she could see to it that he had not died for nothing after all.

She had never told him, not on any of their journeys together, that she could indeed imagine him as he once had been: an officer in the Imperial Service guarding the gate to the Middle Kingdom, wearing the long gown, colored feathers in his thick queue. Or was that only his dream?

Suddenly she felt faint and made her way to the lamppost on the corner. Leaning against its base, she watched the death cart approach. When it had left, men with hoses washed away the blood.

She turned away and went on, up Nanking Road, aimlessly walking. She tried to imagine the boatman in heaven. She saw him instead on the death cart, still bleeding. He had not believed in Jesus, had worshiped idols. He would never inherit the earth, this good man who had run after her to return two baskets of straw. There were millions like him, too poor to buy a shirt, too weak to fight.

Why, Lord, why? Over and over she asked. Again and again, there was no answer.

It was dark when she found herself at the mission school. She had not been here since the parades began. She started to run inside, but the guard, a new one, stopped her.

"Hey, you do not belong here!"

"I have come to see Miss Clayton."

"Not here," he said brusquely. "Gone to the interior."

"But I must see her!"

"Next week! Come back next week!"

She turned away and walked the few steps to the church. The candles on the altar were lit. She sat in the front pew to pray. "Our Father, Who art in heaven, hallowed be Thy Name. Thy Kingdom come, Thy Will be done, on earth—" She stopped and began again. "Our Father—" The words choked her. God did not know her coolie. Poor yellow bastard. Just a Chinese.

The door opened and closed, letting in a gust of cool night air. She shivered, listening to the footsteps that approached her and then stopped across the aisle.

"Our Father, Who art in heaven . . ." a man murmured.

Turning, she stared at him.

"Forgive us our trespasses . . ." he intoned.

And of course it would be so, she thought. God would grant forgiveness to this Christian, this foreigner. Lustrous Jade rose and left the man praying.

It was after midnight when she found herself outside 42 Rue Flaubert. There was a light in her mother's room.

A car drew up beside her. "Lustrous Jade, where have you been?" August Winds held the door open. "Get in. Get in."

She obeyed.

"What is wrong?" He put his arms around her. She did not resist. "I told your mother that you were with me. She expected you home for dinner and called my place. I have been waiting here for you ever since."

At last the tears fell.

"What happened? Why do you cry?"

She said nothing. How could she explain that she grieved for an old boatman? That she mourned her mother's daughter and Miss Clayton's student and, now that she was in his arms, the girl in the dragon boat?

He whispered her name over and over, holding her tight until she cried no more. When she still did not move or speak, he kissed her urgently, as if afraid she would vanish, as if only his passion could detain her.

He knew her well. It was true, she would be going. Perhaps not this year, perhaps not even the next. But she would be going. For a moment she clung to him and nothing mattered except desire, long refused.

But when they drew apart, she saw in his eyes such happiness, such hope, that she was immediately sobered. She touched her hand gently to his lips and shook her head, whispering, "No more, no more." Then, slipping from his grasp, she let herself out of the car.

He called after her, but she was already backing away.

She stood for a moment in the moonlight, halfway between the car and the house, looking up at the lighted window as if to say, Mother is waiting. Then quickly she ran the rest of the way. He did not go until she was safely inside.

Closing the door quietly, she thought again that she would be going. She must not let them hope. Must not break their hearts again and again. Only once.

It was days before she remembered the basket. She had left it on the floor of August Winds' car. There would be no use in asking for it.

Several weeks later, on a day when the daffodils along the Bund were in bloom and the vapors of heaven and earth seemed to harmonize, Lustrous Jade and Resolute Spirit walked briskly toward New China, pushing their way through the afternoon shoppers on Foochow Road. Near the corner of Pearl Street a crowd stopped them.

"Is it an accident?" she asked impatiently, looking up at him.

He shook his head, grinning. "Just a peddler."

"Just a peddler?"

He nodded, then broke into guffaws. Not knowing why, she found herself laughing too. When at last they regained composure, she asked, "What was so funny?"

"Would you buy hair tonic from a bald-headed peddler?"

Laughing again, she knew suddenly that she had waited long enough. "Come, this way," she said, darting down a dingy side street, signaling him to follow. As always, he did so without question. She led him to the tiny Tea Shop of the Nightingale's Lashes, where, having passed by it often, she was quite sure they would find no one they knew.

The old men who sat in the shop every day, smoking or playing mah jong, looked up, frowning at the disturbance, while the portly owner came running from the back room and wiped off the top of an empty table. "Here, please!" He smiled and bowed as the two young people sat down.

"Young Mistress, Young Master, may I serve you some Cloud Mist tea? It is the finest quality, picked by the nimble monkeys on the highest peaks of Kiangsi, steeped in dew collected from the hearts of ten thousand lotuses."

"Your cheapest will be fine," she said before Resolute Spirit could answer.

The owner sighed and, shaking his head, disappeared into the kitchen, while the old men nodded knowingly until the one in gray shouted "P'ung!" and drew the attention of the rest.

"Why have we come here, Young Mistress?"

"Young Sister," she corrected him again. "Remember, we agreed!"

Smiling, he rapped his forehead and pronounced it as empty as a drum.

"Do not talk about yourself that way!"

He shrugged. "You did not answer my ques—"

The owner was back, setting before each of them a cup of half-brewed tea. Brown specks of tea leaves covered the surface of the lukewarm water.

Resolute Spirit did not seem to mind. Spreading his elbows on the table, he peered into the cup and blew the bits of black gently to the bottom. Lustrous Jade pushed hers aside, wondering for the first time what his reaction might be to the idea she had been considering for so many weeks. The plan was logical. It had not occurred to her that he might have objections.

"Older Brother—" Her throat suddenly was dry, and she reached for her cup. "Older Brother," she began again. "Although we have been working together for over a year now, we have never had a personal talk. Still, I feel as if we know each other very well. Do you not agree?"

He smiled again. "Yes, we always agree."

"And are we not the best of friends?"

He blushed and nodded.

She waited for him to say more, but he avoided her eyes, staring instead at the birdcage rack, where the old men had set the pets they had been airing.

It was no use. She would have to ask him a direct question. "My brother?"

"Yes?"

"What do you really think of me?"

He blushed again and lowered his eyes, sipping tea.

"Please tell me."

"People like me are not clever about words. Why must you ask?"

"I must know."

He started to drink again. She put her palm over his cup.

"Please, what do you really think of me?"

"I think . . . I think that—" He cleared his throat.

"Yes?"

"I think, Young Sister, that I would die for you."

She sighed. She had been right. He would marry her. And once married, she would be safe. There would be no going back.

"Older Brother, I do not want you to die for me."

"I mean—" He drew on the wood with a thumbnail. "Why do you ask me such things? I must be blushing like the backside of one of those tea-picking monkeys."

"But you said that we agree on everything."

"About the strikes and the foreigners and things like that. But we are not alike in all the other ways."

"You mean because I am a Hanlin's granddaughter and you are the son of a tenant farmer?"

He nodded. "You read English and write characters faster than I can say them. The only thing in my father's house that matches the number of books in yours is fleas. Your ancestors are all scholars. I am the first born in my family who can even write our name."

She saw an image of the Altar of the Ancestors in Soochow, his peasant family standing incongruously beside it. Quickly she dismissed it. "You do not understand. My rightful place is not with my mother, not with my clan. My rightful place is with the work we do together. I do not care for ancestors. I care for the things you care for. China, not the clan, is my family."

"No." He shook his head emphatically. "No. Even for a modern girl, what you say is not proper." Suddenly he stood up, bumping into the table, knocking over a cup, searching in his pants for money. "From now on we will see each other only at meetings." He put a handful of change on the table. "I am sorry."

Picking up the coins, she gave them back to him. "I do not wish to go yet. Please stay."

Slowly he sat down again in his chair.

Be patient, she told herself. Be patient. She sipped her tea. It was cold. "My brother, this is a new China, and we are not children anymore. We have both signed pledges to marry only those we freely choose for ourselves. Is that not true?"

He glanced around at the old men; one had cupped a hand to his ear, afraid of missing a word. Resolute Spirit moved his chair so that his back was to them, shielding her.

Let them listen, she thought, and repeated, "Is it not true?"

"Yes, but—"

"Resolute Spirit, I want to marry you."

He stared at her. For a moment, she thought he was angry. Then he said, "Are you making sport of me?"

She reached out and touched his hand. "Of course not. It is just that I do not want to marry a stranger of my family's choosing. I want to marry a friend whose ideas are the same as mine."

She paused. "Since you would never ask me, I must ask you."

Now both her hands covered his. "Can you not see that we are well matched?"

He shook his head. "Your mother would never agree."

"She would if she thought I would be always alone, without a home, without children, like Young Granduncle. And that is what I would vow!"

There was wonder in his eyes. "You would do that?"

"Yes, I would. . . ."

"You must not. This is crazy, just crazy talk!"

Again she asked, "Will you be my husband?"

He hesitated, then whispered hoarsely, "No. It would be wrong."

She did not press him further. It would take time.

SOWING
DAWN

❧ 35 ❧

A Print of the Heart

I left home young. I returned old,
Speaking as then, but with hair grown thin;
And my children, meeting me, do not know me.
They smile and say, "Stranger, where do you come from?"
                    —He Chih-chang, Tang Dynasty

CLOUDS HOVERED over Shanghai, the breath of a doomed dragon intent upon revenge. Bold Talent stood with his brush poised above the calligraphy table, unaware of the coming storm, though servants scurried throughout the house, shutting windows.

The room he occupied had once belonged to Spring Moon. For years it had been bare except for the waist-high table and a bookcase where his inks, brushes, papers, and watercolors were stored. Here, he was free to journey to other worlds. Here, like the scholar-poets of the past, he used the calligraphy strokes he had practiced for a lifetime to paint images inspired by memory or vistas seen from mountaintops he would never climb. Thus he enjoyed infinite possibilities, creating balance and coherence. Contentment.

The inspiration to paint had first come to him three years ago, when he returned alone to the house on Bubbling Well Road after Lustrous Jade's graduation and Spring Moon's departure for Soochow. Only the night before there had been the plaintive cry of the child, the whispered "hush" of the woman who had called to him. With them gone, the empty rooms had reverberated with silence, so devoid of sound that its absence jangled his nerves. He had stood for hours at this calligraphy table, but no words had come, the hand that gripped the brush as unsteady as it had been when he left San Francisco.

He could not remember drawing the first leaves, the twig of bamboo. Bamboo that yielded to the wind and thus was never broken. Feverishly, he had painted, sprig after sprig. "Worldly passions are the thieves of life," the old man had said to the Tang painter Ching Hao. "Virtuous men occupy themselves with music, calligraphy, and painting and do not indulge in inordinate lusts."

Hour after hour, he had worked until his brush seemed to fly, moving of its own accord, seizing without hesitation the shape of the narrow blades of bamboo.

Then, night after night, gradually he added to his repertoire—the grove, the sky, the mist, the shadow of moonlight, the figure that dozed—until he had mastered all the forms from the Mustard Seed Garden Manual. To capture their essence, he sometimes waited through an evening, recalling a panorama or a feeling. But once he put brush to paper, the painting was revealed in a spurt of rhythmic energy. The vision completed, he was both exhausted and refreshed.

Tonight he saw a placid pool and carp, chiffon skirts flashing. He soaked his brush in pure water, moistened the tip in the pale ink he had prepared, and pressed down on the paper so that the ink on the tip spread along both sides to outline the watery area. He repeated this for each fish, then added the rock, the porcelain taborets, and, in three vital strokes, a girl with her hand outstretched.

When the memory had been caught, he studied the painting and was satisfied. A print of his heart had been made.

The Sage said once that the soul of a wise man is that of a child. The child in him would always be Spring Moon. In another life, in another season, how could they be apart? Like the moon and the sea, they would forever move in concert. His hand hovered a moment above the flying pigtails, the skirting of red. Then he cleaned his brushes and put them away.

As usual, he went downstairs and asked the servant to bring him tea. When it was served, he sipped it slowly, piping hot. Somehow the taste was never the same as when Golden Virtue brewed it—no matter that the leaves were picked and dried in the same year, by the same hands. At first he had thought it was the water, and his wife had thoughtfully bottled some for him to take back to Shanghai. But it had made no difference.

Golden Virtue had had a nightmare during his last visit home. He had heard her crying as if in pain and had hurried to her chamber to comfort her. After a while she had told him her dream. "I had been baking bread all week, my husband. You came into the kitchen and commanded me to return the loaves to flour and water. I tried and tried but what was done could not be undone. When I reported my failure, you sent me away and I walked and walked, *li* after *li*, in my new high-heeled shoes."

For the rest of the night he had stayed with her, watching her sleep, wondering if she regretted the day he had sent Noble Talent to see her father.

At the thought of his brother, he sighed. When away, Noble Talent wrote long letters, opening his heart, telling of all that troubled him, "a barren life with nothing to show for it." Yet when the soldier was in Shanghai, sitting across the table in this room, hours would go by and not a word pass between them. Perhaps it is my demeanor, he reasoned. Seeing me somehow makes him irritable, as if he thinks that I have failed the Venerable, failed him, failed our cause. Perhaps it is true. I loved the old too much to uproot everything. . . .

His cup was empty. When he poured another, the tea was cold, and he summoned the servant again, to take it away.

Turning out the light, he mounted the stairs. Perhaps, he thought, we scholars see only what we wish, hiding the rest behind a mist, as in the vistas we paint. Impressions, without detail. The man is dwarfed by the mountain; the pain or the joy on his face, the clothes he wears, who can tell? A scene without reality. No battles, no blood.

"We see too far." He spoke aloud. "Perhaps we do not see at all."

Sleep did not come. Always in the late hours when he sought rest, the troubles at New China plagued him, and as the minutes dragged on, more and more he worried about waking early, for that inevitably happened too. Caught between the two prospects, he lay awake, wide awake, so very tired.

He wished he could be done with publishing and its financial difficulties. His friends were losing interest and had hinted more than once that he should sell and give back what he could of their investment. He had resisted their kind offer, hoping each year that he would make a success of it. But then Noble Talent and Lustrous Jade had begun to meddle. Instead of textbooks, they printed and gave away revolutionary tracts that threatened to bring down upon them all the wrath of the warlords or of the Peking clique or of the foreigners, unless substantial bribes were paid.

He shook his head. That was unfair, and he knew it. The press had never made a profit and never would.

All at once the room seemed unbearably stuffy. Who had closed the windows? Had there been a storm? He got up and opened them, standing there a moment watching the moon slip in and out of view among the clouds.

"What is death like?" the boy had asked. He himself wondered now, shaking his head at the thought of the little monkey. His spirits, like Spring Moon's, were irrepressible. Had his own sons been the same when they were his age? He did not know. Their letters came regularly, once a month. Grand Vista studied mathematics at Harvard. Bright Vista had left last year to pursue physics and geology at M.I.T. They could tell him what a mountain was made of, but they had no feeling for it. How different their letters were from those he had written the Venerable. Theirs were—schedules. His, snatches of idle thought.

When his sons were ready to return home, would he be there? It would be his last chance to know them. . . .

Little by little, the idea of returning to Soochow took hold until it became the only thing to do. He would ask August Winds to see to the sale of the house and the press. Or perhaps the orphan would enjoy the role of publisher as he seemed to enjoy everything else, as if life were an amusement, nothing more. No doubt New

China's chances for survival would be better in his hands—if he did not talk someone else into buying it for an outrageous sum. Once more Bold Talent smiled. To think he had once worried that August Winds would grow up to be a field mouse burrowing in the Changs' granary!

He turned up the light and sat for a while, studying the cypress etched on the lid of the cloisonné box on his night table, remembering his father's ghost at the gate.

❧ 36 ❧
The Cadre

Year after year, the popular demonstrations continued. City after city was struck, ports were paralyzed. Coolies laid down their yokes at the command of agitators, or so many claimed.

Year after year, the warlords plundered and fought, and the treaties remained unequal. Tens of millions perished because of the floods and the droughts.

Against such formidable woes, the enemy of an enemy became a friend. Sun Yat-sen, a Christian educated in the West, turned to Russia for hope, and the Comintern ordered the Chinese Communists to subordinate themselves to Sun's Kuomintang Party. Together, Communists and Kuomintang built an army to "eradicate the traitors within and resist the aggression from without." In the summer of the Year of the Tiger, 1926, after Sun's death, Chiang Kai-shek launched in Canton the Northern Expedition to unify China.

But as territory after territory was won, the united front split, each faction wondering how an enemy could be trusted to share the rule when the battle was done. Nowhere was the problem of deciding who was friend and who was enemy more troubling than in Hunan, where Mao Tse-tung, alternate member of the KMT Central Executive Committee and head of the Peasant Department of the CCP, filed this report in the spring of the Year of the Rabbit, 1927.

"A man who owns as little as 50 mous of land is classified as a local ruffian and a man who wears a long gown is denounced as an evil member of the gentry. . . .

"A tall paper hat bearing the characters of Local Tyrant So and So or Evil Gentry Man So and So is placed on the head of

the person to be punished; then he is led on a leash around the village. . . .

"The execution of one shakes the whole country to its foundations and is in fact a very effective instrument in the elimination of feudal influences. . . .

"Shortly several hundred million peasants will rise like a tornado or a tempest, a force so extraordinarily swift and violent that no power, however great, will be able to suppress it. . . .

"They will send all imperialists, warlords, corrupt officials, local bullies, and bad gentry into their graves. All revolutionary parties and all revolutionary comrades will stand before them to be tested."

—Chinese history

HER HEAD LOWERED against the cold wind, Lustrous Jade trudged up the steep, narrow mountain trail, through forests of spruce as thick as fur, toward the Village of Blissful Woods. Her feet were like stones, every step an effort. Ten more *li* to go and only the thought of a bowl of watery rice gruel to sustain her.

She never doubted that she would make it. The girl who had taken little pride in her beauty had grown into a woman quite vain about her strength. Within a month after Resolute Spirit had brought her to these hills, he had dubbed her his Mountain Jade, and the name had pleased her more than all the prizes she had won as Margaret. In the six years since then, she had learned quickly the harsh dialect of Hunan and had thrived as a circuit teacher-organizer in the sectors of the province controlled by the Peasant Association.

She had learned as well to live always with uncertainty and danger, for Resolute Spirit's work was to extort money for the cause from the landlords and merchants on the periphery, and she never knew when he might be betrayed or caught. She had given birth to her son, New Destiny, alone and had carried him on her back everywhere until he was two years old. Only when he contracted a fever that would not abate had she returned briefly to Shanghai to leave him with Spring Moon. Her mother had not recognized her.

At a fork in the trail, she paused to catch her breath, thinking, as she often did, of Miss Clayton. The people at the school had said only that the missionary had died in Hunan, as if it were a spot on the map, a small village. She could have pursued the matter, but the news had come just when she and Resolute Spirit were about to leave Shanghai and there had been so little time. Now it seemed best to go on thinking that her teacher was buried over the next ridge, close by.

It was early afternoon when she reached the Temple of Soaring Spirits, set so high on a precipice that when there were clouds it was hidden from the villagers who tended the fields below. From afar, it looked celestial. Within, it was dingy and damp. But the score of women who were already there, stuffed against the cold with paper and straw, like scarecrows, evidently did not notice. Keeping an eye on their toddlers, they braided hemp or made soles for shoes from scraps of cloth. A few nursed babies. All chatted merrily. In winter, this was the only place where so many could gather and gossip.

"Lai le! Lai le!" Eager hands helped her with her knapsack, pulling her toward the only chair, an ornate rosewood throne confiscated from the landlord's house and placed near the fire for her use. Sister Oong put another stick on the meager flame, and all watched silently while the cadre drew off her mittens to warm her hands. Their breath steamed, rising toward the jagged hole in the temple roof.

After a while old Dew Drop, who was the group leader, pursed her mouth and clucked. "What a terrible trip in this weather. Just to teach us unteachables. We have been stupid so long. Another month will make no difference. Landlord's gone to Shanghai. Lands are all divided. Young toes are all free and wriggling. Everything is fine."

"Not fine to me," shouted a large surly woman in the back.

Dew Drop spat in disgust. "Pay no attention to that one."

But the unhappy one pushed her way through the crowd to confront Dew Drop, in the cadre's presence, with her grievance. "What about my equal share? My mou of rock is not the same as your mou of bottomland."

"Old Mah, you are getting *hoo li hoo too!*" Dew Drop charged, looking to Lustrous Jade for an expert opinion.

She pretended to be busy, warming her hands. Better they fight it out than for her to impose her views—in this matter, anyway. They had had the same argument every month since the lands had been divided. Before that, another subject, but the quarrel endlessly the same.

"Not *hoo li* enough!" Mah shook her fists with fury. "I know better than to be content with a mou of rock when you get a mou of soil!"

Others joined in.

"No more bad talk. Lessons this week."

"It is all the same. All the same."

"You lose face for our village."

The women's voices grew louder and louder until Dew Drop clapped for order. When all was quiet, she said again, "It is all the same."

"If it's all the same, why do you not trade with me? Your mou of land for my mou of rock, Dung Drop!"

Magnanimously Dew Drop ignored the insult and drew herself up in a most dignified way. "Do not be so greedy! What did you have before the Association? A mou of gas!"

Amid laughter, the large woman stomped out, defeated.

Lustrous Jade opened her mouth to call her back, then resisted the impulse. Best to start the lesson, she told herself. Mah would return before long.

As she stood, the women quieted. Patiently she went over last month's work, the writing of their names and the characters for mother, father, sister, brother. There were no pens or paper or books. Each word had to be written on the dirt floor with a forefinger and erased with a sweep of the hand.

Once the old characters had been memorized again, Lustrous Jade traced the new ones for each student. China. Rice. Donkey. Land. Freedom. Feudalism. As always, some got discouraged and drifted to a corner to resume their chatter. Only the most determined memorized all their words. Of these, half would forget them before her next visit. Must remember, she thought, "A prairie fire begins with the striking of a single match." Must remember, it is a beginning.

She stood and stretched, her back aching. Out of the corner of her eyes, she saw that Old Mah had crept back inside and was hiding behind a pillar. She went over and took her hand, leading her to a seat beside the rosewood chair. There was a murmur, but no one objected.

It was her practice during the first class of each week-long visit to tell the women a story when the literacy lesson was finished. Not only was she usually too tired from the trek to conduct political exchanges, which inevitably stirred up passions, but they liked the stories better than anything else, and a week that began with one usually went well. Now, clapping her hands, she announced that today's tale would be that of The Great Silk Factory Fire, which led to Young Huang Organizing the Spinners.

The women cheered and gathered around as she took her seat again. Watching their eager faces, she smiled to herself. The parables she told were so unlike her mother's, yet the spell they cast was the same.

While she waited for the group to settle themselves, one small boy wriggled his way to the front. She thought of New Destiny, sitting at Spring Moon's feet, listening to stories. He would be five years old in a few weeks, and he did not know her. Nor could she see him in her mind's eye. Just a suit of silk so high, no face. She could almost hear August Winds' voice, chiding her. "Even that missionary of yours framed the likenesses of her family, if only to look at them now and then. But you—" She roused herself. The women were waiting.

Patting the head of the boy, who laughed and drew it back like a turtle, she began.

"One day while the women of the Heavenly Silk Factory worked into their twelfth hour, and their children too, the fat owner, lighting his opium pipe, carelessly threw down the match. . . ."

The words never changed, nor did the women's responses: the screams and moans of horror as the flames consumed the workers, the shouts of rage at the capitalist who had locked the factory door lest any employee leave a few minutes early, the determined cheers when the surviving son of one who died vowed to make the owners pay—pay for the one hundred lives lost, pay for the one hundred cisterns of tears shed. . . .

At the end, with a wave of her hand, she brought them to their feet, all together, shouting.

"All power to the masses!"

"All power to the workers!"

"All power to the peasants!"

The meeting was over.

With only an hour or two of light before nightfall, the women hurried toward the village, peeling off in twos and threes, mouths clamped shut against the cold.

It was Sister Oong's turn to be the cadre's host. At the tiny mud-brick house, Lustrous Jade was introduced to the rest of the family, first the father and the brother, then the mother and the grandmother, who had been busy all day preparing for the visit. They openly stared at her as she unwrapped the goatskins that covered her head, shoulders, and feet and washed in the bucket of water they had brought for her from the nearby stream. She was as tall as the men. Her hair, shorn just below the cheeks, was tucked behind her ears.

When she had finished, they offered her a bowl of hot water, for there was no tea. Sister excused herself to prepare the meal, leaving the others sitting on the k'ang, watching the stranger sip.

The old man said, "If only we could offer you some sweets, or melon seeds."

"If only I could have brought you some."

"Soon we will have everything we need to eat. Soon, when all of Hunan is free."

"China," she reminded them. "When all of China is free."

They nodded solemnly.

Her stomach growled. She emptied the bowl. Immediately they offered more. She declined, thanking them profusely. The awkward silence returned.

Suddenly the mother announced, too loudly, "Yes! Before the Peasant Association, we were oppressed, nothing but slaves to the landlord. We worked his fields and he got most of the grain. When our supply was gone, he sold us a few *ching* to eat at heavenly prices. When our money was gone, he loaned us a *cash* or two at the devil's interest. He raped us and then charged us for the pleasure."

The brother spoke up. "If I were not an only son, I would be a revolutionary soldier in the great Northern Expedition."

She knew these recitals by heart, having heard them often, the same words in all the villages she visited. Tonight she was too hungry to give the proper response and merely nodded as, one after another, each member of the family eagerly described the trials they had endured under the landlord, vying for the most colorful incident, exaggerating and reliving the past until all were sincerely angry again.

At last the meal was served. It took only a few minutes to swallow the watery gruel and salted turnips. Then, as the sun set, they went to sleep. There was no lamp.

When first Lustrous Jade had stayed overnight in peasant homes, the sounds and smells of people and chickens packed into a single room were so disturbing that, no matter how tired she was, she would often lie awake until dawn. Now she slept dreamlessly, unaware of Sister Oong snoring beside her, of the baby's whimpering, of the old uncle crying out in his sleep. Sister must have tugged long at her clothing before she was finally awakened. "Please, Teacher, please wake up. You must help me."

"What? Is it morning?"

"No. You must listen. You must help."

She reached out. The girl was trembling. "What is the matter?"

"He would listen to you. You are a big person, a cadre. Not from Blissful Woods. You could make him—"

"Who?"

"My husband. He'd listen to you. Tell him to take me back." Sister Oong sobbed into the quilt. Helplessly Lustrous Jade patted her shoulder, trying to soothe her. "It will be all right. You will see. It will be all right."

After a while the girl went on. "I was just a foolish child. I ate everything when he was in the fields, and when it was gone I stole away to my father's house and asked for more. What did

I know of how a man feels? He lost face. He has a quick temper and beat me. But I have a quicker one and divorced him on the spot, for the Peasant Association had said that everyone was free."

Once again she sobbed, unable to speak. Lustrous Jade waited, knowing full well how the story would end. Once again the cadre would be expected to perform the ancient duties of a go-between.

Finally, Sister Oong continued. "But when I returned here to my home, no one welcomed me. They said I did not belong here anymore. I was just another empty stomach. And it is true. It is true. Until I leave, my brother cannot be married. What would his wife eat? And without a wife, there can be no son, no grandson. You see, you see? You must tell my husband to take me back!"

Lustrous Jade held the woman, rocking her, whispering, "I promise. Tomorrow. I promise. . . ."

Slowly Sister Oong's trembling ceased. "Promise?"

"I will. I promise," Lustrous Jade said again. "Tomorrow."

But the next morning a courier arrived, summoning the cadre back to headquarters.

She hurried to gather her things. The matter must be urgent, whatever it was.

Before leaving, she sought out Sister Oong, who was doing laundry by the stream.

"I will be back, Sister. Soon. And then I shall speak with him, just as I promised."

The peasant girl, beating her brother's shirt against a stone, did not look up.

The return trip took many hours, and by the time she reached headquarters, the *lao chia* of the former landlord, it was late afternoon. She hurried through the two moon gates and past several cobblestone courts to the room where the guard had told her to wait. It was bare except for two stools and a rickety table on which a clock ticked sluggishly. Long ago it must have been a kitchen; the walls were black with soot.

She had been there ten minutes when the door opened and a short man she did not know entered. She jumped to her feet.

"Good day, Comrade." He waved her back to her seat and sat down on the stool across the table from her.

Picking up the clock, he wound it tight, saying nothing. At once, she knew him to be important, one who demanded discipline above all. He was in no hurry to say what he had come to say. She tried to wait impassively for him to speak, but in the end she blurted out, "Is this about my husband? Has something happened to him?"

The man did not answer. Deliberately, he pulled each of his fingers until the knuckle snapped. At last, he shook his head slowly.

Thank God! In her relief, she almost smiled, amazed at her reaction. The old words. What would this man think if she had voiced them?

As the minutes passed, her irritation returned. Petty bureaucrat!

"Are you always this . . . this agitated, Comrade?" He stood up and walked to the small window. "The Party has decided that you and Resolute Spirit are to leave immediately and report to Comrade Chou in Shanghai. He plans another strike to put our people in charge lest the KMT usurp our position when the revolutionary army arrives."

"I thought the strike had already been called, a few weeks after the New Year."

"It failed. The warlords and the foreign police killed hundreds and forced the people back to work. We must try again."

"Resolute Spirit and I will leave tonight."

"Now. You will leave now. Everything is ready. Your husband knows the route and waits at the stable." He turned and held out his hand and, for the first time, smiled. "Good luck, Comrade."

Four days later, Lustrous Jade and Resolute Spirit reached the River Yangtze, which, dividing north from south, connected east and west, and embarked on the seven-day journey downstream to Shanghai. Their boat was flat-bottomed, with transoms made of a single plank jutting above the water, one sail and two oars and a thatched tunnel that formed the main shelter. Resolute Spirit could pace its length in six steps, Lustrous Jade its width in four.

Around them floated vessels as numerous and varied as autumn leaves blown from the forests. Freighters, tugs, lighters, barges, gunboats. Fireboats, barber boats, peddler boats, hay boats, flower boats. Houseboats filled with lepers never allowed to land, and rafts of bamboo tied together in the mountains, destined for construction sites in the cities. Gray steel hulls trailing plumes of coal smoke and flying the Stars and Stripes or the Rising Sun or the Union Jack. Here and there a paper boat launched to propitiate the gods. Their first day on the river, Resolute Spirit scooped up one in peril and sent it safely on its way.

For the first time since they had married, it was he who knew better what must be done and how to do it. He taught her to sail and to steer and to fish, and the best way to unfurl the oilcloth and cleat it against the rain. She learned that deep water is found near a steep bank, that danger lurks near ledges, that swirling waters hide a rock and oil patches often mark a sandbar.

When the plum rain fell, he saw beauty in the ghostly apparitions that loomed in the mist. And when the steamy sun glared at them, he dipped his straw hat in the river and shouted with delight as cooling water trickled from his hair. Sitting on his haunches, he watched the shore for hours without moving.

Often he laughed, and she knew that he was thinking of their son, thinking that soon they would be together. "New Destiny can read now, do you not think, my wife?" he would say. "New Destiny will have cheeks that beg to be pinched, I know." Or, another time, "New Destiny's skin will be smooth and white like yours, I am sure."

At night, when they tied up in the marshes, mosquitoes tormented her but he ignored them, busy fashioning a reed whistle from one of the cattails that flourished along the river.

For Lustrous Jade, sleepless nights made the days long, too long. She bristled at Resolute Spirit's contentment. His attempts to conceal it, as other men concealed their infatuation for a concubine, annoyed her even more. She would catch him smiling at a glimpse of a taut sail or a flight of geese when he thought she was not looking, hear him sigh with pleasure as he smoked his pipe in the moonlight when he thought she was asleep. She thought only of the tasks ahead, and how long the journey.

Did he ever think of such things? If he did, he never said, though when she mentioned the Party and their work, he made all the correct comments.

What can be so wrong, so unbearable, he seemed to ask, if the sun rises and there is enough to eat and we are going together to our son and the river runs out to sea as it always has? She wondered sometimes if he was any different from the rickshaw coolie who drools at the promise of a few *cash* and shrugs off his certain death at a young age. And yet in the mountains there was no one more reliable, more courageous than he.

The fourth morning, after a fitful night during which she had been awakened again and again by the sobs of Sister Oong, she complained that he had kept her up with his snoring.

"But I did not even go to sleep, my wife."

"You did. You snored like a herd of pigs."

"There could have been a herd of pigs on shore, but I was awake. This area is full of bandits. I did not dare sleep." Then, almost as if he had guessed her thoughts, "It is the mosquitoes. You are not used to them. Tomorrow I shall buy some incense from a peddler boat to keep them away from you."

"I tell you, it is not the mosquitoes." Her eyes were moist with chagrin. "Say so again and . . . and I will kick you!"

He nodded, smiling. "Go ahead, kick me. It might make you feel better. It will not hurt me."

Now it was she who read his thoughts: My wife, you are a Hanlin's granddaughter and accustomed to another life. I am a peasant and can get along on nothing.

She kicked the side of the boat instead and stubbed her toe and, hobbling past him, tripped into the mosquito netting.

Later, he took out a needle and thread and sewed up the tear.

❧ 37 ❧
Two Divided

*By the month of the Spring Equinox in the Year of the Rabbit,
1927, Chiang Kai-shek's revolutionary army had driven the soldiers of the warlords from Shanghai and occupied the Chinese
city, while foreign troops protected the Concessions. Now all
the provinces of China south of the Yangtze were under Kuomintang control, and rumors spread of the imminent betrayal of the
right factions by the left. Or of the left factions by the right,
depending on one's loyalties.*

*In Shanghai, Comrade Chou En-lai positioned his men, storing
weapons for possible use against Chiang. But unlike the idealist
Sun, who had trusted Yuan Shih-k'ai and so lost control over
the revolution of 1911, Chiang was not one to have his victory
wrested from him by rivals. Anticipating a possible Communist
insurrection, he ordered the arrest and execution of CCP officials,
strike leaders, and those known or suspected of allegiance to the
radical left. On April 12, squads of armed men fanned out through
the city. Hundreds were killed in the "White Terror."*

*Old enemies of new enemies became friends. Foreign troops,
defecting warlord soldiers, and members of Shanghai's under-
world joined the hunt for those Communist leaders who had
escaped.*

—Chinese history

ON THE EIGHTH DAY of the Fortnight of Pure Brightness, the Patriarch
of the House of Chang hurried down an alley in the Chinese sector

of Shanghai. It was early morning. The streets, lined with tenements, were silent, dark. The scholar's pace never slackened as he lifted his skirt, wading through puddles formed by yesterday's rain. A dog yapped at his heels.

The shot came from nowhere. There was no pain, only curiosity. Bold Talent saw himself falling, saw his body huddled on the cobblestones that paved the narrow alley. In the distance, the shooting continued. But the sound the bullets made against the brick grew increasingly faint—the clicking of tiles.

P'ung, dragons! *P'ung,* bamboos! North. South. One final play. Mah jong.

What am I doing here? he wondered. Oh, yes. He had come to play with his mother in the women's pavilion. The Matriarch arched an eyebrow. Son, you are too old to play here anymore!

Heartbroken, he returned to the dormitory, to the long, echoing room where he would sleep from now on without her, among the cousins. She had sent a packet of his favorite sweets, tied in a silk scarf, to comfort him.

Spring Moon, is that you?

Golden Virtue, do not cry! No, I am glad, I am proud. You, my modern wife with big feet.

Spring Moon, is that you? Today we will learn to count. When I wore a tiger cap and tasseled shoes the Venerable taught me this way. Listen carefully, now!

> One—the Cosmos
> Divided becomes
> One, Two—Yin, Yang,
> Opposites that form the Whole.
> One, two, three, four, five
> Seasons:
> Spring, Summer, Mid-year, Autumn, Winter.
> One, two, three, four, five
> Directions:
> East, South, Center, West, North.
> One, two, three, four, five
> Elements:
> Earth, that gives birth to
> Wood, which is cut by

Metal, that melts with
Fire, which is extinguished by
Water, that is dammed by
Earth. . . .

There is that sound again. What is it? Not mah jong. Louder now. *P'ung! P'ung!* Guns firing. A battle. A war. Not foreigners this time. Chinese against Chinese. Family against family. Revolutionary against revolutionary.

Must warn Lustrous Jade. Must warn Noble Talent. To Shanghai, hurry! No, must not fall. Falling.

No, Enduring Promise, this way. Look, a horizontal *tiao,* a short *pieh,* a rounded *kou.* That is the way to paint the stroke of the chanting insect. A man's calligraphy is a portrait of his character, the work of a lifetime.

He is very like you, Spring Moon. He shares your gift of joy.

It is done, Noble Talent. The Manchu sways on the silken cord. You are safe. So easy to topple a dynasty, after all.

"Bold Talent."

"Yes, Father?"

"Bold Talent, do not become enamored with the process; remember . . ." Remember what?

One—the Cosmos

Divided.

It was twilight when Noble Talent's car entered Shanghai for the first time in a year, passing quickly through the Chinese suburbs, where bodies still littered the execution grounds. Wagons piled high with corpses lumbered down the alleys. Again and again there was a sound not unlike firecrackers. The soldier, a general now, stared straight ahead at the back of his driver, ignoring what he had not wanted to see, longing to be in the quiet of a house untouched by battles that were not battles but betrayals. The car proceeded without incident through the barbed wire that cordoned off the Concessions, where thoroughfares were empty except for the foreign soldiers and the iron tanks.

When he reached 42 Rue Flaubert, it was dark. He did not wait for the vehicle to come to a complete stop before opening the door, pausing only to order the driver back to the barracks.

"Perhaps I should stay, sleep in the car."

"No, it is not necessary. Go. Get a good rest."

The boy saluted. "Thank you, sir."

Noble Talent stood very straight and watched the car move away, wondering what the young man thought of this kind of war, and if he had had a brother in the student underground. Only when the car had turned the corner onto Nanking Road did he approach the mulberry trees, shimmering in the moonlight, that flanked the entrance of the house.

When he reached the door he was suddenly impatient, and he knocked continuously until the hall light came on and he heard footsteps. The door opened just a crack, then wider.

"August Winds?"

The man's face was ashen, and he had dark circles under his eyes. "You . . ." he whispered hoarsely. "I had hoped . . ."

August Winds said nothing more but pulled him quickly inside and led him into the library. On the chesterfield sofa lay the body of Bold Talent. The servants had washed and dressed him, restoring decorum and dignity, and candles flickered on a small table nearby. No artifice could hide the wound in his head, though his features were undisturbed.

A breeze from the open window lifted a strand of white hair. It fluttered above the brow. August Winds reached out to smooth it back.

"How did this happen? What was he doing in Shanghai?" The soldier's voice shook. For a moment, he expected his brother to answer.

August Winds shrugged. "I do not know. Auntie took New Destiny and Enduring Promise to Soochow weeks ago, before the trouble started. The police brought his body to the door, saying only that he had been shot."

"By whom?"

"It could have been anyone."

The clock in the hall began to strike: one, two, three . . . Noble

Talent counted. The last chime hovered in the air. It was nine o'clock.

He whispered, "Does anyone in Soochow know?"

August Winds shook his head. "I had planned to tell them in person. I had planned—"

"Please, will you leave me alone with my brother for a while?"

"Will you be all right?"

He nodded, removing his gloves and holster, setting them carefully on the desk, as if they might explode.

"In that case, I shall take the servants with me to the office. There are arrangements to be made."

Noble Talent nodded again, then knelt. The latch clicked.

Hours later, still alone, the younger brother took from his vest pocket the letter he had begun many weeks before, during the campaign of the Northern Expedition in Chekiang province. He had not had time to finish it. Now he would deliver it himself. Clearing his throat, he read.

"Eldest Brother,

"I am surrounded by my admirable troops and cheering crowds in Hangchow, but I am alone and need to speak to you.

"I have dreamed of such a victory march ever since father sent me to the academy. Now that it is a reality, I know that I enjoyed the dream more.

"The truth is, I abhor the masses we have liberated, their poverty of mind and body, though I realize it is a disease they are born with and cannot cure. The truth is, the filth, vacant passivity, and violent passions of these peasants repulse me more than I dare admit, except to you.

"A child from a hovel by the road runs after me, begging for a ride; the more he squeals, the deeper I dig my spurs into the horse's flank.

"Proclaiming it the ultimate cure, a toothless farmer presses into my hand bread soaked in a murderer's blood, obtained at the instant of his beheading. I kick him away.

"I know that we could not have advanced these seven months

were it not for such people. They feed us, house us, and spy for us. Still, when I must eat among them, I have no appetite.

"I wonder about the Bolsheviks. They give us guns and advice, endless advice. But they are foreigners, blood brothers of the mercenaries who fight beside the warlords. When I see one shoot at a Chinese, my enemy, I want to kill him instead.

"I find myself doubting even my fellows in the Kuomintang, the Communist cadres who march ahead of my army to prepare with slogans and rallies for our entry into towns. I know that Grandniece and her husband are among them, yet even so I am suspicious of their zeal, their talk of evil gentry who will meet their doom at the hands of noble peasants. My sympathies are with the elders they parade in dunce caps across public squares.

"Is this what revolution means?"

He looked up, waiting for the answer he knew would not come. "Is this what revolution means?" He repeated the words. "If so, like you, I do not have the heart for it."

Once more the breeze lifted a strand of the Patriarch's hair. Noble Talent reached out and smoothed it back, weeping.

Later, in the faint light of the false dawn, the soldier stood by the window, smoking a cigarette, absently watching an ordure cart make its way up Rue Flaubert. A big man pushed and a slight one pulled. Perhaps the cart was already full, for they did not stop to collect from any of the pots left by the side doors they passed. Their heads were bowed under the strain of maintaining a steady course through the ruts, around stones loosened by the recent rains.

His thoughts were in Soochow. He would have to tell the women. Now, all widows. He would say only that Bold Talent had died of heart failure. A grim smile touched his lips. Heart failure. It would not be far from the truth. How had Bold Talent put it once? What harm in dreaming, if it eases pain?

There was no reason to recall his nephews from abroad. When

he did return, Grand Vista would be given the cloisonné box, but it would signify only a memory. There would be no new patriarch of the House of Chang.

Suddenly he was alert. The cart had stopped at Number 42. The slight man approached the house, peered through the Judas window. His eyes narrowed. Scum! What did they want? He ran to the hall.

In his hurry, he had trouble with the lock, but then, flinging the door open, he stepped out and shouted into the street. "Hey, you—"

The big one was running toward him, not away. The boy . . . where the devil . . . ?

A sharp pain in his ribs. He looked down and saw the barrel of a gun.

"Back!" Another jab.

Once inside, the big one slammed the door behind him and reached up to pull the cord of the light. Almost at once he whispered, "Noble Talent?"

Blinking in the sudden glare, Noble Talent knew them: Resolute Spirit and Lustrous Jade. It was she who held the weapon.

"Have you gone mad?" He snatched the gun away from her and put it on the table. "I should have known that you two would be part of this!"

For a long time no one moved. Then Lustrous Jade said, in a voice hoarse with fatigue, "Yes, after what I have seen, yes. Perhaps I have gone mad." The hatred in her eyes burned him and he stepped back. She lunged for the gun.

Quickly, Resolute Spirit jumped between them, seizing her, holding her. "You must forgive her. As you may have guessed, we have been running and hiding for two days, two nights."

There was another silence. Then Noble Talent turned on his heels and strode toward the library. "Follow me. In here." He opened the door. The light from the hall fell across the chesterfield.

"He must have heard the two of you were here," he said. His voice cracked. "He must have come from Soochow to help, to protect you."

Lustrous Jade walked slowly toward the body, her steps uncertain, as if she were afraid. For a moment, it seemed that she was not sure who it was. Then she whispered, "Who did it?"

Suddenly, the soldier's control broke. "You did!" he shouted. "You Communists killed my brother!"

Lustrous Jade shook her head, turned to face him. "You are wrong, Granduncle," she said bitterly, each word an arrow. "You are wrong. We would not have killed him. It is your soldiers . . . and their hired gangsters. . . ." She paused, shuddering. "It is your people who do the killing! It was your people who threw young workers alive into the furnaces of locomotives!"

He was about to lash back when he saw that there were tears in her eyes.

"I saw it happen," she whispered. "Do you remember our friend, Hu? We saw him die, heard his screams!"

Could she be telling the truth?

He looked toward the peasant. "Old Friend, is this true?"

The big man nodded slowly. "She speaks the truth. We saw it happen. We heard . . ." He paused as if searching for a word. Finally he said simply, "Screams. We heard the screams."

The nightmare is unending, Noble Talent thought, and shut his eyes, wishing the two were gone. When he opened them again, the room seemed darker. He swayed. Faintly he heard Lustrous Jade call, "Granduncle?" and then the sound of his own voice, as if from a great distance. "Eldest Brother, wake up! wake up! . . ."

His hands had been filthy with the slime of the canal. "How dare you?" the Patriarch had asked. He could hear him so clearly now. "What of your responsibilities to the clan, my brother? To the ancestors? To the clan, my brother. . . ."

The voice faded, and he felt the supportive grip of Resolute Spirit.

Blinking, he saw again the body on the chesterfield, in the bright light of morning. He walked toward it. "Responsibilities to you, my brother," he whispered, "and the clan. I shall pay the debt."

Suddenly, he was alert. He swung toward Resolute Spirit.

"The cart! We must hide the cart!"

They rushed to the front door. Resolute Spirit peered through the window. "Too late. They are coming."

"It could be my men." Noble Talent started forward to see for himself.

Resolute Spirit did not move. "These do not belong to you. They wear no uniforms."

"How many?" Lustrous Jade whispered.

"Five."

Think! The soldier rubbed his hands together, then on his trousers. Think!

First, his grandniece and her husband must hide. He ordered them upstairs. They did not argue. The soldier took command.

When the fugitives had disappeared, he quickly put on his holster and went to the telephone, giving the operator the private number at M.S. & Company.

"Wei?" The voice was August Winds'.

"It is Noble Talent." He spoke quickly, wasting no words. "Do not interrupt. Listen carefully. Send two coolies at once, one tall, one slender. They are to remove the ordure cart they will find in front of this house. Then come yourself, with the hearse. Bring the coffin. Our friends are here."

There was a knock at the door.

"Understood?"

"Understood."

He put down the telephone but made no move. He must not let them know he had seen them coming. The door shook. "Open up! Open up!"

He turned the lock.

Four men, well spaced, stood in a semicircle in front of the house. The fifth, evidently the spokesman, was at the door. A thick-necked ruffian with his left earlobe missing, he was clearly surprised to see an officer. "We have come to search the house."

"On whose orders?"

"Never mind. Step aside." This one was not the kind to be intimidated by any uniform.

Still, Noble Talent did not move. "Do you realize to whom you are speaking?"

"Step aside. Our business is not with you."

The soldier stretched his arms across the doorway. "What are you looking for?"

"Troublemakers!" The man spat.

Noble Talent stared at the spittle in disgust, then into the eyes of the intruder. "There are none here. You have come to the wrong place."

"Let me see for myself." The brute tried to push the soldier's arm away and was surprised to find that he could not.

Ignoring the insolence, Noble Talent spoke again. "This house is in mourning. The departed should be allowed peace."

The man spat again. "Let me see for myself."

Dropping his arm, Noble Talent said, "Certainly. Search this house, search every inch of it. . . . But there will be consequences."

For a moment, the ruffian hesitated. Then he asked, "Who has died?"

"The Patriarch of the House of Chang, whose *lao chia* has been renowned in Soochow since the Ming Dynasty."

"Let me see the body."

Noble Talent did not respond immediately. Then he gave a crisp nod and led the way into the library. Solemnly he knelt before the body. "Close the door when you leave," he said.

He felt the gaze of the intruder move over him, inch by inch, shrewdly assessing his posture. When the man started slowly walking around the couch, still studying him for any hint of unnatural behavior, he gave no sign of concern. The bandit's heels made a clicking sound when he stepped off the rug. The sound approached, then drew away. Noble Talent inclined his head just so, as if in prayer.

Now the man was directly behind him, near the door to the parlor. Probably looking into the other room, Noble Talent thought. He resisted the temptation to check.

Suddenly the bandit approached again and bent down to look into the mourner's face. Noble Talent's eyes never left the body of his brother.

At last, he heard the clicking of boots again, in the hallway.

It stopped. At the foot of the stairs? Noble Talent waited, straining for the next sound.

The sparrows outside. The clock on the desk. His own breathing.

The creak of the stairs.

He wondered if now was the moment to unfasten the holster at his side.

Bang. The door.

No. A trick. He held his position for what seemed an endless time.

At last, the door clicked open and shut and he heard voices outside.

He did not move for another fifteen minutes, his eyes on the hands of the clock. Then he went to the window and carefully looked out between the drapes. The men were still there, standing in a circle on the small terrace, talking. The one without the earlobe had lit a cigar. It seemed that they were in no hurry to leave.

Finally, in the distance, two figures appeared and made their way to the ordure cart. They took their places, the slight one in front, the tall one in back. The cart moved.

"Hey," shouted the bandit leader. "Hey, you there, stop!"

The ordure collectors ran. They did not get far.

Hauled back to the steps of Number 42, they cringed. The bandits tore their shirts open.

"No woman. Nothing but two stinkpots." The leader kicked them away. Noble Talent turned from the window and headed up the stairs.

At dusk, the five men were still watching when the ornate casket was carried to the waiting hearse. The soldier and August Winds walked beside it to a barge on Soochow Creek.

Inside the coffin, the two fugitives.

Beneath the ground near the coal chute lay the remains of the Patriarch.

⋖§ 38 ⁊⋗

Final Payment

What man's land is the graveyard?
It is the crowded home of ghosts—
Wise and foolish shoulder to shoulder.
The King of the Dead claims them all;
Man's fate knows no tarrying.
                              —Burial song

IT WAS MIDNIGHT. On Soochow Creek, fog like a diaphanous shroud enveloped two vessels sailing in tandem, a grand houseboat towing a much smaller craft.

Aboard the houseboat, Noble Talent knelt on deck, pulling on the rope that linked the two, bringing the smaller one alongside, while in the main cabin, August Winds packed books into the empty coffin and the two fugitives rested. Resolute Spirit was first to recover. "I had better go up on deck and help," he said. When Lustrous Jade nodded, he staggered to the door, closing it behind him soundlessly.

Eyes shut, she leaned her head against the bulkhead. Her clothes were wet with perspiration, her limbs stiff, her flesh numb from the confinement. Breathe deeply, slowly, she told herself. Not so fast. One, two, three, she counted. One, two, three. Yes, better. She could feel her heart grow smaller. They were safe. Soon they would be gone, back to the mountains. Safe.

Opening her eyes for a moment, she watched August Winds, who had finished packing the coffin and was sealing it shut. Thus it would be buried, for Golden Virtue must not suspect, must never know that Bold Talent's body lay far from home. She let her lids fall once more.

When she looked again, August Winds sat beside her, gently smiling. "Are you all right?"

His smile was the same as it had been the last time she had seen him, the day she had brought New Destiny to Shanghai.

She nodded but said nothing. The words of gratitude must remain locked within, lest others follow. When their eyes met, his smile faded, then returned.

"Sister, am I so disfigured by the years that you cannot bring yourself to say a kind word?" he asked, teasing.

"You have not changed. I have." She showed him her palms.

He took them in his. "Are you then so proud of your calluses, Lustrous Jade?"

She smiled at that. He knew her well. Quickly she filled the silence, before he could say more. "It has been a long time."

He nodded. After a moment he blurted out, "Have you been happy?"

Happy? Only he would ask such a question. She withdrew her hands and folded her arms against the chill. "I have no time to think of such things."

"There is always time for happiness," he said. When she did not respond, he prompted her. "Perhaps when you are alone with him?"

Why must he ask?

Patiently he waited for an answer.

When she could no longer bear the silence, she said, "My husband and I seldom quarrel, not like you and . . . He is kind to me. I try not to be unkind to him."

At her words he stood up and walked away, stopping at the window to pull back the curtain and look out.

For a while neither spoke. Far apart, they listened to the footsteps on deck, the groaning of wood.

At last he turned to face her. "If mortals wait until the gods remake the world to their liking to be happy, they are already in hell."

It was an accusation, but none of the words had any meaning for her. Not any more, not ever again.

This time it was he who hurried to fill the silence. "Is there nothing you wish to ask of me? Nothing after four years?" When she did not answer, he continued. "All right, if not of me, what of your mother? Your son?" His voice rose.

Silently she begged him, Please do not make me ask. Please. He did not hear.

"Is there nothing you want to know about them?" His voice was full of anger. "Answer me!"

"I cannot. I cannot."

"What do you mean, you cannot?"

"I cannot," she whispered once more. She shut her eyes, remembering the terror on the faces of those who had burned, trying to steel herself against his questions.

"Is it possible that you do not know? Do not know that you broke their hearts when you left them? Every night for weeks your son cried for you, and your mother walked—how many *li?*— pacing the room with him in her arms, trying to comfort him when he wanted only you. Though her golden lilies ached, she would not let anyone else take her place."

He had come toward her as he spoke, and for a moment she thought he would strike her. But he merely stood over her.

"Now I must tell them that I have seen you and that you never even asked what any stranger would: 'Are they well?'"

In her heart she begged him to stop. She hid her face in her hands, but he pulled them away.

"Do you weep, my dear friend? Does a stone cry?"

She looked up.

"For whom are you crying, Comrade? The oppressed masses? Now that is something worth a tear or two."

"You have never understood."

"No, I suppose not," he said wearily. He dropped her hands as if they were soiled. "I am going on deck."

"Wait." She called when he was at the door. "Wait."

He stood still.

"My brother—" She reached out. Her hand was trembling. "My brother, please. If I asked, I would know. If I knew, I would care. If I cared, I could not be what I must be." Her arm fell into her lap. She rubbed the elbow, as if it had been injured and pained her. "You told me once that we had no choice but to be what we are. You were right. Can you not see? The less I know, the less I must forget!"

His expression softened, and when he spoke there was no longer anger in his voice, but pain. "Little Sister, we are so different. You want to know nothing. I want to have something—anything— to remember."

But I must not remember, she thought. My work must be more important than myself. Otherwise, my sacrifices have no meaning. Suddenly she wanted him to understand. "I must not remember. My brother, I must not remember except what serves my cause. I am a Communist. I work—"

"You are an outlaw. You will be trapped in the mountains with lice-infested peasants. Eventually, you will be killed. What will you have accomplished?"

"You are wrong!" She tried to stand but was dizzy and fell back onto the bench. "We will not be killed. We will triumph."

He laughed bitterly. "Even a fool would not wager a single *cash* on that."

"We do not need fools. We have the Party, the people."

Again there was silence. He took out his cigarettes and sat down beside her, offering one to her, choosing one for himself. For a while they smoked, saying nothing.

Are they well? she asked, but not aloud. My boy? My mother? Of course they are, she thought. What danger could there be for them? They were in Soochow, behind garden walls.

Suddenly he laughed again. "No, Little Sister, it is I who am the fool. Risking my life to help Communists. August Winds, the biggest capitalist in Shanghai. I can hear you tell the story now of how I oppress the workers in my factories, of how I oppress my tenants, of how, in fact, I do nothing except oppress the masses twenty-four hours a day. If I were in Hunan you would have me tried by a people's court, paraded in the streets in a tall dunce cap, and executed." He paused, as if waiting for her to argue that it was not so. When she did not, he got up slowly and walked over to the window again. A breath of air stirred the curtain.

She was thinking of another night when they had passed this way, four travelers on deck, laughing.

He turned to face her. "You Communists are right about one thing—we bourgeois are stupid sentimentalists!"

She rose and started toward him, but again she felt faint. When her legs folded, he was holding her. For a moment, they stood together, embracing. Then, saying nothing, he helped her back to her seat.

Must try to make him understand. "My brother, once my heart was like yours. But then I saw that a new China could not be born until the old China was dead. Only by severing old ties would it be possible to achieve the good. I believe—no, I am certain that only when Communism replaces Confucianism will Chinese be of like minds again. Only then will China be great once more."

She went on, explaining. He listened without interrupting, but even as she spoke of the many, she knew he was thinking of one.

When she had finished a second cigarette, she stopped speaking and leaned down to stub it out on the teak floor.

"Another?" he asked.

She nodded.

He reached into his pocket, but when he withdrew his hand, it did not hold the gold case. He stared for a moment at the thick envelope as if he were surprised by what he had found, then tossed it on her lap. "I brought you a present."

It lay there like a coiled snake. She could not take her eyes from it or touch it.

After a time he picked it up and opened it, spreading out the photographs, one by one, upon the bench.

One by one she looked at them, pictures of New Destiny, smiling, growing older before her eyes. New Destiny in satin robes beside one of the dwarf cypresses; New Destiny in a western suit with a telescope in his hand; New Destiny in a fur-lined coat beside

Spring Moon, dressed for the New Year. No more, she begged, silently, as before. Please, no more. Quickly she collected the photographs and hid them again in the envelope.

Before she realized what she was saying, she had asked, "Have you married, my brother?"

"No, but I have a son . . . your son."

The door opened and Resolute Spirit appeared, filling the space. "It is time to go," he said.

Deliberately, Lustrous Jade rose and, laying the envelope on the table, walked past the coffin toward the door.

"My friend," said Resolute Spirit, "my friend, thank you for saving our lives. I shall never forget what you have done."

August Winds nodded.

"One more favor, please."

"Of course."

Resolute Spirit reached into his pocket and took out the reed whistle. "Please give this to my boy."

August Winds took it, glancing toward the envelope, then at Lustrous Jade. She shook her head. "Quickly. We must go quickly," she said.

During a moment when fog blanketed the shore, Lustrous Jade and Resolute Spirit climbed into the smaller boat. They would sail through the canals to the Yangtze, while the others journeyed home.

Three days later the coffin was buried beside Bold Talent's ancestors. The ceremony was a simple one attended only by those members of the family then dwelling in Soochow and by a few of the scholar's friends from the Self-Strengthening Society. The clan did not gather, and there was no procession of priests and musicians through the town. Telegrams were sent to Cambridge, Massachusetts, but in them the Patriarch's sons were told not to return to China. Noble Talent informed the women that he had left instructions: "In life, I have frequently neglected the family's security; in death, I do not wish to jeopardize it further."

When the final kowtow had been performed, Golden Virtue remained on her knees by the new grave. She spoke softly yet clearly, so that, in the stillness, the words hung in the air. "My husband, it was my dearest wish that I go first beyond the Yellow Springs to prepare a welcome for you. Now that you have left, sliding into the earth as silently as common dew, without canopies or drums, I am most—" Her voice trembled. She paused, bowing her head. When finally she spoke again, it was as if nothing had happened, as if during the lapse, time had stopped. ". . . ashamed. So that there may be one who does not forget, one who will always mourn, I shall not depart again from my quarters. Not until it is time for me to sleep beside you forever."

The others, knowing it was useless, did not try to dissuade her. As they did, Golden Virtue discarded her white hemp beside the bronze lions, to keep death from following them home. Then she closed her door to the world.

The morning after the funeral, Noble Talent awoke early to the plaintive cry of the reed whistle. He listened awhile, watching as golden ribbons of sunlight stretched across the room from the cracks in the shutters. Nothing except the scrolls had been changed in the small room since he had left it as a boy to go to the academy. For the first time in many months he felt at peace.

It was the hour of the dragon before he put on his uniform, which had been neatly laid out for him on the camphorwood trunk at the foot of the bed. Once more he walked to the scroll that hung on the wall between the east windows.

Where had he been for the last New Year's? In Nanchang with his men, he supposed. Bold Talent must have hung the scroll then. The calligraphy was his. Standing before it, Noble Talent read aloud the poem by Wang Wei.

> "Friend, I have watched you down the mountain
> Till now in the dark I close my thatch door. . . .
> Grasses return again green in the spring,
> But O my Prince of Friends, do you?"

With a finger, Noble Talent traced a few of the characters, recalling his brother at his calligraphy table—as a young man, as an old one. It had been so much a part of Bold Talent that he had never once asked about his art. Now it was too late.

Slowly he turned away to finish dressing. He found his boots outside the door, soaked by a sudden shower. His servant was nowhere in sight, and he went to the wardrobe, thinking that he had left a pair of boots there—how long ago had it been? He had not looked inside the chest on any of the brief visits he had made to his *lao chia* since he had gone South to join the revolutionaries.

Now, opening it, he was astonished. The odds and ends he had left behind then were gone. In their stead, gowns and jackets of brocade and silk, coats lined with fur. A row of satin slippers. He tried on a pair. They were a perfect fit. Curious about the robes, he measured the blue one against his shoulder, then the gray and the brown. All were the same. Choosing the gray, he undressed and put it on. When he had buttoned the high collar, he was sure. The clothes had been made for him. Could it be that Silken Dawn had continued to sew for him all these years?

On the floor of the wardrobe, precisely in the center, there was a camphorwood box. Wondering, he picked it up and put it on the desk, then opened it. Inside were exquisitely embroidered squares. One by one, he drew them out. The sea horse. The rhinoceros. The panther. The black bear. The unicorn. Insignias of military rank worn on the front and back of the official surcoat when China was still an Empire. His mother's dreams.

Noble Talent returned them to the box. Then, picking up his uniform from the bed, he folded it carefully and laid it neatly away in the closet. He went to his desk and drew out paper and brush. From the porcelain vessel, he poured droplets of water onto the inkstone. Purposefully he ground the inkstick and, taking up the brush, wrote to Chiang Kai-shek asking to be relieved of duty. "Mourning and family responsibilities will keep me in Soochow. Long have I neglected them."

He gave the letter to the porter, then paid a call on his mother. They passed the day quietly, while she sewed.

A few days after the burial, at the hour of the boar, Spring Moon sat on a porcelain taboret by the lotus pond, as she had every night since August Winds and Noble Talent had brought the Patriarch's body home. Why, sleepless, she felt compelled to come here, as if searching for something, she did not know. What she had lost was buried with Bold Talent. There would be no finding it, tonight or any other night.

No one would ever know her so well again, for he had been there always. He had understood her thoughts, her silences. He had shared all but one of her secrets. There would be no recapturing the years for anyone else.

She heard footsteps and turned to see a figure standing in the shadows of the marble screen.

"Who is it?"

"It is August Winds, Auntie. The porter told me that you were here." He walked toward her and bowed. "We must speak."

"Yes, of course." She nodded, wondering what it was, wishing she did not have to know.

"Shall we go into the Hall of Ancestors?" he asked.

"Yes. It is getting chilly."

"It is also where I asked the porter to bring Noble Talent."

She stopped and stood very still, studying his face in the moonlight. Suddenly she was aware of the frogs' croaking, louder, insistent, strangely human.

When they reached the hall, Young Uncle was already there. So he too could not sleep, she thought. They bowed and sat down at the tea table. August Winds offered Noble Talent a cigarette. He lit one for himself and, reaching into the pocket again, brought forth a chocolate bar. "Auntie?"

She laughed, but without mirth. She found it difficult to stop. Wiping her eyes, she replied, "No, thank you." And then, "I find it oddly comforting that despite everything that has happened, you and my mother are still the same."

"What do you mean?"

"Even as a boy, you never went anywhere without hiding bits and pieces of food in your pockets. In the morning, Mother still lingers over her toilette, painting her cheeks, lacquering her hair, deciding which plum-colored dress. She ignores every commotion. I think sometimes that if—" Young Uncle's fingers tapped ner

422

vously on his thigh. He cleared his throat. She stopped. Why was she going on so?

Noble Talent spoke. "Please tell us why you are here, August Winds."

He nodded, then smiled kindly at her as if to say that he did not mind her chatter. Putting out his cigarette, he began. "Rumors are rife in Shanghai. Apparently one of the Communists has joined the other side and given up a list. On the list are many names, including Lustrous Jade's and Resolute Spirit's."

Spring Moon felt her throat thickening.

"This time," August Winds went on, "bribes and connections will not serve. I have already looked into it. An example must be made."

August Winds and Noble Talent each lit a second cigarette. Spring Moon watched them smoke for a while, then slowly rose and walked to the screens that partitioned the hall. Carefully she folded back the center panels, so that a shaft of light from the lamp on the tea table shone upon the altar. With the screen barrier gone, she was almost overcome by the incense. She could not make out the names painted on the Ancestor Tablets that lined the altar wall.

As she stood there the shadows were filled with women, their whispers rustling like dead leaves. On the altar, beside a bowl of fruit, a pear. Faintly she heard the voice of the Matriarch. "It is a sign—the undeniable wish of our wise ancestors."

The message was clear. Depart. They must depart. Spring Moon closed the panels and returned to her chair.

"How much time do you think we have?" she asked.

August Winds shrugged. "At most a week, perhaps only five days."

"We must be gone within three," she said. "It is the only way."

Noble Talent was on his feet now, pacing, his soft slippers barely making a sound on the hardwood floor. Finally, as if he had come to the end of a journey, he stopped. "Where can we go?"

"Hong Kong," replied August Winds.

The soldier thought a moment, then nodded once, deciding. "Yes," he said. And again, more harshly, "Yes."

My daughter, what have you done? Spring Moon thought. You could not have meant to do this. You could not! She shook her head. The thought was too terrible. It was fate. Nothing a mother could have done, could do now, would alter it. It must be that the debts of the House of Chang were so numerous they could only be settled thus.

Looking at the men, she asked no questions, thankful that Bold Talent had been spared the final payment.

Noble Talent cleared his throat again. "There is much to be done," was all he said.

Within the hour, the household was astir. Into the next day, the women packed and sealed the clan treasures in the coffins which had been prepared for the widows. The porters, August Winds, Noble Talent, and Enduring Promise dug around the lotus pool. It was difficult work, for the roots of the cypress still reached deep into the soil of the House of Chang. But before sunset they were done, the treasures buried.

That night, when the courts were quiet, Spring Moon went to pay a call on Golden Virtue. Noble Talent had explained to her that they must leave but had been unable to make her rescind her vow. Her niece would not try. There was only one who could change her mind, and he was dead.

"Please enter."

"Good evening, my aunt."

"Good evening, my niece."

Silently they served each other tea and sipped with eyes lowered.

Are you certain, my aunt, are you truly certain? she thought again and again. But, of course, she did not ask. Perhaps no harm would come to her. Perhaps August Winds was wrong. Perhaps . . .

Golden Virtue spoke first. "My niece, there is one thing I wish you and August Winds to do for me. I include the orphan, for he is younger than Noble Talent and will outlive us all. No others need know."

She nodded.

Awkwardly in her high-heeled shoes, the widow left the room. When she returned she held the cloisonné box. "Please, bury this where it will be safe."

Spring Moon rose and reached out, and for a moment they held the box between them. Then their eyes met, and Golden Virtue said, "It is time for you to go, my niece."

She nodded, took the box, and hurried from the room.

Later, in the garden, August Winds asked, "Where shall I dig?"

"Anywhere. It does not matter."

"Underneath a flagstone? The open area around the pool has all been used."

"Anywhere."

He located a loose stone, pried it out of the walk, and began to dig.

She sat on the taboret, staring at the boughs of the cypress on the box. In the moonlight its copper threads gleamed against the blue like embers. Once buried, would it ever be unearthed again? She wondered. Even if it were, its brilliance could never be restored. Perhaps she should take it with her, along with the other box she had packed that day. It also was blue, the scene of mountains and mist embroidered on it not quite finished—Golden Virtue's gift. In it she had placed her most valued possessions: the ring from America, an antique ivory chess soldier, a brooch of kingfisher feathers and gold, one gold coin, a golden hairpin, a book of poetry by Li Po, letters, a photograph or two.

But she could not take two boxes. And the one she held she had promised to bury.

"Auntie?" August Winds stood beside her, brushing the dirt from his hands.

She looked up. Reluctantly she handed him the chess set and watched as he lowered the box into the ground. Carefully he piled the dirt over the small hole, then packed it tight with the back of the shovel before replacing the flagstone. He rubbed his hands over its surface, smoothing away the traces of earth, then pressed the moss back into the crevices.

"The stones look as they did before," he said. "No one will suspect. Remember, as I shall, that it is the seventh stone in the seventh row. Remember the date of the reunion of the Cowherd and the Weaving Maid."

For a moment she thought she would weep, like a child abandoned.

"Auntie, are you all right?"

"August Winds, I think sometimes the world has gone mad. But then I know it cannot be so. It is only that we are destined to repay old debts."

Her voice broke, and he knelt down and took her hands.

"Auntie, this has nothing to do with what you have done. Or even with what Lustrous Jade has done. It easily could have been the other way round, and Noble Talent the one who led the hunters home."

She shook her head. "You do not know. I have done things you would not dream of. . . ."

"Have you?" he whispered, as if he too were looking back. But then he shrugged and said, "What is life but foolish desires and imperfect choices?" And, more urgently, "Surely if you were faced with the same circumstances, you would do what you did again. . . ."

She had stopped listening, was staring at their joined hands. They wanted only the thread to make a cat's cradle. She had played the game as a child with Plum Blossom, then with Lustrous Jade and Enduring Promise, and now New Destiny. She smiled at the memories.

"I thought so!" August Winds exclaimed. "You would do what you have done."

"I guess I would."

"No regrets?"

"No regrets."

The next afternoon, Spring Moon walked alone to the hill where the ancestors were buried. The pines that framed the Venerable's grave had grown tall, and when the lengthening shadows touched her, she paused for a moment in her climb. How many years had it been? Thirty-six? No, thirty-five. Almost as old as Bold Talent when he had returned from abroad. She smiled at the thought of him, then wondered what her life would have been if he had never taught her to read.

No, it was meant to be exactly as it had been. She was certain

426

of that. She put down the basket and began to weed the graves.

The wind was from the south, unexpectedly warm. The willows swayed. Overhead, the melancholy call of wild geese, flying north. She worked leisurely, savoring the time spent with each kinsman. Most she had never met, but she knew their stories and called each by his rightful name as she tidied the mounds.

She was still at work when the custodian called. "It is time, Young Mistress."

She nodded. "You may go. I shall follow." She watched him as he trotted down the hill toward town, puffing and swaying uncertainly under the twin burdens hanging on the ends of his bamboo shoulder pole. His aged mother, curled in the front basket, called out to her grandchildren in the other, "Be still, my precious dumplings, lest we all fall."

At the new grave, she laid out the bowls of food she had brought, and the sticks of incense, already lit at the altar in the courts. She kowtowed three times. Then she spoke.

"Grandmother said it was foretold that I would live to see five generations under one roof. I believe it is my destiny.

"I have promised that I shall gather our clan to be with thee when the hills are green and the wind is mellow. I shall keep that promise.

"It will not be this year or the next. It may not be this decade or the next. The horizon is hidden by tall grass that sighs and bends with each prevailing wind, and the nights are black.

"But our clan has endured other times when the wine turned to vinegar and incense turned to smoke.

"There is a season for sun, another for shadow. A season to sing, another to be silent. And, in all seasons, parting and reunion.

"In yielding we are like the water, by nature placid, conforming to the hollow of the smallest hand; in time, shaping even the mountains to its will.

"Thus we keep duty and honor. We cherish clan and civilization.

"We are Chinese."

Epilogue

In the eighth moon of the Year of the Dog, 1934, the Communists were isolated in the mountains of Kiangsi, completely surrounded. What hope of survival? None, the enemy thought.

"Not so," cried the Great Helmsman. "It is not the end, but a new beginning."

The soldiers of the Red Army gathered in village squares. A tall cadre hurried from cluster to cluster, encouraging them. "We will be back, comrades! We will survive! We will conquer!" Her voice was as strong as the whirlwind.

It was twilight when her lover, the peasant general, gave the signal to move out. By day and by night they marched, ignoring the bombs that burst in the air and the smell of towns burning.

The cadre saw to the wounded. One cool morning, as the leaves drifted from the trees, a soldier boy of thirteen was given to her care. She had seen him before at meetings, strutting in his oversized uniform and a pair of confiscated leather boots.

She knelt beside the boy in a grove of tall pines, calling to him softly, "Comrade, Comrade." He opened his eyes. Holding his hand, she explained what he must do. "I have asked because I know that you can and want to do it. Am I wrong?"

Tears fell as he shook his head. "No, you are not wrong."

Four men lifted him. The boy screamed in pain. "Please, help me."

The cadre gagged him with a thick rope, and when he nodded for them to proceed, the men lowered him into a basket and hoisted it high up to a lookout in the trees. He waved a grenade. When the cadre waved back, he saluted, his hand to the red star on his cap.

She put on his leather boots and marched ahead.

As the column approached Old Mountain, the line stalled. The grade was so steep that only the rope soles of the soldier ahead could be seen. Night fell. The mountain turned to ice. The cadre shouted to the man who clung to the rock behind her, whimpering with fear, "Look up and count the stars, Comrade. Look up."

Through the first moon of the Year of the Boar, 1935, through the second, and the third and into the fourth, the Red Army marched and fought, unable to escape from Kweichow. Along every pass, at every turn, the enemy waited. The Communists split into columns and sprang diversions, circling until the main file had snaked by, crossing rivers only to double back.

Finally they stood at the banks of the River of Golden Sands. The torrent churned through a mile-high gorge. There was no bridge, and only six boats. For nine days and nine nights the boats plied the river, until all had crossed.

Northward, then, they went, through Yunan and the lands of the Lolos and the Miaos, to the edge of Szechwan province.

There the spring-flooded Tatu River blocked the way. There, twice before, great armies had perished. North of the river, the legions of the Kuomintang waited.

The two armies, Red and White, raced along opposite shores of the Tatu toward the Luting bridge. Like dead men flogged through the nine levels of hell, the Communists marched for three days and three nights, pausing only for ten-minute rests.

They reached the bridge first but found only thirteen iron chains suspended above the abyss, swaying in the wind. The small KMT garrison had torn away most of the wood planks that spanned the 800 feet between the towering cliffs.

At nightfall, the peasant general and twenty-one volunteers started across, inch by inch, hand over hand, swinging from the chains. Shots rang out. A man fell, then another.

At last, some reached the remaining planks. Flames shot up. Through the fire the peasant general rushed the enemy. The Luting was secured.

It was the fifth moon when the Red Army reached the ice peaks of Tibet, seven mountain ranges eternally snow-capped, glistening like white shrouds hung from the heavens to dry. The Red soldiers, dressed in cotton uniforms and straw sandals, pushed on. Thinking they could never survive, the enemy retired.

By the sixth moon, they had reached northwestern Szechwan and rested a month there, gathering strength. Over 100,000 had begun the march. Now, even with new recruits, only 30,000 remained.

When they started out again, the cadre wrote a character on the back of each soldier and taught it to him, and as they marched, each man repeated his word to the one directly behind him. Every day, the soldiers changed places, learning new words.

On entering Mantzu territory, the marchers faced a new enemy. The tribesmen hated Chinese, White or Red, and their queen had ordered all intruders boiled alive and the fields and dwellings stripped. Those who escaped the poisoned arrows of the deadly ghosts of the forests grew faint with hunger.

Ahead the grasslands of Chinghai: not a tree, not a shrub, not a rock. Only grass and bog, exuding a stench stronger than horse urine.

The army advanced cautiously, holding fast to ropes tied to the waists of scouts. At night a few stretched out on dense grass. The rest slept standing, back to back. When the last herbs and mushrooms were gone, they boiled and ate their belts. The cadre shared her boots, the ones she had taken from the boy.

After seven days in the grasslands, the Red Army reached the sanctuary of Yenan. They had marched for 368 days. They had crossed eighteen mountain ranges, twenty-four rivers, and twelve provinces: 25,000 li. More than 6,000 miles.

From these cadres, soldiers, peasants, and boys of the Long March came the comrades who fought the Brown Dwarfs, won the civil war, repulsed the Imperialists, expelled the Polar Bear, and under the leadership of the Great Helmsman imposed order over one fourth of humanity.

Then, once again, there came a time of luan when comrades were divided one against the other and old friends became enemies, old enemies, friends.

For the seed sown in one season takes root; the tree that flowers in another dies. It is the nature of all things.

—Clan story

AFTER TWENTY-FIVE YEARS, Enduring Promise was going home. It would be, at most, a question of days. In his hands he clutched the file that had made it possible for him, special consultant to the White House on the China opening, to be among the first to return.

Only eight months had passed since Henry Kissinger's secret

trip to Peking. The moment it was announced, he had begun planning, seeking favors of superiors and friends he had always been loath to involve in a purely personal matter, never quite daring to believe that he would succeed.

It was Spring Moon he wanted to see; it was of her that he dreamed when he dreamed of home. "Little Brother." He could hear her, teasing. "Little Brother, little man, come and catch me if you can!" In Peking, in Soochow, they had played the game, until in Shanghai he was suddenly a schoolboy, too old for hide-and-seek.

He looked at his watch once more, and at the green wall and the door beneath the portrait of Mao. Patience, he told himself for the hundredth time. Patience. But it was difficult. He had been waiting for more than two hours, since before nine o'clock, when the doors of the Hong Kong office of the China Travel Service had opened and he and the other early arrivals had pressed inside. The Swedes and Germans, an Englishman or two, and several Australians had come for the Canton Fair. All morning they had jostled and shouted around him, demanding travel vouchers and hotel accommodations. All morning the clerks in blue cotton had shuffled grimly between the counter and the stamping machine, ignoring the agony of the businessmen, who alternately shook their visas and their heads. The louder the protests, the slower the Chinese performed. It would be comical, Enduring Promise thought, if he too were not waiting.

It was not the delay that troubled him. His papers were in order, he was sure of that, and too few Americans, even Chinese-Americans, had passed through this office for the procedure yet to be routine. But after twenty-five years, he had expected . . . what? He was not sure. A welcoming smile, perhaps. At least, the same treatment accorded the foreigners going to Canton. Instead, the sallow-faced clerk at the first desk had barely glanced at his credentials. "Take a seat," he had said contemptuously. "Special trips require special attention."

And, no doubt, special clerks, he thought, flipping idly through this month's pictorial with President Nixon and Chairman Mao clasping hands on the cover. Rosy-cheeked peasants and proud factory workers smiled up at him. *Huan yin!* they seemed to say. Welcome. But: Running dog of the imperialists, the clerk's eyes had accused him, as if he had come to partake of the fruits of revolution without having pulled a weed or swatted a fly.

I meant to come back, he had wanted to explain. When I left, I meant to come back.

But when the Communists won the civil war, he could not go back, or so he had told himself. Not with an American wife and a new baby. He had been offered his present position as professor of Chinese history, and he had seized it. He had had no choice, he had told himself then. And had not events proved him right? Of course, or so he told himself.

He threw the magazine on the table, suddenly angry. Damn it, he had no reason to feel ashamed. American passport or not, he was Chinese, and he was coming home.

Once again, he checked the door in the green wall. It was unmarked, but he was certain that behind it was the man he was waiting for.

Unable to sit any longer, he got to his feet and looked out the window, careful as he leaned on the sill not to disturb the thermos bottles lined up on it like ninepins. The sky above Hong Kong was somber, the eerie light that had presaged a storm muted now by gathering clouds. From the streets below, in the hub of the city, the clamor of traffic rose to muffle distant thunder. Pedestrians darted along serpentine alleys, apparently dismissing the threat of rain as if it were merely another moody face among the strangers who hurried past.

As the sky darkened, he saw himself reflected in the window pane and reached up to straighten the glasses he now wore, his only concession to advancing years. At sixty, his hair was still black. The new beige wool suit, tailored overnight at the Mandarin Hotel, fit well. Size 38. His girth had not changed since he had first gone to the United States to meet his wife's family.

Some indefinable change in the sounds behind him made him turn. At last the door in the green wall was open. A thin, middle-aged cadre emerged, holding a cup. Enduring Promise cleared his

hroat. Yes, of course. This was the man in charge. His blue suit
was not cotton, but gabardine.

He waited for the sallow little clerk to give some sign, but the
man busied himself ostentatiously with the papers on his desk
while the cadre approached the window and the thermoses on
the sill. Distractedly Enduring Promise wondered which bottle was
his, and then watched as the man poured himself a cup from the
blue one painted with red roses. The cadre was turning away when
he finally spoke. "Will you help me, please?"

The Cantonese elicited no response. Quickly he repeated the
question in Mandarin and finally in English.

At that the cadre turned and nodded, mildly curious. Enduring
Promise held out the correspondence with the Chinese Ambassador
in Ottawa and his other affidavits.

For a moment the man looked undecided. Then, shrugging, he
put down his cup and took the papers. Interminably he perused
them, without expression, coming last to the American passport,
opening it slowly, deliberately turning to the photo. His eyes flicked
upward, and for seconds he stared into Enduring Promise's face,
unblinking, without warmth. Then, "Come inside," he said, and
led the way into his office.

The room was small, furnished with a large desk, two chairs
and a telephone, and a portrait of Chairman Mao on the wall.
No papers on the desk, except the *Peking Daily*.

The cadre waved Enduring Promise to one of the chairs and
then sat down in the other, reading every document even more
carefully than before, as if searching for some discrepancy.

Again Enduring Promise waited.

Finally the man looked up. Once more, slowly, feature by feature,
he studied the *hua chiao*, his eyes lingering disdainfully on the new
suit, the ring he wore.

"What is the purpose of your visit to Soochow, Dr. Woo?" he
asked, opening the top drawer of his desk and extracting a form.

"To see my sister."

"Her name?"

"Chang, Spring Moon."

"Her age?"

"Ninety."

The eyes flicked up again. "When was the last time you saw one another?"

"In 1947, before I left for America."

"Why?"

The question made no sense, and Enduring Promise hesitated. "Why what?" his children would have retorted. His American children. What would the cadre make of such a remark? He cleared his throat. "I went to New York to meet the family of my wife, an American journalist who had been covering the Japanese War from Chungking."

The man nodded, wrote something, and turned the page. "Have you been in contact with your sister?"

"Indirectly."

"Recently?"

"No, the last time was about six years ago."

Once more the eyes flicked up. "Then she may well be dead."

No, Enduring Promise thought. If she were dead I would know it. But he said merely, "I would like to see her, just the same."

Line by line they completed the forms. As the minutes passed the official's silent disapproval of his answers, of his clothing, of his Chinese face and his American passport seemed to fill the room like cheap incense, until Enduring Promise wondered if he had returned too soon, if everyone he would meet in the People's Republic would feel this way, blaming him for . . . what? For leaving China in the first place, or for returning now after so many years?

And yet, to wait was to risk not being able to return at all. The China opening was fragile and full of perils on both sides.

At last the cadre stamped the application and stood up. "You may obtain your tickets and vouchers at the counter. In three days, you will arrive in Soochow."

"Three days . . . no sooner?"

The cadre went on as if he had not heard. "Things have changed since Liberation," he intoned. "We have rid the country of feudal practices. China has stood up under the wise leadership of Chairman Mao and the Communist Party."

Enduring Promise nodded and turned to leave. Neither offered the other his hand.

Three days later, he was aboard the noon train to Soochow, in the special compartment reserved exclusively for foreign visitors. At every window hung white eyelet lace curtains, stiff from starch and many ironings. Before him on the folding table were a steaming cup of tea, an ashtray filled with stubs, and an almost empty pack of Panda cigarettes.

Now, three days after he had crossed the border of his homeland, he found it a relief to be among foreigners. At least they did not stare at him. Everywhere he had walked in Canton and Shanghai, he had attracted the same silent crowds, as if his skin, too, were pale and his eyes as round and blue as those of the tall Swede in the next compartment. He had tried to engage some of the watchers in conversation, but none had answered him or even smiled. They trailed him cautiously, treating him like an alien from some other world.

It was his clothing, of course, or so he had thought at first. But even as he reassured himself, he did not believe it, and the truth, when he realized it, was bitter. His people were suspicious of the foreigner with a Chinese face. Too curious to run away, too afraid to speak.

For a time he too had been afraid, afraid that Spring Moon would not speak to him, would not claim him as kin. But almost as soon as the fear arose, it had melted away, leaving only the anticipation of seeing her.

He smiled to himself. Spring Moon would hold his hand and, standing on tiptoe, reach up to smooth down his cowlick, as she had done so many times, so long ago.

He had not seen her since 1947, in Chungking, shortly before his own departure for America. He had strapped her into a seat on a battle-scarred military transport headed toward the coast, never dreaming that they would be separated for so many years, that his last glimpse of her would be through the open door of the plane. She had been the sole passenger, a porcelain figurine among wooden crates, unmarked except for the words "special handling."

"It is not too late to change your mind, Sister," he had said.

She shook her head, clutching Golden Virtue's embroidered box in her lap. "My aunt is old and asks for me."

"Perhaps my nephew could obtain passage for you on another flight?"

"No, he was lucky to get even this. Do not fret, my brother." She reached into her pocket and brought out a hardboiled egg. Her eyes danced. "You see? I have come prepared for my first air voyage. Besides, it is said that I shall live to see five generations."

They had written regularly to each other until the outbreak of the Korean War, when correspondence between the People's Republic and the United States became imprudent, if not dangerous, for both of them. By then, Bold Talent's sons were notable figures in the Chinese scientific community, perhaps even working on military projects, while Lustrous Jade and Resolute Spirit stood high within the Party. Perhaps their status would have protected her. Perhaps his wife's family could have protected him from those suspicious of all Chinese-Americans who did not beat the drums for Chiang and the Kuomintang. Perhaps. In any event, neither he nor, apparently, Spring Moon had dared risk calling attention to connections with the other side.

Later, when the political climate was less volatile, he had written to her once a year, sending the letter to a friend in Kowloon, who addressed it and sent it on, postmarked "Hong Kong" instead of the offensive "United States of America." But he had received no word from her until in 1966, a letter had come mailed in Pakistan. It was not long and had obviously been self-censored, but it did contain news of the births of two more great-grandchildren and assurances of the good health of all the family. With it, sepia-toned, as if taken long ago, had been a picture of Spring Moon on the gallery of the Court of Wise Heart. Standing with her was a young girl, identified as Winter Jasmine, the youngest great-grandchild. "She looks very like me," the letter had said, and in the photograph he could see that it was true, though his sister was in her seventies, the child no more than ten. Defying the passage of years, Spring Moon's skin was still smooth, her smile exactly as he remembered it, as it had always been.

There had been no more letters, and as the Cultural Revolution engulfed China, he had stopped writing. He was afraid that any communication from him would imperil her, a mandarin with overseas relations. But always he had thought he would know it if she were gone. Even in the cadre's office in Hong Kong he had not doubted that he would find her waiting for him in the old courts of the House of Chang.

Suddenly, from the loudspeaker over the compartment door came the martial music that had announced the train's arrival at every station since Shanghai. He glanced at his watch. Soochow.

The train slowed. Pulling down his two suitcases from the overhead rack, he hurried to the end of the compartment as if he expected someone to greet him as he disembarked. It was ridiculous. No one could know that he had come.

But the feeling of anticipation would not abate, and when the train coughed to a stop, he got off quickly. Ignoring the staring crowds on the platform, he plunged ahead to the main entrance, where pale green sedans waited to motor foreigners with special vouchers to their destinations. One of the chauffeurs started toward him as soon as he appeared, the only Oriental among the privileged. With the barest of greetings, the driver took the voucher in his white-gloved hand and stowed the bags in the trunk.

Enduring Promise was about to step into the car when he heard a young woman calling him. "Dr. Woo? Wait! Dr. Woo?" In her voice the lilt of the sweetest of all dialects.

I am dreaming, he thought, whipping around, half expecting to see the girl Winter Jasmine running toward him. But it was only the pigtailed train attendant, the one who had asked him politely to lift his feet when she passed the mop through the compartment. In her hand, his Panda cigarettes. "You left these behind."

"Thank you!" He smiled at the earnest young face and reached into his pocket for a tip. No! That was a capitalist custom. "Thank you!" he said again.

The girl nodded stiffly and turned away. He watched as she

marched proudly into the station. After three days he should remember that thanks, like tips, were not paid in the People's Republic. A remnant of the feudal past, a demeaning sign of condescension to show gratitude when a comrade did what was to be expected.

Three cigarettes were left. He lit one and offered another to his driver. The man started to reach for it, then evidently changed his mind and shook his head. Enduring Promise shrugged and climbed into the car, shutting the door against the staring eyes, saying nothing. Why did he keep trying? Casual words that meant little to an American might compromise the report the driver must make to his work committee. Why should the chauffeur suffer unnecessary interrogation by his political cadre because a stranger had made meaningless gestures to lessen the unexpected loneliness that weighed upon his heart at homecoming?

Impatiently he stubbed out the cigarette before it was half smoked and lit another, leaning back to study from his window the city he had left in 1927, searching for landmarks dimly remembered.

With its canals the Heavenly City would never be mistaken for any other town, though here, as in Canton and Shanghai, the people all wore blue, the new buildings were nondescript, and huge billboards towered over the main intersections—parades of nationalities in bright native costumes linking arms, and the calligraphy of the Chairman, bold black against the red background, exhorting comrades to unite.

The waters seemed cleaner than before, reflecting the sunlight instead of absorbing it, and the new boulevards were lined with trees. The beggars were gone. But the banners and the open-air markets and the old men airing birds were gone as well, and shops were so dimly lit that nothing inside them could be seen. Now and then, near the curb, stood a peddler of ice sticks.

The cigarette burned his fingers, and he leaned over to put it out. It was all so different—and yet overloaded carts were still pulled by men bent double, and in the alleys, laundry flapped and torpid tentacles of smoke curled around the tin-pipe chimneys.

Once registered at the Nanlin Hotel, he did not even wait to see his room but returned immediately to the car. "The Ink Pagoda, please."

This time the ride took only minutes. Enduring Promise tried to memorize the way, counting streets, reciting the new names to himself. He felt as he had the first time Spring Moon took him to her *lao chia*—excited, happy, expectant. Like a child.

Suddenly, it was there: the Ink Pagoda and, across the street, the stout gray walls that had once enveloped the House of Chang.

Before the car came to a complete stop, the crowd gathered.

"How long will you be here?" the driver asked.

"You may return to the hotel. I shall not be needing you any more today."

The man hesitated.

"I know the way back. I have official business!"

When the driver still did not move, Enduring Promise turned on his heel and walked away. At the corner he stopped and looked back, half expecting to see the man following, hoping he had not dared to leave the car. The crowd stopped too, when he turned, and he smiled wryly to himself. With all these attendants, there was no need for the chauffeur, and, indeed, the car was moving away.

He turned the corner. Though the lions were gone, and the gates, the opening was where he remembered. He wanted to run toward it as he had done as a child, willow switch in hand, racing to the courtyards and safety from prying eyes. Instead, he straightened and walked slowly along the wall, half reading the slogans now painted on it in bold red letters. "Long Live the Communist Party!" and "Liberate Taiwan!"

At last he reached the entrance. But when he peered inside he was suddenly unsure, wondering if his memory had played a trick and these walls were not the right ones after all. For huddled in the receiving court was a jumble of tiny dwellings jammed one beside the next, filling the space so that there was barely enough room for a thin man to pass between them.

If any man was there. The place was unnaturally silent, like an empty stage, the cakes of charcoal in doorways and the laundry overhead part of the set. He took a step and turned to look back at the entrance. It was the right height and width. And there, in the third stone from the bottom on the left, the first character of his school name. He had had time to carve only the first before his uncle, Bold Talent, had caught him. It had been the last New Year they had spent together in the House of Chang, before Lustrous Jade and Resolute Spirit went to the mountains.

Slowly he made his way down the narrow alley, which twisted this way and that as if it were a pathway through a maze.

"Wei?" he called hoarsely. "Wei?" There was a stirring in the houses, but no answer. Once he looked behind him, but he had left the crowd at the gate. The solitude he had wished for frightened him now, but he walked on, no longer knowing how to return. At one place he thought he saw a fragment of the inner wall of the receiving court, the back wall now of a score of hovels. And one building, larger than the rest, could have been the Hall of Ancestors, though nothing of the red columns remained, and the shutter doors had been replaced by masonry and rows of tiny windows.

Then, rounding a corner, all at once he knew where he was. The Clover Gate was the entrance to another alley now, but by some miracle it had remained unbroken, though the walls on either side were gone. He walked toward it slowly and, passing through it, stood where he had hidden in the shadow the last night before they left the courts, looking back. He had watched Spring Moon and August Winds bury the cloisonné box, so small it had fit under the seventh stone in the seventh row of flagstones. Remember the Weaving Maid and the Cowherd, August Winds had said.

He was sure the other treasures had disappeared long ago. But the box was different. For a moment he wondered if Spring Moon had retrieved it after Liberation, and then knew that she had not. It was still buried somewhere, safe within the courtyards.

He turned away and looked for the Court of Wise Heart. It had been right here, beside the Cypress Garden, but now there was no sign of it.

Suddenly he was afraid, hearing the cadre say, as a matter of fact, "Then she may well be dead. . . ." May well be dead. Had he wished her alive all along? He shook his head. No. If she had died he would have felt the loss as keenly as the loss of his own limb.

"Wei?" he called again. "I need information, please." Arms reached out and closed the shutters.

Do you not know me? he wanted to shout. Do you not know me? I am Chinese.

"Get away, Foreign Devil!" someone shouted.

He swung around. The Clover Gate was filled with onlookers. Were they the same ones he had left at the entrance in the wall? He could not tell who had spoken.

"I used to live here," he said aloud. "I am looking for my sister, named Chang, Spring Moon. Her family lived here for tens of generations."

The crowd gave no sign that they had heard, much less understood. Finally a boy about twelve, with a red scarf tied around his neck, stepped out of the nearest house. His hair was cut short like that of U.S. Marine recruits, and he stood very straight with his hands defiantly on his hips. "The old woman does not live here anymore. We do. We, the proletariat. Go away! You are not welcome here. Your clothes are the clothes of foreigners."

"But this was my sister's *lao chia!*"

The boy spat. *"Lao chia!"* On his lips the words were a curse. "Get away, you monster, you ghost!"

Desperate, Enduring Promise turned again to the watching crowd, pulling from his coat pocket the picture of Spring Moon. "Do any of you know this woman?" An old man held out his hand. The picture was passed from one to another and finally returned, with no sign of recognition.

"Go away, now, all of you," shouted the boy. No one moved. "Go or I will call my brother. He is a soldier in the People's Liberation Army!"

Slowly the crowd began to disperse. The boy watched, implacable, until Enduring Promise, too, walked away, heading toward the spire of the Ink Pagoda.

Why had he been so certain that she would be where he had

always pictured her? Surely they had just missed one another, by a day, at most a week. It might as well have been a lifetime. Now there was nothing to do but return to the hotel and ask for Lustrous Jade or Resolute Spirit. They would know where her ashes were.

But in an alleyway, out of sight of the boy, the old man who had reached out to take the photograph was waiting. He motioned for Enduring Promise to follow, tapping his finger on his mouth for silence.

They did not go far, but the way twisted and turned down alley after alley cut through what had once been the courts of gentry. Finally, in a place so narrow that the evening light scarcely penetrated, the man pointed to a door and backed away, scuttling between two hovels, gone.

Enduring Promise looked around. No one was about. There was no sound except the faint tinkling of bicycle bells from some nearby thoroughfare. He knocked softly on the door. "Sister?" he whispered. "Sister?" He knocked again.

The door opened. A tiny, wizened woman with white hair cut straight across below the ears looked up at him. He did not know her until she took his hand and spoke. "I have been waiting for you," she said. Only her voice was the same. "I have been waiting," she said again, and drew him into the room. He was not tall, yet instinctively he lowered his head lest it graze the ceiling.

They sat across from each other at a small table. She held his hand and studied him, nodding slowly as if to assure herself that it was truly he. Having arrived, having found her, he could not speak. Anxiously he looked around the room, returning again and again to Spring Moon's face. He had been wrong. Her eyes, too, were the same, clear and bright, though wrinkles surrounded them, capturing tears.

There was nothing in the room to show that this was Spring Moon's home. No books, no scrolls of calligraphy, no photographs. Just pots and boxes stacked on the floor, a faded bedspread, limp mustard greens hung on a string. The walls, blackened by the smoke from the portable gas burner, were bare except for a single picture, a calendar with a girl in khaki shorts and toe shoes, leaping.

Nothing to show that Spring Moon lived here except that each shabby belonging was exquisitely tidy and somehow in its place. A single fluorescent tube cast a bluish light.

Suddenly she was speaking, breathlessly reciting a list of things she had prepared to tell him, a list that had grown longer and longer over the years. She talked disjointedly, as if, the moment to unburden herself having finally come, she was afraid that there might not be enough time to say all that she wished. She spoke of Grand Vista and Bright Vista, who swept the laboratories at the science academy now, suspect because they had studied abroad; of New Destiny, who taught school in the countryside; of her great-grandchildren, all three volunteers on the Bumper Harvest Commune in Sinkiang. She told him of the birth there of Winter Jasmine's daughter, Jade Spring, the great-great-granddaughter she had never seen; and she told of August Winds, who . . . she was not sure what he did, but he enjoyed good fortune.

Then, not pausing, she asked about Enduring Promise and his family, studying the pictures he had brought of Nancy, to whom she had taught Chinese in Chungking, and of his children—the girl, Mary, in graduate school now; the twin boys. Smiling and nodding, she repeated their names over and over to herself. How bright and comely they looked! she exclaimed. What treasures they must be to their parents!

She lingered over one photograph in particular, of Mary speaking at her graduation.

"It is a fine likeness," she said.

How could she know? he wondered. Spring Moon had never seen his daughter. Perhaps she too saw the resemblance to Lustrous Jade.

At the thought of his niece, he was suddenly aware that Spring Moon had not mentioned her. Could it be that she still objected, after all these years?

"Heed my warning," she had said to him angrily. "Marry a foreigner and you will have no country. Marry Nancy and you are no longer a Chinese."

All at once he wanted to see Lustrous Jade, to tell her—what?— that she had been right? Perhaps. He remembered her standing next to Chou En-lai, at the press conference. She had come to Chungking to serve as liaison between the Communists and Chiang's people after the United Front was formed to fight the Japanese. He had not recognized her at first. Nor had New Destiny, then in college, although he had seen pictures of his mother. The Long March had aged her face so that she looked almost as old as Spring Moon. But she had still been as tall and slim as when she marched off in the vanguard of her first parade and he had watched through a crack in the curtains, angry because she was leaving him behind. He wondered if she would remember.

"Sister—" he said, and stopped.

Spring Moon still stared at the photograph of Mary, and he noticed that a tear had fallen. Again, fear. Surely . . .

"My niece?" he asked.

Spring Moon shook her head, not looking up from the photograph. "My daughter . . ." she whispered, and he knew that Lustrous Jade was gone. "For a moment I thought that this was she," Spring Moon continued. "But . . ." She looked up at last, and though her eyes still shone with tears, no more escaped. "It is not an easy story to tell," she said.

Carefully she placed the photograph on the table and, prolonging the silence, poured tea from the thermos on the table into the two cups she had set for them. He waited while she sipped slowly. When she spoke again, her voice was muted, as if she were singing a song that demanded a range she could no longer manage.

"After Liberation, we were all together—my daughter, Resolute Spirit, New Destiny and his wife, and I. We lived in the Court of Wise Heart; the rest, and the remaining land, was turned over to the State, for my daughter wanted to set a good example. I did not disagree. After the occupation of Soochow by the Japanese and the war against the Kuomintang many were homeless, and with the passing of the elders and Golden Virtue, we had no need of more.

"My daughter was given great responsibility. After all, she was a Long Marcher and a leading Party member, and her husband, too, was a Hero of the Revolution. New Destiny and his wife taught school. I remained at home and took charge of their children as they were born.

"I made up my mind to adjust to the new. I kept my doubts to myself. Order was returning, after half a century. People were working. Beggars were gone. Bombs were not dropping. And we did not need a wheelbarrow full of banknotes to buy a pair of shoes. That everyone was poor, that we all wore blue cotton, that food was rationed, that children made fun of my golden lilies— none of it mattered. I had seen much in a long life; I was just seeing more. It did not surprise me that the Communists needed time to find out what would work and what would not. China is old, and Chinese are many. I hoped for the best. If I sometimes lacked sympathy for the changes, I had faith in my daughter. . . ."

Spring Moon paused. He wanted to take her in his arms and comfort her, but it was not done. He sat very still.

"Nevertheless," she continued, as if she had not stopped, "life was not without its sweetness. Whatever happened outside our court, within we were"—her voice was again a whisper—"within we were one family, home."

She took a deep breath, held it for what seemed too long a time, then said clearly, no longer whispering, "My daughter's work was secret but most important, for in the spring of 1966, Liu Shao-chi took her with him on a diplomatic mission to Pakistan. I was so proud. I bought silk and had a dress made for her. It was lavender with branches of plum blossoms.

"Upon her return, she gave me a picture of her in the dress, greeting dignitaries. I put it next to my bed."

She paused again, staring now toward the narrow cot in the corner. Vaguely, he remembered reading an account of that state visit; he had forgotten it by the time the letter arrived.

"Later that summer," Spring Moon went on, "I would happen upon the family whispering among themselves. Often they would smile and ask was I not tired and should I not go to take a rest. But their smiles never touched their eyes. The great-grandchildren were often away. Resolute Spirit suddenly looked old. His hair was white. He said that he was not sleeping well. I scolded him for not consulting a doctor, but he merely said that there were no cures for his ills.

"In the fall, New Destiny and his wife did not return to their teaching posts. They said that all the schools were closed. Yet they, like the children, were often gone for weeks at a time. The block meetings, which had been called whenever there was a matter of importance to discuss, were now called almost every night. The cadre said we had to sweep out the 'monsters and ghosts,' capitalist roaders who had sneaked into the Party, the government, the army, the schools. Hour after hour we sat on bamboo stools in a circle and studied the writings of the Chairman, the same passages over and over like the slowest of students. Once a neighbor who had palsy dropped her book accidentally and was made to stand in the takeoff position, her arms spread high above her bent back like the wings of an airplane, until she fainted. No matter how tired or bored, I had to stay alert.

"Throughout, my daughter spent her time writing. She lost weight. Sometimes, she would clench her jaws and grind her teeth; when sweeping, I would find the scraps of paper she had torn up. I thought at first that she was writing an account of the Long March. Later I realized that she was writing her self-criticism to the Party, over and over again."

Spring Moon swallowed hard. Slowly, she raised her teacup to her lips. The droplets fell continuously now, staining her blue cotton jacket. Her hand shook.

Enduring Promise had read many such biographies, reconstructed by refugees who had swum through shark-infested waters to Hong Kong to escape a persecution most did not understand. One owner of a cat that was accidentally burned had accused himself of attacking the Chairman, for "Mao is the homonym for cat."

What could Lustrous Jade have written in her self-criticism, she who had marched with Mao? Had she too had a cat that meowed too loudly? But Spring Moon was speaking again.

"One morning, when all the family were gathered, a dozen Red Guards burst through the door while we were at the breakfast table. 'How dare you?' I shouted, but Lustrous Jade pulled me to my seat and I knew that I must not move or say more. Even Winter Jasmine, who was a Red Guard too, sat very still.

"They smashed a Tang horse that I had bought to remind me of another. . . ." She hesitated. "They burned books in the brazier, and the mementos I had kept in my embroidered box. . . ."

Her hand shook. She reached into her pocket for a handkerchief to cover her eyes. Once more he wanted to comfort her, at least to take her hand. Instead he closed his eyes to give her privacy, seeing her as she had been that day on the plane, smiling up at him, clutching the only thing she could not travel without.

He wondered if he should stop her recital, but when she resumed it she told the story impersonally, as she had told stories to him when he was a child of cruel deeds done by emperors or gods and the most unfilial of men.

"Hour after hour the children shouted, spitting and shaking their fists, and over the windows and walls and doors they painted 'Counterrevolutionary Revisionists' and 'Admirers of the Four Olds' and 'Enemies of the People!'

"Just when the last of them had left, all returned. A fat girl, brandishing scissors, ordered me to stand. Resolute Spirit protested. Three girls struck him from behind with iron pipes. He fell. Quickly, I stood.

"The fat one snatched my gold hairpin, undoing the knot. The tresses that had never been cut were gone, thrown out the window. Then the children, tired of games, paraded away, laughing.

"Even after we were alone, no one spoke, as if we sensed that our words were cleavers that could be thrown someday against us. We tended Resolute Spirit. The blows had hammered him small, so small.

"After that, until night fell, my daughter sat stroking my hair, without a word, without a tear. . . ."

Her voice trailed off.

He waited. The story was not finished, he knew.

Outside there was the sound of water splashing on the cobblestones, muffled voices, a door closing.

"On the first day of the tenth moon my daughter and her husband were arrested. No one asked why or where they were going or when they would be back. Later I learned that the Red Guards had brought them before a mass meeting and accused them of working against the Revolution. The evidence was posted: The cadre had worn a lavender silk dress; the photograph was proof. And a man from Learned Cinders had seen her mail a letter in Pakistan to Imperialist America."

She stopped again, repeating the name Learned Cinders, as if it explained everything. He had heard it before.

"Learned Cinders?" he asked.

"Yes, a little village in the north where, many years ago, a debt was not paid, where . . ."

She spoke now to herself, words he could not discern. He waited, afraid to disturb her. Finally, pronouncing the name of her daughter, she spoke firmly again, although she formed the sentences slowly, forcing them from her lips.

"Lustrous Jade and Resolute Spirit refused to confess or to kneel, asserting again and again their loyalty to the Party. Week after week, they remained in captivity, undergoing questioning, writing denials of their treason.

"One day, against the advice of everyone, I went to the prison to ask them to reconsider their stubborn conduct. There was no other way to gain entrance.

"While the guards watched, I sat across a table from my daughter and her husband, reading the words of the Chairman. 'All our cadres, whatever their rank, are servants of the people, and whatever we do is to serve the people. How then can we be reluctant to discard any of our bad traits?'

"I read and read. 'Every word, every act, and every policy must conform to the people's interests, and if mistakes occur, they must be corrected—that is what being responsible to the people means.' I read another page.

Throughout my eyes were dry. Too many tears, too long withheld, had turned to stone.

"When it was time to leave, I pleaded with them to yield. 'Yield, my daughter, you must yield,' I said, but she only smiled.

"They took the precaution of waiting until a few minutes after midnight on December twenty-seventh, so that their suicides would not coincide with the Chairman's birthday and cause trouble for the family. I never saw their bodies."

Very carefully she folded her handkerchief, corner to corner, and put it away neatly in her pocket. Then, looking up, she said, "Soon I alone remained in the courtyards. But I could not stay. The ghost of my daughter cried to me at night. With her gone, the chain was broken. What the Matriarch had foretold was not my destiny after all."

The next evening, sitting at the table, Spring Moon looked about the small room which had been home for the past five years and thought that for the first time it was indeed a festive place. There were no red silk lanterns, Tang horses, or rosewood chairs. No blind storytellers, no musicians or acrobats. But on her left sat the man who was her son, although he did not know it, and on her right the man who might have been her son-in-law if . . . she shook her head. No ifs. Not tonight.

She broke the wax seal of the vintage *mao tai* and poured a glass for August Winds, who sat at ease, puffing contentedly on his cigarette. He was plump again, as he had been as a child, but his gray wool Mao suit was expertly tailored and from his breast pocket rose an impressive column of ballpoint pens, badges attesting to his unique resources. "How did you do it?" she asked.

His face broke into a dimpled grin but he did not reply, merely shrugging magnanimously.

He will not tell, she thought. Never does, never did. But giddy as the bride she had been at sixteen, she tried to coax the secret from him while she poured some of the strong, colorless liquor for Enduring Promise and herself.

"Yes, August Winds, how did you accomplish this and this and this?" Enduring Promise added his persuasive voice to hers, pointing one after the other to the small plates piled high with shrimp, and pork, chicken, fish, and beef. "From what my sister has told me, this is more meat than any family can hope to buy in a month. I would not be surprised if our dinner tonight cost its weight in *ren min bi!*"

"Ah, my uncle from the Land of Tycoons, you do not realize that money is nothing in a socialist state," August Winds proclaimed.

"However . . ." Spring Moon looked quickly to the right and left, then whispered, "however, ration coupons are dearer than tickets to immortality!"

They laughed.

"Really it was nothing, nothing at all." August Winds sighed. "While the heavens may fall and the earth evaporate, people do not change. And I"—he tapped his nose with a finger—"have the gift for ferreting out exactly the right people to do whatever the deed." Raising his glass, he shouted, "To the people!"

"To the people!"

"To the people!"

Glasses emptied, there was a stillness, a pause that warmed as soothingly as the wine.

Spring Moon's thoughts glanced like a pebble over the years the three of them had shared, over scenes lost to memory until tonight. . . . Sitting between these two at the hotel they had stayed in during the first weeks in Hong Kong, reading aloud the letter from Golden Virtue that told how feigned madness had protected her from those who might harm her or displace her from the House of Chang. . . . New Destiny running into the house flashing the newspaper that had announced the new United Front between the Kuomintang and the Communists. "Grandmother, Grandmother, now we can go back to China, now we can go home!" . . . Noble Talent in his uniform, the day he left them. Even then she had known Young Uncle would not return from the war. Yet he had looked so happy, making a fist over and over. "My arthritis is gone," he had boasted. "I have the Japanese to thank for that, and for the fact that I am a soldier again!" . . . Enduring Promise shyly showing her the dedication in his first book, entitled *The Returned Student.* "To my sister, Spring Moon," it had said, "and to my uncle, Bold Talent, who was among the first to venture and to return." . . . August Winds surrounded by a bevy of shoeshine boys polishing the leather jacket he sported when such garments, worn by the American Flying Tigers, were coveted by noncombatants. In the worst of times, he never forgot to recite the homily appropriate to every occasion and to tip outrageously.

"How many fortunes did you make and lose, August Winds,

in the years we lived in Hong Kong?" she asked, surprised to hear her thoughts spoken aloud.

They tried to recall, counting as they selected morsels with their chopsticks, laughing when they disagreed over what had actually happened.

During Enduring Promise's version of the soybean debacle, August Winds hung his head in shame. "And to think that I took the money from the widows!"

Enduring Promise leaned over and patted him on the back. "But it was your money. Money the women had been recycling for years among themselves at the mah jong table!"

"Besides," Spring Moon reminded him, "you gave them stock certificates in exchange!"

He blushed.

So they *were* worthless! she thought, then quickly came to his rescue. "I remember one week when Second Grandaunt refused to speak to Mother. Not a 'good morning,' not a 'good night.' All because Mother had won at mah jong when you had reported the stocks down, and the next morning you announced a split!"

Suddenly all burst out laughing, even louder than before.

"Shhh!" she cautioned, pointing to the door and the walls. "We must stop. My cheeks hurt so. Let us stop!" Gradually, they quieted and began to eat in earnest.

If I die tonight, I shall die happy, she thought. My son, who bears the name of my first love and the features of my second, is here beside me. It matters no longer that he will never call me "Mother." It matters only that he has fared well.

Enduring Promise filled the glasses once more and said, "Remember our own games, with New Destiny in Chungking?"

"How could I forget?" August Winds pulled the lining from his pockets inside out. "Losses, nothing but losses!"

Spring Moon sighed. "It was the first time I had ever played mah jong! How old was I then? Sixty?"

"And a more deadly game was never played." August Winds shook an accusing finger at her. "You never had less than a pure dragon in your lay-downs."

Yes, she thought. Yes, it was true. "Let them bomb!" she had declared. "I shall not run, not anymore, not after these thousands of *li!*" After all, would the stakes not be the same whether they gambled at the table or in the caves? Since she would not seek shelter, the men had stayed by her side. With blackout curtains drawn, they had played mah jong during the air raids by candlelight.

Raising her glass, she offered a toast. "To pure dragons!"

"We will drink to that!" The two men shouted, emptying their glasses; August Winds promptly filled all three again.

Just as promptly, she raised her glass anew. "To life!"

"To life!"

"To life!"

After the meal, Enduring Promise offered a cigar to August Winds and they smoked in silence while Spring Moon cleared the table, putting the leftovers neatly in a box she kept by the window. She did not rush the task, pretending this was just any night, not a dream. Pretending it was one of many, not unique.

Only when the tea was brewed and she had served each a cup did Enduring Promise end the silence by asking, "August Winds, how is it that Communism seems to agree with you?"

"Ah!" He sat up, eyes twinkling. "But I was never in danger. Do you not see that I am one of those absolutely indispensable to the Revolution? Marx, Lenin, Stalin, and Mao have all ensured my longevity. You must understand that I, the capitalist, the bourgeois, must survive, for with no class enemies, how can there be class struggle?"

"Perhaps in theory, but—"

"Enduring Promise, let me explain," Spring Moon interrupted, pushing her tea aside and hitching her chair closer to the table. "While everyone was throwing jewels and gold into the river for fear of being branded an enemy of the people, August Winds hid his valuables between the covers of the Chairman's writings or behind Mao's portraits, which he had pasted all over the walls of his room. And just to make certain no one became too interested, he scented the room with excrement. Few had the fortitude to enter, much less rifle his things. Still, the most zealous were the girls, and so each day he sat pleasantly, without even the thinnest layer, waiting—"

"You would have laughed to see me, sitting there adorned only with a cigarette!" He guffawed. Then all three were laughing and giggling. As if they were singing a round, when one stopped, another began.

Enduring Promise was the first to regain control. "But why"—he wiped tears of laughter from the corners of his eyes— "why did not others do the same?"

Suddenly, the game ended. On August Winds' face, desolation. Spring Moon thought, seeing it, of that spring when he had come to court her daughter in his Pierce Arrow, of the day of the dragon-boat race. Impulsively, she reached out to touch his hand.

"The others?" August Winds said bitterly. "The others believed, and because they believed . . ." Suddenly he smiled again, too quickly, and shook his head. "I do not know." Then patting his belly lovingly, he continued. "Just as I do not understand why people are afraid of buying on the black market. Always, having safely eaten, I dutifully report myself to the authorities. What more can they do to me than they have already done? They are the very ones who propagate the idea that all bourgeois are corrupt and succumb easily to evil ways!"

Corrupt? Of course, Spring Moon thought. But he is fine, very fine, as a friend.

She looked from one to the other, thinking it was late and almost time for August Winds to walk Enduring Promise back to his hotel. "I never dreamed"—she spoke softly, unable to prevent the catch in her voice—"I never dreamed that I would live to see such a night as this!"

Her eyes filled and she shook her head, forbidding tears. August Winds leaned over and whispered, "My aunt . . ." He hesitated, in his eyes, too, a softness. "My aunt, you are indestructible. Surely you will live to see many more dreams come true."

She shook her head. "No, I will not. Mortals should be content, lest they arouse the jealousy of the gods."

She took each by the hand, and for a long time the three sat again in silence. Then Spring Moon reached up and smoothed down the cowlick in her son's hair, remembering the boy in tiger shoes, wondering about her great-great-granddaughter Jade Spring, a peasant child as Enduring Promise had been, once.

"If only . . ."

"If only what, my auntie?"

"Oh, it is impossible!"

"Sister, we are all too old to think anything is impossible. Tell us, if only what?"

"If only they could be here—everyone together in Soochow—for a week, even an hour."

"The others?"

She nodded, again fighting tears.

Enduring Promise looked away, at the calendar and the girl leaping, but August Winds sprang to his feet. He lit another cigarette, inhaling deeply, pacing the floor, pausing as if for thought between sentences. "It may not be impossible. . . . With such a distinguished Chinese-American visiting . . . perhaps it could be managed." He began to nod, smiling. "I feel lucky tonight. Auntie, please do not fret. Just leave everything to me." Then with a great flourish, he bowed deeply before the younger man and proclaimed, "My esteemed uncle, my honorable uncle, let us be on our way!"

Spring Moon accompanied them to the threshold and stood watching until they disappeared into the shadows. When she finally closed the door, she could still hear their laughter.

On the gentle slope near the city of Soochow, the weeds were tall and the tombs unkempt, the stone markers broken and scattered.

The clansmen had come from across the seas, from the countryside and the borderlands. It was a day when the hills were green and the wind was mellow.

Together the five generations stood.

The mother glanced at her son, then began. "Honored Ancestors, at long last we are here. . . ."

When the ceremonies were over, Spring Moon chose to sit beneath a young cypress that shaded the graveyard from the noon sun. She waited for her family to gather around and hear the story they had asked her to tell. It would not be a new one. All except the youngest, her great-great-grandchild, had heard her tell it before. She would begin at the beginning, with Pan Koo.

Suddenly from the distance came the faint tinkling of bronze bells. She closed her eyes to listen, remembering, seeing the clansmen of the House of Chang pass before her, climbing the hill slowly, with dignity. The men wore black skullcaps and fur-lined satin gowns, the women and children fur-lined jackets, red embroidered skirts, and velvet headbands encrusted with pearls and jade. Each carried a small brass firebox filled with glowing coals.

Opening her eyes, Spring Moon reached out and took the child's hand.

◆ ◆

Author's Afterword

On November 3, 1938 my mother had two important things to do. The first was to send a telegram to my father in Hunan province announcing my arrival in the world. The second was to send for Whai Kung, my maternal grandfather, to tell my fortune.

Although Whai Kung was a herbal doctor, poet and calligrapher, he also practiced the art of prophecy. Carefully, he studied the lines of my palms, the space between my eyebrows, the length of my ear lobes, the nodules on my head and the general placement of details about my face. He also consulted complex charts and maps of the heavens, noting I was born in the Year of the Tiger at three o'clock in the morning. This exact time was crucial for it is then and only then that the essence of being tiger is at its zenith. In addition, my mother was also born in the year of the tiger. And finally, I shared exactly the same birthday with my father and his father.

At last his calculations were finished and Whai Kung announced, "Eldest daughter, I have never seen so many good omens in one tiny child. Her life will be full, her spirits strong. You have absolutely no need to fear. This baby will have a rich passage."

I hardly remember Whai Kung himself, but his prophecy strengthens and comforts me every day. Even during rare depressions I soon rebound, angry and indignant, to remind the fates of their promises. I do not know exactly why grandfather's words have cushioned my journey. Like most Chinese, I am basically a fatalist—too sophisticated for religion and too superstitious to deny the gods. Yet somewhere along the way I was bewitched by the magic of Tao into believing that grandfather's predictions were more than a ritual to please his eldest daughter. And thus far, it is so.

My latest blessing was to have been able to complete one full cycle of my destiny within the spring and summer of my lifetime It began with my birth in China; then continued in America, now home; and culminated in a most propitious return to the land of my ancestors.

Wisely the gods made me wait twenty-seven years before returning. For only at thirty-five was I looking at life from both sides: as mother and daughter, as Chinese and American, as younger and elder, as one person and as a member of a clan, as interested in history as in dreams, no longer thinking that life was without limit and mortality but a word. At that moment when my cup was both half empty and half full I was ready to enter the Chinese landscape. There I heard tales of the ancestors and saw the lives of my relatives—the life I might have led.

The soul of *Spring Moon* lives in that trip—reaching beyond the newspaper headlines, Communist slogans, Western principles, the cultural gap, the political isolation, the language barrier into the hearts and thoughts of my clan. They live throughout China, from Shanghai to Sian. They are newborn and aged, heros of the Communist movement and martyrs of the Cultural Revolution, sweepers and vice-chairmen, downcast and triumphant . . . living and dead.

Once I was deeply saddened to have missed Whai Kung by only three short years. Yet perhaps if our hands had actually touched and our hearts embraced upon homecoming, such happiness would have driven the gods mad with envy. Nothing would have distracted them from a terrible revenge. But this scene never was, and the jealous gods were lulled by the silence of our fateful meeting.

Whai Kung sleeps in the earth near Soochow. He has mountains to shelter him from the wind, green farmlands to gaze upon, the shade of a bamboo grove, the vast tranquility of Tai Hu Lake, and the singing mists just over the horizon. And he has a name.

It is freshly carved in stone. This man was born and lived and died. The stone will not be plowed under or smashed or abandoned or carted away. It will stand. It will endure. For my grandfather. For us. For my Chinese roots. So when one day the children of my children and their children, who won't speak Chinese, look Chinese or know China, visit this lone ancestor they will feel Chinese, as I did that afternoon at his grave.

There I bowed three times. I left chrysanthemums and took away serenity for my mother.

Whai Kung's prophecy still holds true.

Bette Bao Lord

New York
1981

❧ ❦

Chronology

The Dynasties

The Legendary Period		
The Hsia Dynasty	*c.* 1990–1557 B.C.	
The Shang Dynasty	*c.* 1557–1050 B.C.	
The Chou Dynasty	1050–221 B.C.	feudal era
Early Chou	1050–722 B.C.	
Spring & Autumn Period	770–476 B.C.	Confucius teaches philosophy
Warring States Period	475–221 B.C.	Lao Tzu lives?
The Ch'in Dynasty	221–207 B.C.	China united by Emperor Ch'in Shih Huang Ti
		The Great Wall built
The Han Dynasty	206 B.C.–A.D. 220	Model for later dynasties
The Three Kingdoms	221–265	
The Western Tsin Dynasty	265–316	
The Eastern Tsin Dynasty	317–420	
The Southern and Northern Dynasties	420–589	
The Sui Dynasty	589–618	Grand Canal built
The Tang Dynasty	618–907	Golden age of poetry
The Five Dynasties	907–960	
The Sung Dynasty	960–1127	Great age of painting
Partition between N. & S. Sung Dynasty	1127–1279	
The Yuan Dynasty (non-Chinese, Mongol)	1271–1368	Marco Polo journeys to China
The Ming Dynasty	1368–1644	
The Ch'ing Dynasty (non-Chinese, Manchu)	1644–1911	

Modern History

1757 China confines all overseas trade to Canton, imposes restrictions on foreigners

1839 China's attempt to stop British traffic in opium by burning it leads to Opium War

1842 China loses war and signs Treaty of Nanking, first of unequal treaties, opening 5 ports to foreign trade and privileges

1850–64 T'aiping Rebellion led by a mystic, Hung Hsiu-ch'uan, strongly influenced by Christianity

1894 Dr. Sun Yat-sen organizes the first of his secret (anti-Manchu) societies

1894–95 Sino-Japanese War, ended by the Treaty of Shimonoseki

1898 The Hundred Days of Reform are initiated by the Emperor Kuang Hsu and repealed by the Empress Dowager—his aunt, Emperor Hsien-feng's Concubine—with his imprisonment

1900 The Boxer Revolt: the members of the Society of Harmonious Fists attack foreigners and converts, hold foreign legations under siege
The Empress Dowager and Court flee before an international punitive expedition

1902 Court returns to Peking
The Empress Dowager initiates sweeping reforms

1904–05 The Russo-Japanese War

1908 Death of Emperor Kuang Hsu precedes death of Empress Dowager by a day
P'u-i, aged 2, becomes Emperor, reactionary Prince Ch'un named Regent

1911 Outbreak of Chinese revolution
Sun Yat-sen elected President of the United Provinces of China, champions parliamentary government

1912 Abdication of boy emperor
Factionalism pits North against South
Sun Yat-sen resigns to unite country, permitting Yuan Shih-k'ai to be elected provisional president of the Chinese Republic by the National Assembly

1913 Yuan purges Kuomintang members in elected Parliament, ignores National Assembly
Sun Yat-sen's "second revolution" in southern provinces fails

1915 Japan presents her 21 Demands for concessions, including special rights in Shantung, 99-year leases in Manchuria, interests in iron and steel industries, a promise that no part of China's coast would be ceded to any power, appointment of Japanese advisers in economic, political and military affairs. Yuan secretly accepts in part.
Yuan accepts Imperial Office

1916 Death of Yuan Shih-k'ai ushers in warlord period
Schism between the governments of Peking in the north and Canton in the south

1917	China enters World War I on the side of the Allies—Britain, France, Japan and United States
1919	China refuses to sign the Treaty of Versailles, which gives German holdings in China to Japan
	Students lead May 4th ("National Shame Day") Movement to protest treaty
1920–26	Civil war between warlords, strikes
1921	Chinese Communist Party founded in Shanghai
1923	Soviet advisers help reorganize the Kuomintang, which now includes members of the Communist Party
1924	Chiang Kai-shek heads new Whampoa Military Academy, assisted by Chou En-lai, political director
1925	Death of Dr. Sun Yat-sen, Father of the Republic
1926	Northern Expedition to unify China led by Chiang Kai-shek and People's Revolutionary Army with the participation of Communists
1927	Split between Kuomintang and Communists
1930–35	Chiang Kai-shek's "Annihilation Campaigns" against Communist strongholds in Hunan and Kiangsi provinces
1934–35	In the Long March the Communists escape Chiang, retreat to sanctuary in Yenan, in the northwest
1932	Japan occupies Manchuria and installs ex-Emperor P'u-i as regent of "Manchukuo"
1937	Kuomintang and Communists declare United Front against Japan
1937–45	Sino-Japanese War
1938	Canton and Hankow fall to Japanese
1940	Japan installs puppet government in Nanking
1941	Japan bombs Pearl Harbor, United States enters World War II
1943	United Front fails, Civil War resumes
1945	Japan surrenders
1949	Communists take mainland China, Chiang Kai-shek withdraws to Taiwan
1950–53	Korean War
1956	100 Flowers Movement initiated by Communist leadership to regain cooperation of intellectuals
1957	End of 100 Flowers Movement, intellectuals again suspect
1958	Great Leap Forward Movement: "20 years in a day"
1958–59	Sino-Soviet split
1959	Liu Shao-ch'i named President
1966–68	Cultural Revolution begins and hurls China into turmoil
	Liu Shao-ch'i denounced as a counter-revolutionary

1969	Sino-Soviet clashes on the Ussuri River
	Lin Piao designated as Mao Tse-tung's political heir
1970	Mao Tse-tung criticizes Lin Piao
1971	Henry Kissinger makes secret trip to Peking
	Peoples' Republic of China admitted to United Nations in place of Taiwan
	Lin Piao flees and is killed in plane crash
1972	President Nixon visits China
	Anti-Confucius campaign
1973	Teng Hsiao-p'ing, purged in 1967, reemerges as deputy premier
1974	25th anniversary of the Peoples' Republic of China celebrated with Mao and Chou absent
1975	Teng Hsiao-p'ing named Vice-Chairman of Central Committee, Chief of Staff of army
1976	Premier Chou En-lai dies
	Teng Hsiao-p'ing criticized by Mao and purged again
	Major earthquake in Tangshan
	Mao Tse-tung dies
	Leaders of Cultural Revolution, known as the Gang of Four, arrested
	Hua Kuo-feng named Chairman of Chinese Communist Party
1977	Government lifts ban on Beethoven and Shakespeare
	Teng Hsiao-p'ing reinstated as politburo member
	Mao Tse-tung's legacy criticized
1981	Hua Kuo-feng demoted to Vice-Chairman
	Teng Hsiao-p'ing's protege, Hu Yaobang, named Chairman of Chinese Communist Party

Acknowledgments

"The sadness of the Chinese" by Chon Tso-jen, p. 50
   From *A Harp with a Thousand Strings*, compiled by Hsiao Ch'ien and translated by H. Acton and S. H. Ch'en (Pilot Press Ltd.), p. 279.

"Children" by Po Chu-i, p. 60
   From *Translations from the Chinese*, translated by Arthur Waley (Vintage Books, Random House Publishers), p. 232. Copyright © 1919 and renewed 1947 by Arthur Waley. Reprinted by permission of Alfred A. Knopf, Inc., and George Allen & Unwin (Publishers) Ltd.

"Shen Chu-lien's letter to his dead daughter" by Lin Yutang, p. 61
   From *The Importance of Understanding: Translations from the Chinese* (Forum Books, The World Publishing Company). Copyright © 1960 Lin Yutang.

"Pure peace music" by Li Po, pp. 101, 276
   From *The Penguin Book of Chinese Verse*, translated by Robert Kotewall and Norman L. Smith (The Penguin Poets, 1962), p. 14. Translation copyright © Norman L. Smith and Robert Kotewall, 1962. Reprinted by permission of Penguin Books Ltd.

93rd poem, p. 107
   From *The Book of Songs*, translated by Arthur Waley (Grove Press), p. 86. Reprinted by permission of Grove Press. This book is copyright under the Berne Convention.

"Grass" by Ch'en Shan-min, p. 159
   From *The Penguin Book of Chinese Verse*, translated by Robert Kotewall and Norman L. Smith (The Penguin Poets, 1962), p. 53. Translation copyright © Norman L. Smith and Robert Kotewall, 1962. Reprinted by permission of Penguin Books Ltd.

Ch'iu Chin's poem, p. 165
   From *Early Chinese Revolutionaries*, translated by Mary Backus Rankin (Harvard University Press), p. 1. Copyright © 1971 by President and Fellows of Harvard College. Reprinted by permission of Harvard University Press.

"Southeast the peacock flies," p. 173
   From *The White Pony, An Anthology of Chinese Poetry*, edited by Robert Payne (Mentor Book, New American Library), p. 117. Reprinted by permission of Bertha Klausner International Literary Agency, Inc.

"I had long had it in mind" by Yuan Mei, p. 183
   From *Yuan Mei, Eighteenth Century Chinese Poet*, translated by Arthur Waley (Stanford University Press), p. 67. Reprinted by permission of Stanford University Press and George Allen & Unwin (Publishers) Ltd.